It's Onl‸ a Game

Pull up a chair, buy me a beer, and a tale to you I'll tell

Jim Eyre

WILD PLACES
CARDIFF

WILD PLACES PUBLISHING
51 TIMBERS SQUARE
CARDIFF CF24 3SH, UK

First published 2004

All artwork by Jim Eyre

Caving is a potentially dangerous pursuit. The inclusion of stories in this book,
whether relating to incidents underground or on the surface, and whether linked
with caving or otherwise, should not be taken to suggest that the activities involved
are recommended to the reader.

Indeed, any reader who attempts to emulate the exploits described in this book is
warned that these may not be condusive to continued good health. Neither the author
nor publisher accepts any responsibility for any accident or damage, however caused.

MEASUREMENTS
Both imperial measurements (miles, yards, feet and inches) and metric
measurements (kilometres, metres) are used in this book. Generally, older references
– such as the diameter of guns and the depth of shafts in caves – were originally
imperial measurements and these have been retained within the narrative. However,
cave surveys in the UK have, for many years, used metric units and these also appear
in the text.

To convert measurements, a close approximation can be obtained by multiplying
metres by 3.3 to obtain feet, or dividing feet by 3.3 to obtain metres. The imperial
pound weight can be converted to kilograms by dividing by 2.2.

British Library Cataloguing in Publication Data
A catalogue record for this book is available from the British Library

ISBN 0-9526701-6-X

Design and origination by Wild Places Publishing, Cardiff
Printed on Fineblade Extra, an acid-free paper manufactured from
  sustainable sources
Printed in the United Kingdom by CPI, Bath

Contents

Dedication

Writing an autobiography that almost covers a lifetime can be a soul-searching experience that briefly enables one to relive and share sometimes embarrassing adventures with complete strangers. At the same time, it has proved almost impossible to describe in print the tenderness and selfless love I experienced during my second marriage to a delightful, beautiful and loving lady. I wish to dedicate this book to Audrey, who came into my life just when I needed her and stayed for 26 years, charming everyone she met.

Acknowledgements

Special thanks go to Barbara, Eski, Keith and Kev of the Northern Pennine Club, who kick-started this project. Another special thank you goes to Kath Alty, who ensured that the project was kept going by acting as proof-reader and enthusiastic leader (and only member) of my fan club.

For going beyond the call of duty, my thanks and an award for services to caving go to Chris and Judith, who are experts in Italian naval history, the Italian language and West Country folklore, and who can tell the difference between a *diaso* and a *dghajsa*.

Last, but not least, I wish to thank the photographers whose work appears here, including Jim Leach and Bert Bradshaw, and especially Ron Bliss for his many and excellent caving pictures.

Foreword

A **BROKEN, BENT NOSE** loomed towards me. It was a classic – a nose that must have seen a great deal of action, to the extent that you couldn't be sure if the left nostril stayed on the left all the way up. The nose was warped and flattened and attached to a face which emitted a whiff of alcohol as it drew closer. Actually, it was more like the nose was dragging the face in a parody of a weaving paravane in turbulent waters – but more of that later in the book. The nose and face came nearer and the alcohol said:

''Ere, wanna publish a book?'

I FIRST MET JIM EYRE many years before that encounter, but even that tale requires a backward step and another story of a first meeting.

Mendip's finest, the Hunters' Lodge Inn, then as now is oft-filled wall-to-wall with cavers, a roar of noise and an impression of liquid-filled glasses that rise and fall at the same rate as heads nod. When I arrived it was one of those special days – a day when it was even more difficult than usual to forge a route past the first few hairy beings, heading towards the bar.

A photo of mine had recently been published in a caving magazine; it was a set-up picture intended to be funny, to make people laugh at an aspect of the caving world (though the concept of satire would be too strong). I had not until then met one of Mendip's finest denizens, but Tony Jarratt lurched over, almost but not quite spilling his pint. As someone told him my name he pushed his glass into some other caver's hands (an abnormal act in itself) and, without more ado, grabbed me by both ears, drew me close like a footballer with a jug-handled silver trophy, and kissed me full on the lips.

This was not what I had expected.

'Anyone who takes the urine out of them buggers is a friend of mine,' he said (or words to that effect), letting go and staggering back to his pint.

Later that year I was introduced to Jim Eyre. It was well into one of those night-time revelries that truly belong to the caving world that I first saw the nose. It was impressive, as was the fist that engulfed my hand when he shook it.

'Any friend of J-Rat is a friend of mine,' he said.

I do remember thinking, at that first meeting, that I wouldn't want to meet that nose in an alley of a dark night. More exactly, in those circumstances, I wouldn't want there to be enough light to see it coming or for its owner to see me.

Thus began a long-distance friendship that called for spotting each other once every so often as we passed on our ways like – dare I say? – ships in the night. Then, out of the blue, Jim suggested publishing his autobiography. For many, many years I had enjoyed reading his tales of woe and strife, linked inextricably to his caving career. Presented like sporadic pools of pearls in books and magazines, Jim's anecdotes had gained a certain notoriety and the concept of publishing a new collection . . . Well, it was an honour to be asked.

I little knew what publishing Jim's life story meant, in real terms. Turn these pages and you will find neatly arranged, row by row, lines of text flowing around exquisite cartoons that could only come from the pen of Eyre. However, when the manuscript arrived it did so in a bundle neatly wrapped in brown paper and tied up with string. It comprised a similar set of pages to those you see here (only many more of them), with text neatly arrayed and a host of cartoons. Editing and layup should have been a joy, but unfortunately . . .

Jim's computer skills are not up to the same standard as his penmanship. With a newly acquired computer, he had written chapter one then asked his boffin what to do next. 'Have you saved it onto the hard drive?' he was asked.

'Yes.'

'You're fine then, write the next chapter.'

So Jim printed the file and wrote the next chapter, saved it and printed it and wrote another and saved it and printed it . . . The problem was, nobody had told him that he needed a new file for each chapter. Instead, he had written each chapter over the top of the one before, effectively deleting it. I had in front of me a pile of 503 pages with no line spaces or paragraph breaks and only the last chapter on disk. It took more work than I thought possible to bring this to print!

Yet here it is, at last. Even now, *It's Only a Game* represents just the first half of Jim's life, merely taking us to the 1960s – there is more, so much more, to come.

On a personal level I am proud to have been associated in this minuscule way with Jim's story, narrated as it is by one of the finest humorous writers of our time. May his words continue to flow and may we readers ever continue to enjoy the spectacular tales of Jim Eyre.

Chris Howes

Chapter 1

It's Only a Game

SPORTSMEN of the nineteenth century were generally sons of clergymen or the landed gentry born into a life of privilege and leisure. These gentlemen soon adapted their lifestyles to a range of activities designed to liven up their humdrum existence, which enabled them to dress up in weird and wonderful outfits and emit weird and wonderful sounds as they took up rural pursuits such as riding to hounds, riding the odd chambermaid or rampaging around the countryside shooting foxes, deer, pheasants and peasants. Times, alas, have changed; now it is the peasant's turn and 'Sport For All' is compulsory.

All known life on the planet currently revolves around the inane prattle of sports commentators as they pour adulations on sporting personalities. Stars who twinkle in our otherwise dull environment, permanently fixed on the television screen with show-biz luvvies, as they pontificate on world affairs, the latest hairstyles, who is into whose knickers, who has just changed sex, and how to solve the national debt.

Wearing the latest designer trend, profusely greeting the presenter like a long-lost cousin (although they were only on the show four days previously), these masters of Essex-speak explain again why they failed to score the winning goal against Germany six years ago. 'Well, it was like this Michael, if I 'ad turned the other way wiv me left foot, it would 'ave gone in.' To loud cheers from the studio audience who seem to be resurrected from Zombieland, the Star then plugs his latest autobiography which is all about bugger all – his third life story in twelve months, written by someone who can write – and the audience cheers like mad. Gods such as this smile down on us nightly, secure in their Valhalla with their particular skill of doing things with a ball: kicking it, throwing it, pushing it, tapping it, poking it, catching it, dribbling it, running with it or scratching it.

Where did I go wrong? Recovered memory syndrome tells me that it must have been my schooldays.

The playing fields of my youth lay some distance from the school and I rapidly became a deprived child, in the sense that I hardly ever made it there. A gaggle of schoolchildren with two SS guards disguised as schoolteachers was a familiar and disciplined body in those days, but there was always one child who, for some perverted reason, could not resist pushing another through a privet hedge or tripping one up, who also insisted on talking, dawdling, pulling girls' hair, or kicking the odd tin can along the gutter. Strangely enough, I always had the blame, was cuffed around the ears and sent back to school, then told to stand under the clock until the budding sports stars returned.

Consequently, on the rare occasions when I did reach the hallowed playing field turf, I didn't know the rules and got everything wrong. I could never understand why every time I went to kick the football, someone blew a whistle and the game stopped. The teacher leaping up and down on the touchline would blow his whistle with such gusto that it caused his face and neck to expand and change into the colour of a turkeycock, as he excitedly pointed back up the field. Everyone would run back and re-start the game, which proceeded normally until by chance I received the ball again, the whistle blew and the game was stopped. It was all very mysterious, as even the dunce of the class (who is now a millionaire footballer) could kick the ball without the interruption of a demented whistle blower.

Small boy causes teacher to explode!

If I thought football confusing, cricket was, and still remains, a com-pletely baffling and dull affair which for me consisted of sitting on some-thing called the boundary. From there, on a clear day, I could just make out the other players – one throwing the ball and another hitting it with a bat, while the rest threw it back again so the whole procedure could start again.

I would sit there for ages, chew-ing grass and idly daydreaming as I watched the girls bouncing about in their little short skirts playing hockey. This was a much more stimulating pastime, until suddenly a shout broke into daydreams as the cricket ball hurtled my way. A heady moment of glory came when I once caught the ball; the loud cheers took my mind off the pain, for I was sure I had broken three fingers, and I vowed to miss it next time.

I didn't know about Sod's Law in those days, but it was working very well. Every time it was my turn to bat, the whistle blew, the stumps were pulled and we all returned to school, where once again I ended up standing under the school clock in the main hall as punishment for misbehaving on the way back.

Football and cricket, the two main pillars of modern British society, the hierarchy of the great and good, the main topic of conversation, access to knighthoods, parliament and adulation by tabloid editors (and young ladies keen to divulge themselves of their virginity) were denied me. My young developing brain now classed sport as terribly boring periods associated with pain: aching legs from standing under the school clock, and bruised and bleeding knuckles sustained in frenzied attacks from our maths-cum-sports master as he vented his spleen with the sharp edge of a ruler on the back of my clenched fist. This sadistic ritual only stopped when he ran out of breath and could no longer jump up and down with every stroke, as the exertion induced his face to visibly puff up until it disappeared into his neck. During this alarming metamorphosis his bloated features altered chameleon-like from white to red to purple, and I became increasingly worried that one day he would inflate to such an extent that he would burst, a disturbing thought for a small boy. I could imagine the headlines in the local paper: 'Small boy causes teacher to explode!'

Quite by chance, however, while still at junior school I discovered a sport at which I excelled: throwing the hammer. This could be played without continual recourse to the rule book – there was no whistle and I didn't even need a regulation hammer, as mine consisted of a frayed piece of rope with a rusty old eight-inch iron bolt fastened on the end.

Swinging it round and round and letting go at its maximum velocity gave phenomenal results, and the sheer joy of watching that bolt arc into the sky with its rope tail streaming behind was spellbinding. This was especially so on one memorable occasion when, surrounded by an appreciative audience, I let the bolt go from the middle of the local army barracks field. We watched it soar majestically over a large willow tree and disappear through the centre pane of an imposing first floor bay window of a house on the adjoining street.

There was a loud 'Oooo!' of appreciation, followed by a stunned silence from my spectators, before we all scattered.

The following day was obviously going to be a momentous occasion, for a policeman's bicycle was leaning against the school railings and everyone spoke in hushed whispers as we assembled in the school hall. A sudden silence ensued as the imposing figure of the headmaster appeared in the centre of his teaching staff on the raised platform. A chill went through me when he held up a length of tatty rope attached to a large, rusty bolt. He glared at us through his dark-rimmed glasses and spoke in a voice loaded with menace . . .

It was a h-haccident, sir

'This came through my bedroom window! To *whom* does it belong?'

The awed silence was suddenly broken by the shrill, thin piping of a girl's voice: 'It belongs to Jimmy Ers, sir.' I immediately hated all girls.

The headmaster's eyes glistened in triumph, he licked his lips in anticipation before booming out: 'James Eyre, come here!'

Old 'Daddy Dale', as we used to call him, was not a handsome man and close up he looked positively evil. He was heavily jowled with a permanent blue chin, large yellow teeth and cold, black eyes which pierced my very soul as he grabbed me by the scruff of the neck and pulled me close enough to smell his bad breath.

'Well?' he bellowed, 'What have you got to say?'

'It was a h-haccident, sir,' I squeaked.

'Well, you are about to have another,' shouted my genial headmaster, his tongue licking the foam off his lips. 'Bend over, boy!'

I was given a severe thrashing on the backside in front of the entire school, an event never before known in the school's history. Unfortunately, my sore bum was nothing to the thrashing I received from my father when he discovered that he was being charged for replacing a pane of glass. Then I had another clouting from my mother, because: 'You've upset your father!'

MUCH TO THE TOTAL ASTONISHMENT of all the school, I beat the school swot and won a scholarship to the local grammar school. The timing wasn't too good because, when I was just beginning to understand football, I was sent to a school that played rugby and was most amazed when, while I was dribbling the funny-shaped ball towards the goalposts, another boy ran up, picked it up and ran off! Later in the match our goalie seemed to have vanished, so I rushed into the goal mouth to put up a gallant defence only to find that the opposing forward ran around the back of the posts and put the ball down. A big shout from the four spectators, the dreaded whistle, everyone ran back up the field and I was put on the B-team.

Cricket, meanwhile, was just the same as at junior school – only this time I had to wear white flannel trousers and white spiked boots to sit on the boundary. And, worse of all, there was no girls' hockey team to watch!

As a new pupil in an old established school, I soon discovered that it contained an old medieval torture chamber called the gym, and the chief torturer was an ex-regimental sergeant major who had probably suffered a disturbed childhood which had affected his brain. He was a short, balding, pompous individual who was always immaculately attired in a brilliant white vest with blue trim, white trousers and gym shoes. Stiff as a ramrod, he stuck his chest out to impress us puny individuals (we didn't possess a chest between us) and carried an RSM's baton to beat us with.

Any idea I had of representing my country in the Olympics was rapidly dispelled when I discovered that 'physical training' consisted of stripping down to shorts and vests and standing around freezing our balls off, before suddenly being galvanised into action, galloping around the gym, jumping over wooden horses and swinging like monkeys on parallel bars, while being shouted at and beaten by 'Sergeant Bummer'. He was very fit and the first one knew of his presence was a resounding 'thwack' of his stick as he determined to speed up the action, catching us around the legs, arms and head if nothing else was available.

'Why wasn't this sod away fighting the Germans?' I wondered, after a crack behind the left ear. The war would be over in a week. 'Mind you, the Germans are bigger than us and they would probably clout him back.' The pain didn't seem too bad after that thought.

The gym was also the swimming bath. Underneath the boarded floor lurked a pool of dark green water, and when we turned up one day for a swim we discovered it was the coldest bath in England. Our sadistic sergeant had us lined up on the edge for ages, until our knees were knocking like castanets and our bony bodies were turning blue.

'On the command you will dive in,' he said.

'But I can't swim,' squeaked the skinny youth standing next to me, who by this time looked like a blue kipper, almost transparent and shivering violently.

'Don't worry, you'll find it comes naturally,' answered our genial instructor. 'Everyone dive!'

I understood why so many Arctic explorers' names were on the school honours board after I hit that water; it was a good job I could swim or else I would have frozen solid in five minutes, and I suspected that the serpentine colour of those frigid depths was the result of adding antifreeze – I'm sure they had a refrigeration unit attached. Shaking off the anklets of ice, I tore up and down the length of the bath and hauled myself out in a state of shock, then watched the sergeant trying to fish two non-swimmers out with a large net on the end of a long pole. He experienced some difficulty and booted two of us back in to unfreeze them from the bottom, whereupon they were hauled out like two frozen fish fingers, barely breathing.

Sergeant Bummer had another role at the school, which I discovered quite by accident. The school had a system of prefects, handpicked because they were older, larger and nastier than the rest of us. All were boarders with rich daddies, not as bright as the average scholarship boy, but all destined to be feather-bedded in some unexacting job like a member of parliament or boardroom director. Unfortunately, for us lower minions, they could also, according to the school rules, legally beat us up.

Typically, if ever there is anything nasty on the horizon, I'm always one of the first to find out and it wasn't long before I discovered this archaic form of punishment when I was summoned to the prefects' room by a pimply faced yobbo for talking in assembly. I then faced several more pimply faced yobbos, who told me to bend over while the largest one attempted to thrash me with a thick cane.

To me this was totally wrong – I accepted being beaten up by teachers, but not by pimply faced yobbos, so I refused. Two grabbed me, while the other began laying into me with his cane. I hit one and kicked the other, which led to an urgent meeting with the headmaster and Sergeant Bummer, who was the caner-in-chief to the headmaster (his other job). He, under the now well-known maxim of 'I was only obeying orders', administered a heavy beating in the headmaster's study, which I'm sure they both enjoyed. This managed to put me off bureaucracy, PT and PT instructors for life.

Gradually, I adjusted to the strange rituals of the Lancaster Royal Grammar School, with its eccentric masters floating about in tattered gowns over Harris tweed jackets, smelling of pipe tobacco, walking up and down the hill to different classes, some forgetting where they were going. There were the music lessons, where we never made it past the second verse of the *Barcarolle* from *The Tales of Hoffman*, owing to our teacher's inability to tell that we were all tone deaf, and the divinity classes which had a permanent resident in the form of Tiggy, who always sat in the window seat playing tunes on his teeth with his ruler.

Another strange ritual, peculiar to the grammar school, was the Set Run – yet another form of sadomasochism which required pupils to strip down to vests and shorts and run up two very steep hills into the countryside, returning by a circular route of several miles. Weather forecasts were consulted to make sure this event always occurred in conditions below freezing, during a force eight gale or in heavy rain, and all the school had to compete.

Behind a wooden counter, almost buried
under more goods, presided the owner
of Emporium Herbie

This annual event brought great honour to the house that won, so consequently several of the more athletic masters had us staggering round the course on frequent training runs, separating the wheat from the chaff, the fat from the thin and the super fit from the cardiac collapse candidates.

I and my fellow Woodbine smokers soon discovered that, by keeping up with the leaders for half the course, we could then hop over a wall, have a couple of fags, then join in with the tail-end runners without being missed. This made for a pleasant afternoon and we didn't even break into a sweat. After further research we discovered that we could cut out even more of this boring road work by dodging through a copse and along a ditch, to regain the route just before the downhill run to the school. We actually began to look forward to Set Run practice and found that sport can be fun after all.

I should have realised that sport is good for the soul because I came from a sporting family. My father was an ex-sergeant major, a gymnast, boxing instructor and a crack shot, having competed in the King's Hundred at Bisley. Both my parents were also keen followers of the sport of kings and spent most mornings working out very complicated bets, frequently consulting the *Sporting Chronicle* and Mae's cousin, who knew a chap whose sister's husband worked in a stable and often gave Mae, mother's next door neighbour, hot tips. Notwithstanding that the stable the tipster worked in was the one where they kept the canal boat horses, because he was still reckoned to be in the know as he knew another chap who worked in another stable . . .

I never realised that both my parents were mathematical geniuses; compared with them Einstein was a novice. The applied science that went into making a horse bet was a revelation. As I watched them work out the infinite number of times 6d could be employed on a bet my mind boggled. 'Sixpence each way, any back a shilling win, sixpence on a round robin accumulator, a sixpence double on the nose and threepenny flyer, any back four from six, each way, 4.30 Kempton.' And I was struggling with algebra!

As gambling was illegal, my mother had the pseudonym of Ginger II (I never found out who Ginger I was), under which all bets were placed. Every day old Mac, Mae's husband, would come in for the bets and hotfoot it to the bookie's. Mac was what they called a bookie's runner – not very apt in his case as he suffered from bronchitis and emphysema and so he could hardly breathe, let alone run. 'Any bets, Jane?' he would wheeze, and if there was a bet for the first race, generally at 1.30, Mac would have to leave at noon to reach the bookie's in time. That was a terraced house three streets away; he had to stop frequently to hang onto a window sill to catch his breath and have a wheeze and a cigarette while dispersing tips to all and sundry along the way.

The old lady was quite lucky with her gambling; when she had a win old Mac would come staggering in with a neatly folded betting slip, marked with thick blue pencil, which contained the winnings. He would collect his tip and hastily depart before the customary battle took place between my old man and Ginger II, about who had done what and who owed from last week, with my mother generally winning with the immortal words: 'I was going to back that one, but you put me off.'

I DON'T KNOW when I first discovered an aptitude for climbing – perhaps it all stemmed from the time when I was sent to Herbie Brittain's corner shop for a quarter of brawn. Herbies' shop was straight out of Dickens and was a corner shop in the true sense of the word. The door was on the corner of a three-storeyed terraced house,

The higher and more exposed I became the more exposed would be the angels who flew past

which you had to sidle into sideways and work your way past hanging brooms, pots and pans, dishcloths, clogs and tin bath tubs, to reach a small, dingy, triangular room where every inch of the walls and ceiling was covered with every conceivable object that had ever been made in the preceding thirty years, some festooned from above, some nailed to the walls and some stacked in precarious pyramids.

Behind a wooden counter, almost buried under more goods, presided the owner of Emporium Herbie, a round face on top of a round body crowned by a flat, greasy cap on a round, almost bald head. He always wore a suit of a gingerish hue and a collar and tie, all greasy. Around his neck and large belly was tied an apron, which had started off in life as white, but was now so impregnated with black grease that it could have stood up on its own, if ever Herbie took it off.

On the counter under five suspended, yellow flypapers, almost full of dead and dying flies, stood three huge pieces of ham, pork and brawn, and I was always fascinated as Herbie went through his ritual of sharpening his long, thin, razor-sharp, horn-handled knife before grasping the meat with one hand and lovingly carving pieces off. His horny, grubby hands, each with its own set of black matching fingernails, folded up the slices of brawn in a sheet of greaseproof paper pulled from a hook by his head. He then brushed off some cigarette ash which had fallen from the soggy fag end stuck on his lower lip and said, 'Four pence ha'penny.'

On the way back home I couldn't resist eating some, and bumped into my mother who had come looking for me. She grabbed her precious brawn with one hand and cuffed me round the ear with the other. A ginger-headed woman in a rage is a terrible thing to behold, so I dodged round her and ran into the barracks field, then shinned up the giant willow tree opposite our house with an alacrity that would have made Sergeant Bummer proud.

Soon all the street was out as I scrambled upwards, climbing higher than our three-storey house while my dear old ma was doing a war dance down below, threatening to kill me when I got down and crying in despair, 'Our Jimmy, you'll kill yourself if you fall off. Come down love, I won't touch you.'

I climbed higher, away from the staring crowd that had gathered below, until they were obscured by the narrow, light green leaves that glistened in the sun as the thin branches swayed to and fro like the fronds of seaweed in a boisterous sea. It was another world and everything below paled into insignificance with the exhilaration I experienced, even the clouting I would have when I descended.

A blocked gutter was causing problems at the back of the house. The local window cleaner and odd-job man didn't have long enough ladders, so I climbed out of a sky-light and, holding a length of clothes line paid out by Ron, my younger brother, I slid down the grey slate to the gutter and cleaned it out. Leaning over from a steeply sloping roof cannot be recommended, but my precarious position sixty feet up was compensated by a magnificent view of the rooftops of Lancaster and its town hall, and the grand panorama of the Lakeland hills, while down below, across the back street, the equally impressive sight of a young lady's enormous pink bum was revealed in all its glory as she struggled to pull up her voluminous knickers while backing out of an outside lavatory. The effect on me was instant. I never knew that young ladies' bums were that big, or so pink and wobbly, and but for the tightly held clothes line I would have fallen off.

This was the beginning of my sex education, as I later discovered that nearly all the ladies in the smaller terraced houses across the back street sat on their outside loos with the doors open wide, secure in their seclusion behind high backyard walls. Huge thighs and pink wobbly bums were occasionally replaced by younger, more exciting bodies and, on a few rare occasions, glimpses of pubic hair. I wonder if my later fascination for climbing over exposed places was due to this particular episode of my youthful past, perhaps living in hope that the higher and more exposed I became the more exposed would be the angels who flew past with pink wobbly bums and huge thighs.

Needless to say, years later my climbing exploits on the roofs of St Oswald Street came to a dramatic conclusion when, aided and abetted by Ron on the other end of a better class of clothes line, I set to repair the large chimney stack which held five enormous ornate chimney pots and was in danger of falling. We had extinguished all fires and covered all the fireplaces in our house below. I thought it expeditious to drop the smaller pieces of debris down the chimney and was merrily engaged in this task when I was distracted by a chorus of yells from across the street below, and observed what seemed to be three fat female performers from *Show Boat* jumping up and down with rage. Well, I presumed it was rage, because all I could see were six bloodshot eyes and the occasional flash of teeth in what were three extremely black muppets.

It slowly dawned on me that we were working on the wrong chimney, and I was later informed, very concisely and very angrily, that Mrs McRae and her two daughters were having tea when a noise like an express train heralded a fall of soot that extinguished the fire, swept across the room and turned everything and everyone into a set from the *Black and White Minstrel Show*, without the white bits. Profuse apologies, free chimney work and free decorating was the order of the day, and thus ended my climbing exploits in St Oswald Street.

TO BE A YOUNG BOY growing up in the early war years felt like being part of a tremendous adventure that was to change the world. Listening to the wireless in the evenings, we heard of men fighting for their lives; indeed, fighting for our lives, as young men hurled their Spitfires and Hurricanes at the overwhelming mass of German planes that advanced day after day over southern England. These young men were my heroes and made me feel proud to be British; my sole aim in life was to get out of school as soon as possible, join the RAF and become a Spitfire pilot. In the meantime, we had our bikes; straight after school, grab something to eat and off – anywhere – we never made plans.

A bicycle was a form of release, a key to adventure that opened the door to a whole range of activities. With various companions I discovered the Lake District and granite climbs on faraway crags. I discovered stretches of river that I never knew existed. It was inevitable that sooner or later I would fall in and discover how to swim, which led me to the skills of canoeing as we built our own boats from wood or canvas and discovered whitewater canoeing – backwards – and more survival swimming. Roller skating, ice skating, dicing with death on home-made trolleys (two planks on pram wheels) as we careered down the steep hill where I lived and across the busy main road below. Everything began with bikes; old, second-hand 'sit up and begs', until one proud birthday I was presented with a racer, a brand new Hercules which cost my parents eight pounds, a lot of money in those days.

Together with a mate, I set off for Scotland and, after a long hard day, late at night we ended up in a large town. We found a grassy area where we pitched our small tent and, covered with an old, threadbare blanket, we slept fitfully waiting for dawn.

'Want to buy a rabbit, meester?'

I stuck my head out of the tent flap, looked at the owner of the voice – a ragged urchin – and his long-dead rabbit.

'How much?'

'Saxpence.'

'Can you skin it?'

'Och aye,' said the lad, and the deal was done.

A fire was lit and bits of rabbit were boiled for breakfast, a bit tough and underdone as the young urchin remarked after trying a piece. 'Och, it's no fookin' bad, Jimmie,' he said, then quickly disappeared when a large, irate man in uniform loomed on the horizon. This large man gave us a large bollocking in a broad Scottish accent and informed us in no uncertain terms that we were in the middle of one of Edinburgh's finest parks and we had two seconds to shift our arses and our rubbish, punctuating his little tirade with a well-aimed kick from a heavy boot that hit my mate right up the backside. We beat a hasty retreat.

I WAS NOW AN APPRENTICE motor mechanic working for 7/6d a week, patiently waiting for the day when I would become old enough to join the forces. Air raids on Coventry had resulted in a large scale evacuation of Armstrong Siddeley aircraft workers to Lancaster and the roomy upper showroom of the garage I worked in was transformed overnight. Heavy lathes and other machinery were bolted to the concrete floor and the place was soon in full production.

Among my many tasks, I had the job of emptying large tins of swarf, which entailed carrying them down a spiral staircase with the help of another apprentice. There is something in my make-up which is slightly evil, and while struggling with a galvanised bath, filled to the brim with swarf and stinking lubricating liquid, looking down on the other apprentice's worried features peering over the slopping liquid below as we struggled to keep the bath level, I couldn't resist slowly lifting my end up. He gave a horrified yell, ducked, and all this evil-smelling gunge swilled over the garage manager coming up the stairs below. We were both sacked on the spot, though I found a job with the 'war workers' at much better pay and soon became a skilled turner and toolsetter; I felt that I was now helping to win the war.

Nigel, the other sacked apprentice, managed to get himself attached to the works' electrician. Some people are unforgettable and I have carried a picture of Nigel in my mind ever since. He was a likeable character, keen and ever willing to help; his round face, which seemed to be permanently split in two with a wide grin, was topped with an unruly mass of curly hair. In his baggy overalls, which were several sizes too large, and with thick glasses perched on the end of his nose, he looked like a myopic Marx brother.

I was working on a night shift when we had a major power failure. The electrician was nowhere to be found, but Nigel – convinced in his own mind that he was a qualified electrician – said he would sort it out. He approached the huge mains fuse board dragging a large, metal ladder behind him. With all the machines at a standstill, all eyes were on the boy wonder as, perched aloft on his ladder, he unscrewed the safety panel and started poking about inside with his electrician's screwdriver.

Suddenly there was an almighty explosion, and for several seconds Nigel was outlined in a vivid bluish-white flare of high voltage electricity that sent sparks from his suddenly straight hair, before he was lifted off his sparking ladder and hurled across the workshop, as though by some giant unseen hand. He slammed against a wall and slid into a heap on the floor, still clutching the remains of his screwdriver and still wearing his silly, but now bemused, grin. 'Wow!' he said.

The end of the night shift at 6 a.m. on Saturday meant pay day, after which a small group of us would cycle through the town and across the river Lune to the tidal estuary, aptly named 'snatchems', ostensibly to go fishing, but in reality to form a card school. The fluke lines were baited and thrown in the river, and we got down to serious gambling under a clump of trees. Three card brag was a swift way of losing one's wages and always some poor sod would go home broke, but with the consolation prize of most of the fish we caught – and some serious imaginative explaining when his parents found out that they were expected to live on fish for a week.

One card player, who never seemed to lose, was a tall, swarthy, wiry youth with a mouthful of nicotine-stained teeth, which were only partially revealed when he gave his peculiar lopsided grin. Joe Armistead was a youth of few words, but he was particularly skilled in practical matters. Being part gypsy (or 'charber', as we used to say), Joe could handle horses and snare rabbits, and was a fascinating countryman who knew all the different birds and their calls, pointing out things that we were unaware of. He always caught more fish than we did and occasionally went barefoot into the river, carrying a barbed fork on a stick to catch eels. Any particularly big one he would throw at us and give his evil grin as he watched us dive clear of the wriggling, black, slimy creature. We once had eel for breakfast, as Joe, with a Capstan Full Strength cigarette dangling from his mouth, calmly cut the head off and skinned the eel as one would a banana; chopped into manageable pieces and popped into a pan still wriggling, it tasted delicious.

In those days there were wickerwork salmon traps laid out at the mouth of the river and Joe and I sometimes cycled down to catch the early morning ebb tide before the fishermen came to inspect their traps, and often came back with a Lune salmon wriggling in our long saddlebags; once we had to pedal furiously to escape from an irate farmer-cum-fisherman who was chasing us in a tractor.

Joe the charber and I became mates, and as he lived near the quay in Lancaster we made a two-seater wooden canoe in his old man's shed which served as a greengrocer's business. After one or two teething problems (the canoe was unstable and leaked, and once sank with all hands), we managed to make it seaworthy.

One icy morning in January, which some would reason was not the best time for a sea voyage in an untested canoe, we set off down river, paddling past small ice floes floating on the glassy water like soapsuds. It was magic. We drifted down with the strong current, past the shipyards at Glasson Dock, bums wet through and numb with cold, on past Sunderland Point where they used to bring in the slave ships, and headed for the open waters of Morecambe Bay.

We had a plan. It was a bit vague, but we would paddle across the bay to Barrow-in-Furness; it was only eleven miles or so and didn't seem too bad. That was before an inch of ice formed on the canoe deck and we had five inches of cold water slopping around our frozen backsides and legs; we decided to head for shore to bale out and restore circulation to our frozen extremities.

With the canoe upside down on the muddy estuary shore, we began leaping up and down and thrashing our arms about in an attempt to warm up. This strange behaviour attracted the attention of a local coastguard, who approached us with some suspicion.

'What's all this then?' he asked, kicking the canoe with his welly. 'A bit of fresh wreckage you've found?'

When we indignantly told him that it was our canoe, he started laughing.

'We made it ourselves,' said Joe.

'I can see that,' said the coastguard, laughing again. 'Where have you come from?' When we told him Lancaster he said, 'Bloody 'ell', and when we told him we were going to Barrow, he said 'Bloody 'ell' again and burst out laughing so much that he brought on a fit of coughing.

'Barrow! Bbbloody Barrow! You would be lucky if you got past Heysham Deeps in that. Do you know what time it is?'

'No.'

'Do you know what time the tide turns?'

'Er, no.'

'Now,' he said, 'If that thing was seaworthy – which it ain't – and provided it don't capsize – which it probably would – and providing you two don't die of exposure in the meantime, you would either get washed out to sea or get washed up the bay to Arnside. Either way, I don't want to go looking for your bodies. Come with me and my missus will give you a bowl of hot soup and a cup of tea. She likes talking to sailors.' And he burst out laughing again.

After our nautical career was metaphorically dashed on the rocks, Joe and I decided to apply our newly acquired canoeing skills to really dashing ourselves on the rocks by shooting the rapids further up the river. What is now known as whitewater canoeing was just a whirly, bouncing, fast-moving helter-skelter ride into the unknown for us, as Joe's father took us above Kirkby Lonsdale on his old flat back and dropped us off up river, above a well-known set of rapids, and left us to our own devices. As he drove off in a cloud of smoke he shouted: 'I won't expect you home for tea.'

We were soon paddling down river and discovered that a canoeist can hear rapids but can't see them. The roar of falling water and our increasing speed had us both looking ahead for a navigable channel, but by the time we spotted an obvious route the river had us in its grip and we went hurtling down a narrow water chute, hit a rock which spun the canoe round, and within seconds found ourselves careering backwards in a maelstrom of boiling water. Hitting rocks and semi-submerged, we were completely out of control. This was better than any ride on a big dipper – it was sheer exhilaration and, as the river spat us out into calm water, we were both laughing with the heady excitement of our first rapid shoot.

The canoe had a slight leak and we were somewhat waterlogged but still floating as we bailed out most of the water with our hands, listening attentively to an increasing roar as the river tumbled over the last limestone outcrop. Sat in front, I saw the bow of our craft hover momentarily over a six-foot drop of white water, which cascaded and swirled below before plunging over a waterfall.

'Bloody hell,' I remember muttering before we were off on the boat ride of our lives. Gripping the diving, bucking canoe with our hands, knees and feet, we were bashed and buffeted from one rock to another, going completely underwater several times until, half-drowned, half-blinded by the boiling water, I saw Joe hurtling past with a look of total amazement. The battered canoe and I were thrown onto a huge polished outcrop, momentarily spinning slowly high and dry with its bottom stoved in before it slid sideways, depositing me in the river. Hanging onto the wreck like a limpet, I was flushed down the final water chute, then spewed out between two rocks from where I struggled, gasping and coughing, to the river bank and joined my dejected, half-dead companion.

The submerged remains of our once fine craft went careering down the river on a collision course with a portly gentleman in thigh-length green waders, who was happily fly-fishing before his world turned topsy-turvy as the wrecked canoe knocked his legs from under him. The splashing and swearing went on for some time as we slowly slunk away up the greasy, muddy river bank and vanished under the trees.

BEING A SIXTEEN-YEAR-OLD YOUTH in 1941 was brilliant, for although the war seemed a long way from Lancaster there was a sense of adventure and urgency that appeared to create an electric feeling of excitement in the air. We were fortunate indeed to have a statesman of Winston Churchill's calibre to inspire and lead us through those desperate days. Families gathered around their wireless sets for the latest news bulletins and listened enraptured to his stirring oratory as he exhorted us to be steadfast and brave. He was the man of the moment and I often wonder what the outcome would have been if a lesser breed of politician had been in power.

Little mattered in those days. With the world poised on the brink of extinction, my immediate demise didn't seem too important in the grand scheme of things as I dangled by my finger tips from the soaring buttress of Gimmer Crag. With my studded boots skidding and scraping and kicking up the odd spark, I embraced the rough Lakeland granite with the fervour of a long-lost lover as I fought desperately to stay in the land of the living.

Rock climbing, my new sport, was alright if you knew what you were doing, which I certainly didn't. With a grunt of relief I eventually reached a small ledge; I had read somewhere that it was called the Eagle's Nest and I sympathised with the fledglings as I looked at the long length of thin, hairy sisal rope that looped down and down, to disappear round a corner far below.

A faint shout came on the wind: 'Are you up?' accompanied by a hefty tug on the rope, which almost yanked me into space. If I hadn't grabbed a convenient jug-hold I would have been able to answer my impatient mate: 'I was until you pulled me off,' as I passed him on a downward flight path . . .

After a good verbal bollocking I lined my impatient buddy up to the ledge, where we ruminated on the joys of rock climbing and the possibility of the two of us ending our days tied together, becoming skeletons for tourists to gaze at, for neither of us could see a route up the sheer wall overhead. However, as always happens, we managed – more by good luck than skill – to reach the top.

Climbing in those days was dangerous. Our equipment was primitive and the sisal or hemp ropes were glorified clothes lines; they had a very low breaking point when new and were completely useless when a few months old, as they rotted fairly quickly. But, tie a rope around your waist, advance up a seemingly impregnable wall of rock while being held by your trusty companion, who was generally unbelayed a hundred feet below, and you felt invincible.

A fall in those days was serious, with the victim ending up either badly injured or dead, so (unlike modern climbers) we made a point of staying on the rock and I never had a fall, although in several instances I was reduced to a shaking wreck and was left hanging by a knee or an elbow, with finger nails scraping the rock as I tried to defy gravity after misjudging a move.

Cycling or using the irregular bus service up to the Lake District took time, and it was a bit frustrating after spending just a few hours climbing to be faced with a mad dash to return to work in time for the night shift. Our climbing trips therefore became less frequent, especially in winter.

While working at Armstrong Siddeley in 1941 I became friendly with another local youth, Wilf Taylor, who, like me, had volunteered for the Royal Navy and was waiting for his call-up papers. Wilf was a potholer and showed me some well-thumbed, black and white photographs of caves, which I found fascinating. The images of glistening stalactites standing out starkly against a backdrop of dark, mysterious caverns and foaming mountain streams plunging headlong into deep, gaping potholes on the nearby Yorkshire moors, fired my imagination. I became mesmerised by his stories of underground exploration and the lure of dark, dripping shafts and caverns measureless to man, so my first free weekend saw me cycling with Wilf along the road to Settle, to meet his fellow clubmates and be introduced to the joys of caving and potholing with a trip to Hunt Pot.

The weather had turned cold and it was snowing heavily as we skidded down Buck Haw Brow into Settle. Leaning our bikes against the wall, we rushed into The Naked Man cafe and, crouched in front of a roaring fire, thawed out our frozen bodies while a delightful lady served us with a giant teapot full of tea and a plateful of home-made cakes.

Around the corner from the cafe, up a small alley, I entered another world. An old, worn stone stairway led to a paint-peeling door which creaked as Wilf pushed it open.

The dark interior was like something out of a Victorian slum. Peering into the gloom, I could just make out four double-tiered iron bunk beds, two with scruffy striped mattresses, the rest draped with piles of old clothing, socks, muddy boots and trousers with torn or missing legs. Scattered about the room were old rope ladders, a pile of ropes and several compressed cardboard miners' helmets. Everywhere was covered in a thick layer of dried mud and a sharp musty odour that one associates with ancient sewers pervaded the atmosphere; the room looked as though it had been dredged up from the seabed.

'What do you think?' asked Wilf, his eyes sparkling with pride. 'This is our club house – isn't it great?' Before I could think of an answer, a vague character materialised from an adjoining room. He was wreathed in evil-smelling smoke that emanated from a short, blackened pipe stuck in a mouth above a stubbly chin; his hair was unkempt and he was dressed in the casual manner of one raised above common sartorial elegance. Two small black eyes peered at me through the tobacco haze.

'Hello, who are you?' he asked in a well-modulated voice that belied his image. Then he saw Wilf. 'Ah, it's young Wilfred,' he said. 'Have you brought us a new recruit?'

'This is Jim Eyre . . . Jim, this is Bob Leakey,' said Wilf, and thus I was introduced to an extraordinary man whose deeds are legendary. To me, then an innocent, the only clue to this outstanding character lay in his handshake, which felt like shaking hands with a granite statue.

After a vague evening becoming acquainted with more of Wilf's clubmates and drinking large amounts of beer in the nearby pub, I spent an even vaguer night tossing and turning on a damp, lumpy mattress before being awakened by Wilf with a mug of strong tea. The other occupants stirred from their sleeping bags and there was a flurry of activity as men began rummaging in the pile of grubby old clothes and put them on. I picked up what was left on the floor and became a sort of badly dressed mummy before being dragged outside and, with six others and a giant pile of ropes and ladders, piling into Bob's small four-seater car.

It was foggy outside and foggy inside, as Bob, teeth clenched firmly on his smoke-belching pipe, peered through the ice-covered windscreen and the overladen car struggled up the steep, snow-covered road

I became a sort of badly dressed mummy

out of Settle. After what seemed to me a long time in that mobile black hole of Cal-cutta, the car demolished a wall and gate before juddering to a halt in a snowdrift. 'I think this will do,' said our gallant leader and, festooned with ropes and rope ladders, we floundered through the deep snow, following him; our leader, apart from a ruck-sack, didn't seem to be carrying much at all.

Under a leaden sky, the bleak, snow-covered moors seemed never-ending. Bob stop-ped by a partially buried milk churn, opened it, tasted the milk and declared it fresh. Three of us had a drink and were promptly sick.

Our leader, apart from a rucksack, didn't seem to be carrying much at all

Eventually, our struggle through waist-deep snow ended by a small hillock where, thankfully, I threw down my burden and joined the others. The small undulation in the landscape looked down on a black abyss that stood out starkly against the white background – it was the most terrifying thing I had ever seen. This black gash in the earth's crust was seven feet wide and over fifteen feet long, and dropped sheer like the entrance to Hades, dark, bottomless and vibrating with the roar of the swollen stream that hurtled down past fluted, razor-sharp walls into a black nothingness. 'We can't be going down that,' I said to myself, then realised that we were.

My hangover miraculously cleared as I watched the group fastening ladders together, before lowering them down, clattering, into the depths, then belaying the end to a large rock. I watched open-mouthed as a man tied on the lifeline and crept cautiously over the edge, then climbed down the swaying ladders, water cascading off his helmet, before he was swallowed by the gloomy depths.

After a long time a faint whistle signal drifted up and the rope was pulled in – there was no one on the end and it was as though he had never existed. I watched men go down the shaft until it became my turn. 'Don't look down,' said my lifeliner, then he checked that I had tied the correct knot before dispatching me into oblivion. For the first twenty feet I concentrated on putting my feet on the wooden rungs, which were jammed firmly against the smooth walls of the upper shaft; I floundered all over the place as I desperately clung on with my hands, until I learned to push the ladder away from the wall and place my instep on the rung. Then I looked down and nearly fell off the ladder with shock. I was suspended in the centre of a giant rift on rope ladders that stretched below like a spider's thread to melt away into the blackness. There was no sign of the bottom.

The waterfall from above thrashed around like a living entity, a ghostly presence that froze me with its cold breath as it whirled nearer and nearer until I felt the cold, hard spray stinging my face and hands, before the main force of the falling water struck me like a battering ram and almost knocked me off the ladder. With my head down and shoulders hunched, all the world ceased to exist as I was enveloped in a watery cocoon of drumming, beating water; I clung fiercely to the rope ladder and made my way down, rung by rung.

Suddenly, I climbed clear of the main force of water and I could see caving lights, far below, which picked me out like a moth in their beams, holding me, shaking with cold, slowly climbing down with the clumsy unsure movements of the novice, until I landed on a jagged, spray-lashed ledge. A headlamp flashed in my face and I found myself held by unseen hands balanced on the ledge, which ran along the water-worn wall of the shaft. Where the other wall of the entrance rift had been was now the black expanse of a huge chamber; the pounding water arced out from the ledge and, lit by our headlamps, cascaded over the void like millions of sparkling diamonds, to burst on the rock-strewn floor far below.

My companion and I cautiously edged our way along the narrow ledge to where another rope ladder hung over a slender rock flake. I pulled up one end of the doubled rope, tied on and made my way down to the floor, to be greeted warmly by the rest of the team – wondering all the while how the bloody hell I was going to climb out.

Wet through and shivering with cold, I followed the others into the blackness. My cold, clammy clothes clung to my skin and restricted my movement as, stumbling and slipping, I squeezed between huge rocks or slid on my belly through low, water-filled gaps. I couldn't see much as my borrowed light had turned a dull yellow, so I had to make an extra effort to keep up with the group ahead and was carried away by the sound of their echoing voices, scrape of hobnails and flashing lights. These probed overhead and into dark recesses and crevices, picking out sparkling white stalactites and stalagmites. My exertions gradually warmed my skinny body and I began to appreciate the wonder and wild vastness of this subterranean world into which I had intruded.

Later, full of trepidation, I began climbing back up the swinging rope ladder. Looking up, it seemed to go on for ever, so I just concentrated on climbing with my arms wrapped around the ladder, holding the opposite rope sides. As Bob Leakey put it, acting as though I was making love to it. This seemed good advice, as the technique held me more upright and stopped me swinging back, throwing weight onto my arms. Soon I developed my own rhythm and, assisted by the reassuring tug of the lifeline, began to enjoy the climb and looked around at the vast underground cavern in which I dangled, completely exhilarated.

This state of euphoria was soon obliterated by the thundering roar of the waterfall as I climbed into it, stopping dead when the weight of water hit me. The lifeline tied around my chest gave a savage jerk and I was assisted upwards, breaking free of the water like a spluttering, half-drowned rat. I looked up and saw the sky lighting the top of the shaft walls. I was grabbed by helping hands and dragged away from the edge, then someone untied my lifeline as I sat there gasping for breath.

The snow had begun to melt while we were underground and there was now much more water in the shaft than when we descended. I helped on the lifeline, several of us practically pulling the last two men out against a maelstrom of falling water.

'Quite a near do,' said our leader. 'Must be a front coming in . . . Here you are Jim, grab these two ladders and away you go.'

I was assisted upwards, breaking free of the water like a spluttering, half-drowned rat

The heavy, sodden rope ladders were strung around my neck and, laden like pack-horses, we stumbled through the snow with ice forming on our clothes. Later, Wilf and I cycled back to Lancaster to work a twelve-hour night shift, more dead than alive.

The following weekend saw me once again in the Royal Oak in Settle, where I became a member of the grand-sounding British Speleological Association. This entailed drinking lots of pints of beer, smoking lots of fags, singing lots of caving songs and listening to mucky jokes. In fact, it was just like the last time we were in the Royal Oak, except that instead of going to sleep in the hostel we spent the night deep underground digging in a steep, muddy passage somewhere under the Pennines.

There can't be many people who enjoy heaving up buckets of mud and rocks and being plastered in mud from head to toe. However, much as I had become one of them, after two more potholing trips I had to put my new sport on hold until after the war.

Chapter 2

The Royal Navy

REACHING the age of seventeen I was old enough to be accepted as a volunteer in the Royal Navy, much to my dear old man's disgust for we had always been an army family. 'Trust you to do something different,' he said, 'the bloody navy!'

When my papers arrived, ordering me to report at Devonport, I was excited at the thought of becoming a member of the fighting forces and within a few days made my way to our local railway station. The noise and smell of the old coal-burning trains, the dimly lit, overcrowded platforms, shrouded in steam and pungent smoke with half-seen figures lit by the yellow glow from the old gas lamps, huddled on benches or lying on the flat-topped LMS trolleys, trying to snatch some sleep on the top of duffel bags and kitbags, was a scene I would soon become familiar with.

A distant rumble heralded the approach of the train as it crossed the bridge over the river, and the uniformed figures shuffled forward slowly, tired, with eyes red-rimmed through lack of sleep, to crowd at the edge of the platform in vain expectations of claiming a seat.

The clanking steam engine came to a halt with the banging of doors and the shout of the guard as the crowd surged forward, cigarette stubs sparking as they hit the stone slabs. Somehow, everyone squeezed on board, the guard shouted again, blew his whistle and, slowly belching steam and smoke, the train pulled out. Empty platforms, cold and deserted, were left behind as men went to war, many never to return.

I arrived at Devonport as ratings were removing the debris from the previous night's air raid; two of the barrack huts had received direct hits – it was a short war for some.

Duly kitted out with a hammock and pusser's uniform, the latest intake and I went through a brief medical and shower before changing into our new outfits, which were supposed to make us look like sailors. They didn't, unless one includes the crew of *HMS Pinafore*, and we found out later that most ratings bought tailor-made 'tiddly suits' from the many naval outfitters in Plymouth.

It took time to adjust to some of the strange customs and traditions of the Senior Service. Our barracks, for instance, was a ship. It had a foc'sle, which was really the barracks square and had to be saluted every time we walked past it (it was an offence to walk across it). There was a quarterdeck, which was out of bounds, and we had to run everywhere, salute everything that moved, and whitewash everything that didn't. After all the excitement of that first day, I hit my bunk and was soon sound asleep.

WAKEY WAKEY! HEAVE OUT, HEAVE OUT! LASH UP AND STOW . . . *WAKEY WAKEY WAKEY!* TAKE YOUR HANDS OFF YOUR COCKS AND PULL UP YOUR SOCKS!

Some demented sod on the other end of the tannoy was doing a crazy duet with a tone deaf bugler and the volume control had stuck on LOUD! Anyone with a weak heart would have been dead on the first day!

Literally blasted out of bed, staggering around frantically trying to get dressed while severely concussed, my whirling senses were drawn to the open doorway of our hut, which framed the impressive figure of a smartly dressed petty officer with an evil smirk on his face.

'Now you 'orrible set of bastards, we're going for a little light exercise. Out out, double *double!*'

Galloping around the square for the umpteenth time at 6 a.m. seemed a funny way to train sailors. However, this was just a gentle introduction, for more tortures were in store: marching till we dropped, running till we dropped, existing on crap food, being yelled at, insulted, and little extras like running round the square for a couple of hours in the evening, cleaning out the heads (toilets) and various other delights for anyone who showed the least sign of resistance. I was the first.

After a few weeks of this we were allowed to go ashore. The fact that we were already ashore didn't seem to matter and we were duly lined up for inspection. An officer examined us, looking for the slightest excuse to deny us the fleshpots of Plymouth. We were then instructed 'Off caps', and much to my surprise a petty officer smartly marched along the line of extended headgear and plonked a French letter in each!

Being a sailor on shore is much more fun than being a sailor on board. 'This is the life for me,' I thought as I became mixed up in a fairly lively party in the famous 'long bar'. Everything went fairly vague after several pints and somehow I ended up with a three-badge, able seaman – a fellow Lancastrian who had travelled the world and, as the saying goes, 'Been round the Horn three times and caught the clap twice.' This, in my mind, was a fine recommendation for a drinking partner and, together with this most knowledgeable sea dog, I went for a walk on the wild side of wartime Plymouth. We eventually returned back on board HMS *Raleigh*, severely intoxicated but with my education as a seaman vastly improved.

Newly qualified as an Ordinary Seaman Gunner QR3, I was drafted to Hebburn-on-Tyne to help rig merchant ships with anti-torpedo nets – heavy wire mesh which was hand-riveted on the quayside, then hoisted aloft on four specially designed booms. When at sea the booms were lowered by steam-driven winches until they were horizontal to the ship, and the heavy nets were drawn along on guide wires to hang like a steel mesh curtain alongside the ship.

This was but one innovation that helped to win the Battle of the Atlantic and several ships were saved when enemy torpedoes struck the nets and either exploded or became ensnared. There were problems, because when the nets were lowered they reduced the ship's speed. On one occasion, a freighter wallowed in rough seas and a torpedo glanced off the top of a net and landed on its deck, fortunately without exploding but causing a surprise among the crew.

I was lucky to receive such a good posting, although it didn't seem so at the time as I wanted to go to sea – but it was a case of Sod's Law as other ratings I had trained with did have postings to seagoing ships, some that within a short time went to the bottom. Apart from me and three other new ratings who were also on temporary replacement, the rest of the unit comprised men who were all survivors of the war at sea: they had been shipwrecked, blown up, wounded or were unfit for active service. Although not many years older than me, they were physical and mental wrecks and many had a haunted look about them that conveyed the horrors of the Russian and Atlantic convoys. I felt quite humble and awestruck as I got to know them and what they had been through.

In those days Tyneside was a wonderful place. The war economy had transformed the area from the no hope poverty of the Jarrow marchers into an industrial area pulsating with vitality, and the shipyards and docks along the river were working to full capacity. The Geordies were marvellous people: hospitable and generous – the 'salt of the earth' and a marked contrast to the majority of English southerners that I had come across.

The four of us were billeted in civilian digs with a lovely landlady who, although a bit strict, wanted to mother us, even doing our dhobying and ironing our collars until they were as shiny and stiff as boards. Anyone in uniform on Tyneside was fêted like a hero; even when we explained that we were just raw rookies who had never seen action, it made no difference. It was impossible for us to buy beer in local pubs, as someone would always insist on buying it for us and, without fail, after an evening's sing-song around a pub piano, someone would invite us home for supper. A refusal would bring a swift rebuke: 'Hush, Geordie hinny, come on awa' we us me bonny lad.' Lovely people.

I can still remember snatches of Geordie songs from all those years ago:

Keep yor feet still Geordie hinny and be happy through the neet,
Though ye dinna be sae happy through the day.
Keep yor feet still Geordie hinny, keep yor feet still Geordie lad,
And divn't drive me bonny dreams away . . .

Working on the anti-torpedo nets was heavy work; wrestling with the stiff wire and hand-riveting iron templates to form the mesh was the easy bit, the hardest was making the thing work. Hanging onto the end of a forty-foot boom, suspended over the murky waters of the Tyne while being bounced up and down was quite exhilarating, especially after being issued with a pair of heavy leather sea boots which would act like lead weights and guarantee my demise if I fell in.

I soon had the job no one wanted: securing the nets to the top of the boom. This entailed climbing out to its end and hanging on while the winch drivers hauled up the heavy nets. As the weight took hold, the steel boom flexed alarmingly, bouncing around and threatening to throw me off. Once the nets were in position, I had to secure them with a specially designed snatch block and quick-release shackle.

The job was even more dangerous when a ship came in with damaged nets, for this meant that I had to wrap my legs and one arm round the end of the boom and hit the quick-release shackle with a hammer. The effect was alarming, more exciting than any fairground ride. As the shackle opened and dropped several tons of dead weight, the forty-foot boom sprang into the air like a giant fishing rod with me clinging on for dear life to avoid turning into a human cannon ball catapulted across the Tyne.

IN WARTIME, every young lady was attracted to men in uniform, sailors especially (even ugly sods like me) and I was soon madly in love with Mary, a beautiful cuddly blonde from Gateshead. During our innocuous love affair she persuaded me, in spite of a head of steam which we had built up, that she still wished us both to remain virgins. She consoled me as only a cuddly blonde could and I missed the trip to heaven and my train to Hebburn.

Our dear landlady was most emphatic that her door was locked at 11.30 p.m. so, not wishing to disturb the dear soul when I got off the last train in the early hours of the morning, I headed for Simpson's Seaman's Hostel, a grim, brick-built edifice where I had heard, for a shilling, a bed could be had for the night. Arriving bleary-eyed the next morning at my digs, I was looked at with great suspicion by Mrs Jackson, my suddenly not-so-loving landlady.

'Where have you been all night?' she asked.

I explained about missing the train, not wishing to disturb her, and so I had stayed at Simpson's Hostel. I was doing alright until I mentioned Simpson's; if I had said I had stayed in a knocking shop it couldn't have had a worse effect. Dear old Mrs Jackson's face turned white. 'Stay there!' she exclaimed. 'You're not entering my house; Simpson's 'as got fleas!'

So there I was, surrounded by my worldly possessions: one kitbag and one hammock, standing on a windswept street of terrace houses in Hebburn-on-Tyne, flabbergasted and homeless.

Six houses further up the street a door opened and a lady beckoned. 'Hello hinny, has she thrown you out? Come in and have a nice cup of tea.' This lovely lady listened to my tale of woe and said, 'Never mind hinny, you can stay with me.'

Amy was gorgeous, a lovely little Geordie housewife whose husband, Bill, was with Monty in North Africa, and she looked after me like a long-lost son. It wasn't long before another of my fellow shipmates was ejected for breaking Mrs Jackson's curfew, and he joined me.

When pay day came around, Amy refused to accept any money. No matter how we argued or begged, she insisted that we needed it more than she did. I explained that it wasn't our money, it was a billeting allowance to pay her for food and lodging, but she was adamant and refused to accept it. My mate and I solved the impasse by hiding our allowance in the most unlikely places every week: stuffed inside vases, on the top of high cupboards and even under the stair carpet, knowing full well that with her industrious cleaning she would find it sooner or later.

ALL GOOD THINGS come to an end and someone at the Admiralty suddenly realised that four young fit ordinary seamen were enjoying life on Tyneside, so after only a few weeks we were drafted away from Amy's loving care and sent back to Plymouth to HMS *Drake*, known to the boys in blue as Jago's Mansion. Jago was a nickname used in West Country ships and in the RN Barracks, Devonport, to denote the General Mess feeding station. It came from the Warrant Cook who started the system in Devonport Barracks, one Alphonso Jago. At the time I didn't know who Jago was, but the old three-badge ratings used to sing a song that went something like this:

Oh, I wonder, yes I wonder, if the Jaunty made a blunder,
When he made this draft chit out for me.
For I've been a barracks stanchion and I've lived in Jago's Mansion,
So please don't send me out to sea.

These were not my feelings, for, like all transit barracks, HMS *Drake* was a miserable place where kitbags were stuffed in a large rack and often rifled. Ratings came and went all the time, and every hour or so, when a new draft was pinned to the board,

You're not entering my house; Simpson's 'as got fleas!

there was a sudden surge of men to see who was lucky and who had been unlucky in their postings.

That large, black-painted, pin-marked board, festooned with drawing pins and torn pieces of old draft notices, displayed these new sheets giving the name of the ship and a list of ratings being drafted. These innocuous pieces of paper made the difference between living or dying to the men whose names were displayed and who had to report for transit within the hour. My name appeared after two days; I was whisked away to the docks and on my way to Malta, 'the island of goats, bells, rock and smells'.

Several months before I arrived, Malta had been hammered by German and Italian bombers; sunken ships littered the harbour and the tanker *Ohio* lay half-submerged in the harbour entrance, silent witnesses to the desperate and heroic struggle to replenish the almost depleted fuel reserves as the island fought for its life. Valletta, the capital, looked like a giant rubble heap with half-buildings rearing drunkenly out of the debris of pulverised rock. Numerous churches, amazingly, were still standing, although many had holes in their domes and sported scarred and battered walls.

In spite of the bright sunlight reflecting from the white rock, it was a sombre sight and I thought of the many lives lost and the many fine ships blasted apart before sinking to the bottom of the sea on those desperate Malta convoys, and of the unsung heroes who had withstood the non-stop bomber, U-boat and destroyer assaults which decimated convoys and turned the island into a wasteland.

It has been written that Malta was the fox gnawing into the vitals of Italy. It was from Malta that British submarines slid out to take their toll of the Italian convoys supplying Rommel. It was from Malta that destroyers struck out in darkness, leaving death and destruction behind them. It was Malta that had to be destroyed, which the Axis aimed to do by eliminating its airfields, docks and stores, destroying all communications and lines of supply, then laying a minefield in all the island approaches. The plan was thwarted at the final hour in a massive do-or-die attempt to save the beleaguered island, when a massive convoy of merchant ships and defending cruisers and destroyers fought every inch of the way from Gibraltar

German bombs left large areas of Malta in ruins

across the Mediterranean, running the gauntlet of the far superior forces of enemy bombers operating from nearby bases. They attacked, remorselessly, day after day, reducing the supply ships to five: *Brisbane Star*, *Melbourne Star*, *Port Chalmers*, *Rochester Castle* and the *Ohio*.

As we steamed into that battered harbour, past the *Ohio*'s superstructure, I imagined the sky black with smoke as the Stuka dive-bombers came screaming down. I thought of those brave seamen and felt strangely guilty that I hadn't been there with them in 1942, having been born a year too late.

I reported for duty aboard my first ship, HMS *Kimberley*, a battle-class destroyer with a mainly South African crew, having just been recommissioned in South Africa. Aboard a fast destroyer with an illustrious war record, leaving Malta with the bow wave cutting through the deep blue of the Mediterranean was a thrilling experience for a young, raw sailor. I stood on the deck gripping the rail while the engine power increased and the ship vibrated. As the bow momentarily reared up before plunging down into the sea, it created a mass of boiling white foam which spewed over the bows and streamed over me and the forward gun turret, before plunging like a wild stallion into the waves once more.

I staggered below, soaked to the skin.

Chapter 3

HMS Kimberley

AT SEA on the *Kimberley*, I began to feel myself becoming part of the ship and I understood the strange affinity that develops between sailors and the vessels they sail in. The surging power of the engines vibrated through the ship, turning it into a living entity as we ploughed through the sea, sending out a wake of churning white water that boiled up aft of the stern, leaving a white highway that gradually turned glacier blue before being overwhelmed by the darker blue undercurrents of the Mediterranean swell.

It wasn't long before I discovered that there were also undercurrents among the crew, twelve of whom were British, while the rest and the overwhelming majority were South African; it was like the Boer War had never ended. The South Africans were a surly lot who only communicated in English when they had to and reverted to speaking Afrikaans whenever they had the chance. In front of British seamen, on board a British ship, this naturally led to friction as, to our uneducated ears, it sounded like a sort of bastardised German and we took it as an insult.

The similarity between some of our crew and the enemy became more obvious when we called at Ferryville in North Africa to pick up some German prisoners. Herding the Germans on board, we sent them below decks and shoved two South Africans down with them, much to the Germans' amusement when the ratings hammered on the door to be released.

So this was the much vaunted Afrika Korps. They were certainly an impressive bunch: tall, blonde, tanned, they looked the picture of physical fitness; most were not much older than I was, yet they had fought their way through a gruelling desert campaign. I found it hard to believe that these 'supermen' had just been thrashed by the Eighth Army – ordinary blokes like Amy's husband, wearing Dad's Army shorts that extended below their knees.

Once at sea, the prisoners of war were allowed on the aft deck. Being on guard duty, I was soon approached for the inevitable cigarette and began talking to a couple of the Germans who spoke good English and were starved of news of the war. When I told them that we were winning they seemed shocked and became concerned for their families in Stuttgart, for they hadn't seen their parents since they had joined the Hitler Youth brigade, which had been quickly drafted to serve under Rommel.

I swapped a packet of cigarettes for an Afrika Korps belt and received a loud bollocking from one of our South African officers in broken English for fraternising 'wit de enemy'. I definitely preferred the Germans.

It was a strange coincidence that the last time the *Kimberley* had been engaged in picking up defeated troops was during the British withdrawal from Greece, when Greek and British armies were overrun by a highly mechanised advance of German troops through Yugoslavia and Bulgaria. The *Kimberley* had helped evacuate five thousand troops from 24 to 30 April 1941, then again during the Battle of Crete from 1 to 20 May 1941, when I was still at school. Now, the *Kimberley* was once again picking up defeated troops, though this time Germans – some of whom were also probably still at school in 1941.

It was a different crew but the same war and, young as I was, I reflected on the untold misery of the millions of lives ruined by that demented, failed painter called Adolf Hitler. I didn't have time to dwell on this though, as other duties called and I handed over my guard duty to Nobby Stiles, my relief.

HAVING TAKEN THE PRISONERS to another transit camp en route for internment, it was back to Malta and shore leave. As the fort of St Angelo hove into view we rushed for the washroom; there were blokes trying to shave with 'pusser's issue' cut-throat razors, elbows being nudged, throats cut and much blood and swearing.

Best uniform on, I lined up with the shore leave contingent of Red Watch, we were inspected and had DDT powder sprayed down our tunic fronts to combat the outbreak of bubonic disease which a plague of infested rats was carrying, and received a French letter to combat other diseases which over-amorous females might be carrying. Then it was off to the 'Gut', our name for the street called Straight, which was anything but!

Straight Street, Valletta, had ministered to the needs of British seamen since the Knights of St John landed on Malta during the Crusades; indeed, some of their ancestors must still be plonking away on the old pianos in its numerous bars. The narrow, cobbled street sloped steeply down from the centre of the town in a blaze of coloured neon and cacophony of noise from the bars and eating houses that lined each side. Adding to the general hubbub were touts outside each establishment, imploring you to select their wares. Inside they were hot, steamy, smoky and smelt of egg and chips and cheap perfume, which emanated from voluptuous Maltese ladies, while beer fumes and BO emanated from their customers. It was a sailors' version of Shangri-La.

At that time my mate (or as they say in the Navy, oppo: opposite number) was a hard, stockily built Birmingham lad. 'Brummie' and I plonked ourselves down in the Morning Star for our gourmets' delight; our 'instant steak, eggs and chips' arrived almost before we ordered it, with the meat the colour and texture of old cowboy boots, but we shovelled it down before moving on to the more serious business of the evening – getting pissed.

This was our first imperative of shore leave and soon we were in happy land, that pleasant state induced by a full stomach and enough beer to make you happy yet still aware of having a brain. A three-badge stoker was soon belting away on the piano, while his mate, another three-badge stoker, belted away on top of the piano as he went through the motions of shagging Doris, one of the bar girls (though judging by her laughter, he was not quite managing it).

Brummie and I were suddenly partially buried in female flesh as two well-built bar girls landed on our laps, mine whispering sweet nothings in my ear punctuated by frequent requests for 'sherry for the lady', while cutting off the circulation to both my legs and one of my testicles.

After more drinks and some furtive fumbling, Brummie and I decided to explore less of the Maltese and more of Malta. Kissing our lovely ladies farewell we staggered outside, turned smartly one pace right and right-wheeled into another honky-tonk where we were greeted by Johnnie, one of the 'stars' of the establishment into which we had just strayed, affectionately nicknamed the Galvanised Donkey. Johnnie was well known throughout the Med, but alas not by Brummie and me. We were unaware that he was a transvestite, so when this tall, gorgeous-looking female bore down on us, Brummie thought he'd died and gone to heaven.

With a lecherous look on his mottled face, Brummie burbled, 'Come 'ere love,' as this Ava Gardner lookalike hovered alongside. 'Give us a kiss,' said Brummie running his hand up a shapely leg . . . 'Bloody hell! I've got hold of a pair of balls!' yelled my mate, just before Ava hit him with a mighty fist and Brummie passed me going horizontally backwards.

One hour later, he came round in the loving arms of two members of the Navy Police. I don't know what *I* had done, apart from having a bruised hand, but I was under arrest as well – it was strange. We were escorted back to the ship and presented to the Officer of the Watch,

'Attention! Off caps. You are charged with an offence prejudicial to naval discipline. Captain's Report. On caps.'

The following day my duties were interrupted by a call that I would become very familiar with in my services to the monarch. 'All ratings on Captain's Report muster on the aft deck.'

I soon found myself marched smartly with other miscreants, to stand to attention outside the wardroom.

'Ordinary Seaman Wilkinson,' barked the jaunty (the traditional name for the master-at-arms), and off marched Brummie. Whatever justice he received it was quick, for he was out again in a flash.

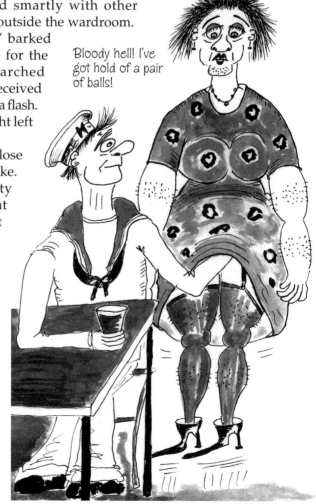

Bloody hell! I've got hold of a pair of balls!

'Ordinary Seaman Eyre. Left right left right, halt, right turn. Off caps.'

I had never seen the captain close up, and he didn't seem a bad bloke. 'Eyes down!' barked the jaunty (bloody hell, I can't even look at him, I thought – I later found out that 'looking' is called dumb insolence and warrants another charge). The jaunty read out the charge. 'By starting a fight, and other actions prejudicial to Naval discipline at the establishment known as the Silver Horse.'

'But I . . .'

'SILENCE!' thundered the jaunty as I tried to defend myself. The captain glared at me and I could feel him memorising my homely features for future reference. 'Fourteen days number elevens and loss of all privileges,' he said.

'On caps,' barked the jaunty. 'Right turn, left right left right . . .'

When I met Brummie, it turned out that he had only received seven days and he started the bloody fight, while I had fourteen and I didn't even remember being in one. There ain't no justice!

I later discovered that a rating being charged cannot speak out in his own defence.

NUMBER ELEVENS meant rising at 5 a.m. and scrubbing out the latrines, plus undertaking various other crappy tasks under the supervision of an equally crappy South African leading seaman. At 6.30 a.m. a quick breakfast and report for normal duties after first clearing up the mess deck, with half an hour for lunch so that you could watch your mates guzzling their rum ration – yours had been stopped. Then fall in with the duty watch and work until the bos'n piped: 'Men under punishment fall in.'

The duty watch was then stood down and men under punishment received two hours' rifle drill, or running on the spot with a rifle at slope arms (which could be quite painful). The piped order 'Men under punishment stand down' came as a blessed relief, which lasted for exactly one hour before the dreaded command 'Men under punishment fall in', and this continued until 9.30 p.m.

Punishment in the Royal Navy meant just that: there was no attempt to show men the error of their ways or to help the misguided and confused, and there were no social workers to plead that you had been abused as a child; there was no attempt at reform or special pleading about discrimination. Homosexuals were a rarity and it would not have been a good career move to complain that the powers that be were homophobic, for they would probably have chucked you over the side!

Ah, the good old days!

If I thought punishment at sea was rather horrid, I was in for a shock when we docked as the punishment there could be more imaginative, such as running around a nearby barracks square with a Lee Enfield rifle on your shoulder in the blazing sun until your white vest was stained red with blood from a shoulder torn open by the continual jolting of the heavy rifle, or until you collapsed from heat exhaustion. However, having 'done the crime and done my time', I was extremely well behaved for a while. Even the jaunty remarked on it.

THE FLOTILLA had received orders to support the Fifth and Eighth Armies, which had invaded Italy and needed the support of our 4.7 inch guns. Just before dusk the *Kimberley* followed the *Lookout* and the *Loyal* as they slipped out of the Grand Harbour, momentarily silhouetted in the liquid gold of a sea bathed in the rays of the setting sun before turning and heading for Naples.

On watch at 1.30 a.m. during the first dog watch, I scanned the faint line of the horizon on a regular sweep. This time the almost imperceptible shades of grey between the sea and sky showed a faint blip. I swung my powerful binoculars back again and made out a very faint line on the horizon.

'Object bearing one five two,' I shouted, and within seconds we were summoned to action stations as the ship heeled over, almost throwing me off the iron ladder as I clambered down to my station on B gun. The ship's speed increased as I struggled into my anti-flash gear and took up my position.

'Load star shells, one and two.'

'Fire.'

The loud crack of the twin 4.7 inch guns and the acrid smell of cordite filled the turret with deafening noise and fumes. The dark sky turned to day revealing the outlines of an Italian cruiser.

'Load H.E. shells.'

The ship vibrated at full speed as we tried to sail within range, knowing all the time that the cruiser, with its superior fire power and range, could at any second blast us out of the water with its battery of 6 inch guns.

'Range closing.' The captain of the gun gave terse instructions to the layer and trainer as he relayed instructions from fire control.

'Closing.'

Silently we waited for the sounds of approaching shells.

'Fire one. Fire two.'

Amid a blast of noise and heat the empty shell casings were ejected from the breech.

'Reload.'

Two more high explosive shells were fed in and the breech block closed.

'Fire.'

'Reload.'

With the gun turret filled with smoke and the blood-stirring smell of cordite, we waited expectantly for the order to fire.

'Range increasing – target out of range.' The gun captain swore. 'The bastard's leaving us . . . bloody Italians!'

At that time the Italian Navy had the fastest ships in the war; with powerful engines and a light superstructure they had sacrificed armament for speed and, coupled with no great desire to tackle three destroyers, the cruiser was soon a faint memory.

We found out through the grapevine that the cruiser was the *Giuseppe Garibaldi*, and the outcome of our brief encounter was not known to me until forty years after the war when my second wife Audrey and I were backpacking on Crete. We stayed for a few days with a delightful couple, a middle-aged Greek and his wife who looked after us like a mother and father, bringing fresh flowers and cups of tea to our room every morning and generally spoiling us with extra meals and drinks in the evenings when we returned. Old Bruno would even go searching for us in his old car if we were overdue from a day's trek.

Bruno noticed my tattoos and with his broken English and my almost non-existent Greek we discovered that we had both been in the services, he as a forced conscript in the Italian Navy. Several drinks later, during a hilarious conversation it turned out that Bruno was serving on the *Giuseppe Garibaldi* when it was attacked by British destroyers. 'But we escape,' said Bruno, 'then we sink in ze 'arbour at Brindisi.'

Bruno dashed off to his room and reappeared with a battered photograph of his ship tied to the harbour wall, its decks awash. When I informed him that I was on one of the destroyers that shelled him, he fell about laughing, kissed Audrey, shook me vigorously by the hand, broke open a bottle of vintage brandy and we all got drunk. Every time I bumped into him after that he would greet me with 'Boom, boom' and a hearty laugh. Dear old Bruno – I still have the dog-eared photograph of his sunken ship, which kept him happily out of the rest of the war.

The Allied advance in Italy was going at a steady pace, with good supply lines, while the Germans had lost most of their Italian support and were fighting bitterly with weak supply lines. They lost none of their aggression as they tried to prevent the

British and American troops pushing remorselessly ever northward, in spite of the confusion of multi-national commands and antagonism between American and British generals. However, on 3 September 1943 the Italian armistice was signed and, although fighting continued in the north, Italy became progressively under Allied control. Naples was captured on 1 October.

The three destroyers pulled into the Bay of Naples, passing under a huge cloud of smoke and ash thrown out by the glowering bulk of Vesuvius; a pyrotechnic display of molten lava explosions lit up the volcano's summit, flickering orange under the black cloud that clung there. The following day a fine layer of ash covered the ship, but otherwise the eruption was quite mild and our skipper soon had the duty watch clearing it off.

We finished refuelling, then followed our two sister ships north past Ischia. Arriving at Livorno we could see the smoke of battle and soon we were engaged in bombarding German positions. It was very similar to target practice and the monotonous crunch of the destroyers' guns was only enlivened when we could see a far off puff of dust as a building toppled or, sad to say, when a church tower collapsed, although in practical terms it would probably have held German snipers.

From our point of view, this was a very antiseptic form of warfare, as in this sector the enemy had no means of hitting back at the ships that were lobbing 4.7 inch shells. The shelling must have been effective, though, as our targets were constantly redirected further north by the British Army fire control. The action eventually ceased and then, line astern and feeling happy with ourselves, we headed back to Naples to replenish our diminished stock of shells.

IN NAPLES the first part of Red Watch was granted shore leave. Having kept my nose clean since my last charge I was in luck, but Brummie wasn't as he was doing another stretch of number elevens for telling our favourite South African leading seaman to 'Shut yor 'ole you foreign bastard!'

Naples was a dump; even without the war damage it was a dirty mess of a city. A few of the more intelligent ratings caught an old ramshackle bus to Pompeii, but I and the less intelligent looked at a couple of ruins, declared them to really be bomb sites and instead decided to sample the foul Italian wine. We had seen signoras give it to babies, so it couldn't be all that strong . . .

Perhaps it was our English stomachs, perhaps it was because we had mixed wine with spaghetti, or perhaps it was those small exotic drinks which came in traffic light colours and tasted of high octane fuel – whatever it was, we all had large purply streaks down the front of our nice white uniforms when we returned to the liberty boat. We woke up the next morning with a healthy respect for vino rosso and discovered that most of us were on a charge. And then I remembered, we had fought with some Yanks. We won.

The following day we were back up the coast. The army had advanced round the next headland and we received fresh orders as we steamed away. It was good to reach the open sea again and the lower deck grapevine had it that we were back on escort duty, heading for Gibraltar. 'Cooks to the galley' piped up. Brummie and I were duty cooks, so I went below.

Destroyers and smaller ships in the Royal Navy possessed a wonderful system whereby each mess had a rota of mess deck cooks – ordinary hands who prepared the main meal of the day and gave it to the cook to cook. The system may seem odd but, considering the fact that the ship only had two cooks, it worked.

Of course, most of the H.O. (hostilities only) ratings had never prepared a meal in their lives and to prevent food poisoning and lynchings one of the older hands or the cook would give advice. Brummie and I were becoming quite good at cooking and, apart from one cock-up when I shoved a chicken in the galley with its arse tied up and its guts still inside, we hadn't done too badly; anyway, it's difficult to bugger up spuds, two veg and a bit of pork. Today I was going to make a sweet. 'Bloody 'ell,' muttered Brummie when he saw me buried in flour, lard, currants and odds and sods.

At the meal the Rum Bos'n served the rum, which is very strong and makes plain cooking seem like cordon bleu.

'Not bad that, Snakey,' said the lads who had eaten the main course. I had acquired the nickname from a newly acquired tattoo, a snake on a dagger. 'What's for duff?'

I proudly went to the galley hatch and the cook handed me my big square tin.

'What's in here? It feels bloody heavy,' said cookie. It was. I plonked it on the mess deck table and the lads looked at it with interest.

'It's got a lot of dead flies in it,' said Big Taff.

'They're not flies, they're currants, you stupid sod,' I answered.

'What is it?'

'Figgy duff.'

'Where's the figs?'

'Underneath somewhere,' I muttered as I took a knife and prepared to cut it into twelve pieces. The knife refused to penetrate. Strange looks from mess mates. Sharper knife. No headway . . . Saw knife. Ah, success. I laboriously sawed the duff into twelve pieces; one fell on the deck – it bounced! It was inedible, rather like chewing golf balls.

'What have you put in this, Snakey? Stewed French letters?' asked Oggie.

'I must have done something wrong.' I ducked as a piece was hurled at my head; it bounced off the deckhead, hit the bulkhead, two South Africans and landed back on the table. It was indestructible. We played cricket with it, football with it, even volley-ball – and then flung the whole lot over the side, much to the surprise of a lone seagull that grabbed a piece and immediately sank beneath the waves. Snakey's figgy duff went down in the annals.

THE MEDITERRANEAN is often regarded as an Italian lake, but it can get rough and life on a destroyer loses its glamour when your whole world is heaving up and down and slewing from side to side. Anything above moderate speed makes the upper decks untenable, as the ship hits a wave the bow lifts and seems to hang momentarily before crashing down, to be completely submerged before rearing up again, spewing sea water the length of the ship.

Most mess decks can become unpleasant in a rough sea, with stuff spilling and swilling around, but our mess deck, where the British crew members were quartered, was the worst on the ship. Mess sixteen, forward lower (or 'the jungle' as we nicknamed it), was always underwater when we were at sea. It was like being on a submarine; the few small portholes or scuttles leaked like sieves and were permanently jammed with towels or discarded clothes in a vain effort to stop the water coming in.

Right in the bows of the ship, at the narrow pointed end, we shared our accommodation with the chain locker, where the anchor chain came down. This was another source of sea water and leaping out of our hammocks in the mornings into three feet of oggin was not unusual when at sea.

Conditions in rough weather were atrocious. The dim night light would reveal a row of hammocks swaying in unison, almost touching the deckhead as the ship rolled and pitched when it hit the waves with the force of a battering ram. The cold, grey, riveted steel plates, seemingly always streaming with condensation, were all that separated us from the sea outside, and the noise of the waves thudding against the hull and the groaning of the ship's plates caused many a sleepless night. A flickering cigarette lighter and stream of blue smoke from one of the other hammocks meant that you were not alone in your sleepless vigil.

Owing to the restricted area of the forward lower, our dining area was situated on the deck overhead, midships near the galley, so this made life more tolerable. The forward lower was also home to some hard cases, seamen who had been in some sort of trouble with authority and glorified in the name of 'skates'; not that I was one, of course, but the way things were going anything was possible. They were a good bunch of mates and a good camaraderie existed between us, cemented by our mutual hatred of Petty Officer Butler.

'Are you awake, Snakey? Gie us a fag.' It was Jock, who leaned over and took the cigarette. 'Gie us a light.' I handed him the lighter. 'Och, it's a fookin awfu nite, it's a fookin guid job this yin was built on the Clyde or we'd be awa' to meet Davy Jones.'

Jock had just joined the ship in Naples after having completed seven days in the cells.

'What did you do seven days for?' I asked as I lit up.

'Och, it were nuthin'. I had a disagreement wi' a killick.' (A killick was a leading seaman.)

'What did you do?' I queried.

'Well, we had had a few drams ashore and we were feelin' a bit happy, ye ken. When I returned on board I pulled his wee beard, just fer a joke like. The fookin wally had nae sense a humour at a', and he put me on a charge.'

'That's a bit much, seven days for pulling a bloke's beard,' I said.

'Well no, I called him a fookin old goat and gie him a wee slap as well. It was a friendly gesture, ye ken. Och, they've nae sense a' fookin humour at a'.'

WHATEVER THE WEATHER, nothing must be allowed to upset the well-oiled machinery and tradition that is the Royal Navy. It mattered not that the ship was bouncing around like a cork and that the denizens of the jungle were trying to do a King Canute by trying to stop the tide coming in through our portholes; life on board His Majesty's Ships must go on.

The captain was making his rounds. This was the equivalent of a visitation from God, or perhaps more aptly it might be compared with a visit from the Mikado and his Lord High Executioner as the retinue advanced towards mess sixteen: the jungle.

'Attention, stand by for inspection.'

Four seamen of low rank, clutching mops and buckets with their trousers rolled up and bare feet in sea water, stood to attention in apprehension as the sea water swished from side to side with the roll of the ship. It was like a bad sketch of spring cleaning day on the *Titanic*.

The captain, with a look of utter disbelief on his well-chiselled features, stepped over the threshold of the watertight doorway and advanced. Between a finger and thumb

Are you trying to tell me my ship's sinking?

he picked a soggy vest off the mess deck table, glared at it as though it had the pox, and dropped it back on the table. He then looked at the assembled humanity before him with a look of utter distaste, before opening several lockers, glancing at the contents as the word 'shit' formed on his well-modulated lips (but which, being too much of a gentleman, he never uttered). He positively glared at the towels wedged in the portholes as though they were an alien life form threatening his ship, looked down at his wet feet and trousers, then scrutinised each one of us in turn: Scouse, Jock, Brummie and me.

'Well, duty officer! What the hell is the meaning of this?' The duty officer turned to the petty officer and demanded an explanation, and the petty officer thought the best persons to supply an answer were us, so he asked us: 'What's all this?'

'We've got a leak,' I said.

'A *leak*!' thundered the captain. 'Are you trying to tell me my ship's sinking?'

' No sir, just leaking. It's the portholes.'

'Silence,' said the petty officer.

'This mess deck is a disgrace and these ratings are improperly dressed. Put these men on a charge.'

The duty officer turned to the petty officer, and said: 'Put these men in the First Lieutenant's Report.'

'Aye aye, sir', said Petty Officer Butler. We had made his day.

THE FOLLOWING MORNING we lined up for the First Lieutenant's Report. There was the usual bunch. 'What you in for this time, Snakey,' asked a pockmarked South African able seaman. 'They're blaming us for the fuckin' ship leaking,' I answered.

'Fuckinell,' he said.

'Ordinary Seaman Eyre,' shouted the Jaunty. 'Left right left right halt left turn. Off caps.' The charge was read out. The First Lieutenant never even looked up from what he was reading. 'Seven days number elevens,' he muttered. 'On caps, right turn left right left right,' yelled the jaunty.

We had picked up four supply ships off Gibraltar and, together with a corvette, were steaming steadily towards Alexandria. At this stage of the war submarine attacks were infrequent, but ships were still being sunk so the Navy could not afford to relax. Butler had us chipping paint off the depth charge mountings while lashed with spray and had just put Jonno on another charge for cursing him.

Suddenly, the action stations alarm sounded and we rapidly cleared the depth charge area and hurried to our positions, Jonno still cursing Butler. The corvette was releasing depth charges as we increased speed and changed course while we waited for the ASDIC (sonar) to detect an echo. Nothing. The ship turned and altered course, but again nothing. 'The bastard's scarpered,' someone said. ASDIC picked up a signal and the depth charge crew fired off six charges in quick succession. We heard a muffled boom, then another and another as huge domes of boiling water lifted out of the sea. More followed in a rapid sequence which vibrated through the ship.

We waited expectantly for evidence of a strike, but nothing came to the surface. I was disappointed, for I had a vision of a U-boat's conning tower emerging from beneath the waves with lots of Conrad Veidt lookalikes waving their arms above their heads and shouting 'Kamerad'.

ASDIC had lost the echo, so after a fruitless search we gave up and followed after the convoy. Heading for Alexandria gave us time to work off our punishment – all except Jonno, of course. In spite of being stalked by Petty Officer Butler, whose aim in life was to make mine a misery, I avoided any more mishaps with authority. With a bit of luck I would manage to go ashore at Alex.

It was an offence to stand still, so if in doubt grab a brush and start sweeping. Butler had been spotted sidling round the gun housing and he suddenly materialised in front of me. Sweeping vigorously, I gave him a sweet smile which meant 'Hello you bastard.' The frustration showed on his face as he searched for something to charge me with.

'You – down to the galley and report to the cook,' he said. 'He wants some gash shifting, a job that will suit you, you're used to rubbish.'

'Aye aye, sir,' I replied, dropping my brush.

'Pick that up,' said Butler.

'Aye aye, sir,' said I, smoothly retrieving my brush. 'Where should I put it?'

ALEXANDRIA – a place I had dreamed about, steeped in history: legends of Cleopatra; Elizabeth Taylor and Richard Burton; the gateway to the Nile and ladies doing naughty things with donkeys. Leaning against the ship's rails, we looked in disbelief at the uninteresting panorama of flat-topped rectangular buildings and the scattered minarets of mosques and clumps of palm trees.

Desert sands merged into the outskirts of the port. We could feel the hot breath of the Sahara and smell the exotic aromas and stench before we passed the sea wall. The wailing cry of the holy men urging the faithful to prayer was interspersed with the clamour of the dockyard, punctuated by the staccato machine-gun-like rattle of the riveters. A forest of cranes, ships' masts, funnels and superstructures highlighted by blue flashes of intense light and fountains of glowing metal from the welding torches hedged us in as we reversed between two other destroyers, the forward spring rope straining and hands lowering collision mats and fenders. Then panic stations – the starboard depth charge carriers were being crushed against a stanchion on the adjacent ship.

We watched horrified as the depth charge was pushed down into the launcher. A leading seaman dashed forward and unscrewed the fuse while everyone stood motionless; in an act of supreme courage he averted disaster, an explosion which would have ripped both ships apart. The depth charge was forced to the bottom of the housing and began to buckle and twist before the two ships pulled apart and the launcher activated, propelling the depth charge into the harbour between the two destroyers.

All this occurred within two or three minutes, yet from my position amidships it was like watching a slow-running film. Then, suddenly, it was over – the film accelerated and a great wave of sound came on as dockyard mateys ran for their lives screaming to Allah, white shirts flapping in the wind as thin brown legs carried them away from what they saw as impending disaster, not realising that the depth charge had been rendered harmless.

The first lieutenant supervised the depth charge retrieval and a disposal unit took it away, as Blue Watch prepared for shore leave while Red Watch began loading stores and I was detailed for sentry duty. Smartly attired in white belt and gaiters with cap perched at the correct angle and chinstrap down, and with my rifle on my shoulder, I should have been a figure of some importance. But no, I was suddenly surrounded by lots of gentlemen in long shirts and funny hats.

'You got cigarettes, Johnny?'

'No, piss off!'

'Baksheesh Johnny, baksheesh.'

'Gold watches – verry cheap Johnny.'

'You want woman?'

'No, sod off, you brown bastards.'

'You want my sister? Verry good, verry tasty, verry young, verry cheap.'

I was overwhelmed by these persistent sods, so I took the rifle off my shoulder and put a round up the spout and pointed it at them. 'Imshi!' I yelled. They all scarpered and I resumed command of the gangway.

'Wily oriental gentlemen' – as we called them in those days – were the world's most persistent salesmen; they would flog their grannies for a few bob, and in fact one did offer me his granny after I had turned his sister down. Within minutes I was approached again by a refugee from Aida, who sidled up to me and with breath like a Pharaoh's jockstrap whispered in my ear: 'You got cigarettes, Johnny? I pay good money, many ackers. You like watch woman with donkey, werry good pokey pokey?'

'You'll get bloody pokey pokey in a minute,' said I, sticking the rifle none too playfully in his guts. He gave a wheezing gasp, his face turned as pale as it could be expected to and he shot back, tripped up and fell on his arse, and everyone scarpered again.

It was a very entertaining couple of hours, until a crew-cutted, bull-necked South African able seaman stood in the bows and began doing a passable imitation of Hitler with his right arm raised in a Nazi salute and ranting away in Afrikaans as he unfurled a Nazi flag. '*Sieg heil*, you bloody bastards, we're coming to get you,' he yelled in English. Within seconds we had a miniature riot on our hands, with me bashing

Arabs off the gangway with my rifle butt and some of the crew turning hosepipes on the rest as more dockyard mateys joined in. They are very excitable people, our wily oriental gentlemen, and peace was only eventually restored when the stupid seaman who had started the rumpus was chucked into the dock by his own mates and the dockyard police appeared and chucked a few of the nightshirted brigade into the back of their jeep and drove off.

With my duty watch over I returned to the mess deck. 'Up spirits' had been piped and we were enjoying our tot of rum when a brown face appeared at the open port.

'Hello Johnny, you like souvenirs, real imitation mummy, jewels for girlfriend, Spanish fly, also for girlfriend, make her very tasty.'

'Fook off ye wee brown bastard, or I'll sink yor fookin boat.' The owner of the brown face obviously understood Glaswegian, because it suddenly vanished – only to reappear at another port to do a deal with Big Taff, who for a packet of fags bought a nice veneered jewel box for his sister. 'Not bad for sixpence,' said Taff.

Tobacco was in great demand and Brummie had a bright idea, resulting in a sudden increase in sales of pound tins of cigarette tobacco from the ship's canteen. We went to work carefully, removing the tin foil seal then taking out the tobacco and replacing it with sawdust, apart from the top two inches which were refilled with tobacco. With the assistance of an electrician, the seal was carefully soldered back in place and, hey presto, one tin of tobacco was made into five.

We were soon doing a roaring trade through the portholes as wads of piastres changed hands with the eager buyers, although there was one tricky moment when one of the traders, who was craftier than the rest opened up a tin. He stuck his fingers into the contents, pulled out some tobacco, rubbed it between his fingers, smelt it and, with big beaming smile pronounced it 'verry good'. If he had dug any deeper it would have been pronounced 'verry bad', our scam would have been blown and we would have had another mini riot on our hands.

Having almost depleted the ship's store of tobacco, the newly made 'piastre millionaires' heaved a sigh of relief when the *Kimberley* was moved to another part of the dock and so we avoided any customers' complaints.

AFTER THREE DAYS' non-stop work on minor repairs, the skipper granted recreation leave to Cairo and a large percentage of the ship's company were soon embarked on the Cairo express, a thing that looked like a coal scuttle on wheels. Several carriages had been reserved for forces personnel and were fairly crowded, but we didn't complain as the other carriages for the locals were completely buried under a swarm of humanity – people hung onto the roof, hung onto the sides and even rode the buffers.

Preceded by a cloud of black smoke, lots of shouting, blowing whistles and flag waving, the train got under way. Standing at the rear of our carriage, I watched an Egyptian man advance precariously across the swaying, jumping buffers with a flat wooden box hanging around his neck and his white 'nightshirt' billowing in the wind. Nimbly, he leapt to our carriage and opened his box to reveal a miniature jeweller's shop, with gold rings and gold watches galore.

'You buy gold watch Johnny, verry good, verry many carrats,' and he began hustling his way down the carriage.

He made his first sale to an army corporal, then approached a sergeant.

'You like gold watch Johnny?'

He gave the salesman a hefty kick up the backside

'No. Piss off,' said the sergeant, obviously not impressed.

'Verry good gold – verry many carrats.'

'You'll get a carrot up your arse in a minute – *imshi*!' yelled the burly sergeant, giving the salesman a hefty kick up the backside. This transformed him into a travelling salesman and propelled him out of the carriage and onto the buffers, where he clung precariously.

'For you,' he said to the sergeant, 'I make verry big discount.'

The sarge obviously knew more than I did, for I bought one. Four days later the gold started to rub off. 'Oh yes,' I thought, 'verry good gold, verry many carrats!'

Cairo was fascinating. The noise and jostling crowds hypnotised us as, with hand on money belt, we headed for the terminal to catch a bus to the Pyramids. Waiting for the bus to start we were plagued by beggars who came to the open windows in a never-ending stream of pathetic, dejected humanity. One young woman patrolled the length of the bus, beseeching money for the sick baby she held in her arms. I was handing her some money when, as she reached for it, the shawl covering the baby's head slipped. I recoiled at the stench and the horrible sight, for the small creature was a dirty grey colour and had obviously been dead some time.

I felt angry that people had been reduced to this by others' greed, for there was opulence galore in Cairo, but the feeling the average Egyptian had for these unfortunates was less than they held for a stray cat. On the bus journey the stark evidence was there in the human bodies that lay in the gutter where they fallen, having been hit by a vehicle and left like so much garbage for the road sweeper.

I was shaken out of my gloom by my four shipmates and we were soon enthralled by Egypt's antiquities. We did the Sphinx, but never solved the riddle. We did the Pyramids, had a ride on a camel and Brummie caught camel fleas.

'You like picture, Johnny?'

'Why not? Take one of the flea as well.' I have it in front of me now, all these years

Some of the crew of HMS Kimberley in Egypt. Jim is in the front row, astride a camel on the left, and Brummie is second from the right in the back row

later. Six soldiers, four artificers and seven Jolly Jack Tars, interspersed with fourteen gentlemen of a dark brown persuasion wrapped in tea towels and nightshirts, all smiling broadly except for one picking his nose, as they tended their camels which we were sitting on. The youth sitting on a camel at the front has his hat stuck on the back of his head, revealing a mass of wavy hair, a slightly aesthetic-looking face spoiled by a sardonic grin and a cigarette stuck in the corner of his mouth, and a display of square ankles where several packs of twenty were stuffed down his socks.

We visited some of the tombs, saw an old, dried-up body lying in a huge stone sarcophagus with a small stalagmite growing on his skull, where the occasional drip of calcite-saturated water must have seeped down through the old limestone capping stones. The Great Pyramid of Cheops had to be climbed, so we raced each other to the top. Standing there in wonder, I gazed at the panorama of ancient Egypt spread out before us and we sat there philosophising as we smoked a couple of fags.

All this culture made us thirsty, so it was back to Cairo and a couple of bars before we headed for the museum, another amazing experience as we looked in awe at the sarcophagi and the great wealth of priceless artefacts contained in this huge, dusty building. Separated only by a thin sheet of glass, the cobalt blue and gold splendour of Tutankhamun's death mask wove me into a magic spell from which there was no escape; the expressionless eyes bore into my soul and I marvelled at the grandeur of those ancient times and contrasted them with modern Egypt and beggars starving in the streets. If I had a wish, it would be to be transported back in time to ancient Egypt and see the land of the Pharaohs as it was.

'Eh. Snakey! All this culture is affecting your brain!'

I was dragged back to reality by my less sensitive buddies. Dehydration was staring us in the face, then luckily we came across a bar, and another. We were saved.

'Eh, Johnny, you want jig a jig?' I looked down at the two small boys.

'No,' I said.

'You jig a jig my sister? Very young, very pretty.'

'No,' I said.

'You jig a jig my mother?'

'Definitely no!'

As soon as we got rid of the urchins we were accosted by more small boys with shoe boxes.

'Shoe shine Johnny?'

'No.'

'I make your shoes verry good, I make your shoes sparkle, verry shiny, *verry* cheap.'

'How much?' asked Big Taff.

'Five piastres.'

'Done!' said Taff, and he and Wilkie put their best foot forward. The two boys worked industriously on one shoe until it gleamed, but the other one remained covered in dust and unpolished polish.

'You like, Johnny?'

'Great,' said Taff. 'How about the other one?'

'Ah, the other one is ten piastres,' said the little sods.

'Stuff you,' said Taff, 'you're getting bugger all now.'

The small boy looked up at this giant of a man in his lovely crisp white uniform, unscrewed a bottle of liquid black polish, and said, 'Ten piastres, or I throw this.' These little wily oriental gentlemen won the day and Taff and Wilkie succumbed, taking great care that the top was screwed tightly on the polish bottle before paying up. The boys grabbed the money and ran. 'Bloody little bastards,' said Taff.

We were sucked into the maelstrom of Cairo, with its bazaars, bars, cafes and restaurants. I can't remember what we ate, but we certainly had plenty of drinks and found ourselves emerging from a narrow alley into a broad avenue on the smart side of town. Considering there was a war on, it was remarkable how many well-heeled Europeans with a predominance of British were around, and we were surprised when an English middle-class gent and his charming wife stopped to talk to us.

'Do come and have a drink with us,' said this lovely woman.

It was wonderful talking to a woman again, especially one who was both beautiful and intelligent, and I realised that I had been cooped up with sweaty sailors too long. They took us into a nearby courtyard, where we sat under palm trees with a slight breeze lending a certain enchantment to the balmy evening, drinking exotic drinks and breathing in the erotic mixture of the perfumed scent of the woman's body. They were very pleasant people and, talking about England and the war, I could have sat there for hours – especially as I sat close to this wonderful female who gazed deep into my eyes and listened intently to everything I said. I think I had reached the point where I was falling in love, when Brummie said, 'Oi you two ain't spoies ar yo?'

It was suddenly, 'Oh, is that the time, we really must dash, it's been wonderful meeting you lads, take care.' With that it was goodbye.

'What did you say that for?' I asked Brummie.

'Well, he asked me what sort of ship I was on,' said Brum.

'Oh,' I said, my romantic vision going up in smoke.

Once in the whirling hubbub of the back streets, we were soon back in the real world as we were accosted at every open doorway of seemingly every bar and cafe in Cairo. Life was good. The Egyptian beer was weak stuff, so we started on the spirits, which was a mistake. Passing one establishment, an enthusiastic 'Salome' invited us in.

'You like steak? You like egg and chips, you like ross bif, you like woman, you like small boy?'

'Just the job,' said Wilkie, 'I'll have small boy and chips.'

Anyway, the food smelt good so we got stuck in to a good nosh and more drinks. And more drinks. I can't remember when the young lady appeared, but we were suddenly talking about massage, manicures and haircuts, and second-hand virgins. At the back of the establishment was a sort of barber-cum-massage parlour, cum-tattooist, cum-manicurist . . . A sort of supermarket for body needs.

Things became a bit vague at this point. Vince was plonked down in one chair and Brummie in the other. They almost disappeared from view as they were surrounded by brown-faced men with beaming smiles and a gaggle of young ladies who knelt at their feet. What followed became even more vague, as the rest of us carried on drinking because we felt we were beautiful enough. I staggered across to see what was going on. Vince and Brummie were sat back like royalty on their thrones, with beaming smiles on their faces, huge cigars stuck in their mouths, very slick haircuts, two gorgeous young ladies each doing their fingernails, and a small boy at each foot polishing their shoes with gusto. I asked if they wanted a drink.

'Yes, bring them across, my man,' said Vince.

I DON'T KNOW when the tattooist became involved, and nor did anyone else. In fact, we didn't know they had been tattooed until the following morning. However, through the mists of time, it appears that Vince and Brummie parted with a wad of 'ackers' from their ill-gotten gains from the tobacco sales, and we staggered and rolled towards a friendly taxi driver who deposited us on the train. Next morning I came to in my hammock with a thumping head. I heard a strangled groan and looked over at Brummie. His mottled face was a strange purply colour and he was looking at his arm.

'What the fuckinell is that?' he yelled.

I rolled over and said, 'That's a bad bruise, when did you get it?'

'I don't know, but it's bloody sore,' came the reply. My eyes had cleared somewhat and, leaning over to his hammock, I slowly focused on what looked like a cross-eyed tabby cat smiling at us, done in bright orange and blue.

'It's . . . it's . . .' I couldn't stop laughing. 'It's a fuckin' tattoo!'

'What!' Brummie tipped out of his hammock and sat on the deck looking at his much maligned arm with a look of total horror on his face. 'What the hell is it?' he asked as he gazed in stupefied shock at the apparition that gazed back.

'It looks like a cat,' I suggested.

'Why the bloody 'ell would I want a fuckin' cat on my arm?' asked Brummie.

'I don't know, perhaps you have one at home,' I ventured. Slowly, Brummie's expression changed, and a faraway trance-like look came into his eyes.

'It's coming back,' he said. 'One of those bloody women said to me, "You like tiger?" I thought she fancied me and I said, yes . . .'

'Oh shit!'

'Tell me, Snakey. Does that look like a bloody tiger to you?'

HAVING LEFT EGYPT more or less intact, apart for the assault on Brummie's arm and two ratings left languishing in a Navy jail, we sailed away from the heat and smell of Alex and headed for the Adriatic, the *Kimberley*'s bow churning through the dark blue water, sending up cool spray that caught on the sea breeze and cleansed the ship from the stench of sewage and filth of the Nile delta. It felt good to be at sea again, and it even moved Vince to eloquence.

'No wonder the Pharaohs died out, living in a fuckin' place like that!'

My shipmate, a taciturn Yorkshireman from Leeds, suddenly launched into a tirade against the 'fez-wearing bastards' and I suspected that he had been done a great wrong by our brown-skinned friends, for he was not normally this garrulous. Leaning against the rear gun turret, enjoying a crafty fag, I waited patiently for Vince to reveal all. Alas, at that moment we were caught red-handed in the act of doing nothing by our soft-shoeing, divisional petty officer who put us on a charge for skiving. Ah, well, it was back to normal and in a strange way I was pleased to see Petty Officer Butler's gimlet-eyed visage again. It meant that the two able seamen who were going to do him in somewhere up a dark alley in Alexandria had failed, possibly because the bastard never went near any dark alleys.

Vince retreated into his monosyllabic self as we headed for Italy. Then one day Vince, who was a betting man, won a bet against the rest of the mess on the result of a boxing match, and was owed 'sippers' all round. The next day the bos'n piped 'Up spirits' and we adjourned to the mess deck, where Vince claimed a portion from every man's rum ration – which varied from a sip to a bloody great gulp. Considering the fact that there were twelve of us in the mess, this meant that together

Tell me, Snakey.
Does that look like
a bloody tiger to
you?

with his own tot Vince consumed an inordinate amount of 60 per cent proof rum in a very short time.

Consequently, after a meal of roast potatoes, Yorkshire pudding and corned dog (we couldn't get the beef), Vince became very expansive and experienced recovered memory syndrome about our night in Cairo. It seems that Vince had a worse aversion to 'arse bandits' than the rest of us. 'So,' burbled Vince, 'just on a whim . . . well I was pissed . . .' and he proceeded to tell us how he had commissioned one of those ancient Egyptians to tattoo two eyes on his arse, 'One on each cheek,' and the words, 'I can see YOU' tattooed underneath. Enough to put anyone off!

He laughed and rose unsteadily to his feet. 'And now,' said Vince, slurring his words, 'all will be revealed!' and he dropped his trousers and undercrackers. There was a stunned silence as we gazed in awe at the sight before us. A hairy, spotted bum is not a pretty sight even when one has not just scoffed a hefty meal, but Vince's bum was something else. The eyes that stared back at us from the bloated, discoloured cheeks bore an uncanny resemblance to the eyes of Nefertiti that we had seen in the Cairo museum, only here one was brown and one was blue and the brown one was crying! Underneath were tattooed the words 'I can see you', but unfortunately one of the e's coincided with the proximity of Vince's anus and had taken on the shape of a squashed 'o' where the tattooist's needle had skidded up Vince's bum. The resultant script read 'I can seo you'.

We fell about laughing while Vince said, 'It's alright for you buggers, but its bloody sore.' After a more scientific appraisal by a two-badge able seaman, it was declared that Vince's bum had been contaminated by a dirty needle and the eye wasn't crying, it was suppurating. I don't care what he said, I'm sure I saw it winking.

SEVERAL DAYS LATER we pulled into the bleak, bomb-damaged harbour of Ancona on the northern Italian seaboard of the Adriatic, before commencing operations about sixty miles further north near Rimini.

The low-lying coastline and sandy beaches seemed desolated as we steamed north, but those villages and small towns that could be discerned through binoculars showed the ravages of artillery fire and it wasn't long before the horizon became smudged with the smoke of battle. Line astern, the three battle-class destroyers moved close to shore and we were piped to action stations. The Germans were entrenched in strong positions on high ground just behind the town and, acting on instructions from Army spotters, we bombarded their positions throughout the day and retreated at night to Ancona. Well out of range of German guns, it was a bit like duck shooting.

Back in Ancona that evening we pulled alongside the ruined jetty to reload with shells, helped by some squaddies who we invited on board for some food and a tot of our stored rum. The lads were existing on corned beef and field rations, so were more than pleased to accept our hospitality. 'Christ, next time there's a bloody war on I'm gonna join the bloody Navy,' was typical of their comments. We promised to be careful where we lobbed our shells before we bid them goodnight.

The bombardment continued for several days and seemed to be having the desired effect, as we moved our range further north. The combined firepower of the three twin turrets with 4.7 inch guns on each of the three destroyers made us feel invincible.

We heard a screeching, whistling roar. At first it caused bemusement, but when it grew louder we realised that it was the noise of a large shell and, simultaneously, there was an explosion and a huge water spout rose only a few feet from the starboard side of the ship. From a lazy sort of duck shoot, we had been suddenly transformed into the target.

Everything happened at once. Accompanied with a sound like an approaching train, a large shell just missed the ship's port side and the *Kimberley* heeled over with the force of the blast as the spout swamped the decks. Thanks to an instant reaction from the bridge we were already going at full speed ahead when the next shell landed, just missing the stern and landing smack between where the other two shots had landed.

This was perfect shooting by the Germans, with a bloody big gun, and the flotilla lost no time in putting up a smokescreen and moving back out of range. I could only imagine the signals between the three skippers, probably starting with: 'What the hell was that?'

This was very exciting stuff for a young lad – it was the first time I had been shot at! The operation took on a different phase as the three ships played cat and mouse with the big gun by nipping in and out of the smokescreen, banging off our guns and making a rapid retreat back into the fog.

As with everything else in wartime, we never found out what was shooting at us until much later when we were informed that the enemy had mounted a 15 inch gun on a railway truck in a tunnel, and it took the combined operation of a pincer movement and several bombing raids to dislodge it.

IT WAS LUCKY for me that I joined the Navy when I did, otherwise Petty Officer Butler, who seemed to be a direct descendant of Captain Bligh, would have had me keelhauled. I could just imagine myself in a Pythonesque sketch, standing there bound hand and foot, waiting to be heaved over the side and only being saved at the last minute by a bloke from the Admiralty who had come to inform Butler that keelhauling had just been banned. I could also picture Butler pleading with the official, 'Oh please sir, let's do it just one more time.'

I don't know why Butler had it in for me. Perhaps he'd heard me taking the piss, or perhaps it all started when I was washing paintwork down and singing a merry little ditty I had picked up:

Oh, I don't give a fuck for the Killick of the top,
Or the Killick of the working party,
For I'll go ashore for my Pompey whore
'Cos I'm pissed up Jack me Hearty.

Butler first told me to pipe down and then asked me where I had heard it. When I answered, 'From some real sailors,' he didn't seem too amused. From there on our relationship became a bit dodgy: me dodging him to prevent him putting me on a charge. Perhaps it was my attitude to discipline or maybe my sardonic wit, but I seemed to rub him up the wrong way and if ever a group of ratings were seen to be not doing what they should have been doing, I was the one singled out for punishment.

I began to hate the bastard, and the tensions on the *Kimberley* between the South Africans and the British were as nothing to the mutual hatred Butler and I had for each other. What made it worse was the fact that he was a fellow Lancastrian, originating from Salford. After facing three petty charges in as many days, all manufactured by

Butler, I lost my temper and said to him, 'After the war I'm going to come to Salford and I'm going to find you, and bloody well fill you in!'

This was not a good career move, as it was immediately translated as threatening an officer – in the First World War I could have been shot. I realised I was in serious trouble and reckoned that I would have the book thrown at me. Surprisingly enough, though, when I was brought up before the captain for insubordination and threatening an officer, he must have realised that Butler was riding me and, coupled with the fact that we were a long way from Malta or Naples, the captain took a more lenient view than I had imagined and lashed me up with everything except a custodial sentence. I considered myself lucky, even though it looked like I would never set foot on dry land again and I would be bound to the ship, like a latter-day Captain Nemo or the crew of the *Flying Dutchman*, doomed to sail the seas for ever with no shore leave.

'You're going to have to keep your nose clean, Snakey,' advised Big Taff. 'You can't win against that bastard.'

I took his advice, kept my head down and my simmering temper and frustration in check. We received fresh orders and headed back towards Naples, passing through the Straits of Messina at night, where rivers of fire flowed down from the smoking summit of Etna, glowing red and gold in the distance. Once through the narrows, still an uneasy and obvious place for a U-boat ambush, we passed the muted lights of Palmi and headed for Stromboli, where continuous eruptions made this one of the most impressive volcanic displays in the western hemisphere. Passing quite close, we could see the molten lava flowing straight into the sea, sending huge clouds of steam from the boiling shoreline. Stromboli at night is one giant firework display.

Naples had become a much busier port since we were last there. The bay was dotted with ships of all descriptions, including several cruisers and aircraft carriers as well as a huge conglomerate of merchant ships clustered near the docks. Reprovisioning with stores and ammunition kept the ship's crew busy for twenty-four hours. Eventually, shore leave was granted for both watches, except of course for me and a few hard cases. We had to be content with an occasional smuggled drink from our returning shipmates and the recounting of their drunken, amorous escapades – all except Geordie, that is, as he had been arrested.

According to Brummie, it seems that he and Geordie had gone looking for a brothel. They had wandered into an area of Naples that was out of bounds and somehow ended up in a bombed-out building with two young Italian ladies. 'One looked like Sophia Loren and the other like Gina Lollobrigida,' said Brummie. 'Anyway, like the start of *Eskimo Nell*: "Pull up a chair and buy me a beer and a tale to you I'll tell."'

Someone supplied the booze and we listened to Brummie's tale of woe. Geordie soon had this gorgeous dark-eyed signorina on the bed in a bomb-damaged room, where one missing wall had been replaced by a sheet of corrugated iron, leaving Brummie in the other half of the room.

'Oh, you lovely creature,' gasped Geordie, as she pulled up her skirt and took off her knickers. He had never seen anything like this before and he went at it with the young sixteen-year-old girl like a donkey with a firecracker up its bum. The young lady obviously enjoyed it because she was soon moaning and groaning and banging her hand against the corrugated iron partition as she writhed about in passion. Brummie, on the other side of the partition with a lady of his own, received a deafening bang in his left ear every time the flexing sheet was struck.

'There I was,' he said, 'with Gina Lollobrigiwotsername and the silly sod next door was sending me deaf. The bed behind the partition creaked and groaned, the lass was moaning and saying, *"Mio amatissimo"* and banging on the bloody iron, Geordie was promising to marry her and shouting his silly head off, and gradually it went quiet.' Then, Brummie said, he could relax and get down to it himself: 'It were the best shag oi ever 'ad in moi loife,' he said.

Brummie sat back and had a long gulp at his beer as he recollected his hour of bliss. Then, Brummie continued, he heard Geordie's girl shouting and struggling: '*Assistenza! Assistenza!*' Christ, he's killing her, thought Brummie. '*Sto soffocando! Assistenza!*' More frantic cries. Pulling up his trousers, Brummie dashed next door to find Geordie sound asleep on top of the young girl with a smile of utter contentment on his face.

But, before Brummie could lift Geordie off the struggling girl, his own partner whispered '*Attenzione,*' and pointed through a hole in the outside wall at two approaching redcaps. 'Shit,' exclaimed Brummie and dived under the bed. The clattering of heavy, large-sized military boots came rattling up the wooden stairs and Brummie watched from under the bed as two pairs of black, shiny boots entered the room.

'Now then, now then,' and 'What have we here? Come on me lad, up you get,' came menacing voices from above. From the bed came a gasp. 'Just a minute, I haven't finished.'

Blimey, he's started again, thought Brummie.

The largest pair of boots advanced towards the bed and stopped inches from Brummie's face. 'You say you haven't finished? You think we're going to stand here while you bounce up and down like a fucking little jackrabbit? When *we* say you're finished, you're *finished*!'

Geordie was plucked off his lovely soft nest and dropped to the floor like a rag doll, trousers still round his ankles and his willy shrinking rapidly like a large pale worm in its death throes as it hit the dusty floorboards. Geordie's bleary eyes gazed in astonishment at Brummie under the bed, before he was whisked to his feet by the redcaps. 'Put tha' 'orrible thing away,' said one, and together they frogmarched him down the stairs and out of sight.

There was a moment's silence then, '*Mamma mia!*' came a relieved sigh from above, to end in a gasp and a scream of terror as Brummie materialised from under the bed. ''Ere you are luv,' said Brummie, 'one tin of corned dog and a packet of fags,' and with cries of '*Grazie, grazie, grazie mille*' ringing in his ears, our hero fled into the night.

We later learned on the grapevine that Geordie was going to spend a few days' rest and recuperation in a Navy jail, as his kit was taken away. His replacement duly arrived on board, an evil-looking sod from Fulham with a scar over one eye and a nose even more bent than mine.

A heavy sea greeted us as we rounded the island of Ischia and headed north towards the Gulf of Genoa. The war was entering a crucial stage, as Allied forces were advancing across northern Europe and the Fifth and Eighth and American Armies were sweeping the Germans out of northern Italy. La Spezia soon bore the brunt of our guns as we returned to the familiar routine of duck shooting, hoping that on this coast the Germans didn't have any surprises in store, as they had at Rimini.

In the north, the Italians had turned on their own forces – their actions would lead to the death of Mussolini and his lover on 28 April 1945, their bodies strung from a street lamp on public display. A buzz went round the ship that another front would soon be opened up and there was an urgent need to clear the harbour at Genoa, where partisans seemed on the verge of taking control.

After several days we left our new base at Livorno and moved up in support of a minesweeper flotilla which was sweeping the heavily mined approaches to Genoa. We had barely settled into our routine when the ship's speakers informed the crew that we were going to Corsica to take on board a certain Right Honourable Winston Churchill, our great wartime leader.

Through a blue haze we watched the mountainous island appear on the horizon and I could smell the scent of maquis and other herbs, although they were miles away. Pulling into the old port of Ajaccio, we sensed the excitement of a historic occasion and, with all hands smartly attired in gleaming white shorts and fronts, we bustled about doing our duties like men possessed. Tied alongside the quay we lined the rails and watched our prime minister clamber sprightly up the gangplank as he was piped aboard. A spontaneous cheer rang out as a surge of patriotism went through my puny chest. The great man clambered onto the bridge, lit a three-foot-long cigar, and we were off to the French Riviera.

With the *Kimberley* cruising at a leisurely speed among the mass of ships lying off the coast of southern France on that fine calm morning, it seemed to me reminiscent of the historic Spithead Review when the monarch inspects England's mighty fleet. I looked up at Churchill, who stood in a prominent position on the bridge giving his famous V-sign and literally sparkling with joy. With a large, beaming smile on his face we passed through the armada of cruisers, destroyers, minesweepers, corvettes and even two ageing battleships.

Early during the First Watch, SAS Red Berets and other specialist troops had landed on the coast and soon overcame what initial resistance there was. Together with the rest of this impressive gathering of warships, the *Kimberley*'s guns had joined in putting up a heavy barrage, designed to obliterate any enemy troops forming a second line of defence further inland, while line after line of landing craft, filled with pale-faced troops, headed for the shoreline, which was now partially obscured in a haze of smoke.

Churchill was in his element. Dressed in his dark, battledress uniform, mouth clamped on a huge cigar, he waved majestically at the American troops, who, jaws chewing frantically on gum or smoking what could be their last cigarette, didn't seem too impressed as they passed by, packed in their landing craft like so many khaki sardines. One or two gave a half-hearted smile of recognition, but no doubt most, thinking of the carnage of the D-Day landings, were more concerned about what lay ahead and couldn't have cared less if it was Betty Grable waving at them.

The Navy guns were soon silenced when it became apparent that the Allied troops were advancing at speed and encountering little opposition. The two battleships, with their big guns and much longer range, still pumped out shells at targets fifteen miles inland, then they too were silenced when a large area inland was overrun and consolidated by the rapidly advancing troops.

The larger supply ships moved closer to the beach and began unloading. Tanks could be seen trundling up the beaches, closely followed by field guns and lorries, The beachhead had been established and the landing was a success. Churchill was right: the Mediterranean coast of Vichy, France, had a soft underbelly, but this 'other D-Day' nevertheless cost the lives of 1,300 Allied soldiers in the first forty-eight hours.

It was quite a day – a long one, but exciting.

THE *KIMBERLEY* left this new theatre of war and returned 'old Winnie' to Corsica. Big Taff and I were detailed to carry the great man's baggage ashore, but when I returned up the gangplank I was immediately put on a charge by the ever-vigilant Butler, who noticed that I was not wearing any socks. I wouldn't have minded if it had been Churchill who rebuked me, unless of course he had sent a secret signal to Butler with his cigar smoke, but somehow I don't think he did as Big Taff wasn't wearing any socks either.

My punishment routine had now developed into an everyday chore. It gave me longer, more hard-working days than anyone else, but as they say: 'Suffering is good for the soul.' Well, it wasn't, but being at sea made it just about bearable.

Anchored offshore on the Italian Riviera, however, was a different matter as I enviously watched my shipmates, nattily attired in their best outfits, lined up for the liberty boat – while I carried on scrubbing decks like a bloody Cinderella! It had been so long since my feet had touched dry land that they were growing barnacles, and I was growing mutinous!

I didn't have a Fletcher Christian to turn to, so I kept my dark thoughts to myself and daydreams of Petty Officer Butler hanging from the yardarm kept me going throughout my bleaker moments.

Returning from shore my mates told stories of gorgeous women, dripping with jewels, who invited them back to their houses for food and drinks. MacMullen, a good-looking sod, even said he had shagged one; I could have killed him as he described lying on silk sheets with this gorgeous naked female writhing in abandoned lust while licking his body all over.

'You lying bastard,' I said.

'No, it's true,' said Smithie, his oppo. 'Well, I saw them disappear into the bedroom and when they came out she had a smile on her face and looked like she had received a good tupping.'

'Bastard,' I said.

'Never mind, Snakey. Here, have a drink of French beer,' said Mac.

At sea the next day I hatched up a plan. Away from Butler's all-seeing eyes, I cornered my fellow miscreants Jock and Oggie.

'How far can you swim?' Jock looked at me in amazement. 'Dunno,' he answered. Oggie asked, 'Why, are we sinking?'

I let them in on my cunning plan. 'Yee are fookin mad!' said Jock. 'Yee'll no git awa' we' it.'

'We'll probably drown. I can't swim two bloody miles,' gasped Oggie.

'Oh well, forget about it,' I said and went back to greasing the davit winch.

Early that afternoon the *Kimberley* anchored in a picturesque bay between Santa Margherita and Rapallo. I leaned against the ship's rail and guessed it would be about two miles to the shore. We had just finished our last muster of the day and all the liberty boats had gone.

'Do you reckon we can do it, Snakey?' asked Oggie, who had just sidled up with his mate.

'Well, if we take it easy . . . and we can float when we're tired . . .'

'Aye, and if we start to drown we can always wave our hands and wait for Butler to rescue us,' interrupted Jock. 'Bugger it, let's have a go.'

We nipped down below, stripped off and put on swimming trunks, then each of us filled a condom with money, two matches and three fags, sealed up the end, stuffed them down our trunks and slipped over the side. Luckily, the sea was calm and we struck out boldly for the faraway shore. After what seemed like hours, we rested.

'I'm knackered,' gasped Oggie, 'and the shore seems further away than ever.'

'Aye, and so's the fookin ship,' spluttered Jock.

After floating on our backs for a while, we struck off for shore again only this time more slowly, conserving our energy. Oggie coughed up some sea water and panicked.

'1 think we're floating out to sea.' Indeed, Rapallo seemed further away than ever.

'Don't get any more fookin ideas, Snakey,' gasped Jock. I was too knackered to answer as, slowly, agonisingly, we swam on until I noticed a palm tree becoming bigger and nearer by the minute. Eventually, we dragged our aching bodies up the beach and lay there gasping like three stranded dolphins.

'We're aw fookin mad,' muttered Jock.

'We'll never make it back,' said Oggie, 'especially when we're pissed.'

Sometime later, the ultra-smart waterfront of Rapallo was treated to the spectacle of three skinny youths staggering with fatigue, plonking their bodies down at an empty table and pulling three French letters from bedraggled swimming trunks, spilling their contents on the table and trying to light bent cigarettes with wet matches.

We had landed at the smart end of what in peacetime is a very fashionable resort surrounded by palm trees, coloured lights and beautiful people; the war didn't seem to exist. Such a transition was unbelievable, and both the ship and the Navy vanished from my thoughts. Oggie gesticulated to the nearest waiter, while I cadged a light for my ciggy from a group of people at the next table. I said 'Saluto' in my best Italian and gestured to my limp cigarette.

While most of the fashionable group looked in a mixture of shock and horror at this apparition in pre-war swimming trunks, one young lady smiled and offered her cigarette. As I leaned over to make contact I found myself looking down the front of her loose, flimsy beach dress at two incredibly beautiful breasts, my hand started shaking and she reached out and held it steady with her own. It was like holding hands with a goddess. I dimly heard her speak. 'You are Eenglish sailor?'

'Si, signorina.'

'You feel very cold.'

'Er, yes,' I said, still talking to her breasts. 'We have been swimming.'

'Why don't you and your friends join us?' asked one of the men. I moved like streaked lightning, dashed across to my mates, downed my beer in one and said, 'Follow me.' The table was soon groaning in food and drink as the Italians insisted on treating us like royalty.

'Where is your ship?' asked a middle-aged woman who was dripping with diamonds.

'There.' Oggie pointed to the distant horizon, where a thin pencil line smudge denoted the existence of the *Kimberley*.

'Where are your clothes?' asked the signora.

'There,' said Oggie, pointing out to sea again. And – having drunk lots of exotic drinks and being slightly overcome with the heady mixture of beautiful women, their sensuous perfume and attention – he told everyone that we were all sub lieutenants and we had gone for a swim, but had been caught in a fierce current that washed us ashore. All very amusing stuff; the Italians that didn't understand him had the story translated (and embellished) by the others.

'I did not know that there are – how you say – currents, here,' laughed one young lady, who was slowly falling out of her bikini as she shook with laughter.

'What for you have 'le condom' with lire and tabac?' asked the dark-eyed one sitting next to me. 'Did you know you would be washed out to sea by these current?'

Ho, ho! We had been rumbled, so we told them the truth – which they found fascinating. 'Ow you get back to your ship?' asked one of the men.

'Swim it,' said Jock.

'Oh, no, you will drown,' said the man with obvious concern.

'More than fookin likely, but it will be worth it 'cos we're in heaven now,' said Jock, looking into the peat-coloured eyes of the young woman next to him. 'I can see heaven in your eyes, so I don't care if I die later.'

'Oh, Meester Jock, you say such a nice thing,' she said sweetly and gave him a kiss.

'Och, noo ahm really in heaven, I've been kissed by an angel,' said Jock, leaning back in his chair and falling completely over, landing spreadeagled with a daft smile on his face.

Our genial hosts insisted that we stayed with them and, later, one would take us back to the ship in his yacht's dinghy. I shall never forget that balmy evening, with the moonlight reflecting off a flat-calm sea and lamplight radiating a warm soft glow. When women like that hold your hand and look deep into your eyes, your mind visits places it has never visited before.

Alas, it soon became time to return to the ship and, like three maritime gooseberries, we staggered along the beach, me with a soft warm arm around my cold clammy body (probably to stop me dying of exposure) as we approached the small jetty. We had already made plans to swim ashore again, when my eyes slowly focused on a group standing near the jetty and the approach of the last liberty boat. Too late, we tried to hide behind our Italian friends.

'Bloody 'ell, there's Snakey,' yelled one of the crew. 'There's Jock, and Oggie.'

'And bloody 'ell, there's fookin Butler,' groaned Jock. We shook hands with our hosts, gave the lovely signorinas a lingering kiss and promised to see them after we came out of chokey or when the war ended, whichever was sooner. Then we waved them goodbye and advanced towards the guillotine in the shape of a deeply satisfied, smirking Petty Officer Butler.

DURING ONE OF MY BLACK DOG DAYS DAYS – an expression that Churchill used to indicate a depressing time – I had put in a request for a transfer to another ship; any ship, even a submarine. There were only a few good officers on the *Kimberley* and the mixed crew and antagonism of the other officers created a mutinous undercurrent. My overriding concern, however, was that I was becoming sorely tempted to take a swing at Petty Officer Butler. That would only put me in a Navy jail, so when my transfer came through I was over the moon.

It was a bit of a drag leaving my old shipmates, but in the forces real friendships never had time to develop and new mates were easy to come by. I was a bit disappointed that Butler wasn't there to see me leave the ship in Malta, for unfortunately he had been badly beaten up – by some Italians, it was said – while enjoying the Freedom of the City which had been granted to the ship's company by the city of Genoa.

Arriving at St Angelo barracks, three able seamen and I were soon processed, received an all-night pass and hailed a nearby *dghajsa* (a Maltese gondola) whose owner rowed us across the Grand Harbour to the old Customs House steps, which we bounced up like men possessed as we headed for the Gut.

Nothing had changed. The honky-tonk pianos were still playing, the bars remained a blaze of light and a cacophony of noise and laughter as 'Jack Me Hearty' got pissed. The four of us grabbed a table and were soon tucking into some dead cat and chips – at least, that's what it tasted like.

Maria, the belle of the Blue Moon soon hove into view. 'Ah, Snakeey, where have you been? When we get married?' and she leapt on my lap with a cry of passion, which nearly gave me a rupture and spilt my beer. 'Oh, don' worry, I bring more, and sherry for the lady.' She gave me a beaming smile, grabbed my British military money, shot off to the bar and returned with a ticket – 'IOU 6d Blue Moon' – plus more bottles and, of course, 'sherry for the lady'. I still have that IOU – I wonder what it's worth now?

After drinking copious amounts of beer I noticed that Maria's voluptuous figure seemed slimmer and more desirable. I decided that I was in love. I was also having difficulty in walking to the bog, and came to the conclusion that I had been so long at sea that my land legs had gone.

Before we left for The Rising Sun I gave Maria a kiss and a cuddle and copped a crafty feel at her lovely wobbly bum. 'Are my arms getting shorter,' I wondered?

'You come to my 'ouse later and stay all night,' she said, flashing her black eyes. It sounded too good to be true. 'I've got a promise,' I said to Vince and the others, 'and . . . and . . . I'm going to . . . er . . . get my . . . er . . . leg over,' I slurred.

Waving them *bonsoir* I staggered off down the Gut towards the warren of dark narrow alleyways at the bottom of the hill. In the early hours of dawn I found no. 15 Nelson Street and knocked on the door. No response. I tried again, only louder. I stepped back and looked up to see if there were any lights. I would have seen plenty if I had stayed where I was! A giant flower tub, complete with soil, hit the spot I had just vacated and exploded like a bomb, showering me with debris. It was a quick way to sober up and I realised that two beings were above – one who didn't like me and the other – my guardian angel – who did.

I guessed my engagement was off.

Chapter 4

HMS Cadmus

MY QUALIFICATIONS as a QR3 Gunnery rating had stood me in good stead. A fleet minesweeper needed a replacement for a QR2 who had been taken ill, and I was being temporarily upgraded to Acting QR2 to take the post. HMS *Cadmus* was part of the 12th Flotilla. She was much smaller than the *Kimberley*, of course, and better for it. I sensed a different atmosphere almost as soon as I walked up the gangplank.

My duties included looking after the ship's armament, which included one 4 inch gun, two sets of Oerlikons, a couple of antique Vickers machine guns, a .525, several .303s, flares and other small arms. I was also in charge of the ammunition lockers and I even had my own small lock-up workshop where the small arms were stored. The crew's quarters were luxurious compared with my previous ship, and I realised that I had dropped in lucky. In the Navy it was a well-known fact that the smaller the ship, the happier the crew and George, the two-badge QR2 who I was replacing, had deferred going into hospital until he had familiarised me with the ship and my duties. One of these was mess deck Rum Bos'n. I had to pinch myself to make sure I was awake!

The 12th Flotilla moved out of Malta line astern, with seven fleet minesweepers followed by four danlayers heading for the Aegean Sea. I familiarised myself with my new toys, checking that I knew all I should about the ship's guns and consulting various manuals if I wasn't sure.

Life aboard the minesweeper was much more relaxed than the destroyer that I had just 'escaped' from. There was a much better atmosphere and a mutual respect between officers and crew. Ships quarters were less cramped and discipline was less enforced. Even the ship behaved differently, waddling and rolling like a friendly duck beneath our feet as we eventually entered the wine dark sea of the ancient Greeks.

Jim on duty with an Oerlikon gun

Approaching the Greek islands on a calm sea in a thin, low-lying mist was an experience I shall never forget. Seen from afar the small islands appeared to float in space, a mirage that remained until the lead ship sailed in closer, but even then an air of unreality remained as the island we were approaching seemed to increase in height, dwarfing the ships until a collision with the giant cliffs appeared imminent. Eventually, the flotilla anchored, tiny ships dwarfed by the bastion of rock that towered above them.

I soon discovered that minesweeping is slow,

tedious work which can be suddenly interrupted by exciting bits – a bit like sleep-walking and unexpectedly waking up to find yourself falling out of a window!

With the motor launch's shallow draughts allowing them to clear a way for the leading fleet minesweeper, the rest of the flotilla took up positions line astern in a stepped pattern, each following the paravane of the ship directly ahead. The paravane was a torpedo-shaped float that was towed so that it snagged the cable tethering a mine. When this happened its graceful progress through the waves would suddenly change; it then bucked up and down and became semi-submerged, while the pennant on top of the float became more lively as the mine wire was dragged towards the cutters. Then, with a lively flourish, the paravane would settle high on the sea and up would surge a spherical monster from below.

Trying to hit the bobbing horns with a .525 gun mounted on the ship's rail wasn't easy, but if one ship's gunner missed then another on the following ship would finish it off. The huge explosion and column of water was ample reward for hitting one of the detonating horns, but a hit near the base of the horns would quite often cause them to sink. Either way, they ceased to be a threat.

I had just detonated my third mine when the smirk of satisfaction was wiped from my face as a seaweed-covered monster rose out of the sea directly ahead of the *Cadmus*. The skipper took prompt evasive action and slowed down the ship's momentum while a few of the crew fended the mine away from the ship's side. Watching a mine bobbing up and down in a heavy swell with those evil-looking horns only inches from the ship's side made me go cold with fear, as I watched four of the crew, armed with wooden oars from the lifeboats, calmly walk down the length of the ship as though they were taking the dog for a walk. Once it was safely clear of the stern, the mine was exploded by a gunner on the following ship.

'Perhaps there's more to this minesweeping lark than I thought,' I mused, little knowing that the following day I would actually hear the horns of one of these monsters scrape along the side of the ship while I was down below. I made it to the upper deck in five seconds flat!

German scientists and their military were con-stantly devising ways of making our lives exciting. After we had spent many days clearing a minefield on the main shipping route through the Dodecanese islands and declaring it safe for shipping, the Germans declared it otherwise by dropping para-chute mines in the cleared channel, one of which crip-pled a merchant ship on the first convoy.

Having dealt with magnetic mines by degausing ships (a method of altering a ship's magnetic field), the Allies found that they had to deal with acoustic mines. These were triggered by the sound of ships' propellers, the frequency of which activated a mecha-nism that released the mine when a ship was directly overhead. The ever-inventive Germans seemed to take a special interest in making life difficult for the crews of enemy minesweepers (us), for they invented anti-personnel mines which were timed to explode

Jim (left) with Tubby Wilson preparing for guard duty in St Angelo, Malta

I don't think many sheep have been to sea in a
rowing boat. This bugger certainly hadn't

alongside the following minesweeper, scattering shrapnel over a wide area. We soon
learned to recognise these 'hobos' as they lacked detonating horns, and as soon as one
popped up we shouted a warning and ducked. There were also mines with clockwork
timing devices, mines that didn't surface, and several mines with cutters on the anchor
wires, designed to cut our sweep wire. All in all it was a continual battle of wits.

I HAD ONLY been on the *Cadmus* for five weeks when I found out that the captain
was a man with a void in his life. His was the only ship in the flotilla that didn't have
a mascot and, unwittingly, Tubby Wilson and I were instrumental in filling that void.

The afternoon watch had just taken over as we dropped anchor off a small deserted
island, the bos'n piped R and R shore leave and most of the crew were soon engaged
in kicking a ball about on the small beach. After a while Tubby and I went for a recce
around the island, and discovered it was not deserted but contained a small house, a
shepherd and a small flock of sheep.

After recovering from his initial shock and realising that we were British, the grizzled
old character invited us into his humble dwelling and offered us a drink of a clear
liquid that looked like water but wasn't. By the time we had to return to the ship,
Tubby and I could speak Greek and the old boy could speak English. We shook hands
and staggered back to the beach.

'If I didn't know better I would have thought you had been drinking – the sun must
have got to you!' said Binks, our petty officer.

'We have, and it hasn't,' I answered with a silly smirk on my face. There are not
many blokes that can get pissed on a desert island and Tubby and I were the envy of
the lower deck – until the sea rose as the wind increased and we both became a bit
green around the gills.

Two days later the *Cadmus* dropped anchor back at Robinson Crusoe's place and I
discovered that we were men on a mission. Accompanied by Jonno the warrant officer,
Tubby and I retraced our steps to visit Dimitri, who welcomed us with open arms.

Dishing out the fags we soon settled down as a cobweb-covered flagon of battery acid was pulled out from under the bed. 'Not for me,' said Jonno. 'Oh you must sir. It's an insult if you refuse,' said I, suddenly an expert on Greek customs.

'Well, just the one,' led to several before Jonno produced a wad of British military currency and asked Dimitri if he could buy a sheep. At first Dimitri didn't understand, but after more arm waving and another drink Dimitri's face lit up and he grabbed an axe and a sack and dashed off outside. '*Ochi, ochi, ochi!*' I shouted and Dimitri stopped with a puzzled look on his face. After more arm waving, drawing on the dirt floor with a stick and another drink so that we all spoke the same language, we eventually made him understand that we didn't want lamb chops, we wanted lamb on legs – a bloody smelly thing covered in wool with legs.

Sometime later we bid *adio* to Dimitri, a happy man with enough money stuffed in his tatty old trousers to retire on, and staggered down to the beach with three of us wrestling a sheep that didn't want to go. A lone able seaman was sitting having a smoke in a solitary whaler. 'Fuckinell!' he exclaimed as we approached. 'You can't take that fuckin' thing on here, you'll capsize us!' Warrant Officer Johnson took command.

'Don't worry, Able Seaman Green. You row, I'll take the helm and Eyre and Wilson will control the sheep.'

I don't think many sheep have been to sea in a rowing boat. This bugger certainly hadn't and it could be safely said that the last thing on this sheep's mind was a sea voyage with three inebriated sailors and another who thought we were totally mad! It struggled and butted and kicked as Tubby and I lifted it bodily, rolled it into the boat and straddled it.

By this time all the ship's company was lining the rails and falling about laughing as Able Seaman Green struggled manfully to row and also stop the boat from capsizing. The poor animal was demented with fear as the whaler rolled from side to side and suddenly, with strength born of desperation, it arched its rear and Tubby shot overboard, leaving me clinging to the sheep like a limpet. Jonno let go of the tiller and straddled the unfortunate beast until we pulled alongside the *Cadmus*, where some of the crew helped us lift it on board and yanked Tubby from the water.

We constructed a makeshift pen under the searchlight platform. The cook brought out stale cabbage and some water and the daft animal began chewing away without a care in the world. HMS *Cadmus* had a mascot.

'**I WONDER** which poor sod is going to look after that?' I queried.

'You are,' came the captain's voice from above.

Why do people associate sheep with shaggers? Why couldn't we have a goat, rabbit, duck, cat or a dog as a mascot? Why do sheep crap so much? I mused on these thoughts as I swept up another load of brown ball-bearings that seemed to emanate in a neverending stream from Phoebe's backside as one of my shipmates looked on .

'You know, shagger, I reckon that sheep fancies you.'

The sheep gave me an adoring glance.

'Of course it does, why do you think I call it Phoebe?' I replied. Smokey Stover was lost for an answer.

The skipper soon began to receive strange signals from the rest of the flotilla, and down below on the mess deck 'signals' took great delight in recounting the gist of these. I didn't know skippers could be so rude.

Pulling into port we received a chorus of 'baaa' from the other ships, and cries of 'Here come the sheep-shaggers' echoing across the harbour made us all think of lamb chops.

THE WAR on the Greek mainland was still raging, with Greek partisans fighting in Piraeus, the port of Athens. The approaches to the Saronic Gulf and Piraeus were heavily mined, so the flotilla was ordered to begin minesweeping to clear the harbour approaches for a naval task force. The operation kept seven ships and crews working from dawn to dusk for a long period, without a break or shore leave, not even any R and R on one of the many islands.

We were joined by a fleet tanker as the *Cadmus* was low on fuel, but there was a heavy swell running – not the most ideal situation in which to pull alongside another ship at sea. With excellent seamanship we closed with the slightly larger ship and the crew began winding in the lifeboats, which on minesweepers are always kept swung out over the ship's sides, ready for instant use.

On board the *Cadmus* was a very junior officer. No doubt trying to look efficient, he ordered Smokey and me to put out rope fenders. I looked at the bridge superstructure of the tanker which had just missed our lifeboat davits and was now twenty feet below us and beginning to make the return journey, and continued furiously winding the davits inboard as we went down and the tanker rose, one ship in the trough of a wave and the other on the crest.

'Stop that! Put out the fenders!' he yelled as we both ignored him and continued frantically winding as the ships pulled slightly apart. No officer likes to be ignored, especially junior ones as it threatens their very existence, and he blew up. 'I am placing you both on a charge of wilfully refusing to carry out an order from a superior officer.' He was referring to mutiny. 'Put out those fenders!'

We did as ordered, then watched horrified as the superstructure of the tanker rising on the swell jammed under our lifeboat davits and bodily lifted the minesweeper, accompanied by the sound of twisting metal.

All hell broke loose as the *Cadmus* listed alarmingly to starboard, before it rolled 45 degrees and the wire hawser holding the ships together snapped and they suddenly separated. There were lots of orders from the bridge, many confused sailors milling around, and one whaler hanging bow-down from a twisted davit.

Warrant Officer Johnson created order out of chaos as the one workable davit was wound inboard and the whaler was lashed down, while the two captains shouted at each other through tannoys. A heaving line was thrown across and we began the manoeuvre again. Slowly, the two ships were fastened together and the refuelling took place. The process of disengagement began but somehow, at the last minute as the fuel line was disconnected, oil gushed out all over our captain's pride and joy, *Cadmus*'s lovely wooden deck.

We had the fuel, we had a knackered lifeboat davit, our white deck was now a black skating rink and we had nearly lost the ship. It was not a good day.

The following day Smokey and I were hauled before the captain on a charge of wilfully disobeying an order from a superior officer and endangering the ship. 'Bloody 'ell, I'll never see my dear old mother again!' I thought. Fortunately for us, the chief petty officer had seen and heard what had occurred and had informed the first lieutenant. He intervened on our behalf and the charge was dismissed. The very junior officer was confined to his cabin and was later transferred to another ship bound for Malta.

PHOEBE WAS BEGINNING TO SMELL. I didn't know if it was the heat or seasickness, because it's difficult to tell when a sheep has seasickness as a sheep's expression does not vary a lot and the doleful look in her eyes still had that same 'what the bloody hell am I doing on a ship' look. I talked to her, but even her responsive bleat seemed off colour and her nose seemed warm.

Being Commander-in-Chief Sheep was an awesome responsibility, so in the manner of all good sheep doctors I examined the other end. It looked decidedly crappy and, just to oblige, Phoebe crapped on my hand. I examined the sheep droppings; they seemed the usual brown, spherical shape and, after holding one to my nose to find that as Charles Dickens would have said, 'it did not give forth odorous fumes', I came to the conclusion that Phoebe stank because she needed a wash. Ho, ho. This was when the fun really started.

The sea was calm, the minesweeping was boring, we had swept a large area all morning and found no mines, so it seemed a good time to become more familiar with Phoebe and give her a shampoo and set.

Aided by Smokey, after a lot of pushing and pulling, we manhandled the bleating, struggling animal down to the seamens' 'heads' (toilets and showers). I fastened a leg lock across her woolly back and Smokey turned the shower on. I was suddenly transformed into an actor in a Wild West movie on fast forward as, in a series of high-flying jumps, Phoebe left the deck like a woolly backed bucking bronco.

'The soap powder, get the soap powder on,' I shouted as, for the third time, I levitated past Smokey, who stood transfixed with his mouth open. The packet of Oxydol was liberally poured over me and the sheep as I vigorously rubbed her woolly back. It was like Aladdin rubbing his magic lamp. Phoebe and I were transformed into a giant, bouncing bubble that bleated every time we bounced. Slipping and sliding over the tiled shower block with Smokey hanging onto the sheep's head, with soap everywhere, I eventually managed to wash the desperately struggling animal. Then, staggering to my feet for the third time, I suddenly experienced a cloven hoof stamped into the middle of my bare foot.

'Ouch, you bastar . . .' but Phoebe was off. As my grip slackened she made a dash for freedom; she skidded on her backside and hit the bulkhead before regaining her feet and, bleating like an out-of-control politician, she headed through the open doorway past a totally amazed ship's cook, trailing a mass of bubbles, towards the officers' wardroom.

Cookie was transfixed. He stood motionless with his left arm outstretched, pointing in the general direction of the trail of soapsuds as two semi-naked men, also covered in suds, hurtled past him.

An officers' wardroom in a Royal Navy ship is a place of decorum, as befits officers and gentlemen. It is a sanctuary from the rough denizens of the lower deck, a haven of peace which common seamen do not enter. The polished table top, the laid-out silver cutlery, the fancy wine glasses, were almost demolished as a huge white mass of bleating soap bubbles hit the table, skidded sideways and spun, legs waving in the air, under the bulkhead seat at the back of the table. Smokey and I dived after it.

The more we tried to calm her down, the more she struggled. There were soapsuds everywhere, laced with sheep droppings and blood from my bleeding foot. Smokey and I were so engaged in our struggle that we failed to hear the call for duty watch to stand down.

'What the hell is going on?'

Through eyes smarting with soap, I looked out from underneath the table at two pairs of highly polished officer's shoes as I recognised the first lieutenant's voice. Hanging on grimly we slid out from under the table, dragging what appeared to be a ton of candyfloss behind us.

'It's Phoebe sir, she got away,' came an apologetic voice from within the soapsuds.

'PHOEBE!' You've given that bloody animal a name?' The Jimmy (Navy slang for first lieutenant) was not amused.

The largest mass of suds, recognising the voice of authority, suddenly jumped to attention, broke from my grasp and, with legs furiously pedalling like a character in a Mack Sennett comedy, Phoebe suddenly reversed direction and rammed the first lieutenant behind the knees. He collapsed on top of us.

I knew that Jimmy was not in favour of having a sheep as a mascot. I also became painfully aware that he was not a sheep lover in any form, except perhaps with mint sauce. His loss of dignity was painful to behold as he struggled to his feet, clutching the sheep by the ears, up to his arse in soapsuds. He glared at me with an intensity that was frightening.

'Acting Leading Seaman Eyre, get that fuckin' sheep out of my wardroom and expect to see me tomorrow. Consider yourself on a charge.'

'Aye, aye, sir,' I mumbled as Phoebe hotfooted along the passage dragging me with her. 'And get this fuckin' mess cleared up,' I heard him shouting to the subbie who was with him. 'And wipe that fuckin' grin off your face!'

After hosing the hog-tied sheep down with several gallons of sea water then finishing her off with fresh water, we found that Phoebe was transformed from a smelly, dejected

Phoebe rammed the first lieutenant behind the knees. He collapsed on top of us

animal into a lovely large, fluffy white poodle. Installed once more in her pen, she gave court to a large string of admirers, including the skipper.

'I've just been hearing about your little run-in with Number One,' he said with a sardonic grin. 'I gather he's not too keen on sheep – especially in the wardroom.'

'I'll tell you what, Snakey, a bit of mascara around those eyes and you wouldn't know the difference between Phoebe and Ava Gardner in a white fur coat,' said Scouse. 'I'll get her a carrot from cookie. And what's this about you and Jimmy having a wrestling match on the wardroom deck?'

'Sod off,' I replied.

'Acting Leading Seaman Eyre, attention, off caps.'

The charge read out by the jaunty was a bit vague: 'Conduct unbecoming to Naval discipline.' The first lieutenant looked up from my record, which he had been studying.

'Eyre, you seem to have a gift for attracting mayhem. How am I going to enter "knocked down by a wet sheep in the wardroom of HMS *Cadmus* on the 8th inst." in my report? If you want to shampoo that bloody animal again, throw it over the side and let it swim on the end of a rope – and you might consider joining it if an incident like this occurs again. Seven days' loss of privileges. Dismiss.'

WE ENTERED THE HARBOUR at Piraeus at dusk, after the final sweep of a long day. The deceptive calm of the semi-deserted town was suddenly shattered by the staccato chattering of a machine gun, and I instinctively ducked when I discerned gun flashes from a nearby rooftop as answering shots cracked out from a smoke-blackened building.

A muffled explosion echoed across the harbour and a pall of smoke rose behind a small church and drifted across the patchwork quilt of old Greek houses, as sporadic rifle shots were answered by the clatter of an automatic. The Greek partisans were still fighting what were probably Greek communists or Greek fascists, or traitors desperate for their lives. The German and Italian armies had retreated into the hills and, wisely, the flotilla pulled back and anchored beyond the harbour mouth.

A flashing Aldis lamp preceded the dark silhouette of a cruiser with a destroyer escort that slid past us and tied up to the sea wall. We could hear the orders coming over the tannoy as marines disembarked and marched along the quay past the warm, beckoning lights of the few tavernas that, being Greek, never seemed to close. Faintly, the evocative sound of Greek music mingled with the soft slap of the waves and we watched, leaning against the ship's rail, drawing on our cigarettes, as a light was born in the harbour and approached, becoming brighter as a small fishing boat pulled out to sea.

The bright gas lamp suspended over its bows illuminated two Greek fishermen who waved at us and shouted a greeting: '*Yiasas*.' We waved and shouted back and watched the wake of the small boat lift and scatter the yellow reflection of the harbour lights into small fragments of light that glinted and sparkled like fireflies, before fading into the darkness.

It was time to turn in.

'**WAKEY, WAKEY, WAKEY**! Rise and shine, the morning's fine. The sun's burning your eyeballs out. Heave out, heave out. Lash up and stow, cooks to the galley has gone long ago. Hands off your cocks and pull up your socks. Heave out, heave out, heave out!'

The different versions of wake-up call could be heard from the other ships of the flotilla and the faint bugle calls from the cruiser were born on the offshore breeze. One thing about the Royal Navy – no one lies in his hammock at reveille. The duty petty officer has an easy way with malingerers – he just pulls on the loose end of the hammock slip-knots and the occupant is tipped onto the deck.

Within minutes the 12th Flotilla was heading out to sea, westwards towards the Corinth Canal to finish clearing the approaches which had been heavily seeded by mine-laying aircraft. With that task accomplished, the flotilla steadily worked its way eastwards and southwards towards the main shipping routes that fanned in from the Myrtoan Sea, anchoring at night at a small barren island off Hydra.

All work and no play makes Jack a dull boy. Whoever said that must have been thinking about the Navy, and it wasn't long before our genial master-at-arms thought up something to entertain the troops. A boxing match.

'Ah, Snakey, just the man. Now, you've done a bit of boxing, haven't you?' asked the jaunty.

'No,' I replied.

'You must 'ave,' he said.

'Never,' said 1.

'Well 'ow did you get that nose then?'

'Fighting, and I'm not very good at it,' I answered.

'Never mind lad, you look the part and it'll give you the chance to improve your pugilistic skills. I'm putting you down for a bout.'

Off he went whistling a merry little ditty from *The Pirates of Penzance*. The buzz soon went round the ship that a boxing match had been arranged and a poster was stuck on the bulletin board. Lightweight: Ferrety Johnson vs Slim MacAverty. Middleweight: Snakey vs The Terrible Turk. Heavyweight: Tiny MacBrindle vs Basher Briggs.

Looking at the poster I suddenly became aware that I was fighting a mystery man. I asked Smithy, who knew everyone on the ship, who the Terrible Turk was. Smithy didn't know. Dodger Brown didn't know. Smokey didn't know. Jonno reckoned that the Turk was one of the stokers, 'and there's some mean bastards down in that engine room.' Cookie had an idea who it might be but wasn't sure. 'Anyway,' he said, 'it doesn't matter. When he clouts you his name will be the last thing you will be worried about.'

On the morning of the boxing match we awoke to grey skies and a stiff breeze. As we began sweeping, the wind increased and the shallow draft minesweepers were soon bouncing around as the sea rose. The paravane vanished in the troughs between the waves with only a little flag jauntily waving at us showing its position. One of the minelayers had reported two rogue mines that had come adrift in the previous night's storm, so several hands were scanning the waves through binoculars, anxious to find the mines before they found us.

'Starboard 18,' shouted one of the lookouts. We just saw a mine appear on the crest of a wave before being swallowed in the trough. 'There's the other bugger,' shouted Dodger as a glistening iron dome bobbed up much nearer the ship.

After five attempts to hit the moving target, I got it with the sixth shot and with a large explosion up it went in a fountain of spray and smoke. The other mine proved more difficult and was eventually left to the marksman on HMS *Circe*, which lay astern, and a black smoke pall soon denoted a hit.

The sea had been gradually building and it looked like this particular operation would have to be postponed. The sweep winch crew began winding in the paravane, then suddenly stopped. 'All hands forward,' came the command over the tannoy. There was a mine jammed in the sweep.

The paravane winch was reversed as the first lieutenant joined the small group on the stern. The horned devil's head of the mine rose out of the sea, water streaming off the dark shape before it disappeared from view; it was only a few feet from the paravane and dangerously close to the stern.

The first lieutenant took charge and dictated the ship's speed, as a petty officer and two ratings worked under his instructions. The paravane was slowly winched closer to the stern and, assembled on the foredeck, we watched the drama unfold.

Jimmy climbed over the stern only feet from the mine, which was tossing up and down. A mistake now would spell death and disaster. The petty officer and one of the ratings held rope fenders between the stern and the lethal horns of the malevolent cast-iron sphere, which was clearly visible to us as the sea lifted it above the height of the deck railings, a mind-numbing sight, before it sank back in a trough out of sight.

Held on by a rope, the first lieutenant grappled with the tangled mass of weed-covered wire as he tried to cut it free from the paravane. An hour passed before the mine was released, only to jam again, now sitting a few yards astern of the paravane, lifting and spinning as it pulled the float over at an angle. The small group at the stern began winching the paravane slowly towards the davits and finally hoisted it out of the water, together with several loops of mine cable which had fouled the cutters. This was slowly cut free and a spontaneous cheer rang out as the last strand parted and the mine drifted away towards the *Circe*, which was lying astern. A loud explosion and a column of black smoke soon denoted a direct hit from the *Circe*'s gunner.

Steaming back to our anchorage in worsening seas, the skipper announced: 'Splice the main brace', in honour of the men who had saved the ship from a sticky situation. This meant an extra tot of rum for the crew, and I was saved from a beating by the Terrible Turk. However, my relief was short-lived as another announcement came over the tannoy: 'All ratings competing in the boxing tournament to assemble at 19.00 hours at the master-at-arms' cabin.'

In spite of the extra tot, the saying that the condemned man ate a hearty meal is a load of rubbish. Perhaps the Terrible Turk ate a hearty meal, but I didn't. The crew had roped off an impromptu boxing ring between the 4 inch gun and the bridge. 'It's a bit small, isn't it,' I complained. 'There's nowhere to run.'

'Never mind, Snakey, catch him off balance,' said Wilkie. Now that was a thought, for even here in the lee of our small island, quite a swell was running and the ship was still lifting and rolling.

'Gladiators to muster,' some wit broadcast over the tannoy. Dressed in white vests and pusser's underpants, we looked a motley crew – apart from the heavyweights, who looked as though they could have given Joe Louis a run for his money.

'Which is the Terrible Turk?' I asked.

'Oh, here he comes now,' said one of the lightweights as a six-foot-six stoker ambled into view, dwarfing the heavyweights as he passed them.

'You're joking,' I gasped.

'No, it's Billy Backhouse, Stoker First Class.'

'Hell! Why do they call him the Terrible Turk?'

Two mines caught in the sweep behind HMS Cadmus, with the first lieutenant in charge and a mine exploding astern

'That's his professional name.'

'*Professional?*'

'Yeah, he was a wrestler originally.'

Oh dear, it got worse. We entered the jaunty's office and he gave us a satisfied smirk as he outlined the rules. 'Three-minute rounds. Three knock-downs or a knockout and you lose. Any questions?'

'Yes,' I said, 'I thought middleweights had to be the same,' looking up at my opponent who towered over me, his head in the clouds.

'Well, it's a matter of weight,' said the jaunty, 'height doesn't count.'

'He's fatter than I am,' I complained. The jaunty agreed.

'He does look to be a better build. Mind you, everyone looks fatter than you, but I'll bet your bones weigh more than his.'

'Yes, and you can weigh them when they chuck my remains over the side,' I muttered.

Watching the lightweights perform didn't do me any good, for they went at it like a couple of Jack Russells and there was blood and snot flying in all directions. By the time the bout was over I was rapidly losing interest in becoming a pugilist.

By this time the ship was jerking on the anchor chain and, as the foc'sle lifted up and down, I staggered into the ring to be fitted into a pair of gloves the size of weather balloons. The bell rang and something hit me on the side of my head, which sent me sprawling across the deck. With flashing lights inside my head and my brain turned to frogspawn, my natural temper inherited from my ginger-headed mother took over.

I launched myself at the sod who had hit me before I was ready.

My arms going round like windmill sails, I stuck my head down and charged, just as the ship lurched. The Terrible Turk and I were both thrown off balance and he somehow found his chin on a direct collision course with one of my weather balloons, which sent him sprawling under the ropes.

I couldn't believe it and I couldn't believe the look on his face as he clambered to his feet. I ducked, I weaved, I ran, but to no avail: he kept bashing his mighty fists in my face and, but for the weather balloons, my good looks would have been blemished. Sinking to the deck under the ferocious onslaught I took a mighty swing at the only bit I could reach – his belly. The effect was amazing! It was almost as if a fairy queen had waved a magic wand. Emitting a cross between a croak and a sigh, he folded up, winded, and my punishment ceased.

With cries of foul coming from the spectators, the bell rang and I staggered to my corner to be given instructions from Smithy, my second. 'Hit him on the chin.'

'I can't reach it.'

'Well, hit him in the belly again, it seemed to work last time.'

Seconds out, the bell went. BANG! The bastard did it again and I was flat on my back with blood spurting from my nose and mouth. He hit me again as I was clambering to my feet and had to be pulled off by the referee, before leaping forward and belting me again. I thought this was supposed to be a friendly contest!

Crouching in pain, I saw two massive legs and his underpants and I launched my secret weapon – I hit him right in the balls and was almost killed when he fell on me. To the sounds of shouting and bell-ringing, we were dragged to our feet, I was disqualified and the Terrible Turk, still in agony and still clutching his balls, was declared the winner.

I vowed to stay clear of the stokers' mess for some time . . .

I hit him right
in the balls

THE 12TH FLOTILLA sailed into Piraeus for the second time. A cruiser and several tank landing craft lay offshore, while two destroyers and three frigates were tied up in the harbour. Pulling alongside the quay, we tied up astern of two merchant navy vessels which were busy unloading much-needed supplies. The seamen were watched intently by a large group of Greeks – women with baskets, men with mules and an ancient battered lorry – who were hopefully waiting to salvage any damaged goods.

Suddenly, an old lady cried out as a sack of flour slid from the unloading net and burst open on the quay. People surged forward with pans, tins, shovels and brushes, and within minutes no trace was left. One of the seamen gestured to another sack which had a slight tear in it and encouraged the Greeks to take it away before the deck officer saw it. They thanked him profusely before spiriting it off on the old flat-back lorry, in a cloud of stinking black exhaust smoke.

The gunmen had fled by now, leaving the population to pick up the pieces of a life ruined by the Germans. They had bled the country dry and systematically inflated the Greek drachma by printing millions of worthless notes, undermining the fragile economy to such an extent that people were starving.

The crew was allowed limited shore leave and we headed for the tavernas that fringed the harbour, drinking weak Greek beer that tasted like gnats' piss and hearing the gen from the squaddies. The men-only atmosphere of the taverna was broken by a woman dressed in the traditional black of a Greek widow, who hesitantly approached a group of army lads. One gave her a small tin of field rations and it was shocking to see her cry with gratitude as she placed a wizened hand gently against her benefactor's cheek before she left, still thanking him.

Three of us stretched our legs around the harbour perimeter, calling at semi-deserted tavernas with run-down stocks in the semi-gloom of the narrow back streets. Chalky White discovered a dusty bottle of pale pink stuff that looked like brake fluid, but it was reasonably palatable and delivered a slow, crafty kick of a mule in carpet slippers. Soon we were all drinking this Cochinella, quickly translated to 'Cocky Nelly', and life perked up tremendously.

It had to happen. The owner of the taverna and another local were in deep conversation and accosted us with the well-known words, 'You want woman?' After a struggled interpretation we became aware that the proffered sex was not for money but for food. We all shook our heads vigorously: we were all young and randy, but we could not take advantage of these poor women who were being forced to prostrate their only asset in order to survive. The tavern owner persisted, telling us that the women were 'very young' and not prostitutes, not realising our distaste until we refused more emphatically.

The bar, like so many in Greece, doubled as a sort of corner shop and we watched a young woman enter with a large shopping basket full of tightly rolled bundles of 10,000 drachma notes – millions of drachmas in all. We watched, fascinated, as the barman piled the rolls on the counter, not offering to check the currency but just counting the number of bundles. For this, once a small fortune, the young woman received a small, stale loaf of bread.

The abject poverty we saw in Greece was awful as people carried around currency of huge denominations, which was almost completely worthless. I saw a Greek pushing a wheelbarrow piled high with the tightly rolled wads of drachmas; what he expected to purchase I could not imagine.

There was a marked change among the crew as we moved operations around the scattered, magical Greek islands, clearing the extensive sea lanes, and there was an unusual demand for tins of corned beef and sardines from the ship's canteen instead of the usual request for goodies like sweets and chocolate. The crew going on shore leave were noticeable for unusual bulges in their tunics and socks.

Barter was the new rule of the Greeks and we were turned into London spivs, early manifestations of the Arthur Daley character later invented for television. Plonk a tin of corned beef on a taverna table top and you were guaranteed free beer for the evening. Tinned food, cigarettes and, strangely enough, soap was the new currency. Offer a tablet of Lux toilet soap to a young lady and it was love at first sight. I have vague memories of a night spent in Madame Zafiria's public house, No. 1 Fokionos Street, Piraeus; what I received in return for three bars of soap was unbelievable. Our canteen manager said that, in all his years in the service, he'd never known such a clean bunch of sods who had a fixation for eating corned dog. Strangely enough, he continued, for all the soap he was selling, we didn't smell any different or look any cleaner.

GERMAN INTELLIGENCE must have been good, for a Junkers mine-laying plane had re-seeded one of the main shipping lanes in the Cyclades group of islands which our flotilla leader had just declared safe for shipping, and a cargo ship had been lost. It was back to square one!

The flotilla was soon engaged in reclaiming one of the busy shipping lanes between the Myrtoan and Aegean seas and the familiar coastline of Andros passed slowly on our starboard side. The flat calm of the sea presented a surreal image of seven ships steaming across the face of a mirror, with their bow waves scarcely disturbing the glasslike reflection, just giving it a faint ripple that slightly distorted the following ship's image.

This dreamlike vision was suddenly broken as a mine surged up a few yards off our bow, rising from the surface and exploding with an ear-splitting bang, showering the ship with shrapnel and shrouding us in a smelly black cloud of TNT fumes. Several more of these hobo mines had been sown by the Junkers among the seven regular high-explosive mines that we cut, as a personal gift to the minesweeper's crews. It was nice that the Jerries thought so highly of us. Bastards!

After successfully clearing and marking several major sea lanes, the flotilla moved to a new base at Chios, one of the larger Aegean islands near the Turkish coast. Doing sentry duty on the gangway, I was accosted by a small excitable group offering me oranges, figs, olives and all sorts of goodies. Being so close to Turkey, they seem to have escaped the attention of the Germans, or so it seemed.

There was a friendly rivalry among the officers and crews in the flotilla: who could bag the most mines, shag the most sheep and so on. Having Phoebe, we rose above that sort of thing; she would disapprove.

I was summoned to the bridge the following morning. This was a first for me – visiting the captain without appearing as 'men under punishment'.

'Ah,' said the great man, 'Eyre, er, how's Phoebe?'

'Oh – great, sir,' secretly hoping she might be coming up on the ship's menu.

'Well, we have received a challenge from the *Fly* (our flotilla leader) and the *Circe* to a shooting match. I'm sure we must have some of the best shots in the flotilla – pick out a team of six good men.'

'Aye aye, sir.' I saluted smartly and left the rarefied atmosphere of the bridge for the less salubrious lower deck. We had some good shots on the *Cadmus* and, with a good showing, I could see me being promoted from Acting Leading Seaman to Leading Seaman Eyre – at this rate I would end up being an Admiral before the war was over.

The next R and R leave saw three of the flotilla's ships anchored off a small island, which was ideal for our competition. I gathered my team of crack shots and we sailed ashore to do battle and uphold the honour of the *Cadmus*. Unfortunately for me and my plans of promotion, however, the island had inhabitants. Clambering up a rocky escarpment, we found a well-used path that took us to a small fishing village, and the small fishing village boasted a small taverna. I tried not to notice it, but my shipmates, with eyes honed to perfection from months spent spotting mines, whooped with glee.

'A fookin pub,' shouted Haggis.

'We can't go in there,' I protested, 'not before a shoot.'

'Och – a wee drink'll no do any harm. Come on Snakey, ye are no a leading seaman yet, ye are only actin.' Against my better judgement I gave in.

The targets had been set up in a small depression among the rocky outcrops behind the village and the *Cadmus* team was the first to shoot: five rounds each. Wilkie hit two bullseyes and three inners. Haggis hit one bull, three inners and one outer. I got three bulls, one inner and one outer. Jonas hit four bulls and one shot went wide; 'I hiccuped,' he muttered. Smokey took two bulls and three inners. Taffy astounded everyone, including himself, by hitting five bulls.

'There ye are Snakey, ah said that beer was like gnat's piss,' said Haggis when the cheering had died down.

The *Cadmus* team easily won the first round, but during the second round things began to go wrong. The targets seemed to be farther away and just slightly fuzzy, and as I lay in the firing position squinting furiously through my gunsight, I thought that perhaps we shouldn't have had that fifth drink. I fired. An inner. I fired again. An outer. My next three shots got me one bullseye, an outer and a miss. My team members fared even worse and Wilkie only just managed to hit the target twice!

'Ah ken yon beer was stronger than we thought,' whispered Haggis. The third and final round was an utter disaster. 'I've seen better shooting from novice nuns,' said the jaunty as Smokey hit the rocks behind the target for the third time and the ricocheting bullets flew over our heads like angry hornets.

Taffy somehow managed to hit two bulls in rapid succession before his other shots went flying over the target, and that was the end of our humiliation. Well, almost. The commander-in-chief, the captain of the *Fly*, took great delight in announcing the results and ended with: 'I believe the *Cadmus* sharpshooters have been granted leave to attend the optician in Chios.' Much chortling from everyone, except our skipper.

'Ah well, it's no the end of the world,' said Haggis as we called at the taverna on the way back to the ship, followed doggedly by half the ship's company.

'I thought you bastards were pissed,' said Geordie. 'You've cost me a couple of quid, you sods – but it was worth it for a laugh.'

'Yes, you nearly got yourself another sheep out there, Snakey – a bloody dead 'un.'

The captain of HMS *Cadmus* stood on the bridge discussing operations with the first lieutenant, when his attention was distracted by singing. This came from the liberty boat containing the shooting party, two of whom were trying to steer the boat with their rifle butts. 'Assemble those ratings on deck number one,' he ordered.

We clambered up the ship's ladder and were met with a greeting party. 'You men fall in over here. Attention!' We stood there swaying like poplars in a breeze.

'Slope arms.' The captain advanced, his face as black as thunder.

'Acting Leading Seaman Eyre, what do you call this rabble?'

'The return of the shooting party, sir.'

'Shooting party – they can't even stand up straight. You are all a disgrace to the ship. Put them in the Captain's Report, First Lieutenant.'

So ended my quest for promotion. I will not dwell on my interview with the captain as it's too painful, but needless to say I had climbed the ladder and slid down the snake and was now an able seaman again – although I did have some satisfaction watching my fellow miscreants, down on their hands and knees, holystoning the wooden deck.

WORKING ON the numerous shipping lanes in the northern Aegean, the flotilla was kept busy minesweeping throughout the day and anchored off a different island each night. It was almost a pleasure cruise, though it was noticeable, as our tally of mines increased, that our trips ashore didn't. A cheer rang out on the lower deck when we were eventually informed over the tannoy by the skipper that, unfortunately, the ship needed to enter dry dock for work on one of the propellers, and we were proceeding to Alexandria.

The vibrations of the ship's engines, the heartbeat of any ship, changed tempo and I went on deck to see the low coastline of North Africa coming closer. It was a depressing

The return of the shooting party

sight after the magnificent backcloth of the Hellenic islands which we had become accustomed to. Soon the stench of Alexandria assailed our nostrils and we were greeted by Egyptian flies, which arrived on the offshore breeze in search of fresh, succulent bodies to feast on. I soon heard the first cry from one of the early victims: 'Piss off you black, six-legged Egyptian bastard.'

The blast-furnace heat of the land hit us as the ship eased into dry dock. The engines stopped and the cacophony of noise that was Alexandria dulled the senses. I immediately longed for sea breezes and to be stood on the bow of the ship watching it slice creamy white waves out of the dark azure depths, with the dull monotonous desert falling fast astern.

I went back down below to see a brown, nightshirt-clad leg disappearing into the small arms locker. I zoomed in after him and grabbed the smelly individual by the scruff of his neck. 'Now, you bastard,' I started.

'Oh no, Johnny, I no steal. Gash, Johnny,' wailed this bundle of rags on legs, waving a dirty five-pound, empty corned beef tin with an improvised wire handle.

'Out, you brown sod,' I yelled as I propelled him along the passageway with a kick up his arse, 'and if I ever catch you down here again . . .' But he was gone. Hello Egypt.

Soon, the ship was transformed as barefoot, brown, nightshirt-dressed gentlemen swarmed all over it. With everyone shouting and talking at once in strange tongues, it was like an invasion from Mars. Sentries were posted on the two gangways, on every entrance to ship's quarters and the bridge.

'Keep your eyes on these crafty little buggers,' said the jaunty, 'they can pinch your underpants without undoing your trousers.'

For several days the ship's company was kept busy loading and unloading and undertaking jobs that were difficult to do at sea. I stripped down the anti-aircraft guns, checked the small arms and the ammunition required. Meal times were difficult, as there was always some little bugger who would invade the mess deck and wave a smelly 'gash' tin under our noses while pleading, 'Gash, Johnny, I have ten children and sick wife.' Taffy said, 'No wonder she's sick, living with you. Here, put this on next time you give her one,' and threw a condom in the Arab's 'gash bucket'. 'That should stop her having number eleven.'

Forty-eight-hour leave passes were eventually handed out to Green Watch and the men on duty watched them line up for inspection, not without some envy. They were, for all the world, like a troop of giggling debutantes at their coming-out ball, little knowing that it would be more than one ball, it would be two if they ended up in the right establishment. They could also end up with a dose of pox as a complimentary gift from ancient Egypt to take back home to the dear wife or girlfriend. Ah well, c'est la vie, as the French would say. It was all part of life's rich pattern.

Meanwhile, Red Watch carried on with shipboard duties and watched the captain having a nervous breakdown as the dockyard mateys began painting his ship. 'My deck, my lovely white deck,' was all we could hear him say as he watched the Arab dockyard workers swarm up the rigging, up the smokestack, up the bridge, over the gun (ensuring that it would never work again) and over the side. All of them carried large tins of battleship grey paint tied to their waists and waved their 'paint brush' around with gusto – this was a bundle of sacking tied on the end of a stick, and an object more remote from a paintbrush was difficult to imagine.

Of course, the net result of all this activity was a completely grey ship, painted in record time by small, hyperactive grey men who seemed to take a delight in being a different colour from that with which they were born. They eventually slithered down the gangways, rolling their eyes and flashing their teeth – their only white bits – as they knocked off work. The captain was in a state of shock as he watched them go; they had almost painted him.

The dockyard around the ship was grey, the water in the bottom of the dry dock was grey, there was grey paint inside the mess deck and there was hardly a rating who had not been daubed. Even poor Phoebe, who I had tied up in the shade of a dockyard crane, had been turned grey as the bastards had used her to wipe their hands on as they passed. Never mind, the little sods were energetic, a far cry from most dockyard mateys and, having our rum ration the next day, Geordie started us off singing a little ditty.

'Oh dockyard matey's children, sitting on the dockyard wall, watching their fathers doing sweet fuckall. When they grow older, they'll be dockyard mateys too, just like their fathers, with sweet fuckall to do.'

'**LIBERTY MEN FALL IN**,' called the tannoy. Red Watch fell in, was inspected, given a French letter each and we were sent on our way to sample the magic of the Near East. As a group we parted company when we left the dockyard, some of the older hands heading for the less salubrious delights of Alexandria where it was said one could watch a woman perform with a donkey with a strategically placed rubber ring on its giant willy.

We stood awhile discussing the merits of this high art form, before deciding to leave these old perverts (who must have been at least twenty-six years old) to their own devices, while we headed for the Cairo express.

During my previous visit, when I was on the *Kimberley*, I was overpowered by the sights and sounds of Egypt in all its forms. Alexandria is a lovely name for a dirty, scruffy hole, yet after calling at a couple of bars it was a vibrant, noisy, ebullient place as we staggered through it before catching the Cairo train That was one thing about Egypt – you couldn't catch the wrong train, because there was only one line.

Arriving in Cairo our group split again, some heading for the Pyramids and some, including me, heading for the fleshpots. First things first, though: we had to have a drink. That's the problem with hot, foreign countries: you become dehydrated by the heat and you find you can't trust the water, so you are forced by circumstance to drink all sorts of strange alcoholic beverages for purely medicinal reasons. This, unfortunately, has side effects.

The best way to avoid these side effects is to have a meal, but during the course of a meal one becomes very thirsty and one is reduced to drinking against one's will, so to speak. So, no matter what one does, one becomes pissed.

We had reached this stage when we found ourselves in a dark, smoky establishment, sat at a ringside table gazing intently at a well-built young lady's belly button, which swayed to and fro in front of our eyes, completely mesmerised as she danced to the sensuous music. Her lovely, lithe hips swung and undulated and the flimsy piece of silk around her thighs slid tantalisingly lower as the rhythm of the music increased. I went into a trance-like state as I stared, hypnotised, waiting for what passed as her knickers to fall down. They never did.

The three musicians, who we had never even noticed, increased the tempo and the dancer's voluptuous breasts bounced up and down and rolled around in a frantic bid to escape from the dainty silken hammock in which they nestled like two large over-ripe pomegranates. The golden brown, beautiful woman twisted and turned before us until I could see the beads of sweat glistening on her flawless skin and small rivulets trickled down from between her breasts. My drink remained untouched as she whirled nearer until the delicate strings of beads which were attached to her hips flicked over our table top, and I stared at her muscular thighs and the fine golden hairs that glistened in the stage spotlight.

Making a superhuman effort I lifted my gaze from her body and peered at her face. She was looking down at me through dark eyes made almost inscrutable with mascara. Her face was beautiful, yet devoid of expression, warmth, humanity, but there was a deep presence of her power as she gyrated in front of us until, suddenly, the drum beat ended in a final loud thump as she thrust her pelvis towards us and I thought I detected a faint scornful smile.

'Bloody 'ell,' said Smokey.

'Jeesus,' said Jock.

'Fuckinell,' uttered Taffy. I just sat there, dry mouthed and speechless.

We sat there a long time, quietly drinking our beer.

'I wonder if she's any relation to Nefertiti,' mused Scouse.

'Who?' asked Jock.

'That bird we've just been ogling – she looked like she could be, did you notice her eyes?' Scouse answered with a faraway look in his own eyes.

'Who's Nefertiti?' asked Smokey.

'That bird in the museum, you know, the one with the big eyes,' said Scouse.

'Oh,' said Smokey. 'Is she a dancer? Funny place for a dancer, a museum.'

'I wonder if she's coming on again?' I queried.

'Who? Nefertiti?' asked Jock.

'No – the bloody dancer.'

'Doubt it.'

'Well, let's awa' then.'

Staggering out into the humid pressure cooker of downtown Cairo, fighting off street beggars and pimps, we ended up in a honky-tonk with a load of squaddies and some lads from the *Orion*, the flagship of the Mediterranean fleet. A three-badge able seaman told us of a bar in the next back street called the Golden Peacock. It had a great floor entertainment, 'But watch your wallet.'

A dimly lit alleyway led down some rickety stone steps to a metal sign hanging on a metal bracket over a curtained doorway. In spite of Geordie insisting that the sign looked like a turkey rather than a peacock, we entered. The bar was dark and smelt of dead skunks, but it was fairly crowded with forces personnel. We grabbed an empty table, sat down and got the beer in. We hadn't been there long when two Arabs carried in a wooden, sloping ramp, which they placed in the centre of the room.

Eastern music began to wail out of speakers as an exotic dancer appeared from the shadows. It would have been better if she had stayed in the shadows, for she was well past her sell-by date, but to make up for her plain visage she had a good body – which she started to show us as she began to strip.

She wriggled and gyrated as off came her bra, revealing two rather saggy breasts then, taking a while longer, she slowly wriggled her flimsy knickers down over her well-proportioned bum and, with a flourish, she spun around and threw the knickers at Smokey. With a show of bravado, and accompanied by raucous cheers, he raised them to his nose and sniffed deeply. The look on his face registered that this was an awful mistake and he chucked them back and took a long drink of beer.

Much braver souls volunteered for much more daring exploits as Arabs came round collecting money; exploits which I will not dwell on, only that one man ended up picking pubic hairs out of his teeth.

The highlight of the act came when the dancer lay down at the foot of the sloping ramp with her legs wide open, inviting the audience to roll ten piastra pieces down the ramp towards her. There is always one silly sod who will spoil an evening's culture, and unfortunately he was with us. For some reason known only to his demented Liverpool brain, Scouse busied himself heating up a ten piastra coin with his cigarette lighter before rolling it with unerring accuracy down the board and scoring a hole in one. The unfortunate woman gave a scream, jumped to her feet and went for Scouse like a tigress, clawing him down one cheek, before we were all jumped on by irate Arabs and forces personnel and heaved out into the alley.

'You stupid sod! – what did you do that for?' I yelled, spitting out blood. Taffy had Scouse by the scruff of his neck and was just about to consign him into oblivion when the rest of us stopped him. Dragging our bruised bodies away from the scene of the crime, Scouse suddenly let out a yell. 'The bloody bastards have nicked my wallet.'

She went for Scouse like a tigress

'Serves you right ye fookin brain-deed Sassenach scouse get!' said Jock, glaring at him with his one good eye while the other one rapidly closed. 'Mind you, ah've never seen a woman spit money out from there before,' he said and burst out laughing.

IT WAS GOOD to return to sea, even minus four of our shipmates who had started a fight in a brothel and put the bloke who ran it in hospital. I heard the gen where all the best conversations take place, in the heads, where I found Bill staring ruefully at his willy.

'How long is it before you can tell if you've caught a dose?' he asked.

'When did you last have a shag?'

'Two days ago,' Bill replied.

'It generally takes about four days,' I said, with the air of one who knows all about these things.

'What's the first signs?'

'Does it itch?' I asked.

'Yes.'

'Well, that could be the beginning. It will itch for a week and then you will start having a discharge if you squeeze it,' said Doc Snakey. 'Then you'll know you've got it.'

'Bloody 'ell! I knew I shouldn't have shagged that bird. But she said she was a virgin – can you get pox from a virgin?' asked Bill.

'Depends which lavatory seat she's been sitting on,' I answered.

Bill then unfolded his tale of woe. The beginning was familiar, as he and his mates had started their shore leave by becoming plastered before ending up in a brothel in a rough off-limits area of Alex. As far as Bill could remember, the girls were very young and quite good-looking.

The trouble started when someone nicked Smithy's wallet when he was on the job – he saw a hand come through a gap in the curtains and his wallet going walkabout. Smithy leapt off the bird and collared the proprietor going down the stairs. He knocked seven bells out of him, took his wallet back then hit him again – harder, which propelled him into space to land in a heap at the foot of the stairs.

By this time three awkward-looking locals had appeared, one wielding a knife. 'We got involved in a hell of a battle, then the redcaps arrived and Big John hit one of those. Jack and I scarpered when more military police appeared. Two of the sods ended up in hospital, one of the MPs has a broken arm and young George did his ankle in. It was a hell of a scrap.'

Looking at Bill's swollen lips and the huge lump of purple bruise around the small slit through which his right eye peered, I believed him.

After a few days the *Cadmus* joined up with the rest of the flotilla and it was back to the routine of minesweeping, plus a new occupation: removing battleship grey paint from everywhere it wasn't supposed to be. I spent a few hours scraping paint off the 4 inch gun and clearing the tracking ring. This involved unbolting a safety stop and, with another rating, digging out the gunge and paint from the rack and pinion as I tracked the gun around. Suddenly, a loudhailer almost deafened us from the bridge.

'Able Seaman Eyre, I trust that gun is unloaded.'

I looked up from what I was doing and saw that I was aiming the gun at the centre of the bridge. I stopped tracking, opened the breech and shouted: 'Gun unloaded, sir,' which received a bit of a chortle from the bridge. 'They must think we're thick,' my mate muttered.

Riding at anchor that evening we were treated to an impressive sunset with ominous-looking clouds building up over the mainland. Brilliant, golden yellow clouds in the west were shot through with streaks of red, mauve, crimson and a luminous translucent blue, colours which changed every few seconds. They were gradually over-whelmed by a glowing purple red that criss-crossed the lighter golds and yellows with a series of diagonal lines, which gradually dulled and thickened like hot metal slowly cooling. 'Looks like a storm brewing' said a two-badge able seaman taking a last smoke before turning in for the night.

We awoke to a dull day, heavy with a calm sea: the storm had not materialised. The flotilla headed north past Lesbos towards Lemnos and took up our sweeping stations. We were beginning sweeps just outside Turkish waters off the Dardanelles when the sea breeze started to strengthen and the calm sea developed a swell. Towards noon the wind increased and the swell broke into waves – the paravane jerked and tugged at the sweeping wire as it plunged beneath the surface time and time again. A signal came from the *Fly*: 'Stop sweeping.' The winch crew wound in the heaving paravane, which smashed against the stern before it could be winched aboard. The pennant went and the paravane was winched in, its streamlined shape a buckled mess. We were glad it wasn't a mine.

The wind strengthened further as, line astern, the flotilla turned to port and headed for base, except for the motor launches and danlayers which, being smaller and of shallow draught, headed for the Turkish island of Gokce Adasi, hoping to find shelter in the lee of the island without running aground or being shot at by Turks.

With the ship bouncing up and down like a bucking bronco, we watched one of the launches being swallowed by the waves, then it stood on end before rolling and twist-ing on its way almost overwhelmed by the sea. The wind suddenly increased to gale force and the rain began – heavy, torrential rain that, driven by the gale, was blinding and, together with the flying spume off the waves, soaked anyone on deck in seconds.

We hadn't seen any rain in eleven months and there was a sudden rush to the oilskin locker. It was empty – some bastard had pinched them. The upper deck was now untenable, awash with seawater. Feeling ill, I stood braced beside the sea door and, through the spray, peered at the ship in front of us. It was unbelievable: all I could see was the funnel and rigging before the ship reared out of the sea and almost stood on end, then it was diving down until I could see the full length of the ship's keel, rusty bottom and twin screws spinning in thin air. I closed the sea door behind me and lurched from side to side along the passage before slumping down in the mess deck along with most of the crew.

During the first dog watch the storm intensified and the ship shuddered with the pounding of every wave. The wind increased until we could hear it screeching through the rigging like a thousand banshees and, what was worse, I could hear Phoebe's plaintive bleat as the terror-stricken animal was thrown from side to side with each roll of the ship. There was nothing I could do.

Handlines were rigged on the upper deck and ratings ventured out when the duty watch was called, sharing a few spare oilskins which had been found in the stores. By the second dog watch the storm had reached a ferocity unknown by anyone on board, even the older hands – some of whom had served in the North Atlantic.

HMS Cadmus *at anchor in the Grand Harbour, Malta*

Below decks were awash with sea water mixed with spew and stuff that had been spilled; it swilled from side to side as the ship rolled and changed direction when it pitched. Everyone was sick to a lesser or greater extent; over half the ship's crew were totally incapacitated. It was a relief to put on wet oilskins from one of the watch being stood down, and force myself out through the half-open hatch before it slammed with the force of the wind.

The upper deck was non-existent. I was standing knee-deep in water when a wave hit me and I hung, coughing and spluttering, grimly clutching the safety line as I fought my way up the ladder to the port lookout station. I reported my presence to the bridge and settled down for my four-hour watch.

Although it was the middle of the night, there was a strange luminous appearance to the sky and white-capped waves. Up here, near the bridge, it was possible to see the bows lifting clear of the sea and the boiling mass of sea water rushing towards the stern as the ship stood almost on end, before shuddering and plunging bows down to vanish in the next trough, leaving only the superstructure visible. My sickness left me and was replaced with sheer exhilaration as, cocooned in my lookout post, in my imagination I rode with the Valkyries on my bucking and rolling steed, far above the raging sea.

The sky was lightening beyond the Turkish mountains in the east when the next watch took over. Then, as I fought my way through the maelstrom of rushing water, past the searchlight platform, I noticed the broken and frayed ropes. Phoebe had gone.

After two more days the storm gradually abated, the incessant wind dropped and the raging sea slowly calmed into a grey, sullen swell. The scudding storm clouds thinned and there was a communal sigh of relief as they parted to reveal the sun. The temperature rose, the sea turned blue and the upper deck was suddenly covered with an assortment of sodden gear being hung out to dry. News filtered down from the bridge that one of the danlayers had run aground on the Turkish coast, and one of the motor launches had been severely damaged, but otherwise the flotilla was more or less intact. We had suffered only slight superficial damage and had lost a couple of floats, plus of course our ship's mascot. Poor Phoebe, though I reasoned it was a blessing in disguise for I'm sure a seagoing sheep was not the happiest of creatures.

The following day, after a period of 'make and mend', life on board returned to normal and the flotilla resumed its sweeping operation. It was immediately faced with the added danger of loose mines that had been torn from their anchors by the storm. The sea watch was doubled and the ship's marksmen were kept busy blowing up rogue mines, which were more of a danger to shipping than the tethered mines owing to their capability of drifting anywhere.

Two weeks later a signal was received from the Commander-in-Chief, Sir John Cunningham, that almost 10,000 mines had been swept by the Mediterranean flotillas and that the 12th was in the lead with almost 2,000 mines accounted for.

This was great news – we celebrated below decks with extra rum.

Chapter 5

Into Italy

THE WAR IN EUROPE was being fought with increasing ferocity towards a final obliteration of the German war machine. The Allies advanced on all fronts and the flotilla received orders to sail to Italy.

'Ah well, here we are again,' said Smokey, as several days later we sailed past the *Ohio* and the superstructure of the *Breconshire*, both wrecks and stark reminders of the Battle for Malta in 1942 and the tremendous loss of life at sea. Easing past the masts of another submerged wreck, we entered Malta's Grand Harbour.

'I'll bet a big, fat, pregnant Maria will be waiting for you on the quay, Smokey,' I said.

'Aye, with a big fat dad, with a big fat shotgun,' said Jock, who had just joined us.

'Sod off,' came the reply.

A lot of work had gone into clearing wrecks from the harbour and removing tons of rubble from the quays; Sliema Creek, which was blocked when we were last there, was now clear.

Malta had been a garrison island ever since the Knights of St John built the fort of St Angelo at the entrance to the harbour during the wars of the Crusades. Under different conquerors it had remained an island fortress ever since, predominately under British rule. Even though the Maltese people are a polyglot mixture of Turkish, Italian, Arab, French and British, they have all the characteristics of a people who have evolved in the claustrophobic confines of a large British barracks. Many Maltese are married or related to British servicemen, many have British sailors as ghostly fathers whom they have never seen, and lots of the really dark-skinned, Eastern-looking dockyard mateys answer to the name of MacTavish. Every Maltese was extremely pro-British, all had a picture of the king and queen in their house and Union Jacks flew everywhere. They were more patriotic than we were, all had cousins who lived in England, and all had brothers who knew the king. And they loved ripping us off.

'Liberty men fall in,' came the order and, duly inspected and armed with a prophylactic defence against over-amorous ladies, we picked our way through the rubble of the docks, skirting one of the newly cleared dry docks which was being filled with sea water.

Reaching the dockyard gates, we showed our passes and were lined up by the Navy police, then inspected as though we had the pox. 'Put yor 'at on straight,' said one well-educated wally. I adjusted my headgear a mini-fraction just to give him a *raison d'être* and realised that we were back in the land of bullshit.

A tinkling off-key piano would have made Les Dawson smile, had he been around in those days. It drew us into a bar and soon we were chomping our way through steak, eggs and chips, the haute cuisine of Jack ashore.

'Ah'm sure this is fookin goat,' said our dour Scot. One of the bar lasses overheard him. 'Ah Jock, you like fookin goat? I get you one you can fook. I bet you look good fookin goat,' she said with her dark eyes sparkling.

'I'd sooner fook you. How much?' queried Jock.

'I only do it for love, but for you I make special price,' said the girl. It was the start of a good night and after Jock was turned down by the girl, who said that she 'would sooner do it with the goat,' we wandered into another bar and bumped into two of my old shipmates from the *Kimberley*. Vince and Brummie were in good form, having been transferred to the *Lookout*, another destroyer, 'and away from those South African bastards.'

'Mind you,' said Brummie, 'some weren't so bad – especially Jonno. After you left, Butler began giving him hell and Jonno eventually caught up with him on shore leave and beat the bastard to a pulp.' It put Butler in hospital for a week.

The bar table was filled with glasses of beer. I downed another pint and felt a warm, rosy glow of complete satisfaction coursing through my body. There is no emotion quite so fulfilling as revenge, even when it is second-hand.

'Here's to Jonno, and the best of luck to him,' said I, raising my glass.

'He's going to need it,' slurped Brummie, guzzling his pint. 'They gave him twelve months.'

After causing mayhem in several bars, things became a bit fuzzy then, after some silly sod decided that we should try the local vino, my brain went out of synchronisation with the rest of my body and walking became difficult.

'Walk straight and try and act sober,' said Smithy as we approached the dockyard gates several hours later. Somehow, we slithered past the MPs, who gave us no more than a cursory glance having their hands full with two other drunks, one of whom had spewed on an MP's lovely shiny boots.

Who's for a swim?

Picking our way through the coils of wire, iron girders and fastidiously avoiding pools of oily sludge, trying to keep our white uniforms white, we approached the dry dock we had earlier noticed being filled. I don't know what happened or why I did it, but I suddenly had an uncontrollable desire to go swimming, so by the light of the silvery moon I staggered to the edge of the dry dock, a ghostly vision in white, then shouted, 'Who's for a swim?' and dived off.

It has been said that in the fleeting moments between life and death, one's whole life passes before one's eyes. This is not true.

As I was flying through the air, doing a passable imitation of Superman, the only thing that passed before my eyes was a dry dock that was dry. In other words, it was devoid of water. In other words, it was unsuitable for swimming. The thought crossed my mind that some bastard had emptied the water out as, narrowly missing the wide, slimy ledges, I plunged thirty feet before hitting the six-foot residue of oil, planks, empty fifty-gallon drums, assorted rubbish and water. There was no shock, no pain, nothing . . . just oblivion.

My drunken shipmates approached the point of my departure from the normal world and peered cautiously over the edge, fearful of what they might see. 'The daft sod, he's killed himself,' said one as they climbed down over the slippery, oily steps towards the gunge pool at the bottom. They could see a body lying full length between two planks of wood, totally unconscious and covered in oil.

Somehow, they brought me to the top of the dry dock and laid me face down as I started mumbling and coughing up spew and oily water. My face was gashed and bleeding, my hands were red with blood, and more blood was seeping through a trouser leg. I was in a mess.

Half-carrying, half-dragging, they took me back to the ship. The officer of the watch looked in disbelief at these refugees from a nuclear disaster.

'What happened to you men?'

'We had an accident, sir.'

'What sort of an accident? You look like you've all been run over by a tar-sprayer. What happened to him?' he asked, pointing at the semi-conscious rag doll (me) that lay at their feet.

'It's Snakey, er, Able Seaman Eyre, sir. He fell in the dry dock.'

'How the hell did he manage that?' asked the duty officer.

'He sort of slipped, sir.' The officer's eyes narrowed as he beckoned over two members of the duty watch.

'Get this rating down to the sickbay and alert the medical officer. You are all on Captain's Report as drunk and disorderly, prejudicial to naval discipline and insulting the king's uniform. Right turn – dismiss!'

My uniform had been cut from my body, both hands and one knee was bandaged and there was a surgical collar around my neck. It hurt to breathe and, where my bruises were just beginning to blossom, my body looked as though it belonged to a very ancient Briton covered in woad.

I had just come round in the sick bay the following morning after my Mary Poppins performance, and the first thing my eyes focused on was a row of discoloured, uneven teeth fixed in the mouth of a grinning medic. The first words that greeted my re-entry into the real world were, 'Well Snakey, you are a silly sod. Fancy launching yourself into a dry dock – it's a good job you were pissed, otherwise you could have been killed.'

'If I hadn't been pissed I wouldn't have done it,' I mumbled, my tongue delicately stroking a loose tooth as I vaguely remembered the night before and laid back with a groan. 'What happened to the water?'

'They emptied it – next time you do a high-dive act, make sure you pick a dock with some water in it.' I groaned again. 'Never mind, Snakey, there's one thing you can be sure of.'

'What?'

'There's no brain damage, because you haven't got a brain.' I tried to laugh, but it hurt.

After a few hours the medical officer appeared, glared at me and prodded me everywhere, asking 'Does that hurt?' Every time I answered 'Yes' he gave a grunt and moved on somewhere else and repeated the process.

'Sit up.'

'I can't.'

'Right, lay down. Roll over.'

'I can't.'

'Right, lift your leg. Now the other one. Bend your knees . . . arms.' The doc glared at me again. 'Fit for duty,' he said and smiled the slow sort of twisted smile that Boris Karloff used when he declared his creature normal.

Four days later, confined to ship and working out my sentence of fourteen days number elevens, I was just beginning to breath without groaning. I had sworn to stop drinking and going out with strange men – such as Smokey, Taffy, Jock and Smithy – when along came Smokey Stover with a smirk on his face.

'Eh, Snakey, you're on the team.'

'What team?'

'The football team. We're playing the Malts.'

'Football? Football? I can hardly fuckin' walk, never mind play football!'

'You're on the list outside the jaunty's office.'

'Bloody 'ell, whose bloody idea was that?'

'Yours – you volunteered for shore recreation when we were in Greece.'

'Balls!'

'Yes, you'll have to watch out for them,' said Smokey. 'These Maltese are high kickers; make the Folies Bergère look like geriatrics.'

'Ah – we're confined to ship,' I said, 'we can't go.'

'Oh yes you can, able seaman,' said the jaunty, who had just appeared. 'I've just added a day to your sentence and given you this one off – and watch out for these Malts, you with your bruises an' all.'

KITTED OUT IN PUSSER'S BOOTS, white knee-length shorts and white tunic-type vests which 'only fit where they touched' as my old mother used to say, we piled into a dockyard lorry and were driven to the football pitch. There is no grass on Malta and, stood beside the gravel pitch, we were amazed when the Maltese team arrived barefooted.

'Oh, this is going to be a pushover. All we have to do is to step on their feet,' said Smithy.

But, pushover it was not. The Maltese were brilliant footballers and made us look and feel quite foolish, wrong footing us on every move. Suddenly, salvation appeared in the shape of Smokey who, like a man possessed, threw himself at the Maltese centre forward as he approached with, as usual, the ball seemingly glued to his foot. Smokey nipped the ball with one foot and, with the finesse of a ballet dancer, leapt into the air and came down with all his weight on his other foot, landing on the Maltese's bare left foot.

This was not a good move as, having your bare foot mashed into the gravel demands retaliation. It came in the shape of two karate kicks, one landing on Smokey's calf muscle and the other, much more lethal, in the groin. Another inch higher and Smokey could have joined a schoolgirls' choir. He fell as though poleaxed and lay, writhing in agony, screaming 'foul' in his new high-octave castrato voice. The foul was promptly awarded by the Maltese ref to the Maltese side!

I cannot say that I have ever been much of a football fan, even though every Saturday I used to put my old dad on the back of my 350cc Velocette, wrapped in an overcoat tied in the middle, with a trilby hat bound tightly to his head using one of mother's scarves, then drove him to either Preston or Blackpool to watch Tom Finney or Stanley Matthews play. Here on Malta, after an hour and a half hobbling around in the blazing sun chasing the fleet-footed opposition, I realised that Tommy and Stanley certainly earned their twenty pounds a week and I wished I had been more attentive, especially when the heavy leather ball landed on my head and ricocheted into the goal.

Amid tumultuous applause and cheering from the five spectators, and although concussed, I was the hero of the match when the final whistle blew. Malts: 25, Brits: 1. With stars still twinkling in my brain, under the watchful eye of the jaunty we were hustled into the lorry and driven back to the ship without even stopping for a beer, much to Jock's annoyance.

'Well, if that is fookin footba', ye can stuff it.' My sentiments entirely.

ROUNDING POINT CAMPANELLA on the Amalfi coast, the cone-shaped summit of Vesuvius dominated the grand sweep of the Bay of Naples. The *Cadmus* steamed past the white limestone cliffs of Capri as we headed into Naples, our new base of operations, and the buzz going round the lower deck was that we would be here for a few days, stocking up on essentials before heading for our new operations in northern Italy.

Shore leave was announced for Blue Watch on the second day in port; the Red Watch duty roster had me down for shore patrol, a thankless task. Dressed for the part with hat jammed firmly on my head, chinstrap in place and with a dark navy blue uniform without collar, blancoed belt and gaiters and black shiny boots, I looked every inch a naval policeman. In my case, a poacher turned gamekeeper.

Issued with our shore patrol armbands, we marched smartly off to uphold law 'n' order among that unruly band of men, Jack me 'earty on shore leave. Once we were marching through the less salubrious quarters of Naple's back alleys, I quite enjoyed admonishing the various drunks. 'Pull yourself together sailor' and 'Put yor 'at on straight' gave me quite a thrill as I uttered these words and watched the recipient drunk quake in his boots. I understood the saying that one should never give power to a working man. I reckoned, a bit more of this and I would turn into a mini-Hitler.

Our patrol leader was suddenly accosted by a group of wildly gesticulating, highly vociferous Italians who said they had been robbed by 'Eengleesh sailors, who ago without apaying theesa bill.'

'Ve afix a pronto,' said our petty officer in his best Italian and off we marched 'Tarantara, Tarantara', just like bobbies in a Gilbert and Sullivan opera. Of course, we never found the miscreants and so, after a trouble-free patrol, we took off our armbands and settled down in a waterfront bar for a coffee before returning to the ship.

The following evening Napoli, the city of songs and romance, was again graced by my presence. This time I had reverted to type and, with a group of shipmates, I was exploring the less frequented, dark back streets of the port – it was not a wise thing to do, which is why they had been declared 'Off Limits to All Personnel'. The sign was displayed in large, prominent letters at the entrance to the alley where we began our journey, like Alice down the rabbit hole – unfortunately for us, though, we were not bumping into mad hatters, but mad Italians.

Naples in 1945 was war-torn and desolate, its inhabitants poor, many corrupt and many on the verge of starvation. For a country that had been overrun by foreign armies twice in three years, and had seen its own troops turned into traitors and labelled as cowards, to say nothing of the forthcoming ignominious death of their leader, Mussolini, it was little wonder that these wretched people were left feeling bitter and full of hatred. What better way to vent this hatred than on these latest swaggering conquerors that were even invading their squalor and misery, drinking and laughing in their bars.

This was how I presumed the Italians were thinking as we met up with some Yanks in a bar by the side of a small, tree-lined square. We had emerged from a maze of filthy alleys that stank of sewage and soggy piles of discarded rubbish, when we bumped into an American soldier urinating. He greeted us like long-lost cousins as he turned round to invite us for a drink with his buddies, finishing his urinating on my foot as he profusely shook us by the hand or slapped us on the back. 'Good job *we're* not having a piss,' one of the lads said, 'the way this excitable sod is waving his hands about he'd probably end up shaking your willy.'

Before they ruled the world the Americans were a likeable race and this bunch of 'guys' were, like us, fairly young (old men don't fight in wars, they only start them). Within minutes we knew them intimately, all on first name terms and all on our way to becoming severely inebriated, especially the Yanks for there is one thing about the Brits, we're the world's best boozers.

The more we drank, the louder we became and I noticed the place filling up with locals who were taking a great interest in us and not drinking – they would not have looked amiss in a Mafia line-up. I warned the others that trouble was brewing so we drank up and left quietly, even the Yanks.

I think the Americans were the attraction, for everyone knew they were loaded in both senses of the word. They carried fat wallets and were staggering drunk – an easy target. The Italians jumped them later, just after we had decided to return to the ship. We heard a shout and turned around to see a gang beating up the Yanks. As we rushed into the fray, their assailants fled, with us in hot pursuit. We caught three of them and I knocked one to the ground. With blood pouring from his nose, he got to his feet, drew a knife and threw it – lucky for me, it missed. As he ran off I followed him again. A grave mistake.

After a wild chase, twisting and turning through the narrow alleyways, we broke out onto a busy road where the pavements on one side were partially blocked by street vendors' handcarts. I took a flying tackle, grabbed him round the neck and we both fell over on top of a cart displaying eggs, fruit and vegetables. We were soon part of a salad as we rolled around, punching each other in the wreckage. By the time my mates arrived on the scene I was in trouble. As I hit one bloke, another two hit me and then the stallholder hit one of them, then my shipmates joined in and we had a full blown riot on our hands.

As with all riots, things got a bit out of control and fists were flying everywhere. In the heat of battle I felt no pain until I had one bloke by the scruff of his neck. I pulled back my free arm to thump him but another Italian grabbed it from behind, twisted it up my back and held it, while another evil sod hit me in the face and knocked me to the ground, flat on my back with the twisted arm underneath. I heard the crack as the bone went and realised the bastards had broken my elbow.

I staggered to my feet in a red haze of hate as I looked at my left arm, swinging uselessly. 'You bastards have broken my arm,' I yelled as I lifted the useless limb and tucked it through the black silk of my uniform and into the top of my tunic. Then, in an uncontrollable rage I tore into the Italians, lashing out with my free fist in my demented thirst for revenge. I have never known such anger. 'You bastards have broken my arm!' I said it over and over again as I lashed out blindly until I was knocked down again.

Sirens and flashing lights heralded the approach of the military police and people ran in a panic, tripping over me as I lay in a pool of blood. I vaguely remember being bundled into the back of a vehicle and mumbling, 'Watch my arm,' before passing out.

Some people are born beautiful and some are just born lucky. I guess I must be one of the luckier ones. I opened my eyes – correction, one eye as the other was having a rest deep inside a large purple bruise. It was obvious to me that I must have suffered some brain damage for I was hallucinating. Somehow, my battered brain had conjured up a vision of a beautiful woman – she had large blue eyes, blonde hair and a beautiful smile, and she was holding my hand. This was a hallucination with feeling, for I sensed this vision touching my hand and bathing my face. This was bliss until the vision accidentally touched the crumpled bone that used to be my nose.

I groaned, opened my eye wider and looked up at this Betty Grable lookalike, dressed in an American nurse's uniform. She smiled a sweet smile and said those much parodied words, 'Hello, sailor,' in a husky southern drawl, then gave my hand a comforting squeeze. I had died and gone to heaven.

I didn't know then how I had ended up in an American Army hospital outside Naples. It turned out that I had been picked up by the driver of an American field ambulance, who had been passing the scene of the mini-riot. 'The doctor is coming to take a look at you, what's your name, honey?' Betty Grable asked as she whispered in my ear.

'Jim,' l answered.

'Well, Jim, you are in good hands here. We will look after you, so don't worry.'

'I won't,' I croaked and tried to smile. A bit of tooth fell out.

The doc soon appeared and checked me over. 'Hi there Jim, you seem to have been involved in a bad accident. Could you tell me what happened?'

'Can't remember,' I croaked, 'but my arm . . .'

'Right Jim, we're going to fix that now,' said the surgeon, before giving the nurse instructions and bustling away.

I came round later with the arm strapped across my chest and in considerable pain when the effects of the anaesthetic wore off. The following day Betty Grable hypnotised me with her big blue eyes as she ministered to my every need and I told her that she looked like Betty Grable; judging by the beaming smile she gave me, this would have put me in good stead if I had been fit and good-looking, which alas, I wasn't.

After a couple more days in this luxurious hospital, being visited by little old American ladies who kept saying 'Y'all' and plying me with magazines, grapes, chocolate and all sorts of goodies, and who were totally amazed at an Englishman being in the

American Army, I didn't want to leave. However, once the swelling had gone down on my face, another surgeon appeared to have a look at my busted nose.

'It sure is a mess, Jim,' he said after prodding it for a while. 'What shape was it before?'

'Well, er, just a nose shape,' I replied as he shone a light up the nostrils. He stood back and scratched his chin, clearly perplexed.

'Now look, Jim, we have one of the finest nose men in this hospital. Tell me what sort of a nose you would like, because this guy can deliver. Would you like your new nose to be aquiline, Roman, snub, Jewish, pert, aristocratic, pinched . . . ?'

I stopped him. 'Just give me a good all-American nose and that will be fine,' I said.

'A good choice, Jim,' the great man said and rushed off on his rounds.

If I was a budding film star or celebrity, I would think twice about having a 'nose job' because knowing what I know now, it's not worth it. It's very painful and also disconcerting when surgeons you can't see stick chisels up your nostrils and start hammering away inside. The local anaesthetic deadens the pain but does not relieve the awful sensation of bone being crunched with pliers, or the feeling of it being twisted and yanked out, a bloody snotty mess just seen through a gap in the bandages. 'Soon be over Jim,' said a voice, before a mighty blow with the hammer on the nose-embedded chisel nearly knocked my head off my shoulders.

Back in the ward, com-

Just give me a good all-American nose

ing round from my ordeal, Betty Grable removed my bandages, closely watched by a group of doctors. 'My, my, that sure is a fine "all-American nose" you got there Jim,' said a tall black man who was the surgeon. 'It's just like mine, only yours has a cute little bend in it.'

WHILE I WAS BEING REPAIRED in hospital, no one had thought to inform the port authorities where I was. My ship's card and identification were in my bloodstained uniform and, when I was fit enough to be discharged, the lovely Betty Grable found my clothes, which had been dry-cleaned and repaired, but no documents or money belt were there. After lots of signals between the American military and the naval harbour master, the documents were located with the Navy police.

There was a slight problem though: I was shipless. The *Cadmus* had sailed two days previously.

More signals ensued. The Americans wanted rid of me and the Navy didn't know what to do with me. After several hours waiting in the hospital canteen another signal came through. I was to leave Naples the following day on an Italian destroyer bound for Rimini on the Adriatic coast of Italy, where I could rejoin my ship. A jeep came to pick me up, I collected my elbow X-rays and was told I needed another operation at a later date. I said goodbye to the hospital staff, gave my nurse a kiss and off I went, like Sinbad on a voyage of discovery.

After the Italian armistice in September 1943 some of its navy's craft – with Italian crews – joined the Allies, mainly for ferrying and light duties. Italian destroyers in those days were built for speed; they had less bulk and armament than their British counterparts and, owing to the extensive use of alloy in their superstructure, they were much lighter, narrower and less seaworthy. A good description by the British was that Italian destroyers were sardine tins or floating coffins, and I was going right round Italy in one – with my arm in a sling. And as I had no kit and no hammock, I was going to have to rough it.

The jeep pulled up at the dockyard beside a decrepit-looking destroyer preparing for sea by covering the dock in black diesel fumes. The ship was even narrower than I had imagined. I clambered on board and handed my papers to an Italian sailor, who hadn't a clue what they were or who I was. A scruffy-looking officer appeared, took the papers, scowled in my direction, said 'Si' and went back up to the bridge and began giving orders. The ropes were cast off, the vessel vibrated like an old washing machine and pulled away from the dockside; we were off.

Once we left the shelter of the harbour the ship began to roll even in the comparative calm of the bay, and I was soon clinging to a handrail near the engine room bulkhead. Suddenly, a series of commands came from the bridge, bells clanged and were answered down in the engine room, and with a tremendous surge of power the bows lifted and the ship took off like a rocket.

The destroyer moved through the waters of the bay like a greyhound unleashed. Hanging grimly onto the rail with my one good hand, I felt the vibrations increase until my whole body shook and the loose tooth jiggled about in my head like a pea in a baby's rattle. I don't know what the Italians had in the engine room – probably a couple of Ferraris, as I had never been on anything that moved so fast. No wonder we hadn't sunk many Italian ships – we couldn't catch them.

The narrowness of the vessel served to heighten the impression of speed. Standing in the centre of the deck, only six feet each side of me a wall of blue-white flecked sea passed by in a continuous fast-moving maelstrom and Capri shot by on the starboard side as we entered the Gulf of Salerno and the Tirreno Sea.

Either the captain was mad or he was trying to get rid of me, for the whine of the engines increased as the ship gained even more speed before it was launched into the white caps of the breaking waves ahead. The effect was dramatic and immediate. The bows hit the rougher sea, lifted twenty degrees, then slammed down in a welter of boiling sea, which sluiced along the deck thigh deep and almost washed me overboard. The destroyer also built up a steady roll, with starboard and then port rails going under several feet of sea. Hanging on grimly, soaked through and being thrown up and down and side to side on a semi-submerged bucking bronco, I thought my end had come.

A sea door opened and one of the crew beckoned me to join him pronto. I skidded along the deck as another wave hit me, and he yanked me inside, slammed the door shut then closed the clips. We were on the top landing of an alloy ladder inside a tin can that rattled, vibrated, rolled, jerked up and down, was hot, stuffy and stank of diesel fumes. What a way to go, I thought.

Following the seaman I clambered down the short flight of steps and joined him and six others, who were sitting on alloy benches around an alloy table which was swilling with vino. I was greeted in Italian and a large mug of vino was passed to me. 'Grazie,' I said and drank it, almost coughing up the liquid when it hit my palate, for it tasted like one cousin removed from vinegar. 'Buono,' said one of the crew as they all laughed. 'Fuckin' awful,' I replied. 'Putrido.' They chortled madly at this and said, 'No, buono,' and offered me another fill.

Either the captain was mad or he was trying to get rid of me

Sat together in this fast-moving hellhole, with legs firmly clamped around the alloy benches to stop us being thrown about, we swigged vino and became buddies. One pointed to my arm and obviously wanted to know how I had done it. 'Italiano – boom, boom.' I demonstrated with my fist and they all gave a cheer, and we all drank to that.

Later, some cold spaghetti appeared, with all sorts of dressing plonked on top. I shovelled as much of this down as I could, followed by more wine, wedged myself in a corner and, copying the others, fell asleep.

It was a sea cruise with a difference. My attitude towards the Italians changed as the ship raced round the toe and heel of Italy, crossing the Gulf of Taranto in record time. The conditions the crew worked under would have provoked mutiny on a British ship: the crew's quarters were squalid, cramped and streaming with condensation and sea water – and the toilets were a place only to be visited under dire stress, when the bladder was at bursting point or the bowels about to erupt in a volcanic frenzy.

A climb down that slippery metal ladder inside that swaying and jumping roller coaster was like a descent into Dante's Inferno when the flames had been put out. The stench was overwhelming and, if you weren't feeling ill when you set off down the ladder, you certainly were by the time you reached its foot. The toilets were the hole-in-the-floor variety and, in most cases, whoever had used them had missed the hole in the middle, rather easy to do considering the violent movements of the ship in which they were contained. In fact, it would be extremely difficult to balance over the hole with trousers down without knowing whether one is crapping on the deck or the bulkhead or the deckhead (walls or ceiling). If, like me, you were successful in hitting the designated target area, you then had to be very nimble when pulling the string flush as a torrent of water shot out of a large pipe, washing away both you and the load you'd dumped in such a fashion that you were convinced that the ship was sinking.

Reaching the Adriatic, the ship pulled in to Brindisi for refuelling and the crew hosed everything down below decks, me included, so I eventually ended up on the gun turret out of everyone's way. I snatched an hour's sleep, to be rudely shaken by an officer who told me in no uncertain terms to get below.

'*Si, si, capitano,*' I said, knowing he wasn't, and scuttled off below just as the ship was pulling out of the harbour only minutes before the captain shouted '*Piena velocità.*' The bow pointed skyward when the Ferraris kicked in and the crew below brought out the twenty-litre vino bottle as once again we became the fastest ship afloat. Well, almost afloat.

Following a long, rough journey I eventually arrived in north-east Italy and was deposited on the quay at Rimini, wet through, stinking to high heaven, half-sloshed, vino-stained, with an arm in a sling hurting like hell and sporting a brand new, all-American nose. I was welcomed back into the arms of my shipmates and given fourteen days' punishment for being absent without leave.

After a prolonged and minute study my shipmates declared the nose looked just like the earlier version, only straighter, and when I talked down it I sounded American.

My shipmates declared the nose looked just like the earlier version

BACK IN 1944 the war on the Italian mainland was fought with great ferocity by the Allies, as they sought to blast the Germans out of the heavily fortified positions to which they tenaciously clung. The battles that raged were paid for with heavy loss of life as the Allied armies advanced yard by yard. Smoke clouds far inland could be seen from the deck of the minesweeper HMS *Cadmus* as she steamed across the Bay of Naples after a successful operation. The ship had needed some minor repairs and the captain had decided that the tiny island of Capri, with its small harbour, was ideal for the task he had in mind.

Pulling alongside the harbour wall, the ship was soon tied up and the gangplank lowered, when much to our captain's astonishment he heard a shout and watched in disbelief as six German soldiers walked down the jetty with their hands held high in the air. He had captured Capri.

Somehow, during the confusion of war, these six soldiers had been left on the island and for whatever reason the war had passed them by. Our skipper was highly chuffed and ever afterwards considered that the island belonged to him.

As a consequence, when our operations in the northern Adriatic in 1945 were completed and the flotilla was recalled to Naples, it was natural that our skipper returned to Capri while the ship's boiler was cleaned. The circumstances were different: the war was almost over in Europe and there had been some changes in the crew, including my addition. Who was I to quibble over six weeks on Capri?

On three sides the white, limestone cliffs of the island rose sheer out of the sea for many hundreds of feet, the only landing places being on the harbour side of the island where the two small villages were joined by a funicular lift. Ideally situated for a fortress, the Roman emperor Tiberius had a palace built here during his reign, and legend has it that this is where the mad Caligula held his orgies, ate newborn babies and threw people to their deaths from the clifftops. On a pleasanter note, the pre-war popular singing star Gracie Fields, who married an Italian and was ostracised by the British, also had a house here. We soon found out that servicemen were always welcome and had the full use of an extensive library and the generous hospitality which 'our Gracie' had arranged for us.

Oh, and there were also several bars and ristorantes. Not a bad place to spend six weeks.

Shore leave was granted and Red Watch was allowed ashore, alas without me as I still had some punishment to work off from an all-night leave in Malta, our last port of call. How could one so young and innocent receive so much punishment? I often asked myself that question, but never heard a satisfactory answer.

It started when Jock, Smokey and I, after having a few beers, wandered over to Sliema where there was an outdoor roller-skating rink where, after a few more beers, we donned skates and began skylarking. In no time at all we had managed to upset several young ladies by grabbing hold and spinning them round until they fell over. Unfortunately, four of the young ladies were in the company of four extremely large marines, who became quite threatening until Jock said, 'Aw awa and bile your heed,' and tripped one up.

The mood of the marines quickly changed from threatening to murderous and we were soon being pursued at high speed around the skating rink by four large marines and two large bouncers. We desperately needed an escape plan, which I spotted on our fifth circuit. On one side of the rink an opening led directly onto seven flights of steep, stone steps that dropped to the harbour. I shouted to my fellow fugitives:

'We're going out the steps on the next circuit.'

'Ye're fookin mad,' said Jock.

As we came abreast of the opening we jumped the perimeter of the rink then up another step, along a flat bit, then had a quick glimpse down the side of an Everest of steps before we were rattling down them. Fortunately, the steps were fairly broad; unfortunately, they were bloody steep and there were three hundred and eighty of them in all, with the harbour at the bottom.

Not for nothing was I known as the boy champion of Prospect Street. My youthful skating skills were still there as I made the bone-jarring descent at high speed, sometimes jumping two steps to avoid hitting the edges. Tremendous concentration was required to maintain balance and judge the distance between each drop and, vaguely, out of a corner of my eye, I saw a flurry of arms and legs and heard an agonising cry, but I couldn't look round and it was impossible to stop. My eyes were blurring, my knees were aching, my ankles were on fire and my brain rattled around inside my skull like that of a punch-drunk fighter, but the steps were almost finished and the black water of the harbour loomed ahead. The last step: I was down and I threw all my energy into a skidding turn that drew sparks from the metal wheels as I missed the edge of the sea wall by a narrow margin. My skates slid from under me and I ended in a heap.

I looked up and, framed by the coloured lights from the rink high above, I saw the sorry spectacle of my two shipmates staggering, falling, skating, swearing and rolling around like marionettes. A crowd looked down from the rink and the two bouncers were slowly clambering towards us. Smokey still had his skates on and he rattled and jumped and fell and cursed his way towards me, but poor Jock had lost a skate and he was doing a hop, slide, slip, fall on his arse routine, being only sustained by his hatred of me.

'I'll fookin kill ye – ye Lancashire bastard – wa' a fookin bloody, stupid idea,' and he fell on his arse again. As Smokey drew nearer, I could see that he was out of control, his eyes had a vacant blurred look about them and his legs were shaking as his speed suddenly increased.

He gave a mighty yell and shot over the edge of the harbour wall

'*Turn*!' I shouted. Too late, he gave a mighty yell and shot over the edge of the harbour wall. There were some boarding steps nearby and I couldn't stop laughing as I watched him trying to swim with metal skates on, until I reached down and dragged him out – just in time to grab his mate, who had put the wrong foot down after the last step and was heading at speed towards the harbour.

We quickly took off our skates and ran like hell for the Gut, where we spent the rest of the evening giggling into our beer. It was a great pity the Maltese authorities didn't possess our wonderful sense of humour, though, because one of us had been recognised and we were brought before the captain and charged with an offence of civil disturbance.

Which was why Jock, Smokey and I were not allowed ashore in Capri. I knew I never should have gone drinking with them.

I DECIDED TO BECOME an exemplary sailor and, once I came off punishment, I impressed lots of the ship's company, baffled some and worried the jaunty, who thought I was ill. With lots of 'Yes sirs, no sirs,' I found life a lot easier on board ship and I suddenly became the petty officer's blue-eyed boy.

'What are ye up to, Snakey?' asked Jock one day. 'Ah dinna trust ye when ye're behavin' yersel.'

Shore leave on Capri was very pleasant. The idle, rich foreigners, who had made the island their own Shangri-La, had been frightened off by the war and were long gone, taking their yachts and trappings of wealth with them. Only the locals and the crew of the *Cadmus* were left to enjoy this idyllic setting.

We caught the funicular up to Anacapri, the top village, and sat outside an opulent ristorante drinking cool glasses of beer. We took in a dazzling panorama of the azure blue of the Bay of Naples, which curved away below us following the sweep of the coastline past Sorrento, the brooding pyramid of Vesuvius and past the sprawl of Naples itself, to continue round to Ischia, which shimmered in the haze eighteen miles away. Taking a clifftop walk along the length of the island, we passed ostentatious villas clinging to the white limestone rock below our feet, a few with people outside who called a greeting as we passed on our way to the ruins of the Roman emperors' palace. It was very picturesque and, looking down through the broken arches and leaning over the crumbling balustrade, taking in the dizzy drop to the sea far below, it was hard to imagine the grim history attached to this seemingly tranquil place.

'Just think of all those wasted virgins,' said Smokey. 'All chucked over the cliff – and we can't even find one!' The spell was broken and we went back for a drink.

A group of fellow crewmen approached as we sat under a green and white sunshade.

'Ah, it's Snakey of the sneakey punch,' said one, taller than the rest. 'I still owe you for that one.' It was the Terrible Turk with some of his fellow stokers.

'What you 'avin?' I asked quickly, remembering that awful clout in the balls I had given him. I soon got the beer in and realised that he bore no grudge.

'I hear you've had your nose modified,' he said, peering at it closely. 'You know, I could have done a better job than that,' he said playfully, prodding it with a mighty fist. 'Where's Gracie Field's place?'

It turned out that the Turk's family came from Rochdale and one of his aunts had worked with Gracie in the mill, and she even remembered Boris, Gracie's husband. For a mill lass to make it from Rochdale to Capri in those days was no mean feat.

There were no distractions on Capri to lead a young man astray and I led a blameless existence. Perhaps it was the atmosphere of the island, but I even got Jock interested in nature. We hired a small boat from one of the fishermen and sailed round the base of one of the massive limestone cliffs and found the famous Blue Grotto. Ducking through the low entrance, quickly guiding the rowing boat in the trough of a swell, the craft just scraped through and we found ourselves in one of the most magnificent sea caves in Europe.

The sea in the grotto was a luminous translucent green which alternated from a pale golden green to pockets of azure blue as the sunlight, filtering through the sea outside, reflected from the floor of the cave. This transmitted the luminosity up from the seabed to the surface inside the dark grotto, to be dispersed into a million facets of sparkling light by the waves, which acted as a prism, directing blue, green and gold splashes of light that danced and flashed like electric fire on the curved roof of the cave twenty feet above. It was breathtaking and even Jock was speechless. Apart from one 'Fookin 'ell,' he sat in awe, completely spellbound as I rowed around the perimeter of the grotto, which was quite extensive.

We suddenly experienced an overwhelming desire for a swim so, leaving the boat drifting, we stripped off and slid over the side. It was magic. Swimming in that strange, luminous, deep and clear water was like floating in space, and the light below and the semi-darkness above was unlike anything either of us had ever experienced.

Suddenly, the dark shape of another boat was silhouetted in the entrance. A local fisherman was bringing some sightseers – two genteel old English ladies and two young girls. Jock and I suddenly heard a thin piping voice from one of the maidens: 'Oh look grandma, mermaids,' as she spotted our pale naked bodies shimmering in the water. We hastily dived underwater and surfaced further away. The old ladies were not convinced.

'They were probably fish, my dear,' one said as the fisherman duly rowed his customers round the grotto, with Jock and me keeping ahead.

'Eh, Snakey, I'm knackered,' said Jock, who slowed down and floated on his back for a breather. Suddenly, the boat and its inquisitive crew came around a bend and two thin, piping voices squeaked in unison: 'There they are, there's two of them. Look grandma, look.'

While we desperately tried to cover our embarrassment, the boat came nearer. 'Look, look,' cried the young girls.

'Oh yes, my dears, we see them. You're right, they must be mermaids,' said the old ladies trying to hide their red faces. 'Go nearer, mister boatman, we can't see their tails,' squeaked the young girls. 'Och, they'll see 'em, too, if they come any nearer,' spluttered Jock, 'an' they won't be where they expect 'em to be.'

The Italian boatman smiled broadly at us and rowed his party away. We hastily clambered back into our boat, put on our undercrackers and rowed out through the entrance before more sightseers came in.

There is also a white grotto on Capri. Rowing further round the island, we passed a line of jagged pinnacles and came upon a cleft in the rock face. Manoeuvring the boat between the jagged fangs of limestone, we entered a high, rift-like cavern which gradually opened into a large cave. This was a natural cavern with large flowstone deposits covering the walls and a shower of water spraying down from the faraway roof. Once a caver, always a caver, and I suddenly experienced the urge to explore.

There was enough light entering the cave for me to see a passage leading off above the flowstone and, after asking Jock to hold the boat against the base of the calcite, I leapt across and began climbing. Bare feet and underpants are not the best rig for exploring caves, and my shipmate thought I had taken leave of my senses as I wedged myself behind one of the huge organ-pipe formations and began working my way up. The formation was old, dry and corroded; it had been there for thousands of years before the Roman emperors, so I experienced a strange sense of wonder because I was probably the only human being to have ever entered the dry, ochre-coloured passage that opened before me.

The light was poor and I waited awhile for my eyes to adjust to the gloom. From down below I heard a frantic cry: 'Are ye alright Snakey?' I answered in the affirmative as I progressed up the steeply sloping passage. The dust of centuries lay undisturbed beneath my feet and the only footprints were mine. 'Leave nothing but footprints, take nothing but time.' Where had I heard that before?

Eventually, with the passage still continuing, I couldn't see what I was doing so I had to retreat, back to my shivering shipmate. He looked at me with a strange expression and said, 'Snakey, ye're fookin mad!'

I couldn't even begin to try to explain the lure of caving to him, so we rowed back to Capri village and, sitting outside one of the bars, settled behind a few beers. As luck would have it, the two old ladies and their young charges came into sight and sat at the next table. We were now in uniform, but that didn't prevent one of the young girls coming across and standing next to Jock, closely peering into his face. 'Hello,' she said,' I know you – you're a mermaid. I saw you in the grotto. And,' she said in a loud voice, 'you had no clothes on.'

Jock's face went bright red when some of the nearby crew heard this and burst out laughing.

'Come away dear,' said one of the sweet old ladies, 'and stop annoying that nice sailor.'

'He's a sailor now – but he's really a mermaid, and I want to know where he's left his tail.'

'What a nice wee lassie,' said Jock to the old ladies as we departed.

IT HAD TO HAPPEN. Fate had decreed that from an early age my life would exist as a series of mishaps, misadventures and happenings over which I had no control. One of these strange tricks of fate occurred three days later when, working in the gun locker on some small arms, I left the door ajar because of the heat. Bill Thompson, one of the sparks (electricians), shouted: 'Can I use your vice, Snakey?'

No lower deck ratings were ever allowed in the gun locker, but Tommo just needed the vice to free a rusty connection so I saw no harm in it. Having loosened his connection while I had my back to him, Tommo must have loosened another one in his brain because he began playing with one of three pistols that were lying on the bench. There was an ear-shattering explosion and a fog of acrid fumes. Tommo stood swaying with a silly, stupefying grin on his face, clutching a smoking starting pistol and looking at a blackened hole in the centre of his other hand before he slumped to the deck.

All hell broke loose. The medics whipped him off to Naples and I was taken before the captain. I was grilled, read the riot act and the rules and regulations laid down concerning guns and ammunition, lower deck ratings and the use of, access to in case of mutiny, and so on and so on. I had unwittingly committed a serious breach of naval discipline, to which I pleaded guilty. I didn't know the stupid sod was going to try to commit hara-kiri . . .

So ended my days of freedom. 'Confined to ship, loss of privileges, fourteen days number elevens, loss of good conduct badge.' And I had only been awarded it the previous week!

A fleet lighter came out to collect Tommo's kit, so we knew we wouldn't see him again. His hand required extensive surgery. 'It's a good job the starting pistol only fired blanks,' I mused, 'otherwise *I* would have needed extensive surgery.' A .22 fired from one of the other pistols would have ricocheted around the gun locker like a demented hornet and, given my luck, it would have hit me. Or, there again, if I had known Tommo was bored I could have let him play with the 4 inch gun and he could have wiped out half of Capri.

I got the black dog, and went about the ship morosely doing my duties as well as the extra punishments, while I brooded on my bad luck. I remember thinking to myself that, if everyone has a guiding star, then mine must be Jiminy Cricket.

Like many other young lads keen to volunteer for service, I came to the conclusion that I was not suited to being a member of His Majesty's Forces. It was not that I didn't like the uniform, or the way of life – that part was brilliant – it was the obeying orders bit that seemed to get me confused. Being born with an enquiring mind, if the orders didn't seem logical I questioned them – not too directly, though, as that was an offence. As I had been warned once by a chief petty officer: 'Hofficers his more hintelligent than ratings, that is why they his hofficers, and whatever they tells you to do, you do it, even if it means disappearing up your own backside.' Words of wisdom.

However, during my time on the *Kimberley* I came to the conclusion that 'Hofficers are not more hintelligent than ratings,' so I ignored the old chief's advice and became a sort of lower deck lawyer. I picked up quite a bit about Navy rules and regulations, mainly because I was always being charged with breaking them. This vast fund of knowledge ensured that I was popular among the crew, but not very popular among the charging officers. When I tried to impress them with my familiarity with the King's Regulations and Admiralty Instructions, I was told in no uncertain terms that: 'It is an offence to quote the King's Regulations and Admiralty Instructions to a superior officer and this is punishable by an increase in your sentence.'

Bloody hell! It was alright for officers to quote these archaic rules at you when you were being charged, but not alright for you to quote them back in your defence. It was very likely that everyone in the Royal Navy who was charged with a breach of regulations since the time Charles Laughton was the Captain of the Bounty, has been found guilty, with the cry: 'Throw that man in the brig!' I once asked to see a copy of the KRs and AIs. It was like dropping a bombshell or asking the Admiral of the Fleet if I could take his daughter skinny dipping.

BEING COOPED UP on board ship can sometimes be a bit of a bore, but cooped up when the ship is tied to a quay is really frustrating. Huddling around a decrepit radio listening to news bulletins of German defeats in Russia and the swift advance of the British and American armies in Germany as battalion after battalion of German troops surrendered made life even worse, because we should have been out there celebrating with our shipmates. I looked around at my fellow reprobates and said, 'Who's for breaking ship and going ashore? The bloody war is nearly over.' Someone had a better idea . . .

We had a whip round and collected a wad of notes, brought the cards out and each of the seven of us cut the deck to see who would break ship to buy some booze. Geordie and I won, or lost depending on your point of view.

We put on uniforms and approached the sentry on the gangway, who happened to be Scouse, and told him of our plan. 'I can hear you talking Wak, but I can't understand what you're saying. Get what I mean Wak? And it'll cost yer a drink,' said Scouse out of the corner of his mouth. This was Liverpool-speak for okay.

Geordie and I walked along the short quay, where a blaze of light and lots of noise indicated the bar. We sidled in past a group stood outside; inside, it was all hustle and bustle as our shipmates busily poured beer and vino down their throats. We had managed to ensconce ourselves in a corner by the bar and consume a couple of beers before we were noticed by our mates and Jonesey, one of our petty officers.

'Now then, lads,' he said. 'I had the impression that you were confined to ship.'

'Well, we should be, but we've come to tell you the good news. *The war is over!*' I shouted. This wasn't quite accurate, but it was near enough.

The bar fell silent as I relayed the gist of the news bulletin and added a few embellishments. 'General Rudsteight has just surrendered and Germany has capitulated,' said I, making up the name and slurping mouthfuls of beer between each word. Everyone cheered and went wild as the drinks flowed freely, then impromptu singing began.

'What did you tell them that for?' asked Geordie. 'The war isn't over.'

'Well, it probably will be by the time we get back on board. Anyway, it's taken attention away from us,' I said with a crafty leer. I collared the barman and pointed to a huge wicker-basket-encased bottle of vino standing behind a curtain that led to the back of the premises.

'Ow much?' He looked at me in amazement. I repeated the question. '*Quanta costa?*' and waved a thick bundle of notes under his nose. '*È certo,*' he said. '*Si,*' I replied, and within minutes the deal was done and Geordie and I sneaked out of the back entrance, lugging the heavy bottle between us.

Keeping to the shadows we reached the ship and huddled near the bow. We tossed a coin to see who was going aboard. I won and, leaving Geordie alone on the quay, clutching the giant bottle of vino, I timed my approach when the sentry (Scouse's relief) had his back to me and slipped aboard – home and safe. I shrugged my uniform off and headed for the forward lower deck, unscrewed a porthole cover and peered at the shadowy figure who was crouching outside with his knees knocking. I unscrewed the inner port and swung it open.

'Is that you, Snakey?' came a whisper.

'It'd better be,' I replied, 'hand me the bottle.'

The wickerwork basket just fitted into the porthole and, after a struggle, we managed to work the bottle through.

'Have you got it, Snakey?' came a whisper.

'Yes,' I replied, when I felt a hand on my shoulder.

'Do you want a lift with that?' came a familiar voice.

My heart dropped into my boots as I glanced at the large hand and uniformed sleeve embellished with three brass buttons. It belonged to our jaunty, the master-at-arms. I was sunk!

The jaunty, a strict but fatherly figure to us young ratings, stood looking at me as though I had taken leave of my senses. Between us, a large dusty bottle encased in its double-handled container stood on the deck. On the one hand there was a smart figure of a man with slightly greying hair atop the ruddy, weathered face of a seagoing Cornishman, dressed immaculately in his master-at-arms uniform, jacket emblazoned with a coat of arms on lapels and upper arms, brass buttons on his sleeves, white peaked cap set squarely on his head, trousers sharply creased and shoes highly polished. In short, a figure of respect and dignity. On the other hand there was me, a skinny, bare-footed, lower deck specimen clad in a stained vest and shorts, stinking of booze.

'What the bloody hell have you got here? If that's vino, you'll get the book thrown at you. Who is outside?'

'Nobody, chief,' I answered.

'WHAT? I've just heard you talking to him.'

'Er, an Italian. I just heard a voice saying "grab this".'

'In Italian, I suppose.'

'Er, no, chief, a sort of broken English.'

'Like Geordie, would it be?'

'Er, no, more like English ice cream man Italian.'

Do you want a lift
with that?

The jaunty looked at me sadly. 'You know, lad, I thought there was more to you than this. You've let me down. Follow me to the rum locker.'

I thought for a moment that he was going to give me a tot of rum because I looked pale, but no, it was to lock the bottle up. 'There's enough raw booze in this bottle to get the whole ship's company drunk,' he muttered as he locked it away. 'Able Seaman Eyre, you are being charged. Get your uniform on and report to my cabin.'

'Aye aye, sir.'

I was hauled before the first lieutenant. 'Off caps,' and the charge read out. 'Breaking ship and entering ship while under punishment and smuggling contraband aboard, contrary to sections 175A and 289B of the King's Regulations.'

The first lieutenant looked at me in disbelief. 'Able Seaman Eyre, do you realise how serious this is?'

'No sir,' I replied, thinking that perhaps this time I had overstepped the mark.

'I am putting you on Captain's Report. Prepare yourself for the worst!'

'Aye aye, sir.'

'On caps, right turn – quick march.'

I made my way back to the mess, informed my mess mates of the disaster and Geordie that he was an Italian ice cream man. They all tried to cheer me up but, to a man, they reckoned that it meant a jail sentence. So did I, just for celebrating the end of the war. Mind, perhaps I *was* a bit premature.

Some of the lads had smuggled some booze back for us, so we had a drink and I settled down to write a letter home. It began, 'Dear Ma and Pa. Having a great time, war nearly over, but don't expect me back for some time.' I then thought 'sod it', and slung my hammock and crawled in.

The following day there was consternation on board as half the crew were still celebrating the end of the war at 7 a.m., thanks to my rumour, which had since been magnified out of all proportions. It was a sorry lot of sailors that staggered back along the jetty, bleary-eyed and stinking of booze while being brought face to face with reality in the form of a very irate officer of the watch.

The *Cadmus* was supposed to head out for sea trials, but the state that some of the crew were in caused the skipper to postpone them and instead he put the whole ship's company on 'clean ship'. This meant everything, from the top of the funnel to the waterline, including holystoning the wooden deck and removing all debris from the quay. I decided to keep a low profile. At noon an announcement came over the tannoy to the effect that all shore leave on Capri had been cancelled until further notice.

THE NEXT DAY the ship sailed north off Ischia conducting sea trials. The sea was calm and at 11 a.m. the order came, 'All men on Captain's Report muster on the aft deck.' With a sick feeling in the pit of my stomach I joined most of Red Watch and we fell in under the stern eyes of the jaunty.

A table and chairs had been set up for the captain and duty officer. The jaunty barked: 'Able Seaman Eyre, six paces forward march. Halt. Attention. Off caps.' The charge was read out. 'While under punishment Able Seaman Eyre did break out of ship and acquired contraband, then broke into ship and smuggled said contraband aboard while being absent without leave, contrary to sections 175A and 289B of King's Regulations and Admiralty Instructions.'

The captain looked up at the jaunty, 'What is this contraband, Master-at-Arms?'

'Vino, sir,' replied the jaunty.

'Bringing drink on board ship is an offence, but I could hardly call it contraband Master-at-Arms. One bottle of vino you say?'

'Yes sir.'

'Where is it?' asked the captain.

'In the rum locker for safety, sir.'

'Have it brought up,' demanded the captain, and a petty officer and a rating were despatched. They returned quickly, lugging the 35 litre bottle in its custom-built basket. There was a murmur of approval from the assembled ranks, quickly silenced by a petty officer.

The captain looked at the bottle, looked at me and looked at the bottle again. 'Do you realise, Able Seaman, that I could charge you with incitement to mutiny?' I gulped. 'There is probably enough vino in this bottle to incapacitate several members of the crew, making them less conducive to obeying orders – in other words, mutinous!' I gulped again and opened my mouth to defend myself before I was hung from the yardarm. 'Silence!' intervened the jaunty.

The captain looked at me in some puzzlement. 'Why did you smuggle all this alcohol on board? Did you want to destabilise the ship?'

'No, sir.'

'Then why in God's name did you do it?' asked the captain in anguish.

'To celebrate the end of the war, sir.'

'Well, Able Seaman Eyre, let me inform you that the war is not yet over, but it probably will be by the time you get out,' and with these dreaded words he uttered worse: 'You are to be placed on remand for a court-martial hearing.'

The rest of the crew on Captain's Report received short shrift from a commanding officer in a foul mood. Charged with being absent without leave, each member of Red Watch who was ashore on that fateful night received fourteen days number elevens. The only light relief came when, later in the day as we were returning to Capri, the jaunty – assisted by one of the crew – opened up the offending bottle, tasted the vino it contained, declared it to be good stuff and promptly poured it over the side. Unseen by him, numerous pans, mess fanny's (tins), buckets and various other utensils were held out of open portholes in the top mess deck. Later that night, Snakey's downfall was toasted with the vino that caused it. Like the jaunty said, it was good stuff – but not worth going to chokey for.

The cell block in Naples was full, as it seemed that the end-of-the-war-syndrome had affected half the fleet, so I was kept on the *Cadmus* until I could be dealt with. By now Hitler was holed up in his bunker. He was quite deranged as he issued conflicting orders and incited what was left of the population of the wasteland that was now Berlin to form a last defence, using a ragged army of children and old people. It would not be long before the bunker fell silent in April 1945, when the Goebbels family, Eva Braun and the fanatical dictator killed himself. But for all this, as the skipper had remarked, the war was not over; instead, it was now a vicious fight for survival against the fanatical Japanese – foot by foot and inch by inch, literally to the last man.

The *Cadmus* eventually returned to Malta and the court martial took place in Fort St Angelo, in front of three very senior officers who wore enough gold braid to start a jeweller's shop, as did my defending officer who had a sash of the stuff tucked through his shoulder lapel. Not to be outdone, I was also dressed for the occasion in my best uniform with my recently returned, gold good conduct badge neatly sewn on. I had lost it that often it would have been better attached with Velcro, but that hadn't yet been invented.

My humiliation was completed by having two of my shipmates, dressed in belts and gaiters, act as an armed escort. They marched me in front of the court, which was set upon the landing area in front of the fort, the scene of many a historic occasion. This was another – at least for me, and one I determined not to repeat.

The hearing was brief and brutal. The charge was read out by the prosecuting officer; the way he presented it made it seem that I was the cousin of Lucky Luciano and Bugsy Malone, bootleggers for the Mafia. My defender was brilliant. 'Able Seaman Eyre pleads guilty,' was all he said. The senior officer announced: 'This court finds you guilty and you will serve seven days in cells, the first three on low diet. Prisoner and escort, right turn, quick march.'

As I was bundled into a truck and driven to Verdala barracks, I suddenly realised what a bloody fool I had been. I shook hands with my shipmates and was handed over to the guards at the entrance to the detention block.

THE PUNISHMENT BEGAN IMMEDIATELY. I was made to pick up my weighty kitbag and hammock, then double across the barracks square towards the cell block administration. 'Attention, empty your kitbag.'

As I started removing each item, I was interrupted. 'Upend it and tip everything on the deck.'

Two of the guards, who had been picked for the job because of their resemblance to Himmler, strewed my kit over the dirt floor. They opened everything that would open and poured the contents out, kicking stuff with their boots or stirring things around with their batons, including the few presents I had purchased. They took an obvious delight in breaking anything that was breakable in an attempt to goad me into some sort of retaliation or outburst.

'Unlash your hammock.'

That was shaken and flung into a corner before these morons tired of trying to humiliate me. 'Right, lash that up and repack your kit.'

I had to stuff everything back inside the kitbag within seconds, helped by one guard putting his boot in it and stamping it down, grinning as he heard things break. 'Pick your gear up. Double march.' I was prodded across the square to the cells. My kit was taken off me. I was made to strip and given a cold shower, before being thrown a coarse white canvas suit and told to put it on and double down a passage to the cells. An iron door opened and I was hustled inside before it slammed shut. I had the feeling of being in a nightmare; I was in an unreal existence.

The cell measured eight feet by six feet. An iron-barred window was set high on one wall. An iron cot, covered in a thin, horsehair mattress with two folded coarse blankets, took up another, while a small corner shelf held a bible, a tin mug of water and two sea biscuits. Under the cot was a metal slop bucket.

The hard tack biscuits were like those kept in lifeboats: they last for ever and are almost inedible. Slowly, I began to realise that the two biscuits and the water to wash them down was what constituted the start of 'my first three days on low diet'. Life was not looking rosy and, as I sat on the cot feeling sorry for myself, I thought, 'Ah well, I can always read the Bible.'

That was before the door was pulled open. A burly guard smirked when he saw the Bible in my hand, and he threw a bundle of tarred hemp rope in front of me. 'You won't have time to read that – you'll be too busy picking this.' I looked at the pieces of rope in obvious bafflement.

'That's your daily task. You have to pick that with your fingernails until I have a nice fluffy pile like spun silk – and at the end of the day, any pieces you haven't picked will added to your task the following day. At the end of your seven days you will stay and pick any oakum left before you are released.' When I opened my mouth to say something he glared at me and continued, 'Prisoners are not allowed to talk, not allowed to smoke – you're not even allowed to shit unless we say so.'

With a look of pure evil he spat on the cell floor and said; 'Clean that fucker up!' and slammed the cell door with a clang that echoed around the cell and my despondent being. I stared into space, totally uncomprehending how my life had so abruptly turned into a bad dream.

I picked up one of the pieces of tarred rope. It was one and a half inches in diameter, a foot long and as stiff as a board. I tried to unravel it or pick bits off, but found the stiff rope unyielding. It was obviously old rope that had been in use, causing the fibre strands to stretch and almost fuse together.

After trial and error I evolved a method of unwinding each strand from the end of the piece – that gave me six thick strands and picking at each one gave me twelve smaller strands, which I pulled apart into a coarse sort of horsehair. I once read that sailors in the seventeenth and eighteenth centuries used to caulk the seams of wooden boats with a mixture of rope fibres (known as oakum) and tar, and I presumed that this was the raw product I was now preparing.

However, what use this old rope fibre had in the twentieth century, I couldn't imagine. I suspected this archaic practice had been reintroduced purely as a mind-destroying task to break a prisoner's spirit. I sat in my cheerless cell like Rumpelstiltskin spinning his cloth of gold, or whatever – only in my case, ruefully looking at my bleeding finger ends as I picked and plucked my way through the seemingly innocuous pile of fossilised rope ends which never seemed to diminish. I realised that I should be thankful that the Royal Navy, which doesn't give up such practices easily, had abandoned the ritual of keelhauling and the use of the cat-o'-nine-tails.

I found the water in the tin mug brackish and the biscuits only just edible if soaked for a long period. There was very little sound coming into the cell from the passage beyond, and nothing at all from the barracks outside. In silence and isolation I picked at the oakum until the light went out, then I crawled underneath a moth-eaten blanket and fell into a dreamless sleep.

My head suddenly exploded with noise and loud banging. I became vaguely aware that the ship had been torpedoed, or we had hit a mine, and I shouted and sat bolt upright, squinting against the bright light.

'Out – out – out. Slop out, you lazy bastard.' Who was this vacant-looking sod staring at me and waving a truncheon in my face? My sleep-fuddled brain slowly cleared as I realised that I was not dreaming and, as my comprehension returned, I lapsed into a deep, dark depression, broken only by a whack on the shoulder by the truncheon-wielding moron, just to make sure that I knew I was a resident of a Navy chokey, the worst hell a sailor could find himself in.

'Come on you bastard. Wake up! Slop out. Chop, chop. Double, double!' In a nauseating trance I picked up the slop bucket and stood at the door of the cell, along with several other creatures of the night. White-faced and dressed in white, shapeless canvas uniforms, they ranged down the corridor like the undead in the bowels of Count Dracula's castle.

'Right turn. Double double double!' We ran the gauntlet of guards as we doubled to the heads, emptied our slops and doubled back, so occupied with dodging playful whacks from their truncheons that no one had time to be introduced to each other. The cell door slammed and that was the day's exercise over.

I stood there rubbing my fresh bruises as the grill opened, more sticks of tarred rope were tossed in and a guard with an Irish accent asked if I would like a smoke. As I approached the grill I was greeted with a puff of second-hand smoke blown into the cell. 'Here, suck on that,' said my tormentor and laughed as he slammed the grill shut. 'Fuck off you Irish ####!' I muttered.

Time and the world outside ceased to function. Inside that cell block all normal behaviour was suspended and prisoners were treated worse than animals. I mused on the fact that, with the war almost over, in many cases we were on the verge of beating better men than those creeps who roamed the corridor outside my cell door.

I went back to my thankless task of picking oakum and vented my anger on those inanimate, turd-like pieces of rope, imagining that I was tearing the guard to pieces. But, by nightfall I realised the futility of it all as I sat contemplating my bleeding fingers.

The grill suddenly slid back and a hoarse Glaswegian voice whispered 'Fancy a drag, Jimmie?' as a glowing cigarette end came arching into the cell to land on the floor in a shower of sparks. I dived on it as the grill slammed shut. It was like manna from heaven. Less than an inch long, I sucked every dreg of nicotine out until I could no longer hold it, so I spat on the glowing end and shoved the remainder in my mouth and chewed it. I didn't care if the donor was dying from an unknown infectious disease or if I ran the risk of developing rabies, scabies, TB or the clap – that wet, dirty little fag end was one of life's luxuries.

A night of dreamless sleep was terminated by banging on the cell door and the light coming on at 6 a.m. This time I was ready. As the cell door was flung open, I was out with the slop bucket and had time to glance at my fellow inmates as they doubled past with their slop buckets. A couple winked at me; it's amazing what a small gesture like that can accomplish. It meant that I was not alone and there were other human beings in the same predicament.

Back in the cell with the door slammed behind me, I eyed the fresh pile of fossilised turds that awaited my attention, kicked them into the wall and swore loud and long. I eventually calmed down and wondered what I should have for breakfast. One nibble at a concrete biscuit, or two? My mind wandered the highways and byways of the pleasanter aspects of my life as I automatically picked and plucked the bloody rope ends to pieces, stopping only to stretch my legs for a three-stride walk and massage my hands, before resuming the monotony.

As the light faded I became aware that I had fulfilled my day's task, leaving only two unfinished pieces from the day before which I determined to complete. At 9.30 p.m. the cell light was switched off, but I continued shredding the last piece until it was undone and fell back, perversely satisfied, on my cot. The sheer misery on the guard's face in the morning when he saw that I had caught up on my quota was reward in itself, until the bastard belted me across the back of the head with his truncheon as I passed by on the slop run. I looked him full in the eyes as I returned, as I wanted to memorise every bit of that ugly pock-marked, weak, weasel-like face with shifty, blood-shot eyes, and swore to myself that I would drive my fist into that slobbering mouth when my sentence was finished.

Having drunk three mugs of crappy water and 'eaten' four sea biscuits, today was the red-letter day when I should be going on full diet. Sure enough, the grill slid back and in came a gourmet's delight: four small, greyish-green tinned potatoes and six peas – stone cold and obviously a second- or third-hand leftover from a canteen meal that the local goats had refused.

I ate the peas and half of one potato and wished I was back on the sea biscuits again.

Was it day four, or was it day three? I lost track of time as everything began to merge into a surrealistic experience that had no beginning and no end. I was concentrating on pulling the rope strands apart when, suddenly, the cell door opened and, lo and behold, there stood an officer. Like his minions he looked a proper bastard, as befitting his illustrious position as chief jailer, but at least he wasn't going to bonk me on the head with a truncheon.

'Haircut,' he bawled, and the door slammed shut.

Within minutes it was thrown open by my favourite guard. 'Out. Left turn. Double double double,' he yelled, hitting me on the back of the legs with his truncheon. 'Halt. Right turn. Sit.'

I sat on a chair in front of a Maltese barber and was just about to say, 'Not too much off the top and just a light trim,' before I was assaulted. This chap could cut for the Olympics. With his high-speed supercharged electric trimmer I was shorn like a sheep in eighty-five seconds.

'Stand. Right turn. Double double double.'

Slam! I was back in my cell, scalped by a Maltese Geronimo and was now a skinhead before my time! I felt the vacant plot where two minutes ago had flourished lovely wavy hair and shuddered as my hand encountered skin and scratch marks. 'Ah well, at least I'll save on Brylcreem,' I mused.

It was all part of the great humiliation process: I was not only a jailbird, I was made to look like one. I felt degraded. 'The bloody bastards,' I swore as I carried on with the interminable oakum-picking. Three of my finger ends were beginning to fester due to fine cuts inflicted by the hemp stands, and I was going through a real downer when the grill opened and a voice said, 'Like a smoke?' I jumped up and a puff of exhaled cigarette smoke was blown in my face. The grill slammed shut again and I heard the guard's maniacal laughter.

Bastard, bastard, bloody Irish bastard. I had never got on too badly with the Irish, especially the Liverpool variety, but this sod I hated with an intensity that was frightening.

As the light began to fade in my gloomy cell I started to hallucinate. I could hear music and singing, and I gradually became aware that it was real. It was coming through a small gap at the top of the window, from beyond the bars set in a sloping recess high in the wall, the relic of an old firing position when the place was part of a fort. I listened intently and could hear what sounded like a party going on, and I became determined to see out.

Rolling a blanket into a tight, narrow roll I stood on the edge of the bed and, after several attempts, managed to thread one end between the bars. I gradually wriggled it down until I was clutching both ends then, hanging onto the blanket, I braced both feet against the wall and climbed to the recess and shimmied up until I could jam myself across and hang onto the bars.

The sound of singing and celebrations came from the administration block across the square, obviously it was a radio on full blast. Pressed against the bars I could hear cockney voices singing 'Knees up muvver brarn, knees up muvver brarn' amid the sounds of a great party. The radio announcer's plummy voice came floating across over the music and happy noises.

'And so the war in Europe is over – this is Victory Day.'

A couple of the guards came staggering out of the block clutching bottles, taking generous swigs and slapping each other on the back. The announcer's voice continued:

'You will always remember this day for the rest of your lives. No one will ever forget where they were on Victory Day.'

'No, I bloody won't – in the bloody cells, that's where I am, and I'm here for celebrating what you silly sods are celebrating today, only I did it a few days early!'

I then slipped off my precarious perch and landed in a heap on the floor, fortunately dropping onto a freshly picked pile of gossamer threads of oakum.

Where was I on VE Day, 8 May 1945? Will I ever forget? Will I hell!

I was scalped by a Maltese Geronimo

Chapter 6

In Limbo

FERRYVILLE. How did I get to Ferryville? Perhaps they had sent me to the wrong place – Ferryville doesn't sound African, yet here I was in North Africa being driven along a desert road towards Tunis by a demented Italian POW singing highlights from various Italian operas while making expressive gestures with his hands as the truck veered from side to side. It didn't seem real, yet as I had found out, most things in the Navy had a Salvador Dali touch and my boundless view of the ocean had suddenly been exchanged for a boundless view of desert sand. Miles of it, stretching as far as the eye could see.

Several weeks previously I had been discharged from chokey along with another miscreant, Ian McTavish, a friendly but short-fused Glaswegian. While in Verdala barracks we became oppos, united in our vision of revenge on a certain pock-faced jail guard and, during a pleasant evening ashore in the Blue Heaven, we became religious as our prayers were answered.

The honky-tonk was heaving with matelots (sailors), the pianist was plonking away, the girls were doing their stuff, we had just eaten steak, eggs and chips, we had drunk several pints, and all we needed to make our world complete came in through the entrance.

With my back to the doorway I was talking to Ian when I noticed his neck becoming thicker and the short hairs at the back bristling. His face suddenly turned very blotchy and his eyes narrowed as he seemed to transform into a very large, wire-haired terrier, before he gave a growl and launched himself past me, knocking over his chair, the table, the drinks and an unfortunate ordinary seaman who was in his way.

I turned around just in time to see the hated Irish jailer being lifted off the floor by a powerful right hook swung by a very powerful, out-of-control Glaswegian. Before he landed he was hit again by a left and a right. As I charged over, the guard's nose was being pulped. There was blood everywhere as Ian straddled the Irishman's limp body and knocked seven bells out of him in a frenzy of bloodlust.

I don't know what the guard had done to my Scottish buddy, but it was apparent that he had picked on the wrong bloke for it took three of us to drag him off the unconscious, blood-soaked figure on the floor.

Before the shore patrol arrived I rapidly hustled Ian away to a bar a long way from the scene. There I had a drink with a man at peace with the world who, with an angelic smile of satisfaction on his face, took a long, deep drink of beer. He wiped the froth from his lips and said, 'You know Jimmie, I really enjoyed that.' Revenge is sweet.

Not long after, Ian was drafted to Trincomalee, in what was then called Ceylon, and I ended up in Tunisia with this bloody Italian doing an imitation of Scarpio trying to have his way with Tosca, and looking at me with dark, limpid, Italian eyes instead of the approaching lorry. Disaster was averted by me grabbing the steering wheel as the two vehicles parted company with their offside driving mirrors.

'You stupid bastard,' I yelled.

'I am a sorry, I get a carried away,' said Bruno.

'We'll both be carried away if you don't keep your eyes on the road,' I muttered.

Ferryville, situated between Algiers and Tunis, was an important depot during the North African campaign. It meant that a large quantity of stores had to be guarded and the depot maintained with the help of several Italian prisoners, who were pleased to have escaped the war and were quite friendly characters.

I had been drafted to relieve a 'stripey' who was due to go home. It was a peaceful – no – a boring existence and the only excitement was the twice-weekly run with Bruno to pick up the mail in Tunis, a job that for some strange reason no one else seemed to want. I had just discovered why when, for the tenth time, I pointed out to my driver that he was supposed to hold the steering wheel with his hands, 'Not your fuckin' knees!'

'Ah, meester Snakey, you a worry too a much,' said Bruno, giving me a dazzling smile as the sun flashed from his three gold teeth and we slewed off the road, almost covering the driver of a camel train in sand. The leading camel staggered with fright and fell, dislodging its load in more ways than one.

With Bruno now attentively wrestling with the wheel and gear lever, we travelled sideways with two wheels on the road and an old camel-owning Arab beating Bruno with his stick and me wiping stinking camel saliva off my uniform, before the wheels gained enough purchase to pull us back onto the highway. With cries of *imshi*, we approached Tunis.

I watched, horrified, as the body went skywards

Bruno had recovered; in fact, he seemed to have enjoyed his encounter with the camel train and I wondered if he was perhaps a sort of Italian kamikaze pilot who self-destructed on camel trains. The light of battle was sparkling in his eyes and he burst once more into song as we approached one of the ornate arched gateways to the city.

With the melodic strains of 'O sol o mieow' ringing in my ears, Bruno flung the truck around a bend and met an Islamic funeral just coming out of the city gateway. The shrouded figures were carrying a body on an open bier on their shoulders, and the surrounding mourners were chanting and wailing – which increased when they looked up and saw a ten-ton truck heading for them. Bruno's 'O sol o mieow' suddenly changed to 'O sol o sheet' as he wrestled with the steering wheel and slammed on the brakes.

I watched, horrified, as the body went skywards in an urgent rush to meet its maker ahead of schedule, the mourners diving for cover on either side and the bier landing with a clatter on the bonnet before bouncing over the roof of the truck. I looked back to see bodies in all directions, but they were all moving and waving fists.

I commanded Bruno to stop, but he ignored me. '*Arresto, arresto*, you Italian prat,' I yelled as we careered through the narrow streets in a cloud of dust.

'No. Eef I stop they a keel me,' said Bruno, his swarthy face turned a greyish white.

'If you don't stop I'll bloody well "keel" you! What if you've killed someone?'

'Oh, I 'ope I only keel one,' said Bruno in his fractured English.

'Well, there was one dead already, but I'll bet he's got up and walked away.'

Bruno reversed the truck and I climbed out and approached the still disorganised funeral party, who saw me coming, dropped the body and began pelting me with stones. I gave them a friendly wave and ran like hell, jumping into the already moving lorry. Bruno later explained. 'If I keel one, that is okay. But if I no keel one, and only injure heem, I have to pay doctor and hospital and feed his family, and that is not okay.'

Coming from someone with Bruno's obvious driving skills, I believed him and wondered what our score would be on the way back.

AFTER A SHORT PERIOD the Army took over and began freighting out the stores. The Naval security force returned to Malta, now a busy transit camp and filled to the seams as men were returned to Britain in increasing numbers. Many spent their last few days in chokey as the excitement became too much and they forgot that they were still in the Navy and did silly things, such as one inebriated rating who bet another inebriated rating that he couldn't climb onto the top girder of a lift and walk along it.

The lift in question was situated against a cliff face at the highest point of Valletta and dropped about 300 feet to sea level. I had been experimenting with the various drinks in coloured bottles that lined the top, cobweb-covered shelf of a dingy bar in a dingy back street in Sliema. There was obviously a hidden ingredient in this exotic fluid that I had consumed which convinced me that I was Son of Spiderman and, after a heated discussion and the exchange of several wads of currency, the bets were on.

I made my unsteady way over a safety barrier and began climbing an iron ladder leading to a network of girders that reached into space over the lift housing. Oblivious to the drop below and the crowd that swiftly gathered, I shakily clambered off the top of the fixed ladder, rose from my knees and slowly stood up on the top six-inch-wide girder and began inching my way along it.

For several minutes I was alone, up there among the stars that twinkled in the black velvet of the Maltese sky. The crowd fell silent and my world existed in the few inches of rusty iron beneath my feet and the lights of the dockyard far, far, below. Somehow I reached the winch housing and clung to it in triumph as I looked down at the crowd, wildly cheering below on the clifftop. I took my cap off and waved in a gesture of bravado; the crowd cheered again and I dropped my hat, which went spiralling down and down until it turned into a little white dot and vanished. Suddenly, as I watched that cap falling, I changed from a carefree, devil-may-care Son of Spiderman into a very sober Son of Jane Eyre as I looked back along the girder and knew, without a doubt, that I could never walk back.

Apart from my buddies shouting encouragement, the crowd below was now silent, sensing that the budding Evel Knievel was about to come to grief. The girder seemed longer and narrower as I took my first tentative step and found I was reluctant to let go of the winch housing.

Calling on all my self-preservation instincts, I slowly, very carefully, crouched down and straddled the girder with my feet gripping the lower, inch-wide flange and my hands gripping the top. In this undignified manner I began my limpet-like progress back to safety.

Wailing sirens and flashing lights heralded the arrival of the Valletta fire brigade when I was halfway across, and two fire tenders hove into view. Grimly continuing my painful sloth-like progress, I was horrified that all these lights, men running around and ladders being raised were due to me, and I tried to wave them away but nearly fell off in the process. I endeavoured to ignore the shouting and long ladders which were raised against the girders over the lift entrance, but I couldn't ignore the ladder that suddenly shot between my legs and almost pushed me into space as I reached the safety of the iron ladder. Try as I might, I couldn't ignore the red-faced fireman on the ladder, who kept trying to grab me as it was rammed into my crutch by his enthusiastic mates below.

For several minutes I was alone, up there among the stars

We had a shouting match, with the fireman wanting to rescue me and thus appear in the *Maltese Times* and me for the same reasons not wishing to be rescued, with my voice becoming higher in the process. 'Can you shift your bloody ladder?' I shouted. 'It's giving me a rupture!'

I eventually struggled down the iron ladder with this zealous chappie hanging onto my collar, until I swung out of reach. Gaining the ground, I looked at the size of the crowd, the converging police and MPs, and saw my mates beckoning. I scuttled around two firemen, dodged two of the shore patrol and scarpered through the crowd to my mates, and we all ran in different directions to avoid being identified.

I did appear in the following edition of the *Maltese Times*, but only as 'Unidentified sailor in dangerous stunt' with a picture of a fireman and the caption: 'Fireman hero rescues sailor'.

A COUPLE OF WEEKS LATER I met some of my old shipmates from the *Kimberley* and a good night was had by all. I don't know whose idea it was to pinch, er, borrow a bus, but it was not a good idea. This is because one of the first things one has to do if one is contemplating stealing, er, borrowing a bus, is to ascertain if one's fellow conspirators are capable of driving it.

I vaguely remember a moonlit night – or rather, early morning – and several marooned sailors with an abandoned lifeboat in the shape of a bus with its keys carelessly left in the dashboard. We were miles from Valletta and we reasoned that all we were doing was parking it somewhere different. With six of us in the driving cab something had to happen. We eventually persuaded it to start before we discovered that none of us could drive a bus.

'It's just a matter of steering,' said Big Taff while Geordie began waving the long black gear lever about. This resulted in lots of grinding noises and little else.

It's just a matter of steering

'I think you're supposed to press one of those pedals,' said Brummie and between us, with the engine revving and the gears grinding and clashing, the bus suddenly shot forward and we left in a series of jerks past an amazed audience of rudely awakened villagers.

Like most Maltese village squares, it was fairly spacious, but not spacious enough for our driving as, with local inhabitants diving out of the way, the bus gave a number of spasmodic lurches, made it halfway round the square, then dived into a shop window. I think this was when the riot started.

I expect most people being wakened in the early hours by someone stealing their favourite bus, and then wrecking it, would be slightly peeved, but I'm sure this slight misunderstanding could have been settled without a riot. However, there it was, a riot – and we were in the middle of it, literally fighting for our lives with our backs to the bus and outnumbered three to one. With fists flying in all directions, I became impervious to pain until a well-aimed house brick hit me just above the right eye and knocked me unconscious. This enraged Big Taff and Brummie, so they laid into the Maltese until they backed off.

After I regained consciousness, we did a deal and paid for the damage, with the bus owner even driving us back to Valletta, bloodied and broke.

SOMEONE EVENTUALLY POSTED a longed-for notice on the draft board, quite near the bottom; it was as though C-in-C Med was reluctant to let me go. 'Able Seaman J. Eyre, destination: HMS *Drake*', it said. At last, I was bound for Britain.

Along with hundreds of other demob-happy ratings, I set sail for Marseilles and boarded a train. This soon made its way through a French countryside gaily bedecked with hundreds of inflated French letters tied to string; they floated and danced over and around the rocking carriages, much to the amusement of the young mademoiselles who gave us wine and flowers at various stations en route.

Arriving in Plymouth in September 1946, I was processed, given demob pay, a chalk-striped demob suit wrapped in brown paper and tied up with string, a railway warrant and, finally, I was released into the great outdoors. Once through the naval gates I took my cap off, gave a loud 'Yahoo' and kicked it high into the air – and was immediately dragged back inside by two burly sentries for 'Insulting the King's uniform.'

I eventually reached Lancaster to find my home full of lodgers. I married one and flogged my uniform, complete with medal ribbons and gold good conduct badge to another, a young naval volunteer who was a crewman on a motor launch in a nearby dock. I invested my demob money on a chestnut filly in the 3.30 at Kempton and made a pile, then went to see my old shipmate Vince in Bradford.

Vince, being an authority on the dog track, helped me to lose everything.

Chapter 7

Post-war: A Brave New World

BEING NEWLY DEMOBBED and newly married was a shock to my system and, after the uncertainty and excitement of service life, I found it difficult to settle down. However, it was a brave new world and there was much to be done; consequently, when my luck on the horses ran out, I applied for retraining under the Interrupted Apprenticeship Scheme. I omitted to mention that mine had been interrupted by emptying a bath full of oil over the boss.

'No call for mechanics,' the man said. 'Everyone's a mechanic these days. We have bricklayers, plumbers, plasterers, joiners, and painters and decorators.'

Well, I thought, the nearest to a mechanic is a plumber. 'Okay, I'll be a plumber,' I said.

'No vacancies on that course – everyone wants to be a plumber,' said the man.

'A bricklayer,' I said in desperation.

'No,' he said after checking the list. 'How about painting and decorating? You look the artistic type.'

There, in a nutshell, was how my destiny was mapped out – by a little man in glasses and a bad case of spots. All in all, I expect he was right. In those days dabbling in paint seemed to be the thing – the fashion statement of the day. We had just been fighting a war caused by a failed art student, and when I reported to Rose, my new wife (who was also a fashion statement) about my new vocation, she curled her lip in disdain.

'A painter and decorator! Hitler was one of them – I hope you're not going to end up like him!'

There's nothing like a bit of encouragement.

My life was saved by a dog-eared postcard which came though the letterbox. It stated, simply: 'BSA meet. Flood Entrance Pot, September 15th'. It was 1947; I had almost forgotten about potholing and this grubby little postcard from the British Speleological Association was the beginning of a love-hate relationship with cave exploration that has lasted all my life. I still can't understand why I should have subjected my body to so much punishment over the years – forcing it through narrow crevices, laying it in freezing water, cutting it on razor-sharp rock, pummelling it with boulders, obliterating it in mud as I blundered about in total darkness. Not to mention the added risks of being struck by falling rocks, falling into bottomless chasms, drowning in bottomless lakes or dying of exposure, pneumonia, blood poisoning, tetanus or histoplasmosis. There must be easier sports!

Nevertheless, one Sunday saw me in the Yorkshire Dales standing outside the narrow cleft in the ground that was Flood Entrance, together with a group of like-minded 'potholers', as we were called in those far-off halcyon days. We were all ex-servicemen, except for a gorgeous young lady who was attired in a floral dress, a direct contrast to the rest of us in our tin helmets, battledress fatigues and odds and sods from the army surplus stores. There was also one dedicated follower of fashion in a chalk-striped demob suit and a trilby hat with a bike lamp fastened on the front using an elastic bandage.

We picked up a motley selection of ropes and rope ladders of pre-war vintage and began passing them down the hole. The cave entrance led via a squeeze through a boulder ruckle into a narrow, vertical, 45 foot deep rift which was aptly named the Letterbox. It was too tight to use rope ladders, so everyone just slid down, including the young lady who was clutching a candle in one hand and the hem of her dress in the other. She slid gracefully out of sight, blonde hair waving goodbye in the draught that blew up from below.

I often wonder what happened to her, for I never saw her again.

Dragging the heavy ropes and ladders through water and mud along a low zigzag crawl soon doubled the weight of everything, as the rope, wood and clothing soaked up water like a sponge. I laddered the next drop, a 48 foot pitch, climbed onto the ladder and smoothly descended to a tuneful clicking sound as, one by one, each wooden rung slid down the rope sides as the old string whipping under each rung disintegrated. I ended up at the bottom of the pitch with a pile of wooden rungs under my feet, two naked ropes stretching above and a very surprised look on my face. Another ladder used as a replacement also had loose rungs, and the size of the party diminished to five while the rest beat a rapid retreat.

We followed the stream down steeply descending passages that twisted and turned before ending at a serrated rock wall which dropped into a wide chamber. The boisterous stream flowed across this and fell into the blackness of an evil-looking elliptical hole, fifteen by twelve feet, and plunged to the bottom of South East Pot in Gaping Gill, some 200 feet lower.

Considering the state of our ladders, we were not too keen on descending this pitch, but such was our enthusiasm that we eventually gained a broad ledge, 140 feet lower down, soaked and battered by the falling water and frightened out of our wits by slipping rungs. We managed to reach the impressive Main Chamber in Gaping Gill, where we stood awhile looking up in awe at the huge entrance shaft, with diffused daylight picking out the grey, swirling curtain of Fell Beck as it dropped a sheer 365 feet, lashing us with its spray.

The return journey was grim. Arriving back at South East Pot, we shouted up the pitch to our staunch lifeline man, who had been left in cold isolation. The strongest member of our group tied on the lifeline, clung to the ladder and swung out over the void before laboriously beginning his ascent. After what seemed an awfully long time, with the roar of falling water interrupted with shouts and whistle blasts, we saw the line come snaking down. I elected to go up next and was soon struggling against the weight of water, three gaps in the ladder where rungs had slipped, and fatigue. With arms aching and gasping for breath, I reached the top of the pitch.

We were there for some time as we brought everyone up and then struggled to pull the sodden ropes and ladders to the top, which now seemed to weigh a ton. Then slowly, almost exhausted, we made our way out. Fortunately, someone had reladdered the 48 foot pitch with a ladder that, with only six slipped rungs, was at least climbable, and once up I continued on my weary way through the low section ahead, dragging my burden of ropes and ladders behind me.

Reaching the foot of the Letterbox, I began chimneying up the smooth walls. I had just reached a tight section when I heard a sound that was a cross between a grunt and a sigh; it seemed to emanate from somewhere above. I shone my light, which wasn't too good by this stage, but I couldn't see anything in its dull yellow glow so I climbed higher until something bumped against my helmet. I twisted my head and looked up.

I was amazed to see a pair of studded boots, wrapped around by several yards of loose, muddy material which I surmised were trousers. Above a pair of soggy red socks, two white, spindly legs extended beyond two pink, scratched, knobbly knees through some grey, dishcloth-like material, to end high above at a blotchy, extremely spotty bum. Beyond this point, vision was obstructed by a cloud of steam. I shouted, the legs gave a feeble twitch and a faint sound like a slowly deflating bagpipe came from above.

'What?' I shouted.

'I'm stuck,' replied a weary voice.

'Well get unstuck,' I yelled.

'I can't – you'll have to try and get past,' said the voice. Silly sod, how the bloody hell was I going to get past him when he was stuck in the only place that was man-sized.

'You'll have to move.'

'I can't.'

'Well, come down.'

'I can't.'

'Well, go up.'

'I can't.' Oh bollocks, I thought as I wriggled my way higher until I was in a position to push the bloke from underneath. As I pushed I muttered sweet words of encouragement: 'Move, you bastard, move!'

He did. The boots and socks flayed to and fro and, with some horrifying wheezing and grunting, the bod moved three feet and stuck again. I pushed once more – nothing happened, and in a fit of exasperation I grabbed his ankles and swung on them with all my weight, grunting: 'If you won't go up, you're coming down.' All this achieved was a wail as his body jammed more tightly.

I was forced to hold a conversation with his bum

I decided it was time to communicate, so I wriggled and pushed and swung on the victim's skinny legs until I was more or less face to face with this pasty, unhealthy-looking bum. I couldn't climb any higher, so I was forced to hold a conversation with his bum, which answered me back when I asked it questions. Perhaps the bloke was a ventriloquist.

It transpired that the unfortunate chappie had become jammed in the cleft four hours before. His light had failed shortly after and, most worrying for me, he was completely exhausted and convinced he was going to die. The rest of my group, who were waiting at the foot of the rift, were becoming impatient and began making all sorts of suggestions – all of which are unprintable – until I realised that something drastic had to be done. I even considered biting his bum, but couldn't quite face up to it, so instead I gave it a vicious nip. A howl came from the body and frenzied movement took it higher. I tried this successful formula again, but only received a kick in the chest from a flailing boot.

Then I heard a shout from the top of the rift and two cavers who had just come in from the surface shone their lights down. I eventually persuaded them to lower a rope and, after a great deal of struggling, I managed to grab the end. Somehow, working mostly by touch, I tied it round the victim's body then shouted up to heave on the rope. The men above heaved, the trouser-wrapped legs swung back and fore, and the body gave a blood-curdling scream.

'Where have you tied the rope?' he yelled. Wow, it was the best reaction yet! No wonder – I had tied it between the poor sod's legs. I retied it, the men above pulled, the body began to rise – and the rope broke! Twelve stone of flaccid humanity hurtled towards me, the feet striking with a stunning blow on my helmet, which knocked me back down the rift. The body ended up where it was originally stuck.

'Oh, sod it!' I retied the rope. A box of matches was thrust into my hand from below while I instructed the men above to pull, but nothing happened. I had a word with the body, which seemed to have lost interest in the proceedings. I instructed the men above to pull again, slow and steady. The body began to grunt and reluctantly moved. I lit a match and gently toasted the pale, spotty bum. It was a miracle. The dead returned to life. With a cry that will haunt me for the rest of my life, the body took off like a rocket!

I had discovered an aptitude for cave rescue.

MY NEW CAREER as a painter and decorator kept me busy and, as I became more proficient, I soon realised that a good living could be made from the upper end of the market, but first I had to learn the hard way. I served my allotted time with a well-established firm before moving around, offering my services to one-man bands – self-employed craftsmen who were always looking for good men during the busy summer months.

I contacted one old boy in Morecambe and offered to work for 6d an hour extra – he nearly had a fit.

'Sixpence an hour over the odds? You had better be good,' he exclaimed. I was; I nearly burned a house down on my first job!

To be fair it wasn't my fault – the silly old sod had insisted that I burned some paint off a bedroom window which was obviously rotten. To compound the risk, I was to do it in a howling gale.

Using extreme caution I tentatively stroked the flame across the window sash and immediately an open joint in the wood glowed red as, helped by the wind, the powdered wood took hold. I watched in horror as sparks blew into the room and began sinking into a feathered eiderdown, sending up little spirals of smoke. There was no time for finesse. I slid down the ladder, threw my brushes out of my brush can, galloped back up the ladder, pulled the smouldering lower window out with my hands, threw it into the yard and emptied the water out of my brush can on to the eiderdown – all in front of two very interested witnesses. My boss and Mrs Black, our customer, stood looking at me open-mouthed.

'I suppose this means I'm sacked,' I said.

No one replied.

Later in my career, when I became much more proficient, I managed to set a fireman's house on fire. Bert, who was a personal friend, was watching telly with his wife when I informed them through the open window that the house was on fire. They just laughed and carried on watching *Gardeners' World*.

'I'm not joking,' I shouted as I began hacking out smouldering wood from the back of a large window. I was soon joined by Bert with his fireman's axe and we started to demolish the window, looking in concern at the smoke billowing from the roof.

'Er, Mavis – you had better call the lads out,' shouted Bert to his wife.

Unfortunately for Bert, 'the lads' thought it was a joke when his wife gave them his address. However, between us we prevented the fire from reaching the roof timbers and had put it out by the time 'the lads' arrived in two large fire engines and a large tender, all laughing their socks off at Bert and me surrounded by smouldering wreckage. Then they did what firemen do, and caused more mayhem than we had.

'Do you want to advertise in our *Fireman's Gazette*?' I was asked.

THE FOLLOWING WEEKEND I had arranged to meet Big Alec, Bill Holden (known as Rocky) and their mates for a BSA meet down Rift Pot. While most of my family thought I was completely barmy for going down these holes in the ground, my brother Ron was vaguely interested so I persuaded him to join us. We found an old mac and some old trousers in the cellar, and one of dad's old trilbies lying on top of the coal; this would do for Ron's caving gear.

Sometime later, after struggling over limestone pavements above Crummack on mist-shrouded Ingleborough, we discerned a small group of cavers standing by an open shaft, and as we approached we heard the rumble of a swollen underground stream welling up from deep below. John L. was there with Gimlet and Rocky and Co. and we had a long discussion about the feasibility of descending in such conditions because there had been heavy rain the day before. We decided to give it a go as the first few pitches should be dry.

It soon became obvious, once away from the daylight entrance shaft, that the whole pothole was like a colander with water spraying in from the sodden moor above, and it was not a good day for potholing. Clad in our old sweaters, cut-down raincoats and ex-miners' helmets, we quickly became soaked to the skin before we even reached the wet pitches. I hadn't seen my brother for a while, but was told he was with Big Alec and in capable hands so I didn't worry too much.

In those days the lower sections of Rift Pot were extremely dangerous, with loose boulders and rocks creating a distinct health hazard. It was down this hole a few years

later, on 19 May 1957, that I had the honour to be leading a group of cavers that included George Band, one of the team which conquered Everest in 1953, when a huge slab of rock detached itself from the wall directly over my delicate body as I was climbing far below. Lucky for me it more or less slid into the arms of George's friend Richard Reynolds, who hugged it tight until he presumed I had taken cover, not knowing that nowhere in the bottom reaches of Rift Pot was safe. The subsequent avalanche of falling rocks caused an immediate lighting up of cigarettes once the turmoil ceased, and then the dreadful silence was broken by Richard's warning cry from high overhead: 'Below!'

George was later asked how he enjoyed his potholing trip. He replied that he had felt much safer on Everest.

One thing about caves and potholes – they never change their nature. Some caves are friendly, some caves are not, and even on those early trips Rift Pot was still a hole to treat with respect.

George Band entering Rift Pot in 1957 and underground (on the right), with Jim Eyre (standing), Tom Sykes and an unknown caver on the left
Photos: Ron Bliss

As has been mentioned earlier, the ladders and ropes used in those early days were, in many cases, older than the cavers using them. Although a fairly inexperienced caver then, I had a great desire to live to be old enough to become experienced and, looking at those ladders which we were threading down the last 145 foot pitch, I was sure they held the promise of a short lifespan to whoever had the temerity to use them. It wasn't going to be me.

John Bancroft turned out to be the man of the moment. A great believer in long underwear, he was nicknamed John L. after the legendary John L. Sullivan who gave his name to longjohns, having worn them for boxing in the late 1880s. 'Our' John L. – even after our warnings of impending doom – advanced onto the ladders which, in spite of our dire predictions, didn't break – at least not until he was 90 feet down. There was a mighty yell and a jerk on the lifeline as one side of the ladder broke. 'Pull me up, pull me up,' came the cry from far below. Three of us grabbed the lifeline and heaved our gallant comrade above the break, where he regained his composure and began climbing towards us. Suddenly there was an action replay as the other side of the ladder broke, and with an almighty yell John was catapulted into space, again fortunately prevented from falling by the lifeline. When the shouting subsided someone remarked, 'You know, I think this ladder's knackered.'

John clung to the remaining strand of ladder

Following these words of wisdom we decided to take no chances and, with four of us on the lifeline, we began to haul him up.

'Heave ho, heave ho . . . shit.' We went flying as the lifeline broke and panic-stricken yells drifted up from below as John clung to the remaining strand of ladder side that had already broken once. We quickly tied another rope to the remains of the lifeline and lowered it to John, then waited anxiously while listening intently over the noise of thundering water, which by now had increased.

'Pull . . .' We heard the weak shout and, too scared to pull in case we snapped the rope, we gently helped him up the pitch and over the edge.

'Fuckinell,' he said (which I'm sure the politically correct will forgive, considering the circumstances). We retreated from the depths and gradually managed to regain the surface, where I found myself looking around for 'our kid'.

Rocky, who at that time didn't know me well and didn't know my brother at all, was standing on the edge of the 125 foot surface pitch. Looking down, he announced to all, 'There's a bloke coming up with a trilby hat on.'

For once Rocky seemed to be at a loss for words. 'Bloody 'ell, he's going down again . . . Hang on, he's coming up again.'

A few more heaves on the rope and my long-lost brother appeared. At least, it looked like him. He seemed smaller when wet through, and something like a small Punjabi as the coal dust secreted in the trilby had washed down over his face, giving him a distinctly Eastern look – so much so that Rocky, on being informed that Ron was indeed my brother, wanted to know if my father was a Bengal Lancer. Ron, on the other hand, wanted to know why we kept pulling him up underneath an overhang, and showed me the lump on his head before he went off in a huff to eat his sandwiches – only to find that Big Alec had pinched them. Ron later told me, quite succinctly and at some length, that he was taking up golf.

There's a bloke coming up with a trilby hat on

I SLOWLY REALISED that marriage had its drawbacks, such as the fact that I was expected to supply dear wifey with housekeeping money and a house to go with it. I therefore found out that much of my time was taken up with earning money and, like all married men, it dawned on me that my life had changed.

I was doggedly following in my wife's footsteps on a shopping expedition in town when I bumped into my old mate, Wilf Taylor. Like me, Wilf had experienced an easy war, but unlike me it had left him with a chip on his shoulder. Struggling to support a wife and family, he was squatting in a disused Nissen hut on an abandoned RAF camp, and had become embittered about the land 'fit for returning heroes', which the new socialist government had promised and which, like socialist promises, had never materialised.

But Wilf, for all his problems, possessed a vintage Sunbeam motorcycle – a means of escape – and he soon had me astride his pillion as we travelled up to Settle in style. Well, not quite in style because it conked out twice and sustained a puncture, which meant stopping every few miles to pump up the rear tyre.

We had the tyre fixed in Settle and met with Johnny Pierce and some of the gang, who told us that the BSA had discovered a large new cave system on Casterton Fell which was so unique that no one was allowed to explore it except a chosen few. We went to see Eli Simpson, the BSA's recorder and general factotum who had an office near the hostel.

Cymmie (pronounced 'Simmie') had been a hard caver and discovered and explored numerous caves in his youth; he was a well-respected figure in the caving world. We entered Cymmie's dingy office to find him sitting in a leather armchair, surrounded by books, plans, journals and cave surveys of all descriptions. Silver-haired with a ruddy face and beaming smile, behind his glasses he was the popular image of every-one's favourite uncle, but there was much more to him than people realised. Very proficient in archaeology and geology, Eli masterminded every aspect of the BSA, dictating which caves should be explored and who should do the exploring. He collected all the resulting information and buried it in his extensive archives like a squirrel hoarding its winter supply of nuts.

Cymmie was also responsible for chucking all the discarded, scrapped rope ladders back in the hostel saying, 'There's nowt wrong with them, we've had them for years.' The only way we could get rid of dangerous equipment was to destroy it before Cymmie could get his hands on it.

However, in spite of all his faults, 'old Cymmie' was probably the most knowledge-able speleologist in England and commanded a lot of respect. Johnny, who was one of Eli's blue-eyed boys, asked about us joining the exploration of the new cave. Cymmie smiled at us and took a long time to light a cigar, obliterating us in blue smoke, before telling us a quite believable story about the new discovery – Lancaster Hole – being so unique that a detailed study was taking place. Builders, joiners and painter and decorators were not required, as the exploration team consisted of cavers who were qualified scientists.

'But lads, here is something you can do,' and he scribbled on a postcard and handed it to Johnny. 'It's very important and could result in exciting new cave discoveries. Draw up a survey and report back to me.'

Outside, we looked at the postcard, edges yellow with age, which contained grid references to three caves in the middle of a bog at Ribblehead. Four hours spent crawl-ing chest-deep in water in eighteen-inch-high passages that ended in a three-inch high crack convinced us that old Cymmie was cleverer than we were. 'No wonder he said these caves are unexplored,' said Rocky, speaking down his nose (he did that in those days, before he took elocution lessons). 'Bugger surveying it – we'll take a few compass bearings and guess it.'

We returned to Cymmie with an impressive looking survey, which brought a benevolent smile to his face and he gave us another postcard on which he had written 'BSA meet Lancaster Hole' dated two weeks ahead. 'Don't tell anyone, this is just for the chosen few.'

I cycled round to Wilf's to find him with his motorbike in pieces in the kitchen, and a very annoyed wife threatening to chuck him and his bloody bike out if he didn't remove it from where it was leaning on her gas stove. I beat a hasty retreat.

Somehow, on the appointed day, with bike back together again and a divorce immi-nent, Wilf and I turned off the A65 and, in a cloud of smoke and screaming gears, tried to ride up a gully-riddled one-in-three dirt road. I jumped off and pushed as Wilf, with throttle wide open and both feet pushing on the road, managed to move thirty feet before his fine machine juddered to a halt. We ended up pushing it.

At the top of the long, steep hill the dirt track stretched away on the flank of a hillside that overlooked Ease Gill, a stream far below. Skidding and floundering through the deep muddy pools in the rutted track, more often off than on, Wilf eventually rounded the last bend to Bull Pot Farm.

Cymmie's words: 'Don't tell anyone, this is just for the chosen few' made me wonder if Cymmie was a relative of Moses, for below us a throng of cavers, tents, bikes and cars encircled the normally isolated farm, everyone waiting to be led into the promised land.

Looking for Rocky's tent among the motley throng, I noticed one that was more decrepit than the rest, with a farmer's chicken clucking away contentedly at scraps of food that the owner of the tent had kindly left outside – he was obviously a bird lover. A hand suddenly shot out of the tent and grabbed the chicken, which only had time for one panic-stricken squawk before it was pulled inside. A couple of feathers lazily floating in the air were the only sign that it had ever existed.

Wilf and I stealthily approached and peered in at Rocky and Big Alec plucking their supper. We pitched our tent and Wilf, who was permanently starving, attached himself to Big Alec in the hope of a chicken leg, only to be told to sod off as he wasn't getting any. He then attached himself to me in the hope of having some of my bacon butties.

During the night a wind blew up and it began to rain. A commotion nearby awoke Wilf who stuck his head outside our tent, and withdrew inside with a smile on his face.

'Rocky and Alec's tent's blown down,' he said with some satisfaction. 'Serves 'em right, the tight sods.'

Contentedly, Wilf clambered back into his threadbare sleeping bag.

Chapter 8

The Discovery of Lancaster Hole

THE DISCOVERY OF LANCASTER HOLE on 29 September 1946 was a momentous event that led to the exploration of the most extensive and unique cave system in the British Isles. Like many important occasions, this had humble origins. It began with the young, rosy-cheeked, tenant farmer's wife of Bull Pot Farm.

She had three lovely children and was in permanent dread of one of her brood straying too near the ominous tree-ringed depression where the farm stream fell into the black, 40 foot deep shaft of the evilly named Bull Pot of the Witches, a pothole so near the farm that she could hear the dull rumbling of its waterfall as it plunged headlong into a subterranean world. Unbeknown to her, this contained large caverns which extended directly under the farm, one within a few feet of the kitchen floor. In fact, one good bounce and she could have been through.

One day a small hole opened on the fell below the farm and, terrified, she asked her husband to contact that nice Mister Simpson of the BSA, who had been caving in the area and had asked them to report anything unusual.

Duly notified, Eli despatched five of his cavers: George Cornes, Les Kitchen, Wes Oakes, Bill Taylor and Wilf Taylor (who was not related to Bill) to go to Bull Pot Farm and reassure the farmer's wife. They did this by rescuing number three son, who was in the act of climbing over the wire fence that surrounded the brink of the 25 foot deep Hidden Pot, then they dug at the new collapse. This revealed a shaft dropping into a cave, Hellot Hole.

Leaving three men pulling out loose rock, George and Bill went walking over the fell, looking for openings in the numerous shakeholes dotted about the heather-covered moor. At first, the pair separated but later came back together beside a huddle of large limestone boulders in a shallow valley below the rift-shaped entrance to Cow Pot. While enjoying the view of the purple-clad moor sweeping down to Ease Gill and beyond, past the silver ribbon of the river meandering down the Lune valley, George mused on the good fortune that had brought him to work in Lancaster, his introduction to the Northern Dales and his late conversion – at thirty-eight years old – to what was essentially a young man's sport.

The warm September sun reflecting from the white limestone boulders highlighted the strange behaviour of a clump of grasses which shimmered and danced with a mysterious energy, although all around was still. Kneeling to investigate, George felt a cold breath of air on his face and, helped by Bill, soon removed the loose plug of soil and grass. A howling gale blew dry dust into the air, releasing the genie of the cave and opening the mythical Pandora's box of secrets. The two men were joined by the others and, tearing at the loose rocks and rubble which were sent crashing into the depths, the group soon enlarged the hole to reveal a deep shaft. Wes tied on a rope and was lowered through the narrow opening to a ledge twelve feet down, from where he reported that the shaft widened and continued below for over one hundred feet. It was every caver's dream.

LANCASTER HOLE turned out to be the most significant cave yet found in the British Isles. Now, just a year after its discovery, standing above the entrance feeling the cold, dank air blowing from below I experienced a feeling of exhilaration as I waited to descend.

Squeezing through the narrow section at the top of the shaft, I found myself swinging freely down the centre, passing walls of black polished limestone, dappled and corroded over millions of years into flutings and razor-sharp flanges, dripping with sparkling droplets that flashed like diamonds as they reflected my passing lamplight, momentarily coming to life after aeons of darkness.

My poetic musing was promptly dispelled as a small, tap-like trickle of water, borne from high overhead, found its way down my neck. The rope ladders twisted their way round the back of a large rock, perched precariously on a jagged ledge and looking as though it was ready to crash down the shaft at any second. It was not a happy thought when I swung underneath it.

The shaft widened into dark recesses as I climbed lower, and the water from above increased as more inlets joined in the race to descend my neck until I was experiencing what cavers call 'heavy rain', but what normal people would call a waterfall.

Thrashing about on the ladder, trying to escape the deluge which was soaking me, I eventually reached the boulder-strewn foot of the pitch, hastily untied my lifeline, blew two blasts on my whistle and scrambled up a short climb into a large passage. Wilf, who had been there for the original discovery, waited for me with a big grin on

his face. Together with Rocky and Big Alec we headed down the large, keyhole-shaped passage until it ended abruptly above a broken rock slope which dropped into a large cavern a hundred feet long and thirty feet wide. Dominating the rugged expanse of broken calcite-covered rock, a magnificent rock bridge extended across the cavern at its widest point, while up above, the roof soared out of sight.

Amid shouts and whistles we clambered down the loose rock slope, which ended in a frozen avalanche against the lower wall of the cavern. A gap in the rock debris beckoned a way on; I inserted my delicate body and removed it quickly when large rocks started to move.

Everyone was poking about looking for new discoveries. I saw a climb up onto the bridge and ascended a sort of spiral staircase that brought me out above the

Theo Wild in Colonnade Chamber during the early BSA explorations. Photo: Jim Leach

flashing lights of the cavers below. A passage attracted me and I was soon reduced to scrabbling over a small rockfall, which gave way to a crescent-shaped chamber.

I stood transfixed. The muddy floor had changed to pure white flowstone, rippling across the floor of the chamber like dappled ice. Beyond, looming out of the darkness like ghosts in the dim lamplight, were majestic columns and slender, white stalagmite pillars, reaching up from a porcelain base to join a roof that was delicately criss-crossed with calcite veins fifteen feet overhead. Everywhere there was glistening calcite and I realised that I had entered the fabulous Colonnade Chamber, described by its discoverers as being 'like a scene from the Arabian Nights'. I carefully crept past the sparkling white floor and went further into the grotto as I breathed in the magical atmosphere, imagining what Wes Oaks and Bill Taylor had felt when they first found the chamber – a sight no one had ever seen before.

That is the essence of caving: illuminating millions of years of darkness to reveal the beginning of time.

I eventually joined the others and we found our way through a maze of large boulders into caverns that became bigger and bigger, until the roof and walls were almost out of sight. A dull roaring came from ahead and, suddenly, the passage was split in two by a huge cavern that fell away on each side into depths we could only guess at.

Carefully traversing across enormous rectangular blocks of limestone that had fallen from the roof of the cave many years earlier, we crossed over the canyon below into a larger continuation of the passage. Following the caver in front, silently walking on an undulating floor of dry mud, was a new experience for everyone, for all the world like walking in a desert at night. It was unbelievable that we were underground, for there were no visual boundaries: no roof and no walls, just a trail in the freshly disturbed glacial deposits of millions of years. Rounding a massive rock, we were brought to a halt at the edge of a void, dominated by a ghostly waterfall falling from a faraway roof that was barely discernible using our combined lights. We watched it whirl and sway, down and down, to crash on huge rocks far below. No one spoke.

My first foray into the unique caverns of Lancaster Hole was mesmerising, but unfortunately my urge to explore was rapidly curtailed when I was collared by Jack Aspin – known as Doc – to be his surveyor's assistant. I soon found myself on the end of a surveying line in huge, tunnel-like passages that intersected others, out of which occasionally appeared Wilf, Rocky and friends, who were having the time of their lives as they found new and amazing sights.

After some time, I decided surveying was not for me and when dear old Jack had me on a very long length of tape I saw my chance. I placed the tape on a large rock, held down by a stone, stuck a lit candle on it in place of my light, and scarpered to the sound of Doc's voice saying, 'Jim? Jim? – Oh, I seem to have lost my assistant.' I soon found Wilf and, much later, found Doc again when we popped out of a cleft in the floor. He had a new assistant and was saying, 'You're much more reliable than the other chap – he just disappeared.'

That first incursion into Lancaster Hole left a very deep impression on me and, although I didn't know it at the time, I was going to be bound inextricably with exploring this lengthy and complicated system. It eventually divulged its secrets, but revealing over 70 kilometres of passages on seven different levels took many years.

Unfortunately, the discovery brought another set of problems. Cymmie, the BSA recorder, who had already restricted exploration to a chosen few, began to act very strangely.

*Poetic Justice, the route that led to the Oxford Pot and Lancaster Hole connection
Photo: Ron Bliss*

Cymmie asked George Cornes to fasten iron ladders in the 110 foot entrance shaft to facilitate exploration eastwards towards Ease Gill and its numerous sinks. The BSA had already taken out a lease controlling access to Lancaster Hole and, when exploration parties discovered a substantial stream entering the cave, Cymmie restricted access still further. What was in Cymmie's mind we shall never know – had he an idea of turning it into a show-cave? Whatever the answer, a point was reached when the lid over the entrance was kept locked and no one was allowed access. Cymmie's excuse was that scientific studies were taking place.

This is when I became a pirate. I used to come up with Wilf and a few other Lancaster cavers and sneak across the fell, wait patiently while Wilf (who helped George design the lock) managed to open the lid with a device he had made, then we all sneaked down the cave, pulled the lid shut and caved all night.

This worked well and every week we extended the cave, until after one particularly hard trip I reached the top of the iron ladders, unlocked the mechanism and found I couldn't lift the lid.

Panic! We were entombed.

Two of us managed to jam ourselves in the tight bit at the top and, both pushing, managed to raise the lid a couple of inches before it slammed shut.

'Funny – there must be a sheep sitting on it,' I remarked. Perhaps it's Phoebe come back to haunt me, I thought as we tried again, but to no avail.

There was a piece of old girder at the bottom of the shaft so I shouted down for someone to bring it up, and we began laboriously levering the lid up, inch by inch while jamming stones to hold it while we levered again. Everyone was completely knackered and I looked down as I had a rest, just in time to see Peter Kitchen rolling off the top ledge, sound asleep. 'Grab him!' I yelled, and Ken Pollit seized the collar of Kitchen's jacket as he went rolling into space.

'Wass up, wass up?' asked a bemused Kitchen, still semi-conscious as Ken wrestled him back. He answered: 'You nearly were.'

'Bloody 'ell.'

Peter looked at us with shock when we told him. 'Bloody 'ell,' he said again, looking remarkably awake.

More levering and then Ken managed to poke his hand out of the entrance.

'*Fuckinell*! There's some bastard shaking me by the hand, I'll fuckin' kill 'em!'

I dropped the piece of girder and watched, horrified, as it hit the iron ladder, sending up a shower of sparks and a tremendous racket as it ricocheted off the shaft walls, taking with it a ton of loose rock before clattering into the ladder again. I saw the lights of my comrades scatter, split seconds before the girder and rocks hit the bottom of the shaft. Then followed a long, deadly silence before a shout from below.

'Missed us . . .'

December 1950 at Eureka Junction in Lancaster Hole, soon after the connection had been made from Oxford Pot. Left to right: Peter Kitchen, Ray Ashbridge, Bill Leyland, Tom Sykes and Ron Bliss
Photo: Ron Bliss

When two of Cymmie's stalwarts rolled back the large boulder they had placed on the lid, it was touch and go that they weren't thrown down the hole. 'It was a joke, Jim – we put it on last night and meant to come and remove it earlier, but we slept in.'

After this incident things became worse. George, who had discovered the cave, received a threatening solicitor's letter and was told to hand in his key. New lids were fitted and blown off with gelignite. In one instance we hid in the heather and watched Bob Leakey fix a new lid in place; as soon as he had gone we removed the wet cement. Threats from Cymmie were ignored and the situation deteriorated until it came to a head one weekend in August 1950, when we found the entrance to Lancaster Hole blocked by concrete.

Eli Simpson had effectively destroyed the thing he thought most of – his own club. The BSA was decimated. By denying access to its own members and blocking the cave, the association's council had effectively invalidated the access agreement. It was later suggested that the lease was not deemed to be a lease at all, as it did not purport to lease any land. It was also suggested that the threats of taking proceedings against trespassers were bluster, for as lessees the BSA was probably only a licensee. As such, the group did not hold a legal interest in the land and, consequently, it had no remedy by civil action against third parties.

This mini-caving-war was spiteful, meaningless and sad. During the time that the entrance to Lancaster Hole was left wide open and the iron ladders allowed access to all and sundry, the unique cave formations sustained a lot of damage. The Northern Pennine Club and Red Rose Cave & Pothole Club were formed to continue the exploration of the cave and any others which entered the system. On 29 October 1950 Ron Bliss and members of the Red Rose found the connecting link in Oxford Pot that tied all the networks together. Lancaster Hole became part of the now world-famous Ease Gill Caverns.

In direct opposition to the actions of the BSA, in line with its newly written constitution that stated that there should be unrestricted circulation of information pertaining to caves, the Northern Pennine Club published the results of all exploration that had taken place up to 1952 in *The Caverns of Upper Ease Gill*. More publications followed as the cave was extended and, in March 1967, the Cave Research Group produced a full survey and topographical description and history of exploration. Today, after more than fifty years of exploration, a complex network of caves spreading for 72 kilometres across three fells and three counties, both above and below the water table, comprises the known extent of the system. That exploration has involved countless cavers. Much has been written of their exploits and in 1989 I documented some of these in *The Ease Gill Cave System*, published by the British Cave Research Association. Much more remains to be written.

WITHOUT THE BSA'S DISCOVERY of Oxford Pot the exploration of Ease Gill Caverns would have taken much longer. It was never an easy entrance as it involves squeezing through some very loose collapsed chunks of limestone to reach a 55 foot pitch, followed by a flat-out, very wet crawl with a permanent gale blowing through it, and then a sod of a passage called the Snake. Narrow, twisting, contorted and undulating from top to bottom, the Snake calls for crawling in a stream, wriggling horizontally with no visible means of support or creeping forward, standing erect, until you find that you are stuck on a sharp bend with the only way onwards down below at foot level. Only, you can't bend down or even see your feet, so reversing and cursing is required to find a wide enough place to lie down in the stream and begin again, crawling forward and then finding that you have crawled past the only place wide enough to stand up.

This was Doc Aspin's nightmare as he was well-built and suffered from cramp very easily, but other than the long underground journey from Lancaster Hole, an entry via Oxford Pot was the only way into the Promised Land. We had to undergo this ordeal on every trip, ensuring that we were cold, wet and knackered before we even started on the real purpose of the expedition. However, there is no gain without pain and we struggled through the agony of the Snake on most weekends.

The Red Rose club possessed one 50 foot rope ladder and 100 feet of rope. The ladder was specially made for Oxford Pot, which was probably our *raison d'être* at that time.

However, all good *raisons d'être* come to an end, as mine almost did when climbing the 55 foot entrance pitch in Oxford Pot after a strenuous day's caving. The entrance to Oxford had been causing concern for some time, partially buried as it was under a pile of rock debris at the foot of a landslip. Two huge slabs of rock overhung the pitch, supporting each other where their tips touched and forming a huge flattened 'V' which seemed to hold everything else up. It also seemed to be the only point from which to hang our ladder.

A good caver is always a pessimist: by assuming that everything that can go wrong will go wrong, that caver will not only remain a good caver, but a live one. Nearing the top of the pitch I looked up at the ladder belay, which I did on every trip for two reasons: one, I didn't trust it, and two, we never used a lifeline. While climbing, my springy steps on the ladder seemed springier than usual and the reason soon became clear as I saw the two slabs slowly opening and the rope belay working its way downwards with every step I took. It was

Jim with his parents and wife Rose in the doorway to 12A St Oswald Street

within two inches of slipping free and I was within two inches of falling 55 feet, accompanied by an unfastened ladder and tons of rock.

I froze . . .

I looked at the opening between the two slabs with the fixed gaze of a snake hypnotising a rat. I reached for the shaft wall and found a hold, then let go of the ladder and spent a very frightening, desperate ten minutes, free-climbing the last few feet before struggling frantically to haul myself into the short entrance crawl.

A couple of the lads were sitting on the surface having a smoke. I told them what was happening, but they said I was seeing things. I reversed back to the head of the pitch, untied the belay and carefully passed the ladder out as I pulled it up the pitch. In fact, it was fortunate that I was the last out that day, because by three days later the entrance to Oxford Pot had collapsed.

We were now reduced to trawling the fells, looking for a pothole that would fit our 50 foot ladder. It was a bit like the Prince looking for Cinderella, for all we could find were the ugly sisters, as we always seemed to end up at the bottom of our ladder with space beneath our feet. It was time for a new beginning.

'**STRAIGHT-GRAINED ASH**,' I said to the man.

'We don't get much call for that. We've got elm, oak and sycamore, and we've got curly-grained ash, but no straight-grained. What do you want it for?'

'Ladders,' I replied.

'They don't make ladders out of straight-grained ash.'

'We do, they're rope ladders,' I said.

'Oh, for a ship,' the man said. 'What you need is oak.'

'It's for potholing.'

'What?'

'Potholing. Going down holes in the ground,' I said.

'Well, you want iron ones for that, for sewers and drains,' said the man, going into a fit of coughing as he lit a cigarette.

'Potholes are not sewers. They are deep natural cavities,' I said.

'Hang on, I'll get Harry. His son's a bricklayer and he'll know about natural cavities. Harry, 'ave you got a minute?'

Harry appeared and I eventually managed to convey the specifications for three hundred pieces of straight-grained ash, complete with drilled holes.

'Do you want them chamfering'?

'No.'

'Do you want them varnishing?'

'No.'

As club treasurer I paid for these and ordered 700 feet of Manila rope. The club was now broke, as was the club treasurer. Although I kept meticulous accounts, I had neglected to bank the money so I had to make up the shortfall – much to Rose's disgust as I had promised her a new three-piece suite and instead all she received was – in her own words – 'A lot of bundles of bloody firewood and yards and yards of hairy rope which was too thick for a washing line!'

It was hard being a pioneer.

A frenzy of activity hit St Oswald Street, normally a quiet respectable place, and its inhabitants were astonished when a bunch of strange-looking men began laying out long lengths of rope on the pavement and riveting pieces of firewood to them. I spliced all the ends and suddenly we were in business: the Red Rose owned 300 feet of new ladders.

Accompanied by a small intrepid band (most of the club members were quite content poking about in small caves, clear in the knowledge that they would not end their days in some bottomless pit), I set off on a voyage of discovery, but where Sinbad found that big monsters can be dangerous, I rapidly found that big 'oles can be even more so.

After a blood-curdling expedition into Lost John's Cave, when we discovered that the old-timer who had named the Wet Pitch had no imagination (it wasn't just wet, or bloody wet: it was a deluge), we also discovered that having lots of ladders and ropes needs lots of men to carry them. My small intrepid band emerged late at night, absolutely knackered, laden with equipment and one war-wounded who had fallen down a hole in the floor and sustained an injured ankle.

Friday night in the Moorlands Hotel was full of tales of our exploits in the depths of Lost John's, and I realised that my team had earned some recreation so a challenge was issued. A fixed bench seat with wooden armrests sat against one wall and I offered free beer to the first one to squeeze through the armrest.

Great fun was had by all as various bods became stuck, but we managed to pull them free. The crunch came when a little thin bloke called Yozzer managed to get through, but fortunately for me he only drank shandy. However, this excited his mate, who always beat Yozzer at everything, and he launched himself at the armrest with vigour. He twisted and turned and wriggled and even deflated his chest until he was on the verge of success, when his bum stopped him.

After lots of heaving and grunting Frank could go neither forwards nor backwards, in spite of our advice and assistance. After an hour, when his face was turning a funny colour, I became concerned and told him to relax while I got some more beer in and went to the bar. The landlord's face also turned a funny colour when I ordered: 'Three pints of bitter, one pint of mild, a shandy and a saw.'

'What does ta want a saw for?' he asked.

'Er, we've got a bloke stuck in the arm of a settee,' I replied a bit sheepishly. Like the Pied Piper of Hamelin I led a group of interested locals round to the back room, where they gazed with interest at Frank who, apart from being stuck, was now quite embarrassed – especially when the landlord shouted for his wife.

'Eh, Gladys – come and look at this, you won't believe it. I always said these bloody potholers is daft.'

A saw was produced and a joiner to go with it, as the landlord reckoned: 'Yon daft lot would probably saw their mate's 'ead off!' But Frank was freed.

After the collapse of Oxford Pot a new entrance was required. While some of us were engaged in an orgy of caving with our new ladders, others were ferreting about in the bed of Ease Gill, looking for an easy entrance. Having already made some dye-traces, one known sink tested with rhodamine (a red dye) produced results inside the cave where a inlet emitted a flow 'like a slaughterhouse effluent' which entered the main passage of Oxford Pot. Members of the Northern Pennine Club soon opened up a low bedding crawl – Slaughterhouse Drain – which was later shortened to Rosy Sink.

Bert Bradshaw and his mate Norman Dunnington were suitably impressed with their handiwork, which gave us an easy dry-weather entrance, but a flood trap when it rained. The roof of the passage reminded me of scenes from an Edgar Allan Poe film, where the roof slowly slides down onto the unfortunate victims below – only in our case it was large square blocks which slid down like enormous guillotines. One monster denied us access at first, but Bert blew the end off it and this enabled us to crawl underneath. In my case this meant lying on my back, looking up at this 'hanging death'. When I complained to Bert he replied, 'You worry too much – it's as safe as a row of houses.'

Bert probably said the same thing when, a few weeks later, he appeared on the fell with a real live ambassador. I don't know where Bert found him
– obviously not in Nottingham

Eh, Gladys – come and look at this. I always said these bloody potholers is daft

where Bert lived, but who knows where one finds ambassadors. I've been wined and dined by a Dutch ambassador's wife and been taught to ski by a Norwegian ambassador's wife, but I've never met one in Lancaster. But, there again, there could have been one in Nottingham.

Anyway, Bert persuaded this gentleman to squeeze his portly, well-fed body under this Sword of Damocles and took the poor, unsuspecting chappie on a

Ted Hodgson (left), George Cornes, Johnny Pierce, Ron Bliss and Harry Bewes digging at Oxford Pot. Photo: Ron Bliss

caving trip. Bert and Norman brought him back after a good experience, as cavers do with novices, completely knackered with his plumed hat in ruins.

On the way out, as Norman was squeezing under the errant block, it became more errant and slipped, trapping Norman by the legs. Fortunately, he was fairly skinny and, after a mighty effort, he struggled free but Bert and the genial ambassador were now firmly imprisoned. 'I say,' said the ambassador, no longer quite so genial, 'what do we do now?'

'Buggered if I know,' said Bert. 'Are you religious?'

'As a matter of fact, I am,' answered the stout chappie.

'Well, pray it doesn't rain,' answered Bert, gloomily eyeing the trickle of water entering the restricted passage. Luckily for our entombed heroes, digging out the floor with tools brought from outside gained a few inches before we encountered solid rock, and Bert emerged first. 'Just in case,' he said. 'I didn't want to get stuck on the wrong side of him.'

Then after a mighty struggle we retrieved Bert's ambassador, who crawled past us like a bedraggled roly-poly pudding – not speaking, not even to say goodbye.

Not very diplomatic for an ambassador.

Chapter 9

A New Hudson and New Caves

TRANSPORT TO GO CAVING was a problem in the early days. Lifts on the back of Wilf's Sunbeam could not always be relied on because, just like sunbeams, it sometimes faded away. But, once we became well established at Bull Pot Farm with the use of a room kindly loaned by Walter Pearson and his wife Kathleen, we had a system: Walter would collect us from the bus terminus at Kirkby Lonsdale, often with a trailer containing sheep, and take us to the farm.

Walter always made sure that young ladies in the group received preference and joined him in the Land Rover, while other unfortunates and I ended up in the trailer being squashed by sheep or, in one case, with a demented, enormous sow. If you have never had the pleasure of sharing a trailer with a pig, being bounced along a one-in-three, rough dirt track and down three miles of a switchback, semi-submerged mud lane, you haven't lived.

One fateful day the doorbell rang. My mother answered it: 'It's one of them potoilers,' she shouted. It was Wilf. 'Do you want to buy a motorbike?'

The story unfolded, like so many in my life, with the fateful words: 'I know a bloke.' Every time I hear that phrase it's always about an offer you can't refuse – a bargain, a give-away, or his wife doesn't like it, or it needs a good home – and I fall for it every time.

'It's a 1931 New Hudson.'

'New?'

'It's a five hundred.'

'What, pounds?'

'No, *ccs*.'

'How much?'

'He's giving it away.'

'How much?'

'Twenty-five quid – a bargain.'

It turned out that this bloke worked at the nearby mental hospital. Wilf wasn't quite sure on this point – perhaps he was a patient. 'I'll get him to bring it round,' said Wilf and vanished.

The following evening I had a visitor. A small, dapper chap in a black beret and a very long oversize coat, he looked a bit like a small Spanish onion seller who had just found an Oxfam bargain.

'Are you Jim?' he asked.

'Yes,' I said, wondering how a small onion seller knew my name.

'I've brought it for you to have a look at.' Behind him stood a vision in maroon and aluminium paint – it was more like Flash Gordon's rocket ship than a motorbike; it was the biggest, ugliest, most powerful looking machine I had ever seen in my life. I immediately put on that knowledgeable look, the one that all would-be purchasers of second-hand cars and motorbikes wear. I slowly walked around the monster and fiddled with this and that while the proud owner informed me, 'That's the choke, and that's the advance and retard, clutch brakes, throttle . . . don't give it too much or it will throw you, goes like a rocket.'

I believed him as I looked at the huge twin fishtail exhausts that swept the full length of the machine.

'Well, yes, it looks alright. New Hudson. Hmm, not seen many of those about.'

'No, they are quite rare, especially this model. They stopped making them in 1933.'

'Why?' I asked.

'Demand couldn't keep up with supply.'

'Oh,' I said, not really listening. 'What's this file handle for?'

'Oh, that's the hand change gear lever.'

'It's not, it's a file handle.'

'Well, the knob came off and I fixed it with a file handle.'

At this moment Rose appeared. 'What's that?' she exclaimed in horror.

'This is that New Hudson I was telling you about.'

'It's a bit big for you, isn't it? What's this on the back?' Rose asked, pointing to a black-painted rectangular piece of wood mounted on four bed springs which were bolted to the mudguard.

'It's the pillion,' l said. 'Try it for size.'

'I've never seen one like that,' said Rose.

'Well, no, I modified it,' said the onion seller. Wives have a tendency to put second-hand motorcycle salesmen off.

'Jump on, I'll take you for a spin,' he said. With that he fiddled with the controls, jumped up in the air and landed with both feet on the kick-start. The huge engine burst into life, the whole machine shook and throbbed like a prehistoric predator about to leap on its prey, blue flames and smoke came out of the exhausts, and we were off.

It was awesome. I can understand some women having orgasms while riding a motorbike – I nearly had one hanging onto the onion seller as we took to the open road, with that great throbbing machine beneath us, the wind whistling through my hair and the countryside speeding past in a blur.

After half an hour of breathless excitement he deposited me back at 12A and I decided to buy it. I borrowed ten quid from Rose, who 'didn't think it a good idea', rushed outside and gave the onion seller the money and he promised to deliver the New Hudson the following evening.

I nearly had an orgasm hanging onto the onion seller

The next day I arrived home late to find my mother going mad. 'Get that thing off my front – it's leaking oil all over my flags.' Making a mess on the paving stones was a serious crime, because all the ladies on our street got down on their hands and knees and scrubbed the pavements outside their respective houses, then bleached them until they were white, and woe betide anyone who walked over them before they were dry.

I went to the front of the house and, with some misgivings, viewed the New Hudson leaning against the stonework underneath the bay window. Newspapers spread underneath the machine held a pool of oil and a note was stuck on the brake lever. 'Rear stand fell off, see Frank Shepherd, tell him I sent you. Harry,' the note said.

I pulled the bike away from the wall and was astounded at how heavy it was. I sat astride it and decided to freewheel five houses down to our back street, then push it into the yard as it would be difficult to start without a stand, living as we did on a steep hill.

I silently whistled down the hill, braked and slowly turned, then slowly toppled over with the heavy bike on top of me. I asked my father to help me shove it up the back street and into the yard. He never said much, my old man, but when he did it generally made sense.

'I think you've bought a pig in a poke there,' he said. He was right.

My maiden voyage was arranged for the following Saturday, which turned out to be a heatwave. My wife and her friend were despatched on the bus to Heysham for a day on the beach, where Wilf and I would be waiting having arrived before them on my flying machine. Duly kitted out in several sweaters, ex-Army greatcoats, berets, goggles and wellies, we set off down the hill astride my smooth-running New Hudson. It was smooth-running because we couldn't start the engine.

As we approached the main road at the bottom of the hill Wilf began doing something with the file handle, er, gear lever. This resulted in three loud explosions, which caused an old lady to fall over while sheets of flames and black smoke came out of the twin exhausts. The bike made an awful clunking noise and hopped across the busy main road like a demented kangaroo, before coming to a halt in front of an approaching double-decker bus.

It was not a good start and after the bus driver unleashed a string of swear words, some of which were new even to me, we carried on 'freewheeling' into town. We were accompanied by frenzied action on the gear lever and resounding whirring and clunking noises from inside the gearbox, with an occasional flash of flame and explosion, as we made our gravity-driven ride to the river and the quay, the lowest point in the area. After Wilf had fiddled about with everything that would turn or twist, or push in or pull out, he stood astride the bike and gave the kick-start a mighty belt. With a loud bang the engine misfired, the kick-start kicked him back and Wilf went flying over the handlebars.

'The fuckin' bastard,' he said nursing a sore ankle. ''Ere, you 'ave a go, it's your fuckin' bike.'

Wilf Taylor was not a man who usually used strong language and I was shocked. Stood astride I gave the kick-start a tentative kick and it lashed back with venom.

'Bloody 'ell,' I said.

'Advance the timing,' said Wilf, so I followed his instructions, twiddled a lever on the handlebars and gave the kick-start a mighty kick. The engine gave a sort of asthmatic cough and strong-smelling fumes came out of the carburettor.

'You've got it,' said Wilf. 'Right, give it some welly.' I did as he suggested and, much to my amazement, with a mighty roar the engine burst into life.

'Try and put it in gear,' said Wilf. I pushed the file handle down, which resulted in an awful screeching of tortured metal.

'The clutch, the clutch,' shouted Wilf. 'Pull the fuckin' clutch in!' I pulled it and wiggled the file handle about again; the bike shot forward amid lots of clunking noises with Wilf hobbling after me shouting, 'The clutch, the clutch.' I pulled the clutch lever again, the noise of mangled machinery stopped and I managed to find neutral.

Fortunately for us we were quite near one of Lancaster's well-known motorbike mechanics, who Wilf knew personally. In fact, every motorcyclist in Lancaster knew Phil personally, because that's how motorcycles were in those days: totally unreliable and sooner or later they required a visit to Phil Barton. Though not quite the special agent of the popular radio series, he was certainly the special agent for sick motor-cyclists and their ailing machines.

Wrapped in our arctic clothing and dripping with sweat, we pushed the heavy machine to Phil's and leaned it against the wall. Phil, a slightly balding, plump character looked up from a customer's bike and said: ''Ello, 'ello, what have we here? Blow me – it's a New Hudson! I haven't seen one of those since before the war.'

Being an enthusiast, Phil left what he was doing and came over to look at my machine. 'They were marvellous bikes – whose is it?'

'Mine,' I answered proudly.

'Where did you get it from?'

'Off an onion seller,' I replied. Phil gave me a funny look and turned to Wilf.

'Who's he?'

'My mate,' said Wilf.

'Should be in a museum,' said Phil.

'Who? My mate?' asked Wilf.

'No – his bike,' answered Phil as he went back to what he was doing.

'Er, can you have a look at it?' I asked.

'Seen it,' said Phil.

'We think there's something wrong with the gearbox,' I said. Phil ambled across again, went down on his haunches and took a long hard look at the gearbox.

'You know that's an original Moss gearbox – there's not many of those about now.' He looked at me and said, 'That's one of the best gearboxes ever made. There's six gears in there, all put together with precision engineering. Like a Swiss watch. Hardly ever go wrong.'

'This has,' I said.

'Ah,' said Phil, giving a lugubrious shake of the head. 'That's the trouble with precision engineering, it can be temperamental. Like women,' and he gave a gravely laugh.

'Can you fix it?' I asked.

'No,' said Phil. 'That's the trouble with precision engineering – you can't fix it.'

That was the beginning of my motorcycling career and almost the end of my married career, as I had forgotten about my wife sitting on the sands at Heysham waiting patiently for us and the picnic parcel tied to the back of the bike.

After three long, hard miles of uphill struggle, pushing a bike that must have weighed four hundredweight, wearing sweaters, long coats and wellies, we eventually got the New Hudson to Wilf's Nissen hut where he had a spare three-speed Burman gearbox and an irate wife who greeted him with the loving words, 'Where the bloody 'ell have you been? You think more of 'im and your bloody mates than you do of your family.' And so on and so on. All in all it was not a good day.

Two weeks of cowboy engineering took place in Bailrigg Woods, as Wilf and I took out the Moss gearbox and tried to replace it with the Burman box, which was much bigger and not intended to fit on a New Hudson. However, after a great deal of struggling, welding and drilling, we had it fixed to the frame, but found that it wouldn't connect to the driving sprocket. We therefore bent the bike frame with a couple of large crowbars to accommodate it.

We made it work, but something was wrong. It was time to call in the expert: George Cornes. George was one of those rare breeds of men who could fix anything, no matter how technically difficult, while telling a funny story, reading instructions written in a foreign language, philosophising on the merits of communism and whistling bits of Faust. If he didn't have the part for a repair, he would make it. In short, George was a genius with a bit of the mechanic from *Last of the Summer Wine* thrown in.

A week later I was the proud possessor of a motorbike with a transplant and a unique feature: when driven in a straight line in snow, it left two sets of tyre marks.

THE FOLLOWING WEEKEND it was hey, ho for the open road. With caving gear strapped on the back of my trusty steed and fond farewells from a wife who was convinced that she would never see me again, I started up the machine after narrowly averting a broken ankle from a kick-start that kicked back like a mule every time you touched it. I went juddering down the road in a series of jerks as I struggled to master the clutch and gear lever. When I stamped on the back brake to avoid a suicidal dog I discovered that it was lethal and experienced my first skid, which sent me down the road sideways. 'They should be banned,' shouted an old dear as I narrowly missed her shopping basket.

Once out of town, heading for Red Well to pick up an unsuspecting young caver, I began to gain confidence and found that, once going in the right direction in the right gear, the New Hudson could move. Then it began to rain and I determined several things at once. One, I couldn't see because my German tank commander's goggles had steamed up. Two, I began receiving electric shocks from the handlebars. Three, I couldn't slow down or stop.

My clubmates were sat waiting for me on a wall outside the Red Well Inn when they heard the sound of an approaching helicopter. 'He's low,' said Bill. Then, as it appeared over the brow of the hill they saw a motorcycle approaching at a hell of a speed. 'It's not a helicopter, it's Jim!' and they watched in astonishment as the apparition hurtled towards them with a beret rammed down onto a bent nose, orange goggles askew and an ex-Army greatcoat flying in the wind, shouting 'I can't stop' as it disappeared over the horizon.

'That's funny,' said Bill.

The faster I went, the worse the electric shocks. I had to stop somehow, but no matter how I twiddled on the twist-grip throttle, nothing happened. I was on a runaway motorbike! I had to either stall the engine or turn the bike round. Approaching a crossroads I pulled in the clutch and applied the brakes. The noise of the screaming engine was deafening as I slewed the bike around, smoke issued from the brakes and the engine felt red hot and sounded as though it was going to explode or seize up as I let the clutch back in and began charging back towards my clubmates, who were still standing on the roadside completely nonplussed.

'I can hear him coming back,' said Bill, seconds before the throbbing machine appeared over the brow of the hill and again, without stopping or attempting to wave, the apparition disappeared, except that this time a silencer fell off which increased the noise factor by several decibels. One of the group rushed to pick up the fishtail silencer from the road and quickly dropped it as though it was red hot – it was!

I was now an accident waiting to happen, as a blowlamp-type flame was licking my left leg where it was whooshing out of an open port. I had to cock my leg to avoid it being barbecued, while at the same time I was slowly being electrocuted. I knew I had to slow down and stop before I hit Lancaster. Approaching the main road with a slipping clutch, smoking brakes and a screaming engine, I managed at last, after several unsuccessful attempts, to reach the petrol tap and turn it off, but the bike continued hurtling towards the highway. In desperation I pulled a handkerchief out of my trouser pocket and jammed it into the carburettor. Emitting a loud explosion, the engine finally stopped and I leaned the smouldering wreck against a nearby lamp-post, sat down on the kerb and lit a cigarette.

After several near-death experiences, not including minor injuries due to the bike falling on me, a red hot silencer branding my leg, losing half a trouser leg and a finger end in the whirring chains (the cover had been removed in another accident), I came to the conclusion that the onion seller was of a higher intellect than I was. But I was still living and, thanks to the attentions of George Cornes, so was the Bomb, as it had been christened by my fellow cavers.

'Ah, it's Ers,' George would say in his lovely Oxford accent when I rolled up to his corrugated iron-roofed wooden garage. Always wearing a boiler suit and a broad grin on his ruddy face, and always buried in something mechanical, George was always the same.

Within minutes he would be sorting out my mechanical problems and discussing our next caving trip while outperforming Spike Milligan with incredible, surrealistic inventive anecdotes, such as his views on cave rescue, in which we were both involved. 'Now, if all cavers were made to wear large earrings, they would be easier to rescue.'

IT WAS A LOVELY LATE OCTOBER MORNING, with an early frost and patchy mist giving way to sunlight. I thought, 'It's great to be alive' as I bowled along on the Bomb, which was running well since George had stroked it with his magic fingers. Today we were going to scale one of the stream inlets in the Far Series of Ease Gill Caverns. Exploring new cave was always exciting, realising that you were looking at sights nobody else had ever seen and treading where no one else had trod.

My mind was on such things as I came onto a stretch of old Roman road that I knew was dead straight, so wondering what the Bomb would do flat-out, I gave it the gun. The speedo zoomed from fifty to sixty and hung about just under seventy as I headed for a little patch of mist that still clung to the road. I knew there was a corner coming up, but I wasn't there yet – oh yes I was, for the mist suddenly lifted and there was a Z-bend. I jammed on the brakes, the bike slid sideways and threw a vicious wobble as I struggled to keep it upright, then shot from under me as I went sliding, rolling and tumbling along the road with the heavy machine skidding along behind me, threatening to catch me up.

I came to with my head inches from a milestone and the clutch lever of the Bomb inches from my jugular vein. I surveyed the damage. There was blood running from a cut above my right eye, my nose was bleeding and it felt as though it had been modified again. I had lost both trouser legs at the knees, but luckily my legs, although badly scoured, were still attached to the rest of me.

The Bomb had been completely remodified. The handlebars looked like something out of *Easy Rider*, the footrests, kick-start and other odds and sods had all been sheared off on one side, the pillion had disappeared and, all in all, the Bomb looked like a scrap job.

As in all the good Westerns, along came the US Cavalry in the shape of George Cornes. In his green plastic mac and on his green BSA combination, he looked more like an overgrown leprechaun than a cavalry officer, but much more useful. George approached a nearby farm and returned with some sticking plaster to hold my nose on and a borrowed crowbar to lever the handlebars into a more practical shape. We pushed the wreckage to the farm and told the farmer's wife that we would return later and fix it. The nice lady wanted me to go inside and sit down while she made me a cup of tea.

'Oh no,' said George, 'I can't let him go in there – he'd be chasing you up into the bedroom. Ee be a proper Don Juan ee be.' The look of incomprehension on the lady's face was a picture. 'Besides,' said George, 'I need him to explore a new cave.'

'What, like that, with all those cuts and bruises? Look at his legs!' said the dear lady in horror.

'I know, they're 'orrible, aren't they,' said my incorrigible mate. 'But we'll wrap 'em up when we gets there,' and we waved farewell to the good lady, who by this time must have thought that we were both a couple of head cases.

Several pain-wracked hours later I found myself, aching from top to bottom and with a throbbing headache, staring up at a fifteen-foot waterfall that sprayed down from the airy blackness of a high aven in the Far Series of Ease Gill. The previous week I had tried to free-climb it, but the weight of water was too much and I fell off. I now watched George, Bert Bradshaw and Bill Leyland screwing together several sections of heavy, galvanised iron pipe, which we had laboriously dragged through half a mile of tortuous passages. It was assembled into a T-shaped arrangement with a light-weight ladder fastened on the short cross-section.

George stood braced in the spray at the foot of the waterfall, while I climbed on his back. Bert handed me the heavy array of iron piping; I hoisted everything aloft and tried to achieve our objective: to jam the T-piece above the waterfall and climb up the ladder. It was too short, top heavy and I was thrown off balance and fell, almost laying out Bill in the process.

Plan B was called into action. I climbed onto George's shoulders and then climbed higher on the rock face in the direct flow of the water. Bert now climbed onto George's shoulders, Bill handed Bert the T-piece, and Bert handed it up to me then held me in place while I balanced on two minuscule footholds and manoeuvred the pipes into position. I had just started to climb up the ladder when the pipes failed to grip. I gave a mighty yell and swung the pipes over my head, away from the men below, mere seconds before we all fell in a heap in the pool at the foot of the waterfall. Luckily, no one was hurt and we tried again, this time with success thanks to my guardian angel because, just as I reached the top of the climb, one end of the T-section came away from the rock. I grabbed the lip of the waterfall and held the ladder in place while I struggled up and secured it for the others.

From here, we managed to climb higher to reach a succession of small ledges and the foot of a steep water chute. I tried to bridge the heavy torrent, but found it difficult to grip the smooth, water-polished walls and eventually slipped, to be grabbed by the men below.

Bert had been poking about on the left-hand wall and saw a possible climb higher up. I handed him the rope and we pushed him onto a small ledge from where he made his way to the top of the water chute, then threw the rope down. Aided by the rope it was an easy climb, and we were soon clambering into a roomy passage which led to several hundred yards of steeply ascending stream passage. In turn this took us to a magnificent chamber covered in beautiful and unusual black-and-white formations. We christened it Magpie Chamber.

Turning back, we told Bert to loop the rope around a bollard-shaped rock so that he could easily descend on the double rope once we had reached the bottom, and then we could pull the rope down after him. Simple. Only, for some reason Bert couldn't make it work so he chucked the rope down, reasoning that he could descend the water chute with enough friction to slow him and avoid falling.

Now, being a mining engineer Bert should know all about these things. The rope came down and then we heard a mighty yell: 'Support me, Jim!' I saw a pair of hob-nailed boots approaching at high velocity. Bill and I braced for impact and hurled ourselves at the out-of-control body as it came into reach after fifty foot of free-fall, which threw us all backwards into a deep pool, hysterical with laughter.

The hysterical laughter wore off after sitting on the back of George's bike, heading back to the farm. Then, having worked in the dark, I was placed on my New Hudson. Clutching my petrol tank with my lacerated knees, holding onto twisted handlebars and pulling a piece of string to accelerate, trying desperately to keep George Cornes' rear light in view in thick fog while all the time hoping that no one would run into my lightless wreck from the rear, concentrated the mind wonderfully.

'Look at his legs!' said the dear lady in horror

Chapter 10

Bang and Bedsteads

CAVING MUST BE THE ONLY SPORT ever created for fearless halfwits, bold explorers, raving lunatics, frustrated inventors, harmless eccentrics, scientists, masochists and cross-dressers who are able to see in the dark. In those days it was the only sport around where you didn't need to buy expensive gear; in fact, it was ideal for tramps who, after all, are used to wearing cast-off clothing and boots with soles hanging off, and trousers split up the seam, held up with braces and lengths of string.

If there had ever been a Sportsman of the Year Award in the 1950s (which fortunately, there wasn't) it would never have been won by a caver, partly because as a spectator sport it vies with jam-making and partly because of our appearance. My wife said it appealed to me because I always was a scruffy sod.

Despite that hurtful remark, underneath our tramp-like appearance and strange clothes (which in some instances included ladies' silk underwear and in one extreme case some of Nora Batty's cast-off nylons), and underneath all those string vests, John L. longjohns, old sweaters and thick trousers, were some hard men. They had to be, to survive the cold, wet conditions of British caves, which on a good day were unpleasant – but on a bad day, when they were lashed by cold, wet winds and thundering water, they were lethal. The ideal build for a caver would be that of a fat Arnold Schwarzenegger – but then, of course, he wouldn't be able to get into the caves, so that is why most cavers look like the seven stone weaklings in the old adverts, who used to have sand kicked in their faces by Charles Atlas.

Our newest recruit was such a lad. Quiet and unassuming, every Friday evening Bill Leyland used to arrive on his 50cc James two-stroke at the Moorlands Hotel in Lancaster. Friday nights were Red Rose club nights and, ensconced in the little back room, we would talk about crumpet, motorbikes and caving, while I, as club treasurer, would collect a shilling subs from everyone, write it down in my little red book and then spend it on beer. Somehow we always seemed to consume a lot of this, including Bill who, at closing time, would be steered outside, gently placed upon his bike and pointed in the general direction of Red Well. We used to watch him wobbling his unsteady way down Quarry Road, never expecting to see him again, but we always did as the following week he would turn up like clockwork.

Bill developed an inordinate interest in the Bomb, as he did in all things that exploded or burst into flames, which the Bomb frequently did. He once experimented in making home-made explosives, succeeded in blowing up his old man's garden shed (unfortunately when he was still inside it) and, of course, when we began to acquire gelignite, Bill took an unholy interest in that. Gelignite had become the caver's friend. It was fairly difficult to get hold of, unless you had a cousin in the IRA or knew someone who worked in the quarries, but once acquired it revolutionised caving.

Our gelignite store was a cupboard next to the fireplace up at Bull Pot Farm, where Bill kept his gramophone and jazz records. The pink, soft, putty-like stuff smelled strangely like marzipan and every time I looked in that cupboard it caused me to shudder as some of it was becoming old and weeping nitroglycerine. It also seemed to have wandered onto Bill's records, so when he played Benny Goodman's 'One O'Clock Jump' I thought that we would experience a real one as I watched pieces of pink gelignite going round and round and slithering under that sharp needle. The jelly needed using, and an opportunity arose a couple of weeks later when we were forcing the restricted depths of Pippikin Pot on Leck Fell.

Wilf Taylor and I were convinced that this small pothole, midway between the well-known Lost John's Cave and Ease Gill Caverns, would join the two caves together. As a

At Pippikin Pot in 1952: Peter Kitchen (left), 'Dicky' Bird, Harry Bewes, Bill Leyland, Jim Eyre, Wilf Taylor and Roland Johnson enjoying gin and cigars pinched from Bill's parents. Photo: Ron Bliss

consequence, we spent considerable effort hammering and chiselling in a small twisting passage that led onwards. A small group of us, with Bill carrying the gel, set off for Pippikin. Bill was noticeably given a wide berth when we found that he was also carrying the detonators – 'Wrapped up safely with the gelignite,' as Bill put it.

After preparing everything for blasting, we made the unhappy discovery that the detonator wires were only ten feet long and would only reach around a corner into a small chamber containing a roof of hanging death (loose boulders). This was a disaster, as we had intended to detonate the explosive from outside the pothole, until Bill volunteered to do the deed down below accompanied by another head case . . . er, fearless caver.

We waited with baited breath in a nearby shakehole until a muffled explosion and thick, noxious fumes came rolling out of the narrow confines of Pippikin Pot, but there was no sign of our two volunteers. We waited a while and then, braving the fumes, entered the cave to find Bill and his mate crouched in a little alcove surrounded by huge rocks which had fallen out of the roof, both in a state of shock. Bill was still clutching his battery and detonator wires, staring blankly into space.

'Are you alright?' I asked.

'What?'

'Are you alright?'

'What?'

They were both as deaf as a post. We pushed past them and found that a large flake of rock had been removed, enabling us to squeeze through for another fifty feet before the passage narrowed again. More work was required.

They were both in a state of shock. Bill was still clutching his battery
and detonator wires, staring blankly into space

In those pre-breathalyser days of only light traffic and lots of personal freedom, it was customary – nay, compulsory – to end the day's caving in a local pub. In the case of Leck Fell this was the Whoop Hall, where, in our rough clothes and mud-stained features, we became a sort of tourist attraction – especially after we had drunk several pints. That exposed a latent thespianism and we would end up on the stage singing mucky songs and telling risqué monologues. This particular evening was especially jolly, because a couple of coach parties were in and we were all enjoying ourselves, except Bill and his mate whose ears were still ringing from the explosion.

All good things come to an end and, as we went outside to mount our bikes, Bill found that he couldn't walk straight. Using sign language he told me that the explosion had affected his balance; I replied, still in sign language, that it was the beer. But, sat on his bike, Bill kept falling over, so we got him to grip his handlebars while two of us drove our bikes each side of him with one hand on our handlebars and the other on Bill's shoulders. In this manner we made our slow though erratic way to Red Well where we deposited him on his doorstep.

It should be mentioned at this point that this mode of travel is not now encouraged.

FOLLOWING OUR SUCCESS at scaling T-Piece Passage, we turned our attention to other major inlets in Ease Gill Caverns. Most of these presented a daunting challenge, especially in the vicinity of the original Oxford Pot breakthrough where three streams enter Pierce's Passage, a large stream passage that joins with the master cave. After managing to climb some leads, with varying degrees of success, I became more ambitious. Most weekends found me scrabbling desperately on wet, polished rock in my hobnailed boots as I thrust and chimneyed my way high above the stream passage next to thundering waterfalls, which lured me upwards like the sirens lured fishermen of old to their fate.

Following one episode, when I had my team of three spaced out on a loose and almost vertical boulder slope, I lost all credibility when several huge rocks moved at once just as we were forty feet above the floor. Fortunately, no one was hurt, but my caving companions began to show less enthusiasm for my projects. My attention was diverted to the two waterfalls thundering from the dark roof of Trident Passage and I began experimenting with small ledges and clinging to small nobbles of rock. I realised as I climbed higher that I was a solo act and a new approach was required.

At this time there was a new fashion in furnishing and people were throwing out their old cast-iron beds. The fact was not lost on Ray Barker, a recent and highly inventive member who hit upon the idea of making scaling ladders from them. With some ingenuity, Ray soon fashioned several six-foot-long metal ladders, held together with cut-down nails used as rivets; it was not good engineering practice, but it was good enough for us.

Soon, accompanied by Ray and a few more enthusiasts, we began our assault on the Trident inlets, using the mini-ladders to gain access to small ledges and then pulling up the ladders behind us. When the ledges petered out we bolted three sections of ladder together and, surprisingly easily, gained a high-level passage. After another short climb we emerged, much to our delight, above a waterfall that thundered into the passage forty feet below, where the lights of our clubmates flashed up at us in amazement.

Abandoning the ladders we went splashing up the stream passage, shouting and whistling in anticipation of great discoveries. However, our exuberance was short-lived as the passageway subdivided into smaller ones and ended up choked by round boulders that had been forced in from the surface.

Returning to the lip of the waterfall, I suddenly realised that when viewed from below there were *two* waterfalls. Where was the other one? By gingerly traversing over the plunging water and peering round a bulge in the chamber wall, I saw the heavier volume of water churning out from beneath an overhang some twenty feet lower, and seemingly inaccessible. Unfortunately, exploration fever is a terrible disease and I had caught it. There is no antidote and I knew my only hope of a cure lay in that passage below me, which I therefore determined to reach.

'You're bloody mad,' said Mike Bateson. 'If you think I'm going over that, you can think again!'

'But you're the lightest,' I said.

'Yes, and I'll be the deadest if I set foot on that contraption,' muttered Mike. He gazed in horror at my innovation: four flimsy ladders made from bed-ends were balanced precariously over a sloping bulge and hanging into nowhere with a flexible ladder tied on the end. 'It's like a fuckin' fishing rod,' said Mike. 'As soon as you put weight on that it's going to bend.'

I must admit that it didn't exactly inspire one with confidence and, after a great deal of discussion, it was decided that two of my stalwart supporters would act as ballast by sitting on one end while I advanced into space and descended the flexible ladder

The more I advanced, the more the ladders bent

on the other end. I began creeping across the flexing metal. 'Watch that it doesn't slide sideways,' I said, just as the contraption did. I rapidly jumped off.

'It needs modifying,' I said to my team. 'I hadn't allowed for the lateral thrust caused by the gravitational pull of placing a rigid object on a sloping surface.'

'Bloody 'ell,' said Mike, 'you mean it slipped.'

We eventually secured a rope belay to stop the ladders moving and me sliding into oblivion, then once again I tentatively made my way along the ladder. This was alright up to the point where it rested on the bulge which jutted out from the shaft wall, but beyond this fulcrum things became decidedly dodgy. The more I advanced, the more the ladders bent and I wondered if perhaps I was being a little foolish. Creeping like a cat I moved slowly, one rung at a time, accompanied by an awful screeching noise as the frail ladders bent more and more under the strain.

By the time I reached the end I was on a downward curve with my feet hooked over a rung to stop me from overbalancing. My mates were struck dumb as, feeling very vulnerable, I carefully swung, sloth-like, underneath the metal ladder and climbed onto the rope one. The metal was flexing and groaning in an alarming fashion and, as I moved down the rope ladder, it began to bounce until I was suspended like a puppet on a spring above the white water plunging out of the lower passage.

What was more horrifying was the fact that I was suspended in space, four feet from the passage.

With my nerves on edge I started swinging, hoping that my frail support would take the strain. I eventually managed to pendulum into the passage, where I thankfully belayed the ladder to a flake of rock. Wow! I had made it!

Fired with an excess of adrenalin I clambered up the steeply ascending passage, water spraying above my knees, and entered a complicated series of tunnels criss-crossing over one another that led to several large chambers. It was almost a miniature cave system in its own right and, after becoming momentarily lost, I eventually returned to my clubmates, spotting on the way back a safer route that could be laddered in the conventional manner.

The following weekend, with a stronger team and more hastily made bedstead ladders, I returned to finish the exploration. There had been considerable rain during the week, the surface stream was swollen and the caves below were rumbling with noise and draughting with air displaced by the subterranean inlets, waterfalls and streams. The crashing, falling water and spray carried on a strong, wet wind greeted us as we entered Trident Passage, pushing against knee-deep water until, rounding a bend, we came in sight of the chamber and the two waterfalls.

They were totally unrecognisable from the week before. A foaming mass of water formed a solid wall that thundered down with no sign of the two separate waterfalls of the previous week, and as we stood there another deluge fell from above, soaking us through. Behind us a curtain of water was suddenly drawn across the passage and water sprayed inwards, everywhere. The equipment was left and we made a rapid, disorderly, sodden, panic-stricken retreat, finding the surface stream flooding into the entrance as we emerged coughing and spluttering, fighting against the flash flood.

We had always considered Ease Gill a safe, all-weather cave and Mother Nature had just reminded us otherwise. In fact, there is no such thing as 'safe'.

'I'M NOT GOING UP THAT – you're bloody barmy if you think I'm going up that!'

So spoke Ray Barker two weeks later. Three of us were perched on a ledge twenty feet up in a sixty-foot-high aven, holding onto a long bedstead ladder that sloped at an alarming angle across a thirty-foot-wide gap.

We had returned to the Trident high-level extensions that I had discovered, where the object of the exercise was to gain access to a passage forty feet up on the opposite wall. I had already made one attempt, but when the top of the ladder moved sideways and the bottom of the ladder slipped off the ledge, I was lucky to escape unscathed as the cast-iron bedstead went screeching down the wall and fell, clattering loudly, into the stream.

We had modified our approach and belayed the foot of the ladder to prevent a reoccurrence. I magnanimously offered Ray a go at the climb, but he declined my generous offer of caving fame. As he remarked in his lugubrious fashion, 'It's no good being famous if you're dead.'

'But these ladders are your invention – don't you want to try them out?' I asked.

'No,' said Ray. 'You're the test pilot.'

My fate was sealed. I tested everything in the time-honoured fashion by giving it a kick, declared the contraption safe, and advanced boldly to where no one had gone before. The angle of the ladder was well outside the safety zone established for the building trade; forty-five degrees did seem a bit dodgy, and the higher I advanced the more the ladders bent and the farther down the wall the top of the ladder slid, with an ominous screeching of tortured metal.

Suddenly, there was a mighty noise like a gunshot. Then another, as two bolts snapped and the ladder collapsed with the top half flattening against the cave wall. The half I was on dropped against the wall and rapidly slid down it as the top section folded back on itself and fell backwards, threatening to make me the filling in a metal sandwich. All this happened in seconds and I have never climbed down a ladder so fast in my life. I jumped the last few feet and Ray grabbed me as I clutched hold of the ledge, just as the mass of twisted metal narrowly missed us and clattered on its way down into the stream again!

This was becoming monotonous. It was back to the drawing board – or rather, back to the back streets to collect more bed frames . . .

The following week we returned again with more ladders, more modifications and more interested observers, for my renown as an underground Blondin was spreading. After several hours' preparation, we looked with satisfaction at the longest ladder we had yet conceived. It towered up from the ledge at a good angle into the darkness overhead, with the top above the beckoning passage.

It looked foolproof. With a couple of wire ladders clipped to my sling, I climbed slowly up the bedstead ladder which, although it was flexing and bending, did not worry me too much – perhaps I was becoming immune. Then, just at the halfway point, the ladder gave a groan and bent even more. Looking up, I watched with interest as the top of the ladder slid down the wall until it was inches from falling into the passage that I was trying to reach. I stopped and the ladder stopped moving. I crept up very slowly and the top of the ladder stayed put.

I had almost reached the top when the bloody thing gave a metallic chuckle, slid off the wall and fell into the passage, landing on a large round boulder, then it pivoted and turned over as I scrambled clear and clawed my way into the passage. Within seconds my only visible means of support slowly toppled sideways and crashed down with a horrendous noise, narrowly missing the men below.

Silence . . .

'Are you alright, Jim?' The voice from below brought me round from my state of shock. Having answered, I thanked my lucky stars that I had brought two ladders up with me.

Having informed the group below, I set off on a lone exploration. The passage ahead was six feet high and three feet wide with a dry mud floor covering loose rocks. After forty feet I entered what appeared to be a wide chamber, but before I became too excited and started rushing about with explorer's fever I noticed that the floor of broken rock and loose slabs felt rather unstable. Everything seemed to move beneath my feet as I advanced and there were several black gaps between some of the larger blocks. Peering down, I made out the faint pinpricks of moving lights far below and slowly realised that I was looking at the cavers in the lower stream passage a hundred feet beneath me. I was standing on a false floor that was liable to collapse at any moment!

There is one thing about caving: it is never boring – especially when I discovered that there was nothing solid to which I could fasten my ladders. I looked like becoming a high-level Robinson Crusoe until I found a long, thin slab of rock which I jammed across the passage. I secured the ladders to it, taking great care not to touch the monster at the passage mouth. That rock looked as though it could fall at any second, so I climbed down the ladder very carefully in an attempt not to dislodge my improvised belay.

I rejoined the others and we unanimously decided to spend a couple of weekends climbing in the Lake District – it was safer, much safer.

THE GENIE THAT LIVED IN THE BOMB appeared again when, laden with ropes and ladders and an unsuspecting passenger on the pillion, the New Hudson was flogging up a long, steep hill and my passenger began complaining about his legs become hot. I ignored him for a while, until he began moaning.

'It's the silencers, they tend to get hot on steep hills,' I shouted over the noise of the labouring engine.

'We're on fire!'

'What?'

'We're on fire!'

I stopped. My passenger leapt off and began beating his trousers, which were on fire. Still straddling the machine I could smell something cooking and I realised it was burnt Jim – *my* legs were on fire, as was the bike. Flames were shooting out of the carburettor onto a leaking petrol tap, where more flames were greedily licking the underside of a full tank. I stopped the engine and stood there almost enveloped in flames.

'Grass. Grab some wet grass,' I shouted to Tom, my erstwhile passenger. I couldn't let go of the machine as it (still) didn't have a stand, and if I dropped it that would probably result in an explosion. Thankfully, the long grass by the roadside had been saturated by a recent rain shower and Tom hurriedly packed armfuls of the stuff around the flames and put them out. Leaving the smoking bike leaning against a wall to cool down, we sat and had a fag to calm our shattered nerves.

Once it had cooled, I restarted the engine. A flame shot out of the carburettor and it burst into flames again.

'Wet grass?' asked Tom.

'Wet grass,' I answered. That was when the Bomb and I decided to part company, so I sold it to Bill Leyland for fifteen pounds and bought myself a 350cc MAC Velocette. The only losers were the residents of Red Well, whose peace was shattered by a demented being, tearing round a field on a noisy, flame-spitting monster like a born-again Toad of Toad Hall who laughed gleefully every time he fell off.

Chapter 11

Jumpina Gulf

I **DON'T KNOW** what first attracted me to Juniper Gulf – perhaps it was the name, or its translation to Jumpina Gulf by one of my more colourful colleagues. However, one misty October morning saw a group of heavily laden potholers walking across the barren Allotment area of Ingleborough searching for the hole, which was proving hard to find on the featureless moor.

Eventually, the top of a stunted juniper tree loomed out of the mist and led us to a narrow, elongated rift out of which it grew, clinging to the weather-beaten lip of a 75 foot deep shaft. A boisterous stream could just be seen flowing across its floor, before being swallowed by an evil-looking cleft at the foot of the shaft wall. An old wooden stake, which looked as though it had been placed by the original explorers, was given a kick and declared safe. The fact that the Gritstone Club drove the stake into the moor in 1924 didn't give my clubmates much confidence so, as usual, I was elected test pilot.

The entrance pitch proved to be an easy climb and I descended the ladder, passing smooth walls decorated with ferns such as Hart's-tongue and other more exotic rock plants. The stream flowed along the flat, shingle-covered floor of the shaft and fell down a dicey-looking boulder slope that overhung a narrow, rift-like passage.

I heard shouts from above: 'What's it look like, Jim? Is it wet?' Juniper had a fearsome reputation – it was classified as a 'very arduous and dangerous pothole', and when it was wet some of the lower sections of the pothole became impassable. There had been rain throughout the week, though not enough to worry us.

Water was our primary concern during those days of the late 1950s, as we had no such thing as waterproof clothing and, no matter how many sweaters we piled on, we became saturated in no time at all. The average temperature in British caves varies from eight degrees to three degrees Celsius and, near the base of underground waterfalls or in a cave in spate, the wind-chill factor can quickly lower the cooling rate to minus nine degrees.

Other than polar and high-altitude exploration, there is nothing that can sap your body heat more quickly than the depths of a pothole in flood in winter. When you are soaked to the skin and wet, clammy clothing clings to your body, it feels like an embrace with a corpse. Water is everywhere: you stand in it, it hangs in the air, it rains on your head. Complete saturation in near-freezing temperatures can soon reduce an inactive caver to a miserable, weak human being, incapable of replenishing lost body heat. Co-ordination is lost and the downward slide to the onset of hypothermia leads rapidly to a serious situation.

Being of the skinny variety, I hit upon the idea of covering my body with Vaseline before entering a wet cave. Though messy, it certainly helped, but one of my contemporaries – a Preston plumber – thought of rubbing his body with Fiery Jack, a so-called remedy for rheumatism. My friend, also called Jack, rubbed the lotion all over his body and remarked in his broad Lancashire accent, 'By gum Jim, it's great. I can feel my body fair glowing with heat!' But, suddenly, Jack's smile turned to a look of anguish when he accidentally rubbed some on his balls. He became a real Fiery Jack as he plunged naked into the cold cave stream in an effort to obtain relief. We could almost see steam rising off him!

We soon assembled a mighty pile of ropes and rope ladders at the base of the daylight pitch and a small group of hard men pushed ahead to begin laddering the underground drops, while the bulk of the team followed with the rest of the equipment. Sprayed by water, I hastily clambered down the rockfall, trying to keep as dry as possible for as long as possible, when suddenly a large rock moved and went crashing into the rift below. I heard a shout and another rumble of falling rocks; the whole boulder slope seemed to move, some boulders crashing past me as I sought refuge in the passage below.

The pungent smell given off by the broken limestone hung upon the air, as lots of confused shouting from above informed me that a man had been injured. Leaving my ladders, I cautiously climbed back up, dislodging another rock in the process.

Harry Johnson's leg was badly gashed. We tore his shirt flap off and tried to stem the bleeding, then sent him out with his mate to have it cleaned up. This was not a good start: we were still in daylight, one man was injured and the team was two men short.

Cautiously, we climbed back down the teetering rock slope and began working our way out along a high, narrow rift passage as the stream boiled beneath our feet. It went deeper and deeper in the narrow confines below the only passable route, a slightly wider section where it was possible to traverse by straddling the underground canyon. Carefully placing our feet on small ledges, we proceeded slowly along with ropes slung around our necks, clutching a 25 foot rope ladder in each hand. There was a yell from behind: Wilky had dropped a ladder.

'You silly sod,' shouted Johnno as we all stopped to gaze at one of our brand new ladders, jammed fifteen feet below.

He became a real Fiery Jack. We could almost see steam rising off him!

'Tha dropped it, so tha can climb down and get it,' said Johnno, a broad-speaking Yorkshire member of the Northern Pennine Club who was helping on the joint meet with the Red Rose. We watched the unfortunate Wilky slide down into the tight cleft and slowly grind to a halt as he became stuck. 'I can't reach it', he shouted. 'Use your feet – hook it with your feet,' someone else yelled.

After a lot of confused grunting and muttering, during which Wilky turned almost upside down, the ladder was passed up to Johnno. He slid into the rift above Wilky and passed the ladder up to the bloke above. Suddenly, there was a panic-stricken yell from Wilky:

'I'm stuck, I'm stuck . . . Bloody 'ell – I'm slipping lower!'

This was great entertainment until we realised that the silly sod, struggling to reach the ladder, had slowly slid down the smooth walls of the narrow canyon and was now securely jammed.

'You stupid bastard,' I shouted somewhat unkindly, and instructed Johnno to undo a rope ladder and pass one end down to the distraught Wilky, who was making matters worse by his futile attempts to free himself. By calming him down and persuading him to get a firm grip on the ladder, three of us managed to pull Wilky from the embrace of the smooth walls, like freeing a reluctant cork out of a bottle.

Beyond this point the canyon-like aspects of Juniper Gulf became more apparent. The walls stretched farther apart and the rift grew higher and deeper, with the stream now only faintly discernible over a hundred feet lower. We were soon reduced to 'back and footing' (feet on one wall, backs on the other), which was a bit unsettling over the airy drop with each hand grasping a heavy ladder, making it impossible to grab anything if we slipped.

The canyon widened dramatically; it was almost devoid of holds and I was forced to climb higher looking for the way on. A voice from one of our more well-read members informed us all that this must be the Bad Step mentioned in the original exploration accounts written by the Gritstone Club members.

Things became a little tricky at this point, involving some high-level traversing on smooth walls to enable me to gain a recess above a 40 foot pitch. My clubmates had watched my progress over the void with interest, especially how my studded boots slipped and scraped on the smooth, undercut walls. Two of our newer members were completely unnerved by this performance and volunteered to stay and man the life-line. They watched with the rest of the group, perched like so many twittering budgies above the chasm, lights flashing off the wet dappled walls while I rigged the drop from a belaying point which, as seemed to be the practice in those days, involved a long discussion about whether it was safe or not.

The end of the ladder was swinging in space, a narrow canyon still dropping to a barely distinguishable stream rumbling below. The way ahead at this level consisted of a wide traverse. I swung off onto a sloping ledge and made a recce, soon finding that the traverse became wider until I was nearly at full stretch. With my shoulders on one wall and my feet on the other, I wondered how Mike Bateson would manage as he was considerably shorter than the rest of us.

While the lads were lowering the rest of the tackle, I carefully traversed down towards the stream to see if there was an easier route. There wasn't, for the rift narrowed and I struggled back up to be confronted with the look of total incredulity on Mike's face. 'If you th-th-think I'm going a-a-across that, you had better th-th-think again,' said Mike, who when excited tended to stutter. Faced with the prospect that lay ahead, who could blame him. It almost got me going . . .

Grabbing two ladders and garlanding a rope around my neck, I moved along the traverse until it suddenly finished in a seemingly impossible gap where the walls became undercut. I scrabbled desperately upwards to a sloping shelf of rock and found a dodgy move, a sort of half-straddle, half-jump accompanied by some praying, that took me across the gap into an easier traverse ahead.

I informed the others. With men straddled across the traverse, we passed all the tackle across and even brought Mike over – he seemed to increase in stature by several inches, with frenzied stretching in his efforts to bridge the gap.

'That's the b-b-Bad Step, not the other one,' said Mike, hurling himself into the comparative safety of the passage ahead.

The next section of traverse was easier. It led us along a high-level crawl, which soon had us sweating and swearing, to a window-like opening directly on to an 80 foot pitch. After a long delay in the tight confines of the crawl while we tied four ladders together and checked all the knots (reef knots and two half-hitches were the order of the day), we passed the ladders forward to find two granny knots had some-how got in there.

Mike seemed to
increase in stature
by several inches

'Oo the fff— tied this!'

'Which belay do you want Jim?'

'A short one.'

'We've only got a fifty and a hundred.'

'Use the fifty.'

Things went quiet for a while, until we discovered that Ray Barker had the lifeline in a knot. I thought I had time for a cigarette, so produced a battered packet from inside my helmet and took a few soothing pulls on my weed, causing a paroxysm of coughing and cursing from behind as the smoke blew into the restricted crawl.

At last, the eighty was rigged and we all descended, apart from another two stalwart volunteers who chose to remain as the lifeline party. More traversing led us back under our route until we encountered the stream issuing from a narrow passage in a circular chamber. Here, the nature of the cave changed as we followed the stream, ducking under large boulders jammed in the passage. It was much colder with damp air swirling along our route and we became aware of the dull rumbling noise of falling water.

The turbulent stream suddenly fell down a series of small cascades and disappeared into an ominous blackness – the big pitch. A dry oxbow took us away from the falling water into a low, broken bedding, which gave us a good view of the spectacular shaft dropping away and the stream shooting across, spraying off the black walls, directly onto where we were about to hang our ladders. It was going to be a rough ride!

Crouched under that dripping overhang of black rock my team began unrolling the stiff new ladders, whose rope sides kinked and twisted making it slow, cold work. In the background Ray and Arthur Woodall wrestled with a 280 foot length of one-and-five-eighths inch Manila rope.

'This is a bloody silly game,' said Mike, water dripping off his nose.

'Jim – I can't find a belay – all these rocks are loose,' shouted Tom Sykes.

'Keep looking – there's got to be something.'

'Fuckall,' came a voice.

'Oh, bollocks. There's got to be something. How do you think the Gritstone got down?'

I left what I was doing and shuffled towards the back of the bedding, looking for anything that would serve as a belaying point. There was nothing; everything moved. Way back against the far wall a piece of rock had cracked away, revealing a small fissure round the back. I gave it a shake – it moved, but I couldn't see my body weight dragging it towards the pitch.

'Shove the belay round that, and if it moves when I'm climbing – sit on it,' I said and continued laddering the pitch.

Was it my imagination, or had the cave become noisier? I looked across at the water falling down the pitch and it did seem heavier – well, perhaps not, it could be my imagination . . .

The clicking of wooden rungs against the rock as we lowered them into the depths and the 'wet forest' smell of the new rope overcame my trepidation and, once I had tied on my stout lifeline with a bowline and a half-hitch, I knew nothing could go wrong. 'Keep a tight rope, lads,' I said as I set off down the pitch with a bit of old towel wrapped tightly round my neck then stuffed into my Royal Navy pusser's sweater in a futile attempt to keep dry.

The kinks in the rope ladders straightened out as I put my weight on them. Within a few feet I was swinging free from the wall and was struck by a powerful deluge of extremely wet, cold water. With chin tucked in and head bowed, I went into automatic drive, hanging with arms crossed around the back of the ladder and looking down as my feet found rung after rung after rung. It went on for ever, while I was encompassed in the centre of a deluge that battered my body and dulled my senses.

Problems. I was suddenly hanging by my arms and my feet were thrashing in space. I looked down at the biggest, mightiest bunch of bastards that I had ever seen in my life.

The new ladders had taken on a life of their own and were contorted into a giant knot beneath my feet. I stopped and looked at the enormous tangle; unfortunately, my mates up above didn't realise this and continued paying out the heavy lifeline, which descended in a huge loop below me. I fumbled for my trusty whistle and blew a mighty blast, but it sounded like a bubble pipe. Nothing happened, so I blew again.

The lifeline stopped moving.

I blew two distinct blasts.

The lifeline gave a sort of a 'what the hell does that mean' judder, then went back up. As soon as the loop straightened out, I blew one blast and the line stopped. I managed to clear the knot so I blew three more blasts and started climbing down again, with the lifeline comfortably tugging at my waist. Ah, the Red Rose were well trained in those days!

The weight of water increased, drumming on my helmet, pouring down my neck, up my sleeves, down my chest, back and out of my trouser legs – this was central cooling with a vengeance! Christ, it was cold.

Everything below me was almost obliterated by the falling water and I kept going automatically, trying to ignore the white, bloodless hands that gripped the ladders. After a while, feeling like I had been flushed down a drain, the force of water hitting my skinny, ice-cold body diminished, having been dissipated into a mere monsoon rainfall by its long fall.

Looking down, I was greeted with the sight of another gigantic knot where the new ropes had twisted and kinked even worse than before. Kicking savagely at the wooden rungs and occasionally leaning down and untwisting the knotted mess, I swore to myself that I would never again put new rope ladders down a pitch like this without first stretching them.

Spinning wildly, with my lifeline twisting around the ladders above and me becoming weaker by the minute as the water increased, I realised that desperate measures were called for. I took my feet off the ladder and swung free, held by the lifeline as I pulled up the ladders and untangled them until the bottom rung reached a ledge, from where I hoped that I could climb to the bottom of the shaft.

My faithful lifeline team, up above in the land of the living, was by this time very confused. There had been no sign of life from their gallant leader for some time and, according to what was happening to the rope, this meant that I must have fallen off the ladder – so even though I was now back on it, they decided to pull me up!

'Stop, stop, you silly sods,' l shouted, but they couldn't hear me. I groped for my whistle again and blew a thunderous blast as I pulled on the rope. Message understood. The rope went suddenly slack and I almost fell off.

I scurried down the last few rungs and was suddenly held tight only one foot from the ledge. I blew three blasts and the rope came looping down around my neck. I hastily untied, scuttled off the ledge and climbed down, then ducked under another waterfall and reached an alcove where I crouched, a shivering wreck, as I watched the hairy Manila twist and twirl its way upwards.

Knowing that it was going to be a long wait, I made my way across the rock-strewn floor of a high, cathedral-like cavern which ended in a fissure after a hundred feet. Here, another stream entered and joined the main stream before flowing into a miserable-looking slot in a corner of the chamber. There was nothing happening above and, apart from an occasional flash of light way up in the vault of the roof, I could have been on the moon.

Having concentrated on trying to keep my body warm – that is, one step up from a corpse – I noticed the ladder twitching and slowly, ever so slowly, I made out the caplight of another silly sod coming down. The light seemed to go out as the caver above became enveloped in the deluge of water and the bottom of the ladders twitched more vigorously. I heard vague shouting and whistle blasts before I discerned the stocky figure of Ray in his unmistakable bright green boiler suit descending gradually towards me. He reached the ledge and stood there nonplussed.

'Climb down,' I shouted. He reached my side, his normal ruddy features now the colour of putty.

'Bloody hell, what a bloody pitch!' he gasped as he untied the rope, which sailed away out of sight.

While we waited for the next man down, Ray and I inserted our reluctant bodies into the narrow, low crevice where the stream flowed between froth-covered slimy walls. We were soon forced onto our hands and knees until, after a couple of hundred feet or so, the mighty Juniper Gulf ended where a foamy pool met the roof in this miserable cleft.

Returning to the foot of the pitch, we could see the end of the lifeline thrashing around in the water, which had dramatically increased in volume. I tied on, blew my whistle and began climbing, head down against the deluge. The force of water was incredible – without the lifeline, I felt sure that I would have been knocked off by its sheer weight.

About eighty feet up I suddenly realised that the lifeline had threaded its way between the rungs of the ladder. I blew a blast on the whistle. The line stopped. I had two choices: untie the lifeline and unthread it from the rungs, then retie it – which, in the present circumstances of being cold, tired and pounded by a heavy waterfall while hanging onto the rungs was a recipe for disaster – or go down again. I chose the latter.

I shouted up the pitch from the bottom and thought that the men up top understood what had happened. Sure enough, the rope went up and was lowered again with a canvas bag containing a rock tied to the end, to prevent a reoccurrence of the problem. Having good caving mates with common sense can make all the difference in situations like this.

Ray tied on, taking the bag with him after throwing out the rock. Soon, he was in trouble with lots of shouting and whistle-blowing, and he seemed to take an awfully long time to reach the top.

My light was starting to yellow when the bag came sailing down like a grey, headless ghost. I tied on, stuffed the bag down my jacket, blew my whistle and set off, concentrating on gripping the rope sides, leaning into the ladder, keeping my head down and preventing water from entering my mouth.

A couple of times the weight of water knocked me sideways and left me hanging on one hand, off-balance as I reached upwards, desperately clawing for the next rung. I could hear nothing and see nothing except the ladder in front of me and I seemed to be climbing for ever, until my head and shoulders broke through a seemingly solid wall of water at the head of the fall, the volume of which had increased threefold and which had the ominous colour of peat-stained floodwater.

I was literally dragged the last few feet and hauled over the lip of the pitch like a sack of wet coal. 'Bloody 'ell,' I gasped. Crawling away from the head of the drop, I took off my helmet, the only place I could keep my cigarettes and a cardboard 6d bell battery dry. I opened my cigarette tin and revealed a soup of tobacco; my bell battery's stout cardboard outer covering had been reduced to papier mâché, as had my compressed-fibre miner's helmet. This could be shaped into anything and, in its wet soggy state, could even have been used for origami.

This cheered everyone up. However, I managed to scrounge a fag from Tom and a bit of string to tie my three battery cells together. We realised we had picked the wrong day: Jumpina Gulf was really jumping. We would have to abandon our tackle and return the next weekend to let more members bottom the pot and retrieve our tackle, assisted if need be by some of the Northern Pennine Club lads. The journey to the foot of the 80 foot pitch was a nightmare as the power of the stream coming down the narrow passage forced us to traverse above the water, and where before we could crouch under rocks we now had to chimney up the smooth walls and climb over them.

One place worried me. I remembered a large rock that almost blocked the passage, which I knew we would have to crawl under as there was no way over. Reduced to crouching with water up to my chest, I came across the huge slab. I was right – water was welling up from beneath and the way out was blocked. With my fading light I could see that the rock was jammed under an overhang, but on one side an irregularity revealed a narrow gap. I chimneyed up and found to my delight that we could get out, and we were soon at the foot of the eighty, much to the relief of the lads we had left there. The traverses were swilling with water, noise and a howling draught; I had torn a trouser leg on the ladders and it was split from ankle to crutch, flapping about like a fashion model's kilt. When I tripped over it and nearly did a nose dive off the Bad Step, I tore off the flapping piece of cloth.

Nearing the entrance we looked like refugees from a war. Three were without lights and two were almost minus boots as their soles had come apart, revealing in one case a length of red sock that hung out like a dog's tongue. The boulder slope at the foot of the entrance pitch was unrecognisable with water spewing out from between the blocks.

We emerged late at night to greet a howling wind and driving rain, then set off for Crummack in thick cloud. We got lost and ended up in Clapham. All in all it was a good day out, especially as we had no tackle for three weeks because it never stopped raining.

Oh, the joys of caving.

Chapter 12

Holes that Bite

D**URING THE FIFTIES** the strange pastime of potholing suddenly began hitting the headlines. In those days people hadn't quite lost their marbles – there were no squawking pop singers, no 'celebrities', no television personalities, and footballers had day jobs. The only queer buggers around were potholers and we were the darlings of the press as, being in a very primitive stage of development, we hadn't quite mastered the technique of getting in and out of potholes safely and we kept having accidents.

A cave rescue was manna from heaven for the press because they generally happened at week-ends. This guaranteed at least a two-day spread with lurid headlines such as 'Fight for life in hell hole' or 'Trapped in darkness as water rises', accompanied by a spread of photographs of all sorts of people dressed in caving gear, stood outside some pub. If the reporters couldn't find the right story they used to invent one, with a lurid diagram showing a few balloons – representing a cave – and an arrow denoting 'Trapped caver here' and another showing 'Rescuers here'.

It was all good fun and, if you could persuade a young lady to become stuck in a cave . . . Wow! You had hit the jackpot – it was free beer for a week. One unfortunate lass did manage to get herself stuck tight in an undulating passage, and the fact that she possessed an undulating body probably had something to do with it, because when she slipped her undulating bits didn't match the cave's undulating bits.

When I explained all these details to the pack of news hounds waiting outside the cave, they began drooling at the mouth and begged to be given her vital statistics in exchange for a donation to the rescue team – which I did, but neglected to tell them that she had a hump back!

I BECAME INVOLVED IN CAVE RESCUE in a very casual way. It started when George Cornes appeared at 12A one Monday morning.

Her undulating bits didn't match the cave's undulating bits

'Jim, there's a gentleman to see you.' My father's voice floated up the stairs and penetrated my subconscious state, just as I was waking up. 'He wants you to go potholing.'

Knowing that I don't go potholing on Mondays, I staggered downstairs to be confronted by George's genial face.

'I thought you said there was a gentleman to see me,' I muttered.

"Ello, Ers, you look lovely in the mornin' – get your gear, we're off to Penyghent Pot.'

Surrounded by caving gear, I was fastened into George's sidecar and driven at break-neck speed towards Ribblesdale. Penyghent Pot, a recent discovery by the Northern Pennine Club, was a hard and notorious cave with an entrance involving a low, wet, 300 yard long canal-like crawl and thirteen wet pitches. The mile-long cave system had been the scene of a fatality three weeks earlier, when a young caver had died of hypothermia. This grim scenario looked like being repeated as another young caver had fallen on one of the pitches, and a full-scale rescue was taking place when George and I arrived, together with numerous other cavers who were converging on the hole.

The bleak fell in the shadow of Penyghent was littered with a scattering of small tents, rucksacks, bundles of clothes and tired cavers, wet and mud-stained, who were trying to snatch some sleep after working in the cave all night.

A group of us were organised by Reg Hainsworth, the Cave Rescue Organisation leader, and we were soon on our hands and knees in the cold, chest-deep water of the canal. We worked our way through 300 yards of abject misery, with the water splashing off the cave walls and making a mocking echo as it slurped along the passage ahead, mixed with the grunts and weak attempts at humour from the group.

A flat-out section gave us more anguish as we slid along like muddy seals, coughing and spitting out the muddy water, and I wondered how we were going to bring the injured caver out. It was a sod of a place.

Reaching the big pitch, we relieved some tired cavers and sent them out. The rescuers had been working in relays throughout the night, all except one, Bob Leakey, who had been on the rescue from the beginning and refused to leave the stretcher. Positioning for the big pull up the pitch, we could hear Bob giving orders and we were soon heaving on the straining ropes that held the stretcher. I didn't realise how heavy a casualty and stretcher could be, or how many men were required to retrieve an injured victim. Pulling the stretcher over the lip of the drop, I looked at the ashen, almost lifeless face under the bandaged head and thought of the agony to come.

There was a wide trench in the cave floor. Volunteers were asked to bridge it with their bodies, one of which turned out to be my brother Ron who, in spite of his declaration never to go underground again, had relented when he heard the urgent BBC radio bulletin requests asking for potholers to assist in the rescue, as there was a dramatic shortage of men.

Half-dragging, half-carrying, to the sound of hammer blows of men ahead knocking off rock projections in the narrow passage, we brought the stretcher to the foot of a small, eighteen-foot pitch; like all the pitches in the pothole, it had a strong volume of water flowing over it. The site was awkward, with jagged fangs of black rock jutting out everywhere, and it was narrow at the top.

The stretcher kept jamming. George, the man of the moment, solved this problem by climbing up the short ladder, which was held rigid by some of the team, while others balanced the casualty on George's broad back. Yet more men pulled supporting ropes from above, where willing hands lifted the stretcher off George's back and over the obstructions.

The next pitch was dealt with in a similar fashion, only this time several of the team were required to stand neck-deep in a pool at the foot of the pitch. It was here, as we were preparing for the lift, that I noticed the casualty staring at a lone helmet lying in a recess, a relic of the failed attempt to save a young caver's life only three weeks previously.

The helmet belonged to the dead caver. I wondered if our victim knew – then he said, tonelessly, 'That was William's helmet.'

We reassured him, then more volunteers arrived with hot drinks and soup – at least, they had set off as hot drinks, but many had come to grief in the crawl. At least we managed to put some nourishment into our patient, as he was going to need it. He was in considerable pain and obviously very weak and cold, with his core temperature dropping steadily in his immobile state.

Someone had the brilliant idea of bringing in a car tyre inner tube, which we inflated and placed under the stretcher in the wet crawl. Ropes tied to the head of the stretcher were taken along the crawl to where men could pull, and the stretcher was to be guided by a 'driver' at the rear.

With men each side and men ahead, the order was given to move. Stumbling and slithering through the muddy water, we began the long trek. After some distance the passage narrowed and several of us were forced to let go. We watched the victim and two men leaving, crawling along the miserable passage in a welter of brown, peat-stained water which broke over their shoulders. We returned to the end of the crawl to wait and joined the long queue of rescuers, sitting on ledges, half out of the water while trying to ignore the numbing cold. Time passed. All cigarettes had been smoked and even the most imaginative had run out of jokes when, preceded by a faint splashing, the cry came from the crawl: 'He's out!'

We cheered. After thirty-six hours, the injured man had reached the surface.

THE RIGOURS OF PENYGHENT POT were felt again several months later, when I found myself ploughing through the wet crawl once more. During a prolonged period of very wet weather some ladders had been left in the hole and I had been asked to help retrieve them. If I had been born a woman, I would have been a lady of easy virtue because, like the singer in the song, 'I can't say no.' I am also an opportunist and, with this group of hard cavers, I would be able to bottom the cave without having to drag our own club tackle in, so it would be a fairly easy trip. At least, that was my reasoning . . .

It was now the depths of winter and the higher fells were covered in snow, some of which was melting and flowing into the low, miserable confines of the entrance crawl. I began to regret my hasty decision immediately my body hit that icy water. That's the trouble with decisions made in pubs.

I followed the backside of the bloke in front, and his never-ending moan: 'Effin hell, it's cold – we must be bloody mad. We want our fuckin' 'eds testing.' Splash, splash. 'Bloody 'ell, it's cold.'

'Shut up and go faster. I'm freezing my bloody balls off,' I muttered.

Eventually, we all plopped over the rock barrier at the end of the crawl and worked our way down into the cave, seemingly never out of the water as all the pitches had water streaming over them. Some of the ladders were twisted and kinked by being battered by weeks of floods; some had broken rungs and lifelines had been washed away but, fortunately, most of the pitches were small, though we took care as cavers only seem to fall off small pitches.

Towards the lower reaches the cave became wetter as we splashed along in waist-deep water, crouching crab-like along a low tunnel section then climbing above the

Rose with Ma and Pa

stream along a dry section. However, this respite was short-lived and we soon plunged back into the water again. It was the wettest, most uninviting cave that I had ever been in, and we had to keep moving to stay one step in front of the undertaker as our chattering teeth sounded like a Spanish dance group on speed.

More inlets in the lower cave turned the last two pitches into miniature Niagaras and there were only two silly sods, self included, who bothered descending the last pitch into the sump. As one of our wiser comrades put it, 'I can't see any point in going down a forty-foot pitch with a bloody river on your head when you can see what's down there from here, and that's bugger all.' Words of wisdom.

While pulling up the ladder from the last pitch we mused on the fact that we were 527 feet down, with thirteen pitches to climb and over a mile of wet, cold cave to negotiate. That concentrated our minds wonderfully – that and our cold, wet bodies. We splashed through water and were half-drowned on the pitches, hardly feeling any discomfort as we were kept 'warm' by our exertions, and it was only when we had to stop to derig pitches and coil up ladders that we started to feel Ole Rigor Mortis breathing down our necks.

We took a break at the top of the biggest pitches, as we had by now accumulated a large pile of equipment and were slightly knackered. Two small climbs and then we were in the crawl; the going was slow because we were laden like packhorses and, in the tight bit, reduced to lying full-length, almost covered in freezing water. We pushed and juggled our burden in front, then we kicked and wriggled as we sloshed our way through after it like giant, landed fish wrapped in flapping rags, floundering on a sandbank.

Everything is relative and so, by the time I reached the hands-and-knees section, I found it somewhat better than the last bit. This was possibly because I could move faster, and possibly because I now had no feeling in my hands or legs. With a coil of rope around my neck, a heavy rope ladder in each hand, the sole of a boot hanging off, my cut-down raincoat even more cut down – well, shredded would be a better term – tears in my trousers and my light a dull, yellow glow, I only had one thought in my head: 'Let's get the hell out of here.' I went steaming along that crawl to the sound of clonking wooden rungs hitting the rock floor, the swishing and splashing of displaced water, and another knocking noise which I couldn't quite place. Reaching the surface, I was greeted by my wife Rose, who had been walking in the area. She gave a smile at my bedraggled appearance and then a look of horror (perhaps she's gone off me, I thought)

'Good God!' she exclaimed. 'Look at your knees!'

Jim (right) at Penyghent Pot with fellow members of the Red Rose Cave & Pothole Club

I looked down at the flapping cloth that used to be trousers, where two gaping tears at knee-level revealed two deathly white kneecaps completely stripped of skin. As we all looked at the pulpy sores they slowly began to ooze blood. What a mess! The rest of the group had cuts and abrasions, and one had a knee similar to mine. However, as a past winner of many knobbly knee contests, I was in a much worse state than anyone else. I couldn't feel anything as I began to tear off my wet rags, but once my body began to warm up it was a case of 'Ooch, ouch' when I tried to move and blood began to pour out of what looked like kneecaps. I didn't know bones could bleed.

Rose was a good wife – extremely efficient and highly organised, as one would be with the German surname of Backhouse. Within seconds she had me standing to attention as she tore off my shirt tail and some of her knickers, wrapped up my knees, dressed me and called me a bloody fool, then packed my rucksack and, before carrying me off the fell, turned round to the others and said: 'You're all bloody fools. Anyone else want bandaging? Any one else want their gear carrying down the fell?'

'No, Rose,' they answered meekly, for she was that sort of a woman.

'Right, I'm taking him to hospital and I want one of you to accompany me off the fell and help me start his bike, and then lift him on it.'

'Right, Rose,' they answered.

A PAINTER AND DECORATOR has to be, to a certain extent, a fairly nimble sort of fellow, but after my trip down Penyghent I was about as much use as the proverbial one-armed paperhanger. In fact, I was the no-legs paperhanger. I was now self-employed and, having received a bollocking from Rose and the hospital doctor, I received one from an irate customer when I explained to him that I could only decorate the top half of his lounge. I couldn't bend so, 'Would he mind painting the skirting boards?' He was not amused and became even less amused when I tried to convince him that I had damaged my knees praying.

They say necessity is the mother of invention. Having become sick of trawling jumble sales for old, cast-off clothes which shredded after one trip, I decided to make my own caving suit out of sailmaker's canvas. As Rose used to be a dressmaker and was also sick of having muddy 'clothing' hanging on her washing line, she soon drew up a pattern and left me to it.

The canvas was tough stuff and guaranteed several years' trouble-free caving – if I could cut it. After ruining my best paperhanging scissors and almost knackering my wife's sewing machine, I fetched out my sailmaker's needle and palm from my Navy days and ended up with an indestructible suit.

We had just discovered a new cave. It was wet and involved lots of crawling and climbing, and was ideal for the launch of the Eyre Wonder Suit, which would revolutionise caving. The lads were suitably impressed when, after a mighty struggle assisted by a dresser, I was attired in my dazzling white outfit and set off into the cave. Strangely enough, I found bending slightly difficult and put it down to the suit being dry – it would be alright when wet.

Lying full length in the shallow stream, crawling over sharp rocks and cobbles, I felt quite comfy, whereas my companions were in obvious discomfort. The further we progressed the better I felt, as I was pleasantly warm. In fact, I was becoming quite hot and I slid gratefully into a deep pool that stretched across the cave passage. We were soon able to make our way at a half-crouch, which was hard work, and then thankfully the roof lifted and we could all stand erect. Well, all except me that is, for something seemed to have happened to my suit and the neck and shoulders were forcing me to walk like Quasimodo.

This was brilliant entertainment for everyone but me. Then, when we came to climb up into a higher passage, I found that I couldn't lift my arms above my shoulders or bend my knees. The bloody suit was shrinking!

My mates were falling about laughing as I struggled up the climb with steam coming out of the arm gussets, which had split open. The new canvas had soaked up the water and its fibres had swelled, trapping me inside a man-eating suit.

Eventually, with the suit wide open at the front, I crawled out of the cave like a well-wrapped mummy and found that as well as not being able to stand up straight, or move my arms and legs more than a few inches, I couldn't take it off! Even assisted by two undressers I couldn't get out of it. It was a snug design, with the front only opening to the waist. Now with it shrinking, the crutch threatened me with a sex change every time my two assistants tried to pull up my collar to slide it off my shoulders.

'Jim – I think Rose has stitched you up,' said one comedian.

'Ho, ho. Anybody got a knife?'

After a painful interval a Swiss Army knife was produced along with a troop of Boy Scouts who were fell walking, and they took a great delight in finding out which gadget on the knife was best for removing a bloke with a bent nose from the confines of a bent canvas suit.

Lying there in my longjohns, I felt like I was reborn having just escaped from the womb, and I shook the Boy Scouts by the hand and informed the Scout Master that there should be a badge for this sort of thing. He said that he would ask his wife to design one.

I was saved from further embarrassment by the ex-Army stores, which suddenly became the cavers' Mecca when it was discovered that they sold rubber survival suits *which were completely waterproof*! Complete with neck and wrist seals, and with built-in feet, a waterproof willy hole and a hood, they were a caver's dream.

Kitted out in the new goon suits, we were as different from the old cave explorers as George Mallory was from Edmund Hillary. Caving ceased to be an ultimate experience for masochists and, suddenly, became an enjoyable sport as we cast off all the weight of sweaters and old, cut-down jackets, and replaced them with a single boiler suit to protect the delicate rubber of our survival suits. Our old studded boots were discarded in favour of new Vibram soles, and lacerated knees and lightless caving trips were suddenly a thing of the past when miners' kneepads and rechargeable accumulators came on the scene. Caving became a sport for sissies as we floated along deep, wet canals and slid through cold, wet crawls with ease, snug and dry inside our bright yellow cocoons. Wet pitches held no more terrors for us: up with the snugly fitting hood, and away we went.

It was almost virtual reality caving, but we soon found that there were drawbacks. I discovered this when climbing a notoriously wet pitch in Diccan Pot, when my neck seal developed a leak and my legs began to fill up with water. I suddenly inflated like a Michelin Man, stood motionless on the ladders unable to go up or down. Ignominiously, I was lowered down and cuts were made in the goon suit legs to let the water out before I could continue.

The built-in feet were great, but we decided they had to go when, swimming along an underground and fairly deep stream passage, three cavers were suddenly turned into two as one sank without even saying goodbye. With

I informed the Scout Master that there should be a badge for this sort of thing

This is bloody ridiculous – we need lightweight equipment

a struggle he was retrieved and his suit made rapidly non-leak-proof, so that any water which entered could also drain out.

The technological advances of wartime ensured that strong, lightweight alloys and high-tensile aero-cable soon became available, and Lewis Railton – a well-known, respected caver and scientist, and member of the South Wales Caving Club – came up with a specification for lightweight caving ladders.

During a retreat from the depths of Lost John's Cave, when four of us were carrying out all the equipment (which really needed eight sherpas), we had stopped for a smoke above Dome pitch when a voice came out of a huge coil of wet, one-and-five-eighths inch Manila rope. It was Ray Barker. We couldn't see him, but I knew it was Ray because, being a strong lad, I had given him the 180 foot rope to carry. From the depths of the coil came: 'This is bloody ridiculous – we need lightweight equipment.'

'We can't afford it,' I answered.

'I can make it,' said Ray.

'But it will cost a lot just to buy the material,' said I.

'Put the subs up,' said Ray.

'Are you sure you can make it? How about the jigs and all that?'

'I can make those too,' said Ray.

So the amazing Ray did as he promised and, helped by some club members, made 500 feet of new 'electron' ladders. He also acquired from the RAF, of which he was a recent member, 1,000 feet of plaited nylon, glider towing-rope. Thanks to Ray, at that time the Red Rose Cave & Pothole Club was the best equipped group in the north of England, and probably Britain. We were about to make our mark in the caving world.

ANY SANE PERSON wishing to make a mark in the caving world would have picked somewhere else, but I dabbled with the devil, Old Nick, and picked his favourite hole: Nick Pot.

They used to frighten young cavers with stories about Nick. It had the deepest underground pitch in Britain: 280 feet was a daunting prospect and, to make it even more daunting, it had a 280 foot waterfall dropping down it. And coupled with that fact, the 80 foot pitch immediately preceding the big one was reputed to be the loosest, most dangerous pitch in the Dales. That made it more daunting than ever.

So why did we want to go down it? Because we needed to train for the 365 foot deep shaft of Gaping Gill, the deepest in Britain. In response to numerous queries of 'Why' from my clubmates, I was speechless. I couldn't say, 'Because it's there,' because somebody had already said that, so I answered lamely, 'Well, it seems a shame, now we've got all this new tackle, not to use it.'

'You're mad, totally stark staring bonkers,' said Dave Raines, our newest recruit. He drank his pint and stared at me with his bloodshot eyes in a very strange sort of way, then went off and joined the Northern Pennine Club – the members of which, in those days, were all mad!

The small entrance to Nick Pot, high on the southern flank of Ingleborough, offers no clue to the vast cavern that lies a few feet beneath the moor. During the original exploration by the Northern Cavern and Fell Club in 1935, the bulky rope ladders were uncoiled and threaded through to the pitch, as the top section of Nick consists of a tight, shattered mess with nowhere to attach them. Progress was difficult enough for us as we struggled through the awkward confines of the jagged crawl, even with our new lightweight ladders.

The 80 foot pitch was a nightmare and I peeled a huge chunk of rock from the cave roof before we could even think about rigging the pitch; it went crashing down, taking large slabs off the unstable walls as it fell.

With the ladder belayed outside the cave, I carefully climbed down, gardening as I went, peeling loose sections of rock from the walls of the narrow shaft as I passed. The noise could be heard outside on the moor.

'It's only Jim, quarrying,' said Ray.

Thankful to be down the first pitch, I dived for cover under a wide shale band that led directly onto the big pitch. Stood alone in the wide, flat-roofed chamber, trying to ignore the noise of falling rocks, I looked at the heavy stream which flowed down a gully and poured over the lip of a huge black hole that seemed to have no end. There was no roof, no walls and nothing but blackness below.

This shaft was nearly twice the depth of the big pitch in Juniper; it was time for a fag. Sat on a rock, puffing away at my Capstan, I watched my mates bringing the tackle under the shale band, still followed by the sound of falling rock. When we were all assembled and the cries of 'Bloody 'ell' and 'Jeesus Kerist' had subsided, we began to rig the pitch.

The stream gully contained an old wooden dam with a primitive sluice gate. Mike Bateson was entranced. 'It's t-t-the original dam, made by t-t-the C-Cavern a-and Fell Club,' he stuttered, wild with excitement. 'This was built in 1935,' he exclaimed and, with loving hands, stroked the ancient timbers before he belted the sluice gate with a rock, declaring to all and sundry that he could fix it.

Within seconds Mike was oblivious to everything else as he set to, trying to repair the ancient and, it seemed, fairly essential dam. Engrossed in laddering the huge shaft we forgot about Mike and I concentrated on encouraging the ladders past a steep, V-shaped notch in the walls eighty feet lower. They kept catching, so I decided to climb down and thread the ladders past the obstruction. The cave suddenly went quiet, the noise of falling water ceased and a triumphant cry from the gully announced to the world that: 'I've fixed it!' Brilliant – a dry climb would make the descent quite enjoyable.

I began climbing down to the V-shaped ledge when suddenly, giving a tremendous roar, a wall of water shot across the pitch and hit me with the force of a fireman's hose. With arms and legs wrapped around the ladder, I hurled doubts on Mike's ancestry.

'Er, s-s-sorry Jim, s-s-slight adjustment needed.'

I asked Mike to leave the sluice gate open while I was perched in the line of fire, as I preferred a steady downpour to infrequent torrential blasts.

'Okay, I'll leave it open,' said Mike and I was enveloped in water again.

Without the dam the pitch would be a difficult and dangerous climb as, even out of the full force of the flow while perched on the ledge, I was being hammered by the water. I asked Mike to try again. What a relief when he turned the water off! Unfortunately, my relief was short-lived for, preceded by a warning shout, I was again struck by a miniature monsoon.

However, in spite of 'Archimedes', I got the pitch rigged. Looking down at the torrent that almost immersed the ladders, we wandered across to see if we could help Mike with the dam. With four of us crouched around the wooden structure, I marvelled at the ingenuity of the Cavern and Fell Club members. They had built a wooden frame into a natural cross-fault in the gully and jammed it in with small stones. The wooden sluice gate had deteriorated over the years and two slats were missing, but after numerous experiments and a sort of Handy Andy repair with rocks, a canvas tackle bag and a bootlace, we made the dam work and it was all systems go.

With my gallant team in place I tied the plaited, nylon glider towrope around my waist and began climbing into the depths of the big pitch. The weight of so much ladder trailing over the V-shaped ledge pulled the top eighty feet at an angle, held rigidly away from the wall. This made climbing difficult as I tended to swing under the ladder and I was thankful when I reached the lip. I had a good light and looked down at this awesome drop and the wire ladders descending into the gloom as far as the eye could see.

Checking that my lifeline wasn't twisted round the ladder above, I stepped over the edge and began working my way down just as a muffled shout preceded the roar of approaching water. Within seconds I was engulfed in a torrent of water that obliterated everything, except the need to cling onto that ladder. Motionless, I held on until the flood abated; then, as suddenly as it had started, it stopped.

I continued climbing down, swinging clear of the smooth, black fluting of the wall, before I heard another muffled shout. Once again I was hit by a deluge, but this time it didn't stop and I realised that the old dam must have collapsed. With water beating me about my head and shoulders, enveloped in a grey, icy cocoon in the centre of the downpour, I continued down, carefully placing my feet on the round alloy rungs and concentrating on rhythm and balance.

Suddenly, my progress was halted by a savage jerk on the lifeline and I was held suspended. I blew several blasts on my whistle. The line twitched and I began climbing again to be abruptly brought to another halt. With water pouring on my head, halfway down a 280 foot pitch, it was not the best of places to be. I put all my weight on the lifeline and heaved my way down a couple of rungs before being held tightly by the rope once more. The downpour stopped briefly as lights shone down and I heard a shout, 'Stuck,' before the flood began again.

I swore at the men above as I tugged on the lifeline, which suddenly came free from whatever obstruction had snagged it. Thankfully, I carried on climbing down, and thankfully someone managed to turn off the tap. The water stopped pouring on my head.

The cold, clear air in the shaft brought everything into sharp relief. Below, the glistening alloy of the ladders stood out like silver against the dark backcloth of the smooth walls of the chasm. Far below I could make out the rock-strewn floor of the pitch, and a huge, black fluting of razor-sharp rock which rose out of the depths like a shark's dorsal fin.

I felt very exposed and remember thinking, 'If I fall and hit that knife-edged rock, it would cut me in two with the ease of a bacon slicer.' Such morbid thoughts were rapidly dispelled by an ominous roaring and a cold blast of displaced air. I wrapped my arms and legs tightly around the ladder, seconds before I was hit by a huge cascade of water, the force of which tore one hand free of the ladder. I was momentarily hanging by one hand as I was spun around by the impact.

With the worst of the deluge over, I carried on climbing down. Then, with a shock colder than the water, I realised that my lifeline was non-existent – it was hanging below me in a gigantic loop.

I clung to the ladder and blew the signal for up. Nothing happened. The water still poured on my head, I was shaking with cold and my hands looked as though they belonged to a dead person. In fact, one slip and I would be just that. It was obvious that I needed to get down and off that ladder, before I fell off from sheer fatigue.

Slowly, the loop of rope below was pulled back up and, happy to have my lifeline reinstated, I continued climbing down – but not for long. The plaited nylon rope jammed again and I was held immobile, 180 feet down and 100 feet from the floor, while way up above – almost in heaven – four of my team-mates were desperately trying to undo the biggest knot that they had ever seen in their lives! Mike frantically worked on the dam like a neurotic beaver, while Tom Sykes tried to communicate with the dead: me.

During a brief interval, while Mike stopped the water flowing down the pitch, I was informed that the situation was hopeless and that I had better come back up. Then communications ceased as another torrent came crashing down the pitch and, head tucked into my shoulders, I began to plod back up, swearing a different swear word on every rung. That was until the rope jammed again and I was left hanging with another giant loop beneath my feet.

I was in a serious situation so, preparing for the worst, I unclipped my sling, threaded it through the ladder and refastened it around my waist. Relieved, I took my hands off the ladder, leaned back in my sling and beat some life into my hands and aching arms.

There was a mighty knot at the head of the pitch, another bunch of knotted bastards fifty feet lower, and somehow the rope had been twisted several times around the ladder below the V-shaped ledge. I knew nothing of this, until I was hit by a particularly heavy flood followed by a momentary silence when the whole shaft was illuminated by a magnesium flare. This frightened me to death, as I thought I had gone to heaven – then wished I had when I looked around at my airy surroundings where I hung like a spider in the dome of Saint Paul's.

It was our photographer, Ron Bliss, who provided the illumination to highlight where the rope was stuck, and after three more dam releases I was allowed to go down again and I reached the foot of the pitch at last. I found a dry alcove and crawled in, an object of sheer, frozen misery.

Hang-gliding hadn't been invented then. If it had, I would have taken it up as nothing could be worse than potholing with a load of slap-happy cavers and an elasticated rope that magically ties itself into knots!

SOME PEOPLE NEVER LEARN from their mistakes. Perhaps I am one, for a few weeks later I assembled my trusty team at Gaping Gill. Everyone in the club was going to descend the 365 foot shaft – that is, until we fastened the ladders together and stretched them across the fell. We could hardly see the bloke on the other end and all our volunteers were suddenly reduced to four.

Ray Barker had acquired an old Land Rover, which he parked on a funnel-shaped depression above the open hole. He casually hooked the end of the ladders around his towbar and said: 'Ready when you are, Jim.'

'No, ready when you are, Ray,' I replied. 'You made most of the ladders and it's your Land Rover, so I think you can have the honour of being the first man ever to descend Gaping Gill on electron ladders.'

We had discarded the plaited nylon after the Nick Pot fiasco, especially because on the return up the pitch Tom, who was tied on and waiting for the slack on the lifeline to be taken in, was talking to me one minute and the next he suddenly became airborne. He took off in a gigantic leap that would have done justice to Bugs Bunny. Frantically clawing at the ladders while yo-yoing up the pitch on the elasticated rope, Tom swears he ascended it in four huge leaps as he was intermittently plucked off the ladder. As a direct consequence, here we were tying all the club's ropes together, ancient and modern – which sounds a bit like the hymn book. Indeed, looking at the ropes invoked the need for a prayer or two because, somehow, someone's mother's washing line was in the heap.

Soon, a pale-faced Ray was ushered over the brink and he commenced his descent. He was about 100 feet down when I noticed he was being followed by his Land Rover, which was trundling down the slope towards him. It stopped in a series of jerks and disgorged three shrieking women. One, who had knocked it out of gear, had a very surprised look on her face – although she could never have been as surprised as Ray when he found his ladders were transformed into a moving staircase and he was descending Gaping Gill without moving his legs.

Terrified shouts and enough whistle signals to form the *William Tell Overture* came floating up from below, indicating that Ray was not too happy with this innovation. Then, after a suitable interval, a faint whistle told us that Ray was down and we hauled up the ropes: there was one-inch Manila, one-and-a-half-inch hemp, a length of old climbing rope, someone's towrope and, as stated, something that looked suspiciously like a clothes line.

'Anyone want to go next?' I asked, being the perfect gentleman. 'No?'

I tied on and began climbing past the still dripping walls from our stream diversion. At forty feet I found the line holding me back, so I shouted for more slack. This was my first mistake. I climbed steadily downwards until I came into the roof of the Main Chamber, 500 feet long and 100 feet wide. It was breathtaking. I stopped climbing to take in the magnificent sight from my airy perch as I gently swayed to and fro, 250 feet above the rock-strewn floor, grey and ghostly in the light filtering down into this vast cavern.

This was my second mistake, for I slowly became aware of another grey and ghostly presence – that of my lifeline, which was still descending and looping in heavy coils around my neck and over my arms. I shouted and blew my whistle, but this only spurred my enthusiastic team on to greater efforts and the rope descended from above with even greater speed. I was now fighting to free myself from coils of heavy, wet rope, which was winding itself around me and threatening to pull me off the ladder with its weight.

Congratulating themselves on a job well done, and me on such a speedy descent, my lifeline team chucked the rest of the rope down the hole and settled back on the moor for a well-earned rest and a fag. A faint shout from below from the diminutive figure of Ray informed me that most of my lifeline was on the floor and 'Don't fall off.'

Fighting my way down the swinging ladders while heaving coils of rope off my neck, I eventually joined Ray and collapsed in an exhausted heap, my arms like strings of spaghetti . . . I must be the only caver who has climbed down Gaping Gill carrying his lifeline on his back.

We were soon joined by Tom Sykes, and Ray took the lifeline and returned up the pitch. Then, after a long interval, we discerned the figure of Mike Bateson hovering into view. Grabbing the lifeline, I had a surprisingly easy and painless climb out, which took only six minutes. However . . .

There was always a however with the Red Rose. Looking at the gaping mouth of Gaping Gill, one wouldn't believe it possible that if a bloody great coil of rope was thrown down this bloody big hole that it wouldn't hit the bottom. Yet this is what happened – or didn't happen, depending on which way you look at it.

We chucked the rope down in a bloody great bundle. We carefully laid out coils on the moor and threw them down one by one. We threaded it down –

I must be the only caver who has climbed down Gaping Gill carrying his lifeline on his back all to no avail. Every time we chucked the rope down we had to heave it back up, and it was heavy and wet. After several attempts, with one caver nearly being dragged to his death in a loop of rope, we were becoming tired and desperate.

It was growing dark and my spirits were sinking with the setting sun when Mike's wife became anxious and accused me of putting her newly married husband in peril. The faint whistle signals that came from below were becoming intermittent and off-key, and we were seriously considering laddering Bar Pot, an alternative way into the cave, to retrieve our missing members. We couldn't very well go home without them . . .

For some time now we had been fruitlessly lowering a kitbag containing a couple of rocks, trying to reach the bottom. 'That's it,' I said. 'Pull it up and we'll ladder Bar Pot.'

We heaved the heavy rope up and were completely astonished when we found Tom on the end. He swore he'd never even touched the ladder. After more 'fishing' we also retrieved Mike and, towards midnight and very weary, a much wiser band of potholers came down off the fell and headed for home.

Chapter 13

Cave Rescues and Crazy Customers

JIMMY LEACH WAS PLONKING AWAY on the piano, his sardonic grin wreathed in smoke from the cigarette stuck in the corner of his mouth. His mate Budge, as well as Buzzer, Colin, Hairy Bert and a few other members of the Northern Pennine Club, were grouped around the old upright – a sort of barber-shop quartet, singing *The Ball of Kirriemuir* as they swung their slopping pint glasses in unison with the rhythm.

The bar was packed and it was difficult to see who else was in through the thick haze of tobacco smoke. I recognised some of the Bradford Pothole Club members over by the window, and some from the Red Rose playing darts. Struggling to get served, trying to push my way through the crowd, I shouted my order to one of the barmaids while holding three conversations at once with various other cavers.

The door opened and a blast of fresh air sucked some of the fag smoke out as some of the Craven cavers entered. Jim suddenly changed tune as the Northern Pennine cavers began singing, 'Oh, the Craven Pothole Club are a rotten set of bastards,' and everyone joined in, including the Craven lads.

It was a typical Saturday night in an Ingleton pub. We had been exploring some new, high-level passages in Notts Pot and, after a good day's caving, what better than to finish it off in one of the pubs? See who was in and swap experiences, tell the latest jokes (which I could never remember) or exaggerate the latest find (which I was soon doing, with one or two extra embellishments). There was a great camaraderie in those days; most cavers knew each other and each club had its own 'characters'.

Much of what was going on in the caving world was passed on by word of mouth, as only a couple of the old pre-war clubs published journals. The newer clubs, like ours, tried to print a newsletter on antique Roneo duplicator now and again, but the results were generally unreadable. When I tried to draw cartoons for publication it was hilarious, for the technique required X-ray vision as it involved drawing on a piece of greaseproof paper with a wooden skewer. It was impossible to see the result until it was printed and almost all the finished drawings had pieces missing – eyes, noses, ears – even legs and arms in some cases – so our literary merits were shelved for a later date.

I was telling George Cornes about our latest find when a burst of laughter drew our attention to Wilky, who was on his hands and knees proposing to Sue, one of the local lasses. Wilky did this frequently when he was pissed, which was often – and within minutes Sue's boyfriend, who was a big lad, hoisted him onto a table while Sue egged him on to 'Show us what you've got to offer.' So Wilky started stripping and was down to his grubby string vest and matching Y-fronts when the door opened and the village bobby walked in.

'We've had a callout for Ireby Fell, lads. Some cavers are overdue.'

Pints were downed and the bar emptied, and the Queen's highway was suddenly awash with swaying motorcyclists driving hell for leather out of the village and onto the dirt lane leading up towards Gragareth and Ireby Fell. Two bikes were already in the ditch as we roared up the steep, greasy track, awash with mud and loose rocks and streaming with water.

In bottom gear, with the engine racing and the back wheel slewing sideways, we arrived at the top of the steep track. Reg Hainsworth was standing by the cave rescue trailer, which contained what little equipment we had and a couple of Neil Robertson stretchers.

I was one of the underground rescue controllers and Reg gave me the details as I stripped off in the cold, driving rain, struggling to cover my body in the wet caving clothes that I had taken off earlier in the day. The idea of standing in a gale force wind, in pouring rain, bollock-naked while wringing out sodden garments prior to putting them on your freezing body, may strike some people as highly amusing. It was about as amusing to us as being a competitor in a Japanese TV survival show, but it was essential.

Ireby Fell Cavern is over 400 feet deep and almost a mile long. Its short, easy entrance pitches attract novice cavers, but thanks to lots of newly dug drainage ditches it also attracted plenty of water. This quickly ran off the moors when it rained, turning the cave into a flood trap and one of our busiest venues.

Grabbing some ropes and a stretcher, I set off across the fell with Harold 'Budge' Burgess, another rescue controller. By this time the mist was solidly down and visibility was reduced as we stumbled along, heads lowered against the driving rain. We worked on memory alone as we searched for 'the cavern', which we knew from previous experience was hard to find. Less than an hour previously we had been enjoying ourselves in a comfy pub; now, here we were, at eleven hundred feet, walking in circles on a mist-shrouded fell in driving rain. Isn't life strange.

We stumbled onto an old, broken wall and we knew where we were. Soon, we came across the luminous glow of white water and we staggered down the gully, together with rocks loosened by the torrent, and ducked into the low entrance and small chamber to join four others crouching there. A sheet of water thundered from an inlet overhead and joined with the surface stream to continue down the first pitch, where a caving ladder hung.

Gordon Batty, one of our hard men, and Mike Warren decided to push through the solid sheet of water and on down the fifteen-foot pitch where a dog-leg ledge led to a roomier section above the other pitches. I held the line while Gordon ducked through and vanished from sight. I felt the weight go off the line and pulled it up. Mike tied on, and he too disappeared.

We had no communications and I stood there holding the line until I felt a tug. Assisted by the others, we heaved on the rope and up popped a very bedraggled, white-faced youth.

One up, four to go.

We lowered the line and, after a long interval, we hoisted up another. Two up, three to go.

The next one proved more difficult as something was going wrong; I could tell by the feel of the rope. I slackened off a fraction, then suddenly I felt two violent tugs and we heaved up another one and handed him over to Brian Boardman, our St John first-aid man, who sat him with the others.

Three up, two to go.

Meanwhile, down below, a life-and-death struggle was taking place. One of the trapped cavers had started to climb out without a lifeline, then panicked when the full force of the water hit him. His foot slipped and his leg had gone between the rungs of the ladder. He hung on desperately for a while, until the waterfall loosened his grip and he fell backwards, suspended by his leg and upside down in a raging torrent.

Prompt action by Gordon and Mike averted a tragedy, as Gordon climbed up over the lad and freed his leg while Mike held his weight from below. During the commotion the lad fell a few more feet and banged his head, which caused him to lose all interest in the proceedings. Meanwhile, up above we retrieved the fourth lad, who told us what had happened and, 'Could we please lower the stretcher down?'

Four up and one not going anywhere.

After an almighty effort we managed to bring the stretchered casualty up the pitch, with a spluttering, half-drowned Gordon steering him from behind. Soon all were up and the rescue was over.

Not according to Brian Boardman, it wasn't.

The conditions outside the cave had worsened: the wind had increased, there was snow and sleet mixed with the driving rain, and Brian didn't think the rescued lads were fit enough to walk across the fell, as they were very cold and weak. More of the rescue team were bringing two Thomas carrying stretchers to the cave and, Brian reasoned in the comparative shelter of the cave entrance, it would be prudent to wait.

After some time, accompanied by two trundling rocks, Johnno appeared and looked at us in amazement. 'Where's the stretcher party?' he asked 'They set off ages ago!' Of course, the stretcher party was walking around in circles on the mist-shrouded fell, completely lost in almost zero visibility. Then Chester and two others appeared.

'They're laying flashing signal lights across the fell. We've lost half of the fuckin' rescue team – what a night!' said Chester.

We borrowed Chester's leg and jammed it across the rift

I decided that we should make a move by starting to carry the lad in the stretcher and assist the two strongest survivors. Once up the stream gully we were faced with the full onslaught of the wind, driving the heavy rain almost horizontally, hitting our faces with stinging liquid arrows. We could see about three feet; beyond that lay a wall of mist.

Having agreed that we would keep the wind in our right ears, we set off across the featureless fell, six of us grouped around the Neil Rob with two others helping the two lads avoid the numerous drainage channels, bogs and ankle-trappers.

Chester, our favourite monoped, had lost a leg as a child, but could do amazing things with his 'tin leg'. He was a very useful member of the team and, on one occasion, indispensable. When exploring a new find, we were once stopped by a narrow rift with smooth walls where there was nowhere to belay our ladders. After some argument we borrowed Chester's leg and jammed it across the rift, then hung the ladders on that. The gallant Chester proved very reliable as our lifeline man, as he couldn't bugger off and leave us.

Unfortunately, on this occasion, although the gallant Chester was still reliable, his leg wasn't; it must have had metal fatigue or something. One minute he was there, clip-clopping alongside me, when suddenly he fell over. 'Me bloody leg's gone,' he exclaimed. He struggled to his feet (er, foot), picked up his broken leg and tucked it under his arm – now, there's not many people who can do that! – then leaned on my shoulder and continued as if nothing had happened. It looked like a scene from the First World War as we staggered through the mist until we found an old broken wall and knew that we were heading in the right direction.

A light glimmered ahead – it was one of the policemen who, recognising my voice, shouted: 'This way Jim!' As we approached out of the gloom he began to say something, then stopped speechless as he looked at Chester's bedraggled features. His gaze turned to open-mouthed horror as he took in the booted leg tucked under Chester's arm, coupled with the empty, flapping trouser leg.

'Hell'! he exclaimed and his face went ashen. He swayed and almost passed out, until Chester waved the leg under his nose and said, 'It's only a tin 'un, you daft sod!'

With the casualties whisked away in the ambulance, the police inspector came across just as I was struggling to get dressed. 'Tell the lads that Jack's opening up the bar again – go in the back door.'

Hot soup and beer wasn't bad at four o'clock in the morning.

THIS WAS HOW CAVE RESCUE WORKED. A quick trawl through the pubs and club huts formed the first line of defence, while the police at Settle rang around the few cavers who owned a telephone, who then contacted others, and a white flag was hung out at Settle police station to alert cavers who were on their way home. Any cavers on the official rescue list were contacted through their local police.

Before I owned a telephone, I enjoyed having policemen cycle up from Lancaster and rattle on my letterbox at all sorts of odd times. I would be wrapped in my wife's dressing gown having a piece of paper thrust in my hand, giving me details of the location and nature of the incident and the time of callout. With the Lancaster police not being familiar with cave names, I sometimes had to make an educated guess and change Saint John's to Lost John's and Alan Pot to Alum Pot. I could imagine two broad-speaking sergeants easily translating Rowten Pot to Rotten Pot, but we used to get there in the end.

We had one obliging sergeant who threw pebbles at my bedroom window, in order 'not to disturb anybody'. His finest hour came when he committed an act of coitus interruptus and then shouted up to me: 'There's been an accident, can you come quick?'

Those were the days. And where was the accident? Disappointment Pot.

I HAD MADE SEVERAL NEW DISCOVERIES and been involved in quite a few cave rescues, which attracted considerable comments in the national press. These generally ranged from the Margery Ploops and Priscilla Bog type of columnists who almost experienced orgasms as they demanded 'Why do they do it' in 'They should be banned' articles, to the twittering of some MP who had worked out that each rescue cost ten thousand pounds, when in fact they cost nothing apart from lost wages and the loss of a job for some.

It was obvious that our fame was spreading when, one day, my parent's humble abode was graced by the presence of a 'purple Rolls Royce' which, according to my mother, contained 'two toffs'.

'They were proper gentlemen – you could tell by the way they spoke,' she said. Then she looked at me with suspicion and asked, 'How come you know people like that?' It was almost as though I was dealing with the Mafia.

I eventually met the gentlemen and it turned out that they were keen cavers, but needed to advance their caving experiences beyond the single, old ship's ladder and rope that they owned. They had heard about the local club and its marvellous equipment, and they were keen to join. Oh, it wasn't my sweet personality that had attracted them – it was my tackle they were after.

Richard and Henry were invited to join our club and they soon became enthusiastic and popular members. They were also the source of much amusement when we discovered that Richard's dear old nanny used to wash and iron his caving clothes, and 'couldn't for the world understand how he got them in such a mess'. This was slightly different from the rest of us, who just dried them and then shook the mud off. Tom Sykes used to spread his on the top of a privet hedge along the back street, 'Until a bloody rag and bone man took them!'

However, caving, like climbing, was a great leveller and when we discovered that Richard's guardian angel, in the form of his dear old nanny, always sent him out with a good supply of cooked pheasant legs nicely wrapped in foil, and that the toffs were quite hard, they soon became part of the gang. There was one strange side effect. I started to be concerned when, after a few hard caving trips, Richard and Henry's well-modulated speech had coarsened while ours had become more refined.

After achieving Richard and Henry's ambition to 'bottom' Lost John's, we were happily ensconced in a pub when Richard blew some froth off his pint, took a deep gulp and turned his mud-streaked face to me and said, 'I say Jim, I believe you are a decorator. Would you like to do a small job for my mother?'

'Yes – where does she live?'

'Leighton Hall.'

'Where's that?'

'Warton.'

'Whereabouts?'

'Oh, up the hill – just ask anyone,' answered Richard vaguely. 'Call anytime.'

One day, therefore, the residents of Warton were enlivened by the sight of a bent-nosed character riding a combination (a battered Matchless twin motorcycle with a wooden, coffin-shaped box attached) with his white overalls tucked into his wellies, numerous cans of paint in the box, buckets swinging from the ladders and a plank draped over the box with a bit of old rag tied on the end as a hazard warning to other road users.

I pulled up outside the pub and was directed to the crossroads, up the hill and through a wood, to where a house stood by an imposing gateway. This must be where Richard's mum lives . . . I knocked on the door and a man in a flat cap appeared; must be Richard's dad, I thought.

'Hello. Is Mrs Reynolds in?' I asked.

The man looked at me strangely and said in a Polish accent, 'She doesn't live here, she lives there,' and pointed up the drive to a large house with mock battlements and Gothic windows.

'Oh.' I thanked the man, started up my bike and rattled my way along the drive, to pull up alongside a purple Bentley (it was not a Rolls Royce). I was greeted like a long-lost cousin by a lovely, flamboyant lady in a very large hat and billowing flowered dress.

'Ah, you must be Jim,' she said. 'Richard has told me all about you.' I was then plied with tea and cakes before being taken on a marathon walk through the rambling house, past paintings of Richard's ancestors and huge stuffed heads of animals that had eaten Richard's ancestors, to the bedroom that needed redecorating. Richard's 'small job' was a room so high that clouds obscured the ceiling. This was a big change from redecorating bungalows. I took out my notebook, scratched my head, put on an intelligent look and began working out an estimate.

'Oh, don't worry about that, Jim,' said Mrs Reynolds. 'Just let me know how much wallpaper I need. I'm flying to Paris on Wednesday; I shall buy it there.'

So began a sequence of events that have continued over the years. Richard's family had acquired an eccentric decorator who almost became part of the household as he called in at frequent intervals to redecorate the stately home.

Richard also introduced me to a more stylistic approach to rock climbing, which made my present method of attacking the rock with knees, elbows, fingernails and teeth seem somewhat primitive. It all started when I was decorating one of the rooms and Richard appeared in the doorway.

'It's much too nice to be indoors on a day like this, Jim – fancy a bit of climbing?' Overalls were thrown off and I was whisked away in Richard's nippy little sports car to Hardwick Buttress and Gimmer Crag, wearing size-nine gym shoes with their toes stuffed with newspaper, borrowed from Richard. While we were clinging to the warm rock, dear Mrs Reynolds was clinging to a tea tray containing a silver teapot, sugar bowl, milk jug, a plate of cakes and a dinky little cup and saucer, shouting: 'Jim, Jim! Has anyone seen Jim? Oh, I seem to have lost my decorator.'

It wasn't long before I was also undertaking some decorating for Henry's wife. It was an unusual job because, for some reason, Henry had taken up the floorboards and I hung wallpaper while balanced on the joists.

'Ah, Jim, you're a nautical man,' said Henry. 'How would you like a sail on my yacht?'

'Well, er, yes,' I replied in some pain, as my foot had just slipped and I was straddled across the joists. 'Could we talk about it later?'

I didn't quite know what to expect, as the term 'yacht' means different things to different people and Henry was certainly different as he had just been telling me about his punt gun.

Punt guns were invented in the nineteenth century by a gentleman who was either a rotten shot or lazy, and who had an inordinate fondness for eating duck. Henry had a great-great-uncle who was a great exponent of the art and had acquired (pinched) a large gun during the Spanish Civil War, or some other conflict in which his ancestors dabbled. (At times like these I wish that I had ancestors who dabbled in wars and things, but the nearest I can manage is a cobbler in Northampton who mended King Charles' boots when he was on the run.)

Anyway, Henry's ancestor fixed this huge gun barrel to a flat-bottomed boat (punt) and used it for shooting ducks. Henry found the old gun barrel one day and restored it to its former glory, then mounted it upon a punt, whence he and Richard sailed forth on the River Kent at Sandside.

The idea of a punt gun is to lie flat and quietly propel the punt forward to within shooting distance of the happy little ducks floating on the water, quacking and doing what ducks do. When you fire an ordinary gun you light the fuse and stand back, but you can't do this with a punt gun because you've nowhere to go – as Richard and Henry found out.

The gun had been loaded with shot and a large charge of black powder, then at the right moment Henry lit the touch hole. I was told that there was a mighty explosion, every duck within a mile was obliterated, those behind the gun died of shock and Richard and Henry were propelled backwards like *Bluebird* in reverse. They shot across the Kent and were violently ejected when the shattered wreck hit the reeds by the bank on the other side.

And Henry wanted me to sail on his yacht.

Duly appointed as press-gang officer by Captain Henry, I arrived in Morecambe on one fateful day with a crew consisting of two Yorkshire types: Stewart May and Colin Thwaites, plus Rose my wife and A.N. Other, whose name I can't remember because he probably fell overboard.

Having expected something out of *Treasure Island*, I was pleasantly surprised at Henry's yacht. It was obviously his pride and joy, and sparkled from bow to stern. We clambered aboard and were introduced to Zoë, Henry's small daughter and obviously second in command.

It was a gorgeous day in early October: warm, sunny, not even a zephyr of a breeze and the sea was like a mirror, reflecting the Lakeland hills turning mauve in the autumn haze. As there was no wind we decided to trawl for fish, so we chugged out into the bay, cast out the trawling net and began sweeping up and down off the Cumbrian coast.

Henry was in fine form and regaled us with amusing anecdotes, but Zoë soon sorted us out and had us doing this and that.

'Jim, coil that rope. Colin, stow the anchor properly.'

'Aye, aye, Zoë.'

As the temperature rose a light sea mist began to form, clinging to the surface of the calm water, and a heat haze blocked out the shoreline. The yacht seemed to be floating in space as the horizon softened.

Henry let me take the helm and pointed out a little white buoy in the hazy distance between sky and sea, dully reflecting on the glassy surface, and told me to head for it. Our idyll was eventually broken when the skipper mustered all hands aft to pull in the trawl – which our lot, being cavers, did with gusto. We banged the ship's side and scoured the ship's deck with the trawl board before Colin chucked it on the deck, where it scratched a housing as the catch was released.

Poor Henry. His lovely deck, his carefully applied varnish, his flawless ship's side.

'My deck, watch my deck, don't throw it down . . . look you've scratched my varnish . . . Oh, that was a bloody thing to do, you will have to be more careful. Oh bloody hell!'

Colin, being a quiet lad and not used to being shouted at, looked at Henry in amazement. Also a landlubber, he didn't realise the pain felt by a yachtsman when his boat has been almost mortally wounded. He and Stewart sorted out the catch in silence.

Rose was given an extremely large basket full of leaping shrimps and, escorted by Zoë to the ship's galley, she was told to cook them – which is what they do with fresh shrimps. Meanwhile, the trawl was dropped over the stern again and the captain turned his attention to the wheelhouse, curious about the ship's zigzag course.

'Jim, what are you doing? I told you to steer for that buoy.'

'I am,' I said, pointing at the little white dot on the horizon.

'Then why is our course so erratic?' demanded an exasperated Henry.

'Because it keeps moving,' I said.

Henry looked at me in complete bewilderment. 'Buoys don't move.'

'This bugger does.'

Henry squinted his eyes as he stared at the distant object, then took out his binoculars and looked through them before snorting, 'That's not a buoy! That's a bloody seagull!'

Before Henry could throw me over the side a mighty scream came from the galley, followed by Zoë laughing her head off. Henry stormed away to find the galley covered in steam and Rose covered in shrimps. They were leaping out of the cooking pot and landing in her hair, on her clothes, down the front of her dress and even further. There were shrimps down her wellies and shrimps all over the floor. Three small, bewhiskered pink faces peered out of the top of her bra and looked at Henry with their little black eyes, wondering what was going on. Shrimps aren't intended to live down women's breasts (they're extremely comfortable, but too warm).

'Bloody hell, woman!' shouted Henry. 'What are you doing? I said boil them, not give them a warm bath.'

Of course, Henry knew that you plunge shrimps into boiling water, but he obviously didn't understand women like my wife and he hastily ducked as a heavy ladle skimmed his left eyebrow. If Rose could have lifted the heavy cooking pot she would have thrown that as well.

'I'm not a bloody ship's deckhand,' she said, 'so don't talk to me as if I am!' There followed something about stuff your boat and stuff your shrimps (some of which were still clinging to her in an adoring fashion), and she stormed out of the galley to join me at the wheel. 'Who does he think he is – Captain Bligh?'

I eventually calmed her down as we did another trawl while I chatted to Henry about nautical matters as one old salt to another, saying things like, 'When does the tide turn?'

'Oh, plenty of time yet,' said Henry. 'Besides, I know this bay like the back of my hand. I can always navigate the gullies.'

It was time to pull in the next catch so I left the wheel with someone else and went to help my fellow deckhands. Something went wrong, for the weighted trawler board was dragged against the hull and took some varnish off a nearby hatch – again.

Not surprisingly, Henry became very excited. 'My boat, my boat, you clumsy oafs!'

'That's it – I've had enough,' said Colin.

'Me too Stanley, er, Colin,' said his mate, and they both downed tools (or fish, or whatever they were holding) and stormed off to stand brooding on the bows.

We began sorting out the fish and shrimps in an ominous silence. I picked up a large flounder, which suddenly twisted and flipped out of my hands, up in the air and disappeared through an open hatch into the engine compartment. Zoë gave a little squeak, stuck her head down the hatch and shouted with glee, 'Henry, Henry, Jim has just dropped a big fish and it's gone under the engine.'

It seems that I had committed the cardinal sin, for any fish that slips under the engine is difficult to retrieve and is often doomed to remain there, stinking to high heaven until it rots away. Henry went spare. He poked about under the engine, laying on his back with his red face and staring eyes looking up at me as he fiddled and prodded with a bit of wire. A look of total despair came over his face. 'Oh Lord, it's gone in the bilges. What a bloody disaster.'

'It's Jim's fault, it's Jim's fault,' shouted Zoë in her high-pitched squeaky voice.

'Oh, shut up, Zoë,' I said.

'Henry, Henry, Jim's shouted at me,' she squeaked.

I too walked away and joined the mutineers on the bows. Mutiny on the high seas was a treasonable offence, but this was a different category because I noticed that the

I said boil them, not give them a warm bath

tide was running out and we had just passed a fellow yacht perched high and dry on a sandbank. Its skipper was looking over the side with a 'Where did all the water go?' look, scratching his head in disbelief as we cruised by.

The tides in Morecambe Bay are quite treacherous. At low tide the bay is almost drained of water and, apart from a few gullies, is just a large expanse of wet sand. When the tide turns the reverse happens and the sea rushes in as a tidal bore, faster than a man can run. We were in the former situation, where the plug had just been pulled.

'Henry, Henry – the tide's going out,' shouted Zoë.

'Don't worry dear, Henry will look after you,' said our unflappable skipper as he navigated the yacht skilfully up the twisting, rapidly diminishing channel. The sea was rushing past us at speed in its race to reach the Irish Sea, and the sandbanks on either side were growing higher by the minute. We could make out our jetty as Henry swung the yacht towards the shore; he was like the *Lord of the Rings* for the boat seemed to be sailing on dry land. It was – after a couple of little shudders, we ran aground.

After a suitable interval Henry approached.

'Hello chaps – been a rather strange tide today. Never seen one go out so quickly. Fancy a drink?'

The mutiny was quelled and the mutineers meekly followed Henry to the cabin where he miraculously produced a bottle of Glenfiddich.

We sat in the cabin and found it quite pleasant, watching the sun change to orange as it sank towards the horizon, casting long shadows across the sandbanks, highlighting the ripples and sculptures left by the receding tide as the golden fingers of light stretched out into the approaching mists. Well, perhaps my poetic musings were brought on by the sheer ethereal quality of our surroundings – or perhaps it was the Glenfiddich.

The last plaintive cries of the seabirds echoed our plight as the sun went down and, on a more serious note, so did the Glenfiddich. The sea mist rolled in, it became dark and even Henry's fund of tall stories was beginning to dry up when I noticed a flashing light coming from the shore.

'Ah – obviously someone signalling,' said Henry. 'Mmm, I can't quite make it out. I'll ask him to repeat his message.'

Henry took out his Aldis lamp and began signalling the shore as he rattled away on the trigger. 'Ah, that seems to work,' said Henry as the light on shore ceased. There was a brief interval before a thin, piping voice came echoing across the wet sand.

'Are you stuck, mister?' It was a small boy with a torch.

Fortunately, it was a calm night and the lights of Morecambe, Silverdale and Grange reflected in the wet surface of the bay, encircling the stranded yacht like a string of sparkling jewels. The moon rose, brightening our surroundings with a cold light which illuminated another stranded yacht. That gave us some comfort, knowing that we were not the only silly sods. Henry sent a signal with his Aldis and received a prompt reply. He burst out laughing.

'It's the Howsons,' he said to Zoë.

'Oh, aren't they silly. Fancy getting stuck in the mud,' answered the bright little thing.

After a while Rose appeared from the galley with cups of tea. 'Anyone fancy some shrimps?' she asked. There were no takers.

Our imprisonment didn't seem too long and, sat near the stern looking at the silver reflection of moonlight on the faraway sea, I became aware of the soft whispering of approaching water. Looking down, I saw the gully gradually filling – the tide was turning.

The whispering slowly changed into a dull murmur, which increased in volume until it became a roar as the gullies filled and the incoming tide began racing over the wide expanse of flat sand in a small tidal wave. Suddenly, the wet desert metamorphosed into a shallow sea with choppy waves, thrashed upwards by the fast-moving current. The yacht gave a lurch and began tugging at the anchor chain, like a lively dog eager to be unleashed.

With the mist rolling in over the cold sea, Henry, once more in command, delayed moving until he knew the channel was deep enough, then he gave the order to weigh anchor. This caused Colin to scratch the deck again. Slowly, the yacht was skilfully navigated along the twisting gully until we could make out the curved end of the old wooden jetty, festooned with seaweed, with the current slapping against its timbers.

Henry took the yacht as close as he dared and gave the order to drop anchor. We watched the sea rise until it reached the walkway on top of the jetty. Henry put me in charge of the little 'pram' dinghy and asked me to begin rowing the 'crew' ashore, two at a time with the baskets of fish.

The steep curve of the jetty meant that I had to row further every time because the tide was now rising rapidly. I also had to row the dinghy against the flow to prevent being swamped as the bows were pushed up onto the wooden planks.

The mist was thickening and, by the time I had landed the crew, the tide was racing, pushing up a bow wave against the jetty and threatening to carry me off to Arnside as I fought against the strong current to pick up our gallant skipper. Henry and his basket of fish were quickly taken aboard, and we both realised that the dinghy was now no match for the strong current of this high, autumn tide.

'Let the current carry us up onto the jetty, then jump off quickly,' said Henry. I rowed diagonally from the yacht then I turned towards the jetty and let the tide take us. We approached like a mini motor boat. I stowed the oars and jumped just as the bows of the dinghy went up in the air and it slid onto the jetty. As the bows went up, the stern, complete with Henry, went down and the boat was swamped.

Soaking wet and swearing, Henry scuttled out of the dinghy and, together, we pulled it onto the jetty and secured it.

The mist had now thickened and visibility was down to a few yards by the time we made our tentative way up the old jetty. Clutching our baskets of fish in front of us, I came across three wide gaps where the old planking had rotted. Striding across on the centre spar, I shouted to Henry behind: 'Look out for . . .' I was interrupted by a grunt and a cry of 'What the bloody hell!' and Henry sat below in the sand, surrounded by flapping fish and covered in shrimps.

'Oh, Henry's fallen down a hole,' cried Zoë gleefully.

Standing on the prom, we shared out the spoils. Henry said, 'Brilliant, we must all do this again.' Colin said, 'Yes, see you in the spring,' and set off for Leeds in his A4 van with flounders flapping around his feet. It gave a new meaning to the terms 'spongy clutch,' and 'spongy brakes'.

SIX YOUNG CAVERS decided to go caving and, on a day of torrential rain when going underground should have been out of the question, they descended Providence Pot near Kettlewell. They intended to complete a through-trip by following the complicated series of passages that eventually emerges at Dow Cave on the other side of Great Whernside, an undertaking of almost a mile of difficult route-finding in a flood-prone cave.

Their decision to descend Providence Pot at 2 p.m. on Saturday 7 December 1957 was to have far-reaching consequences. After taking several wrong turns, the group reached a point approximately halfway between the caves; then things began to go wrong. The rain increased to such an extent that the torrent of floodwater pouring down Hag Dyke loosened huge boulders, causing the Providence Pot entrance to collapse under a large pile of rubble.

At Dow Cave the water spewing out of the entrance made the cave impassable. The young cavers were effectively sealed in what could be an underground tomb but, perhaps fortunately, they were unaware of this as they had more immediate problems. The water in the underground stream had risen dramatically and, struggling along the flooded passage, one member dropped a plastic bag containing watches and spare batteries into the fast-flowing stream, which carried them away.

The four youths and two girls, one only sixteen, became lost and desperately tired as they tried to find their way back and escape from the rapidly rising water. With lights almost non-existent, they managed to find refuge in a high-level chamber.

I wonder what their thoughts were – probably something along the lines of, 'Some-one will call out the rescue team, which will come looking for us.' I wonder what their thoughts would have been if they had known that both entrances were effectively sealed and that no one could come looking.

The Upper Wharfedale Fell Rescue Association team rapidly assessed the seriousness of the situation and asked the Cave Rescue Organisation to assist them, as lots of manpower would be needed. Like the effect of a pebble thrown into a pond, the vibrations reached Lancaster and I managed to contact five other cavers. We were faced with a horrendous motorcycle ride. Rain was coming down like stair-rods, the wind was blowing in 40 m.p.h. gusts and, according to our information, many of the

'Oh, Henry's fallen down a hole,' cried Zoë gleefully

roads were flooded; it was also bitterly cold. I was just about to leave when the telephone rang – Arthur Woodall's father had offered to take us in his car.

The comfort of warm, leather upholstery soon became a distant memory as, chest-deep in icy water, we fought our way upstream in Dow Cave. A large body of men was working in shifts to clear the massive blockage at Providence Pot. Meanwhile, cave divers had passed the sump in Dow Cave and reported that it might be passable with a free-dive.

Wrestling against the strong current, we were eventually faced with a blank, dripping wall with dark-brown floodwater welling up from beneath it, a liquid dome of menace. Somewhere under it lay a passage that, under normal conditions, could be passed with a short 'duck' – a few feet of face-in-the-water gurgling. However, the rescue team faced the prospect of standing back, up to the chest in water, then diving down against a strong flow of water, locating the submerged passage and swimming its full length against the force of the flood.

None of us knew the cave. I was the leader and I wished I was at home in bed. Wearing my bright yellow goon suit under my overalls, I took a deep breath, dived and battled against the buoyancy of the air trapped in my suit, only to return to the surface with much coughing and spitting, having achieved nothing. I opened the neck seal of the survival suit, crouched in the water and forced out all the air.

Clutching a plastic bag, which contained food for the trapped cavers, I dived again. Working my way down the rock wall I located the flooded passage and forced my way into it. Half-swimming, half-pushing my way with my feet, I struggled in a swirl-ing, silent nightmare of brown water. I noticed that a small stalactite in the roof of the passage remained in the same position, no matter how hard I tried, and I realised that I was not moving. I was on the verge of drowning as the last bubbles of air exhaled from my tortured lungs. I grabbed the stalactite and pulled and kicked my way forward, swallowing water. My groping hand felt the roof rise; it was suddenly grasped and I was bodily dragged up, retching and coughing, by Ken Pearce, one of the cave divers.

The cursed plastic bag, which had contributed to my near demise, was full of soggy sandwiches and chocolate bars, floating in a soup of wrappers, paste and crumbs. I was sick.

More problems lay ahead. I had never met Hardy and I'm sure I never will, and I will never learn what the horror was that lurked in the submerged tube ahead called Hardy's Horror. It was impassable and the only alternative lay twenty feet higher, in the roof of a very tight, smooth-walled crack. Eight cavers forced a way through the flooded duck, but only two of us managed to climb this difficult chimney.

I remember a sharp, pointed rock on which I balanced on one foot while reaching out over the stream to scrabble for a handhold, before leaping into space and straining frantically to jam my body between those smooth, greasy walls. I hung there, panting for breath, before fighting my way upwards.

A small bedding plane continued against the roof of the passage and I hung on there while Tom Sykes, the only other survivor of my rescue team, joined me. Surrounded by mist, Tom grappled his way up. 'I'm bloody knackered,' he said. 'These fuckin' plastic bags don't help.'

I agreed and began working my way along the traverse which lay ahead; it was reputed to be the worst in the country and was indeed called the Terrible Traverse. The brief description we had been given was on the conservative side, because we were soon floundering in a widening rift where the few small holds became non-existent. Below us, the smooth walls belled out and we could plainly see the roaring white water of the stream thirty feet below. One slip, and that would be it.

With feet on one wall and shoulders on the other, swinging those cursed plastic bags of slosh beneath us, we progressed slowly, a foot at a time. I thought we were too high, as the walls were unmarked, but I couldn't see a viable route down, apart from falling off.

The way ahead looked impossible, until a slight bulge in the wall gave purchase to a shallow recess and then a wider section, and so on. The smooth, black walls continued interminably and the holds disappeared, yet we continued; I was convinced that I couldn't possibly fall off – a sort of 'walking on water' syndrome. I had become psychologically immune to the drop below, when I noticed a general widening beneath us. We seemed to be in the roof of a chamber and I thought I detected movement.

'It must be the kids,' 1 thought and shouted down. I received no reply.

'This must be Brew Chamber,' said Tom. This was the place where local experts reasoned the trapped cavers might be. Tom also thought he detected movement down near the stream, so we took turns in shouting.

Nothing. We were whistling in the wind. The only answer we received was the mocking echo of our own voices and the dull, ominous rumbling of the stream. The walls we clung to eventually became too far apart: we were too high and would have to retrace our 'steps' and find a lower traverse which could take us down. Our lights were fading and so was my companion; he suddenly slipped and scrabbled desperately for a hold on the featureless walls.

'Drop the bag, Tom,' I shouted. 'Drop the fuckin' bag.' He did, and I traversed above him and pulled him back up from the featureless void.

We were both very tired and realised that becoming two more casualties would not endear us to the rest of the rescue team, so we retreated, almost feeling our way along that awful traverse.

There is nothing in this world so comforting as the light of another caver when you are tired, cold, knackered and lightless, even when it was Randy Coe, one of the Craven.

'Here, get this down you,' he said, offering us a hot drink, 'and chuck that bloody rubbish away.' He dumped my plastic bag of mashed-up goodies into the stream.

'Have they found them?' I asked.

'No,' said Randy. 'Here, have a fag.'

After a cigarette and a rest Tom and I slid down the chimney and dived into the flooded duck, allowing the floodwater to flush us out the other end. It was much easier than when we entered. Passing other cavers heading inwards, we eventually emerged into the light of day. With ice forming on our saturated clothing, and staggering with the gait of the physically exhausted, we were stopped by two reporters. One panned a camera on our homely, frost-covered visages while the other asked, 'Have you been in the cave?'

'What a fuckin' stupid question. Piss off,' said Tom.

Later that day the Providence Pot team managed to open a precarious gap between the loose blocks and two rescue groups began the search. The rain stopped and, with the floodwaters dropping, more rescuers were able to enter Dow Cave. A local hostel crammed with 150 rescuers resembled a field hospital as men tried to snatch a few hours of sleep. We joined them, after first being attended to by those lovely ladies in the Women's Voluntary Service.

The 'gentlemen' of the press were, on this occasion, a complete pain in the arse. They commandeered all the available accommodation and blocked the telephone lines, and one prat even went round the hostel taking photographs of sleeping cavers, until he was unfortunate enough to pop off a flashbulb in the face of John L. who, like his namesake, packed a considerable punch. They say the reporter was unconscious before he hit the floor.

The trapped cavers were eventually rescued at 11 p.m. on the Monday night, after spending 57 hours underground. The rescue generated a great deal of sensational press coverage and it was the first time that a rescue was reported on television. The incident was highlighted later that evening when, throughout the land, a silent black-and-white picture of two bedraggled cavers staggering jerkily towards the camera appeared on household screens.

'Eh, you're on telly,' said Tom's wife. 'You don't look too happy – what were you saying?'

THE TENSE DRAMA acted out on the Dow–Providence rescue was the forerunner of many more. The fifty-seven hours' duration of the rescue, plus the additional ingredients of rockfalls, floods and the fact that young people were involved, especially two girls, was manna from heaven for the reporters. Instead of putting the young and adventurous off caving, not unnaturally the media exposure made them all the more keen to be involved in such adventure – especially as the press, which now had the added sensationalism of television, portrayed the victims as heroes.

The real heroes of cave rescue mostly go unobserved, suffering discomfort and risking life and limb to save lives, then, after a protracted rescue such as this, return to work to find that in reward for their public-spirited, selfless act, they are greeted not with a handshake but with their P45 (the sack). I was, fortunately, self-employed so only lost money, and when I returned to work to find my customers still covered in dust sheets, they never complained. I was always treated as a hero and given extra biscuits with my tea. 'Seen you on telly, ooo – don't you ever get frightened?'

Being a self-employed decorator provided me with a fascinating insight into people's lives and, in many instances, I became a friend as well as a father confessor, a confidant and counsellor as they regaled me with their hopes and fears over morning coffee. It was tea in the poorer households, where some dear little old lady had often been baking cakes especially for me. Some unfortunate children grew up with me while I decorated for their parents, and then for them as they became married. I met some very interesting people – and some very strange ones.

A psychiatrist needed my services but, instead of me going to his house to look at the work required, he insisted that I went to his office. 'Perhaps he thinks your head needs looking at,' chortled my wife.

'Come in Mister Eyre,' called the voice. I entered the room and stood looking at the chap sitting behind the desk with his eyes shut. He never opened his eyes all the time he was talking to me, which I put down to normal psychiatric behaviour. This became really weird when he began looking at the colour cards and pattern books with his eyes shut. It became even weirder when, halfway through decorating his lounge, he suddenly decided that paying me a shilling a roll for wallpapering was too much and he was going to deduct something from the account 'because I was working so fast'.

Brother, you had to work fast sticking paper on for a shilling a roll!

The psychiatrist was most astonished and his long-suffering wife – who seemed quite normal – had hysterics when I opened the window, threw out the remaining six rolls of wallpaper and all my equipment, then drove off leaving his room half-decorated and him with no chance of obtaining the same wallpaper again. Now *that* opened his eyes.

I returned home early and said to Rose, 'You were right, I do need my head looking at. I don't work for any more psychiatrists.'

After this incident I steered clear of the psychiatric profession, but bumped into a mad professor. I should have known he was mad when I first went to see him. He looked mad. Well, strange. He stood in the doorway of his house looking at me through thick glasses and said, 'Hello, who are you?'

'I'm the decorator.'

'Yes, what do you want?'

'You telephoned me.'

'Did I? Hmm.'

'I'm Mr Eyre.'

'Ah – you've come to fix the leak.'

'No, I'm a decorator.'

'Oh. You don't do leaks?'

'No.'

'I suppose you had better come in then,' he said. I should have turned and run.

I followed the slight, diminutive figure into his large, well-decorated house – from what I could see of it, for every room was stacked almost to the ceiling with large cardboard boxes.

'Have you just moved in?' I asked.

'No, I've been here fifteen years,' answered the little chap.

'Oh.' Some people are naturally slow at unpacking. I didn't dare ask what was in the boxes – probably dead decorators.

He took me upstairs past all the unfurnished rooms, up a narrow staircase to a small attic where paper was literally hanging off the ceiling and was draped across a desk. Cobwebs almost obscured the daylight filtering through the small skylight, and the floor was thick with old flakes of whitewash which had peeled off the ceiling and walls.

'This is my office,' he proudly announced. 'I think it could do with a lick of paint.'

This must have been the understatement of the year. I wondered if I had stumbled onto a *Candid Camera* programme on the telly and looked closely at the little man, who peered at me intently from behind his thick glasses. No, I didn't recognise him – he must be genuine.

The outside of his house also needed some repairs and repainting. The professor was completely useless at doing anything practical, so I began to feel sorry for him and I took myself off to the local do-it-yourself merchant, bought the materials and did the repairs before starting painting. I gave him the list of materials I had purchased; he looked at it and asked me to add up the cost. I thought he was joking and burst out laughing, until he explained that he couldn't add it up because he 'didn't do that sort of maths'. He only dealt with abstruse forms of abstract numerics.

I had me a rare bird indeed – a mad maths professor who couldn't add up a shopping list. I told him how much he owed and waited with bated breath to see if he

This is my office. I think it could do with a lick of paint

understood what money was. He didn't. 'Oh, I never deal in money. Can I write you a cheque?'

I snatched it from his quivering hand before the ink was dry and zoomed to the bank to ensure that he was solvent before painting the outside of the house.

A large Irish lady used to call in twice a week, 'To look after the poor wee soul,' as she put it. 'He can't even boil water,' she said. Over a cup of tea she informed me that the prof was harmless, but 'as mad as a march hare – completely daft – though up at the uni' they think he's bloody brilliant.'

Assisted by the professor and his helper, we struggled down the narrow attic staircase with his heavy filing cabinets. I pulled off the dangling paper and washed off the old whitewash, ready for decorating. Down in the kitchen I discovered the professor trying to boil a kettle without lighting the gas; the place was thick with gas fumes. I asked him for a sweeping brush and shovel.

'What for?'

'To sweep up the mess,' I replied. He looked at me very strangely.

'There shouldn't be any mess. What have you done?' Not bothering to answer, I took the brush and shovel, went back to the attic and began clearing up. Suddenly, I felt a presence and looked up to see the professor glaring at me.

'What have you done?' he yelled in a high-pitched, quavering voice. 'I didn't want the paper taken off!' and he came tearing across the room and snatched the brush from me. I was flabbergasted (this is not a word I use often). 'I wanted you to paint over it,' said the irate little man. I realised that I was dealing with a strange person and carefully explained that it is very difficult to paint over wallpaper when it is swinging in the breeze.

'I never told you to take it off,' he yelled as I retrieved the brush and carried on cleaning up. 'What are you going to do about it?' I glanced up and saw a creature completely demented. His eyes behind the thick glasses were rolling around like ping-pong balls in a bingo caller's machine. His stiffened body was shaking violently.

'Well, one thing's for sure,' said I, trying to introduce some levity into the proceedings, 'I can't stick it back on!' He obviously had no sense of humour because, intent on what I was doing, I never noticed him turning into a miniature Bela Lugosi until I felt something at my neck. I looked down and there was this mini-vampire hanging onto my throat, his eyes now spinning round like marbles in a glass dish.

It was ludicrous. I lifted him down, placed him in a corner and said slowly and clearly. 'Now, I'm going to clean up and go, and I'm not going to charge you, do you understand?'

'You can't leave me,' he yelled and turned into Bela Lugosi again, once more launching himself at my throat. I caught him in full flight, carried him down the stairs and gave him the address of the psychiatrist I had just worked for. I went home, poured a stiff whisky and said to the wife: 'Add mad professors to the list.'

I needed to relax. I picked up the phone and contacted one of my old regulars, then zoomed off to Hest Bank to do a job for old Andrew. He was an old Scot who

There was this mini-vampire hanging onto my throat

lived in South Africa for years and had a South African wife. They were two of the most interesting people I have ever met. She used to tell me stories about the Transvaal, about how her ancestors lived, and every day at 4.30 p.m. they would make me stop whatever I was doing with the cry, 'It's sundowners' time, Jim.' Then they would bring out the malt whisky and old Andrew would recount his exploits from the First World War, when he was a pilot. It was fascinating stuff, as he was a real-life Biggles.

The pilots in those days were incredible. Planes were held together with cloth and string and the only armaments were handguns; aerial combat with the Germans meant shooting at each other with pistols!

I don't know whether it was the whisky or the fascinating stories, but listening to how Andrew shot down observer balloons over the trenches was unforgettable. He had become a pilot because he was in the cavalry, and when the first planes came out the top brass reckoned that anyone who could ride a horse should be able to fly a plane. It was no big deal, they were simple machines, said Andrew, and all you had to do was get rid of the balloons that were directing the German gunfire.

The trouble was that shooting at a balloon with a pistol wasn't very effective, because to hit the balloon you had to fly very close and the balloon sites were always ringed with anti-aircraft guns. Then, if you did hit the balloon the pistol bullet went straight through, 'Doing about as much damage as a bee sting,' as Andrew put it. You therefore had to try to shoot the poor bugger crouching in the wicker basket below, while the crew on the ground furiously wound the balloon down.

'Here, have another dram, Jim,' and I would end up driving home three sheets to the wind, to use an old nautical expression.

I had lots of customers like this. Unbelievably, one of the old boys had been a gold miner in the Klondike. When I said he was pulling my leg he gave me a booklet he had written about his experiences, under the pen name Wanderlust. Another old codger owned property all over Morecambe and seemed a typical money-grabbing landlord, until I got to know him better. He lived in a lovely house in the Lyth Valley in the Lake District and one day, when he was feeling expansive, we sat down on his porch overlooking a wonderful view of the bay. Over a couple of beers he told me how, in his younger days, he was a hobo (a tramp) and spent many years riding the rails across the States and Canada. He had served time in jail, had stowed away on board ship to avoid capture by the police, and sailed from Vancouver to Japan – then as a crewman to Australia, where he made his money, and eventually ended up in Morecambe, paying me to decorate for him.

He didn't know that one of his properties was being used as a brothel. I was working at a house doing some work on the staircase when a door opened and a young lady popped her head out and said 'Would you like a cup of tea, love?' I answered, 'Yes,' in a very faint voice when I realised a very ample breast had also popped out of her open dressing gown. She beckoned me in and sat me down at the table as she busied herself with the teapot, floating to and fro with her dressing gown wide open and not a stitch on underneath. With tea and cakes laid out before me, she stood there and gave me a sweet smile and asked, 'Is there anything else you would like, love?'

Looking at her pubic hairs, which were dark, bushy, curly and about three inches from my nose, I answered faintly, 'No thanks, love.'

The hairs nudged closer, until I could smell bath salts and soap. 'Why,' she said in a teasing voice as my teacup began rattling in my saucer, 'you're trembling.'

A FEW YEARS LATER I was decorating in London, making money faster than I could spend it as people kept throwing wads of the stuff at me. However, London town was not my idea of fun and I asked my wife to come down as I needed a good meal. Once my reputation was established, I worked for artists, musicians, doctors of all descriptions, singers, opera and otherwise. One lovely lady once sang with Duke Ellington and his band, not much in the scheme of things but one that I found exciting, especially when she sang to me and rolled her big, dark eyes.

Another of my regular customers was a dentist. A huge shopping complex was being built next to his surgery and one night I received an urgent telephone call, followed by the arrival of a builder, who took me to a meeting with the developers. They were piledriving beside the surgery and cracks were appearing in the surgery walls. The assessors were coming the following day and would probably stop the operation, unless I could camouflage the cracks to appear less severe than they were. 'You can name your own price,' they said.

I spent the long night plastering up cracks that were widening by the minute, as the building shook and groaned with every thud of the piledriver. It was ridiculous, for it was obvious to me that the building was going to fall down, because the cracks became wider and wider. The big boss kept popping his head in and hastily withdrawing it. I kept telling him that it was futile and that the building was going to fall down. 'You're okay, lad, you're doing a good job. We've got the lads shoring it up.'

Half an hour after his visit the building gave a groan. The top storey's main crack, which was now two inches wide, opened up another inch! I flew down the staircase without touching it and joined the group outside, which had just manoeuvred a huge baulk of timber into position.

'It's alright now, we've cracked it,' said the man, and I reluctantly returned indoors just as the piledrivers began again, making the whole building move as though it was on a waterbed. The cracks had all opened up again and they gave me an Irish labourer to mix the plaster while I furiously chucked it into the cracks before skimming them over.

'Oh bejabbers, this is bloody dangerous. We'll be like them there Egyptian mummies if this lot goes,' said Paddy.

As daylight appeared, the building looked like a patchwork quilt. What was obviously a very important group of people ascended the stairs, looked at Paddy and me covered in plaster and looked at the horrendous display of structural cracks which no amount of plaster could hide. They had a hurried conference, thanked me and said I could go home. With the familiar refrain of 'name your own price', the piledrivers started up again.

'You aren't going to charge all that for one night's work?' Rose exclaimed. So I knocked a bit off and went to see the man. 'This is no good,' he said, 'double it.'

That's the trouble with workers like me, brought up with the maxim of a fair day's work for a fair day's pay– we don't know how to overcharge, even when we're told to.

Chapter 14

Digs and Disasters

CAVE EXPLORATION is one of the few areas where it is possible for the average person to experience the ultimate thrill of seeing something no one has ever seen before, and entering a newly discovered cave or cave passage for the first time is almost like being born into a new dimension. Glistening stalactites and flowstone cascades are brought to life as your light probes ahead, highlighting the dark recesses and unexplored passages that lie beyond, awaiting your entry into a part of the world that is yours. This is your domain; you are the lord of all you survey.

After the initial, frenzied exploration there comes an insatiable desire to photograph the new discovery. However, once I entered the strange world of the cave photographer, I realised that the one essential factor it required was one thing I lacked: patience.

We had a brilliant photographer in the club: Ron Bliss. He was not very popular with the rest of us because he insisted on suspending his models (us) on ladders under waterfalls – or making us lie full-length in cold pools or crouched in abject fear under loose boulders – trying to look as though we were enjoying it.

Ron took me under his wing and showed me the rudiments of cave photography, which in those days of flashpowder was fairly basic, mainly knowing how much powder to use for a particular shot. Together we did a practice 'shoot' on some stalactite formations in a stream passage we had found. Ron set up his camera on a tripod – I, not owning such a device, stuck my camera on a ledge with the aid of a blob of mud. We both poured out the appropriate pile of flashpowder, lit the touchpaper, switched off our lights and opened the camera shutter before, in total darkness, fumbling our way out of range.

I could just make out my touchpaper spluttering and fizzing – then nothing. Ron had taken his picture and shouted for me to relight my fuse. I groped back and leaned over the pile of powder, just as it gave a faint splutter and went off with a tremendous bang and a flare of brilliant white light. I was blown backwards, minus sight, eyebrows and moustache; my camera was ejected from the ledge into the stream.

By the time I had stopped shaking and smoked two fags, amid the pungent smell of burnt hair, my eyesight had returned and I decided to leave cave photography to Ron for a while. This was fortunate for me, because on our next caving trip we almost lost Ron.

The upper series of Lancaster Hole contains many holes and rifts that drop into the stream passage, a long way below. Ron was set to take a photograph and had three of us lined up as models in front of a glorious bank of flowstone.

'Lights out,' commanded our photographer. We sat in pitch blackness watching Ron, silhouetted by the flare of a match as he lit the touchpaper. Wishing to appear on the photograph, Ron gave a brief flash with his light to find his bearings, then scrambled across to us in complete darkness. I thought I heard a grunt just before the flashpowder went off in a dazzling flare.

Jim Eyre (left), Harry Bewes, Peter Kitchen and Harry Saunders in Ron Bliss' first underground photo, taken in Montagu West Passage on 11 June 1950 during one of the Red Rose pirate trips into Lancaster Hole

Having sat in the dark for a while, I asked Ron if we could switch our lights back on, but received no reply. Cautiously shading my light from the camera lens, I switched on. Ron had vanished, just like a stage magician, gone in a puff of his own smoke.

'Strange,' said Ray.

'Funny,' said Tom.

'I wonder if it's something I said,' I remarked as we shone our lights around the cavern. 'It's not like Ron to go off like that, especially in the dark.'

Then we became aware of a faint wailing noise, which seemed to emanate from behind a large rock. We wandered around the back, but couldn't see anything that would account for the wailing. Then we heard it again, like a banshee with toothache, coming from a small funnel-shaped depression beneath our feet. The funnel led to a small, black hole and the wailing came from there. Looking down, I saw a light and our very bemused photographer, who we eventually retrieved.

Fortunately for Ron he had picked the right hole to fall down – an adjacent hole, two feet away, dropped sheer to the stream passage sixty feet below.

Later, as I became more proficient in underground photography, I became the proud owner of several cave photographs showing stalagmites leaning drunkenly, a close-up of a piece of rock which resembled a moonscape, three stalactites taken in a fog, a caver's left leg, and three indistinct figures seemingly struck by lightning. In spite of all this, word had spread round my relatives that I was a sort of cross between Lord Snowdon and Lord Lichfield in the art of portrait photography, and my dear mother had promised Auntie Doris that I would take the official photographs at the christening party of Doris' latest offspring.

Having been fog-bound in a cave for three hours when we filled it with thick smoke from end to end, I was quite pleased when my local photographer announced that a new 'smokeless' flashpowder had arrived on the scene and, with this in my possession, full of confidence I arrived at the christening. I arranged everyone around the table where, standing in the centre on a brilliant white tablecloth, stood a large christening cake, resplendent in ornate white icing.

Around this masterpiece lay bowls of trifle, glistening jellies, cakes piled on glass stands, a silver tea service and brilliant white china cups (borrowed from Auntie Alice). Everything glistened and sparkled – it would make a lovely picture. I sat the doting parents, complete with baby in a dazzling white christening gown, in the centre foreground of the small dining room and asked Uncle Walter to draw the curtains.

'Ee, I've never heard of that before,' said Auntie Gladys. 'I've been to lots of christenings and we've never been asked to sit in the dark.'

'Oh, this a new technique,' I muttered as I carefully measured out the correct amount of 'smokeless' powder, set up the camera, opened the shutter and said, 'Smile, and don't move,' as I lit the touchpaper.

The paper fizzled and spluttered, and suddenly there was a mighty whoosh. The room was lit in a stark white glare, freezing the fixed smiles and staring eyes for ever. There was an unearthly yowl from the cat, which flew at the curtains and clung to Auntie Doris' best velvet with its hairs standing on end. The baby started screaming, Auntie Gladys started coughing and Uncle Walter (always good in an emergency) opened the curtains to reveal a scene of desolation.

What daylight that could filter through revealed a room filled with smoke and a fine drizzle of ash, which covered the baby, the cakes, jellies, tablecloth, trifles, the glorious christening cake and all the people in a fine charcoal texture.

I half expected everyone to start singing 'Way down upon de Swannee Ribber,' and broke into uncontrollable laughter as cries of rage, shock and 'Open the window, open the back door,' rang out while they all rushed outside and stood in the yard. It was like a Laurel and Hardy comedy and, still laughing, I hastily began putting my camera and the 'smokeless' flashpowder away.

'You, you, you bloody idiot,' said Auntie Doris, trying to soothe her sooty baby and flick dust off its now grey christening gown. Big Taffy, her husband, threatened to punch me on the nose, until I soothed him by telling him that 'It would be a brilliant picture.'

'How could it be, man, we'll all be covered in bloody soot. We'll all look like bloody coal miners!'

In the end I managed to convince everyone that the photograph would be wonderful and they all set about trying to remove the ash from the food. I suggested that cutting

The paper fizzled and spluttered, and suddenly there was a mighty whoosh

the top off the jelly would help: 'Consider the little black bits among the little coloured balls as little black balls of liquorice or something, and blow on the mince pies before you eat them.'

My dear mother exploded. 'You've shown me up – you're a disgrace to our family,' and she turned to Auntie Doris: 'Our Jimmy's always been bloody daft – it's all that bloody potholing that's affected his brain!' She took a swing at me but, thanks to years of experience, I ducked at the right moment, hastily departed, jumped on my bike and shot off in a cloud of blue smoke.

The photograph *was* brilliant! Tommy Steele later sang a hit song titled *Flash Bang Wallop*, which went: 'Oh, what a picture! What a picture! What a photograph! Rum tiddley um bum, bum, bum, bum, stick it in your fam-lee album.'

Boom boom.

IN MARCH 1959 a caving tragedy unfurled in a slow build-up of unforeseeable events. I overheard a news bulletin about a caver trapped in a Derbyshire cave, but took little notice until a later report confirmed that no rescue had been achieved. I rang up Reg Hainsworth, leader of the Cave Rescue Organisation in the Dales; he told me that he was in touch with the Derbyshire police and had offered the services of the CRO, but they seemed to think that the rescue could be resolved by local volunteers. Nevertheless, Reg placed all CRO members on standby.

The countdown to disaster had begun at 1 p.m. on Sunday 22 March, when a small group of cavers went underground to explore a new extension in Peak Cavern. The narrow, twisting shaft, which had been discovered two weeks previously, lay in the wall of a chamber at the end of a long, muddy crawl. Climbing up from the miserable hands-and-knees crawl of Pickering's Passage, the group lowered seventy-five feet of ladder down the shaft, which had been explored to forty feet and was known to continue. Neil Moss, a young twenty-year-old caver, volunteered to try to descend further.

At 3.30 p.m. Neil forced himself down the restricted shaft, kicking the surplus ladder in front of him. He had no difficulty sliding down the ladders as the mud on his overalls acted as a lubricant. He landed on a pile of loose rock and excess ladder, and shouted up that he might be able to push the loose rocks down the shaft and clear the way. After struggling for some time he managed to move a few of the rocks but, unfortunately, in doing so he jammed the loose ladder below him. Assisted from above, he tried to free it and managed to move the rock with his feet, but only succeeded in further jamming the ladder. After more struggling Neil shouted up that he was tired and that he would come up to let someone else have a go.

After ten minutes Neil had not appeared and it became apparent that he was having difficulty in climbing the elliptical tube. The ladder rungs were spaced a foot apart and, being six feet tall and fairly well built, Neil found that the restricted shaft (which was eighteen inches wide at its widest) prevented him from raising his leg high enough to place his foot on the next rung.

The group had not taken a rope with them and a difficult situation was developing, which the inexperienced young caver could not cope with. He soon tired more and, standing on a ladder rung, he asked the five cavers above if they could pull up the ladder with him on it. He was raised a few feet, then he jammed.

Two of the team climbed into the top section of the shaft, where it twisted down an inclined bedding, and tried to assist Neil from there. During the struggle they saw that Neil's helmet-mounted carbide lamp – which burned acetylene gas to produce a small flame in a reflector – was nearly out. The air was becoming foul and one of the lads began to feel ill, so he returned to the chamber above to be joined later by his friend, leaving Neil alone, apparently stuck, lightless and weak from his exertions to free himself.

The six cavers in the chamber realised that they had a very serious problem on their hands, so one hurried back to obtain a handline from a climb further back in the cave. The old hemp rope was lowered to Neil by a caver lying in the inclined bedding directly above the stricken youth, and he was told to tie it round his body. Neil replied that he couldn't pass the line round his body, as the shaft was too constricted. Leaning out from the bedding, one of the group managed to tie the rope to a ladder rung, hoping to pull the ladder free. With five men at the top and one in the shaft, they heaved on the rope which, being old, broke and sent the men above sprawling.

Again a rope end was lowered to Neil, this time tied in a loop. Neil managed to place it under his arms and the men above pulled, raising the hapless victim for a few feet before the rope broke again. Neil, who must have been extremely weak by this time, slid back down the shaft. The broken end was lowered once more, Neil tied the two ends together, but as soon as pressure was applied from above, the rope again broke.

It was now over four hours since the party had entered the cave; Neil had been trapped in the shaft for two hours. The situation continued to deteriorate while two of the group rushed out of the cave for assistance. Another attempt to pull Neil free ended with him jamming again and the rope breaking.

The air in the shaft was now heavily polluted with carbon dioxide, and Neil's behaviour became irrational as the bulk of his body cut off what slight flow of air there might have been. His carbide lamp further depleted the oxygen before going out.

At 6.45 p.m. the Derbyshire Cave Rescue Organisation was alerted and one of Neil's team-mates returned with two ropes and more men. At 7.15 p.m. the Castleton police were alerted and an hour later two cavers entered the shaft and struggled along the downward-sloping bedding. They pushed the new rope down towards Neil, who unfortunately could not respond as he had lapsed into unconsciousness.

Two more attempts were made to help the victim, which resulted in one caver being hauled out of the upper shaft in a state of collapse due to the effects of carbon dioxide. During the sequence of events thus far it had not even been thought necessary to initiate a full Derbyshire callout, or to even to alert the CRO, which was the most experienced cave rescue team in Britain and only two hours' drive away.

It was past 10 p.m. before the police were contacted with urgent requests for oxygen and a hose. A full-scale Derbyshire CRO callout then ensued. With Neil unconscious and the shaft totally polluted with carbon dioxide, the situation was almost hopeless; there was nothing anyone could do except wait for oxygen bottles in the mistaken belief that releasing it down the shaft would revive the unconscious caver and clear away the carbon dioxide.

The first oxygen arrived just after midnight on Monday morning and a desperate attempt was made by a caver going into the shaft on a line, alternately breathing oxygen from an open bottle and then lowering it down the shaft towards the unconscious caver below. Several attempts were made, all to no avail.

The system of rescue callout in the Derbyshire area was new and untested in a serious situation. It was a foggy night, few of the team were on the phone and the local police were unable to cope – and all this time CRO team members were kicking their heels while Reg Hainsworth kept trying to obtain information about what was going on. Most of us were awake all night, waiting for a call.

At 1.25 a.m. the Derbyshire CRO secretary informed the police that all available men had been called out, but reliefs were urgently needed. Reg and the Settle police found it difficult to determine what was happening and we debated whether we should head for the Peak District without an official callout. Then, eventually, Reg managed to contact someone at the scene and a strong CRO team left for Castleton.

At five in the morning a lightly built caver wearing the minimum of clothing and breathing directly from an oxygen bottle made a determined attempt to reach Neil, but had to be pulled out in a distressed condition. At seven in the morning the police initiated bulletins on BBC radio and television to try to contact more cavers, as the manpower shortage was now desperate.

At noon on Monday, Ron Peters made another attempt to descend the shaft. Breathing oxygen from a rubber tube held in his teeth, he managed to tie another rope to the broken one that was still around Neil. After this gallant attempt, Ron was hauled out and collapsed on reaching the chamber.

Arriving at Castleton we found chaos. Literally hundreds of cavers and reporters were hanging about outside the cave, the village was blocked solid with sightseer's cars and everywhere there seemed total confusion, with no one in charge. We waited impatiently as Reg Hainsworth tried to find out what was happening and, still unclear of the situation, several of us picked up oxygen and compressed air bottles and followed other cavers, floundering in a slowly moving human jam as we struggled through the thick, glutinous mud of Pickering's Passage.

Reaching the chamber, a feeling of futility and resignation struck us immediately. A wire ladder and taught rope hung in the elliptical fissure in the wall of the chamber and the walls,

The last rescuers to leave Peak Cavern after the death of Neil Moss: Jim (left), with Ron Penhale and Michael Booth

ladder and rope were smothered in mud. Below us, the ladder and rope twisted down until they reached an indistinct, muddy blockage that was Neil Moss.

Listening intently, we could hear Neil's faint, laboured breathing. We tried to move the ladder and pulled on the rope, but were told that he was firmly jammed in an immovable position, with an arm forced into a recess under a ladder rung in the efforts to free him. I looked around at the mud-covered cavers and faces of men who had struggled and lost all hope, and I felt the air of despondency that hung over the chamber. Everything had been tried to release the unfortunate caver clinging to life far below us, and everything had failed.

But we were fresh and felt we should try again, so we opened a compressed air bottle and lowered it down the shaft to blow out the poisonous mixture, then unfastened the rope and ladder and slackened them off to allow a lightly built caver to go down. He tried to push the unconscious victim lower with his feet, out of the narrow bottleneck in which he had become tightly jammed.

However, it was impossible to move Neil from the cavern's vice-like grip and the distraught volunteer was pulled up. In sheer desperation, we started excavating lower down the slope in the chamber, in the hope that a crack or small connecting fissure could be enlarged enough to enable us to enter the rift below Neil. We felt better doing something and were soon tearing the chamber apart, until we hit large blocks which needed blasting – in the circumstances, that was out of the question.

It had been raining incessantly all day and we were told that we could become trapped by rising water and were ordered to withdraw. Men started to make their weary way out. As we waited I sat at the top of the shaft, together with an RAF doctor. We listened to the vague sound of increasingly laboured breathing before leaving the chamber and its faint spark of human life, trapped in its cold embrace.

Outside Peak Cavern the morbid crowds, enquiring reporters, glory seekers and listless groups of cavers created a macabre atmosphere that I likened to the tragedy of Floyd Collins, an American hillbilly who became trapped while exploring Kentucky's Sand Cave in 1925. Floyd became a celebrity as tourists gathered in beer tents and around fairground attractions, waiting for his rescue or death; sadly, it turned out to be the latter.

The threat of the cave passage flooding proved to be a false alarm and a small group of us returned with the doctor, Flt. Lt. Carter. We sat for some time listening silently to the faint sound of laboured breathing that whispered up the shaft before it faltered and then finally stopped. Neil Moss, a brave young caver, was dead.

This was the first time we had failed to retrieve a fellow caver, injured or dead, and we all experienced a great feeling of sadness and a sense of failure as we emerged from Peak Cavern carrying an empty stretcher.

There have been many reappraisals of the Neil Moss tragedy. Would the outcome have been any different if the CRO had been called out immediately? Perhaps, but with hindsight the crucial factor that decided the outcome, and which none of us realised at the time, was the fact that it only took two or three hours before Neil was overcome by the foul air, and in that time his friends were powerless without a decent rope. If Neil had been more experienced, in the very early stages he could possibly have been talked out of the situation, when he was still fairly strong, by encouraging him to raise his body weight on his arms alone. This might have been enough to bring him past the tight section, which may have allowed the slight air current to keep flowing while a decent rope was obtained and two rope stirrups were lowered for his feet, allowing his eventual haul upwards and release.

This is all conjecture, but some years later a caver in an almost identical situation was rescued from a Yorkshire pothole when he was trapped beyond a bottleneck in bad air. Divers' bottles were used to purge the area of bad air, the trapped caver changed his wetsuit for a polythene bag with neck- and armholes cut in it to reduce friction and, with the aid of two foot-stirrups and a rope around his chest, he was gradually eased out inch by inch – screaming and kicking, but alive!

The Peak tragedy left me feeling depressed and the act of sealing the narrow shaft with rocks, turning it into Neil Moss's tomb, is something that I shall always remember. However, as a direct result of the incident the Derbyshire CRO was reorganised and a better system of communications was established between the country's various groups, police and local authorities. It saw the beginning of a more comprehensive national rescue system.

MANILA AND HEMP ROPES, with their constant history of breaking (the rotten rope was a significant factor in the Neil Moss tragedy), were discontinued as new man-made fibre ropes became available. However, the material that really changed caving was neoprene. Almost overnight this light rubber, honeycombed with small air cells, revolutionised the sport.

I saw some neoprene advertised and rushed out to spend a few quid on a brown paper pattern and several sheets of this weird stuff. Helped by Rose, I soon made a primitive suit which I powdered with her talcum powder – you had to, due to its inherent friction. I struggled into the suit. Rose had hysterics and couldn't stop laughing: 'You look like a member of the Oomegoolie tribe, suffering from malnutrition.'

I walked around the garden in my suit and the lady next door, who was hanging her washing out, gave a scream of horror, broke her washing line and tripped over her washing basket. Her large Alsatian dog came halfway through the hedge, growling furiously and intent on protecting its mistress from the black marauder from Planet X.

When our neighbour recovered she said ,'You look a right bugger in that – I always thought you were kinky!'

I took the suit for a test drive in Cow Dub, a cold, black sink in Ease Gill where, watched by my fellow cavers, who were waiting for me to either sink or die of exposure being clad only in my black shroud, the suit proved a success. I felt surprisingly warm.

After my demonstration the Yorkshire Dales were soon covered in black, matchstick men who laughed at wet caves. Wet pitches were there purely to stop us overheating. Cave exploration increased in leaps and bounds and what was previously thought impossible now became probable, as tight squeezes were overcome and low, wet crawls were pushed to extremes, often revealing new caves.

There are always drawbacks to every new discovery and some cavers simply refused to believe that it was possible to swim in a wetsuit while carrying two metal ladders and wearing boots and a heavy miner's battery pack. My mate Kevin was one. While caving in Wales, I discovered to my total amazement that this staunch buddy of mine had followed me into Dan yr Ogof clutching two large, empty plastic water bottles.

'What do you want the plastic water bottles for, Kevin?'

'The Green Canal – these are flotation devices,' answered my favourite Yorkshireman somewhat brusquely as he lit another fag.

'Don't be ridiculous, you can't sink in a wetsuit,' I said, making a grab at his bottles.

'I can, and if you try to take them off me, I shall modify your nose,' said Kev, turning ugly. He was bigger than I was and there's nothing worse than a man deprived of his water bottles, so I desisted – until we reached the Green Canal.

We entered the water like black seals – all except Kevin that is, who enjoyed his last cigarette as though he was going 'over the top'. Clinging to his plastic bottles, he entered the water like Aphrodite with lead boots. Soon, we were all swimming along and I turned to Kevin as I floated on my back.

'See, it's impossible to sink in a wetsuit,' I said.

'I can,' answered the struggling figure from behind a bottle.

'Rubbish. You're no different from the rest of us.'

'I am,' answered Kevin and stunned us with the phrase: 'I've got negative buoyancy.' It sounded like some horrible disease.

'What's that mean?' I asked.

I've got negative buoyancy

'It means if I let go this bloody bottle, I sink,' said Kev.

'Bollocks,' said I, remembering my physics class from school. 'It's nerves – you have to learn to relax.' I began talking to him in a low voice which, being out of character, unnerved him straight away. I think I must have hypnotised him, because he loosened his grip on the bottles and I took them away; the rest of us began playing water polo with them.

'There you are, Kevin, I told you that you wouldn't sink,' I said, spinning round. But Kevin wasn't there. I turned to Steve and asked, 'What's negative buoyancy?'

'It means you can't float,' answered Steve, who was very knowledgeable.

'Oh, er, where's Kevin?' I asked, shining my light around.

'Down there,' someone said. Looking down through the clear, green water, we could see Kevin bottom-walking – he didn't seem too happy. We hastily pulled him up and gave him his bottles back, but he wasn't a bit grateful for our having saved his life. When he had finished coughing he said, 'As soon as I get onto dry land, I'm going to kill you, Eyre.'

I didn't dare tell him that there was a dry way which bypassed the canal, for he would have really killed me.

TO REPLACE OUR CAVING ROPES we opted for the new Courlene made from bright orange polypropylene, which meant that we couldn't lose it. The rope was light, strong and non-absorbent, so it would float on water – unlike nylon – plus it was cheap and didn't stretch, making it ideal.

We discussed changing the ropes on the stretchers for one of the new synthetics at a CRO committee meeting. Dick Hylton, one of our older respected controllers (who had lost a leg at Anzio), stood up with a length of Courlene in his hand and said in his broad Yorkshire accent, 'Now look, I'm going to show you something.' Dick then proceeded to tie an unslippable bowline knot in the rope.

'Watch,' he said, and began to shake the rope gently for a few seconds. We watched in amazement as the bowline knot slowly untied itself!

'Now, apart from its ability to untie itself,' said Dick sagely, 'it also melts in the sun. Mind you, tha doesn't see much sun in a pot'ole, so it should be alright if tha sticks a couple of half-hitches behind the bowline.'

We immediately opted to use a different type of rope for rerigging the stretchers. However, having bought hundreds of feet of Courlene rope, I contacted the manufacturer. The rep confirmed that prolonged exposure to ultraviolet light caused a loss of tensile strength; he asked me what the rope would be used for.

'Potholing,' I replied.

'Ah,' the man said, 'it should be an ideal rope for your purpose, because tha doesn't see much sun in a pot'ole.' I wondered if he was a relative of Dick Hylton.

There are some potholes where you don't see much of anything. Slit Sinks could hardly be called a pothole, as it was only a narrow slit just above the bed of Ease Gill. After it was dug out, the slit revealed a series of tight squeezes and a small, torturous passage ending at a fifty-foot pitch.

Returning the following weekend to continue the exploration, we were dismayed when, at seven in the morning, a violent thunderstorm broke over the area. This put paid to any underground exploration, as a swollen Ease Gill would flood all the caves in its catchment.

The storm eventually passed and the sky cleared to give promise of a beautiful day, so we walked across to the gill anyway. We were soon in the midst of heather that hung with sparkling jewels, where the sun shone through droplets of rainwater and produced miniature circular rainbows in each, to be scattered into a cascade of flashing light as we brushed past.

We came upon the gill to find, to our astonishment, that it was bone dry! It had been dry for weeks, but after the violent storm and heavy rain of only a few hours before, we expected to see a raging torrent. We were completely baffled. After some discussion we reasoned that the heavy rain had soaked into the dry ground and we decided to head into Slit Sinks.

I was still mystified and somewhat uneasy as I led the way through the narrow, twisting passage; today, it seemed to take us longer to reach the pitch. We soon had it laddered and I was about to go down when young Ted, a keen novice caver, asked if he could be first as he was very excited at the thought of making a discovery.

I was not too happy about the idea of a novice dashing on in front, so I said he could go first down the pitch provided he waited for me at the bottom. I tied him on and lifelined him down the roomy drop.

I watched Ted's slow progress, his light illuminating the clean walls of a lovely circular shaft. He stopped and reported another drop below, then his words were cut short by the sound of a muffled explosion which sounded like a quarry blast. I had never heard anything like that underground and my blood ran cold as I heard a faint rumbling noise coming from a circular, four-foot diameter passage on the other side of the pitch. The rumble intensified with each second and was accompanied by a strong draught of displaced air – the cave was flooding!

I shouted down, 'Ted, come up!' and yanked on the lifeline.

'Why?'

'Come up!' and I began hauling him bodily as the thundering roar of approaching water reverberated around the cave.

'What's that noise?' shouted Ted as two of us heaved desperately on the rope.

'Climb faster, the bloody hole's flooding.' I heaved the white-faced youth off the ladder in the nick of time as, accompanied by a howling gale and an awful noise that I never want to hear again, a wall of water containing tree branches and rocks appeared out of the round borehole and thundered down the pitch, inches from him.

My mind was racing. Where had the sudden flood come from? It could only have entered through a sink higher up the gill, which meant that Ease Gill itself was also flooding.

All my fellow cavers had scrambled madly into the roof of the chamber, gaining a shallow aven. As the rest of the cave reverberated, I listened at the small passage through which we had entered. It was silent – if we hurried we had a chance to escape.

'I'm going to try to get out,' I yelled to the others and launched myself into the narrow confines in a desperate race against time. I had to reach the entrance before the flood, which I was sure was boring down the valley. Before I knew it the others were snapping at my heels with cries of, 'Hurry up, Jim', as I struggled round tight, awkward corners, half expecting to be overwhelmed by floodwater on each tortuous bend.

In my panic, I struggled round one corner and became stuck. 'Back up,' I shouted, 'I'm stuck!' Panic-stricken shouts from behind were accompanied by a reluctant backwards shuffling; it was a horrible moment as everyone was completely at the mercy of fate, jammed together in that restricted passage that could become a watery grave.

I twisted my body round, dropped my camera and wriggled free into the low, tight entrance crawl. There was no hope at all if water came in now.

'Daylight ahead,' I shouted, as much for my own benefit as for the men behind, who had become strangely silent. I heaved myself through the last few feet and lay full length on the dry, warm rock of the sun-warmed streambed, promising to go to church every Sunday.

The sky was blue and the skylarks were singing, and it was good to be alive. But we were only just alive, as a small, six-inch high wave of water came down the gill. I shouted a warning as I hastily improvised a dam of rocks and sods to deflect the water for as long as possible.

Bill Leyland was the last out. As he wrestled in the tight entrance the floodwater poured in around him; we grasped his arms and pulled, and then sat silently watching the stream, now four feet deep, swirling its way down the valley past the now completely submerged entrance to Slit Sinks. I shuddered. Another few minutes . . .

This practical lesson on flash-flooding after a prolonged dry spell, which nearly caused my early retirement from caving, was a salutary reminder that a large amount of water does not immediately soak into dry soil, but runs off. From the beginning of the thunderstorm, rainwater had collected in the large catchment area of Crag Hill. It then started to run down the valley before we even walked across the fell – had we known that it was rapidly approaching our personal plughole, we would certainly have stayed on the surface.

Unfortunately, having a lousy memory, I soon forgot about this object lesson and a few months later I was happily engaged in heaving rocks out of a large rift just below Ease Gill Kirk. This waterfall is situated in the lower part of the valley and only runs in very extreme wet weather, as the higher reaches of Ease Gill generally sink underground.

There was a promising draught blowing out from gaps between the boulders, and the smooth, water-polished walls denoted a major sink. We were therefore spurred on in our task and, after a couple of weekends, made the breakthrough when we pushed the last few boulders down and slid into the twenty-foot deep rift to emerge in a surprisingly large passage. Unfortunately, the passage was blocked with rockfalls at both ends, so we probed about looking for a way on. Then one of the surface team appeared at the foot of the entrance rift and shouted, 'Come out quickly,' and promptly disappeared. Not knowing what to expect, we scarpered across the rock-strewn floor and quickly chimneyed up the rift to the surface.

Climbing the dry waterfall of the Kirk, we joined the others. They were standing in a group looking along the dry, boulder-covered streambed that stretched up the valley for a mile before reaching Cow Dub – at that time, the last major sink in upper Ease Gill.

'Can you hear it, Jim?' asked Mike Bateson.

I listened. There was a faint rumbling sound that signalled the approach of running water. The group stood transfixed as the noise became louder, then a wave of peat-coloured water swept into view, crashing over the mossy-green boulders with a spume of frothy scum that blew in the wind like dirty soapsuds. The crest of the two-foot high leading edge of the wall of water bore down towards us.

Where the valley widened the flow seemed to lose its impetus as it spread across the valley floor, to suddenly deepen and speed up again upon entering the narrowing channel above Ease Gill Kirk. It crashed onwards in a brown, solid mass with a noise like thunder.

Standing on the edge of the fifteen-foot drop, I was awestruck as I watched the flood charge around the basin below, picking up old tree trunks and swirling them round and round in concentric circles of debris, froth and scum in an ever-deepening pool. Then the flood plunged down the open rift that we had just vacated, pulling down a thick tree trunk. It jammed upended like a gnarled totem pole in the centre of a whirl-pool, which gradually slowed as the cave filled. The telltale scum's streaky lines pointed towards the next drop towards the valley bottom, and the swollen stream, now more like a miniature river, crashed on and on in its unstoppable path towards its ultimate goal – the sea.

Tom and Mike joined me; we sat and looked at each other. Tom said, 'Bloody 'ell – give us a fag!' We were privileged to witness this display of nature's might. The reason for the sudden surge was that it had built up on a fell already saturated after weeks of rain. The peat bogs were full, the cave sinks further up the valley had reached capacity, and the heavy downpour of the previous twenty-four hours was forced into the old, dry watercourse, sinking in old inactive sinks and filling them before continu-ing downstream.

If our small digging group had been without clubmates on the surface, we would have been unaware of the impending flood until it came pouring in on our heads. With this thought, I fetched the cigarettes out again . . .

Two young cavers from Leeds were not so lucky. They were exploring Pegleg Pot when a similar flood occurred. The cave is situated a couple of hundred yards further up the dry section of lower Ease Gill and is named after its discoverer Dick Hylton, a member of the Northern Pennine Club.

The entrance to Pegleg lies in the dry streambed. The two cavers, unfortunately, picked the wrong day to explore it, because just after they entered the restricted low entrance passage at 3 p.m. on a cold February afternoon, it started raining. By the time they reached the roomier caverns below, the rain had become heavy and prolonged, so much so that I was called out to assist in a rescue down Spectacle Pot in Kingsdale. Here, four cavers were trapped beyond a low, tight section aptly named Splutter Crawl. It was more than 'splutter' that night, it had filled up. One caver was a stretcher case and the others were not feeling too good after their long, cold, wet confinement. However, after diverting the entrance stream, we managed to pull them through the crawl on ropes and the rescue was a success.

It was 1 a.m. We were wet, cold and tired when a call on the radio stated that two University of Leeds students were overdue, having entered Pegleg. This was the last place on earth to be in a flood and we were all aware of the seriousness of the situation as we scrounged around Ingleton for sandbags, corrugated iron sheets, picks, crowbars and other items.

Gordon Batty and I were the first to reach Bull Pot Farm. We staggered across the fell in blinding rain to be confronted by a swollen, twenty-foot wide stream. Pegleg Pot was submerged under five feet of water, the only clue to its whereabouts being two sodden rucksacks that floated in an adjacent pool. The situation looked grim and the survival of cavers in the restricted cave below, underneath the flooded stream, seemed extremely unlikely. I had a gloomy vision that we would bring bodies out.

However, there have been many cases of cavers surviving against all odds so I put my negative thoughts to the back of my mind. More of the rescue team arrived and I sent a runner back to the farm to inform Reg Hainsworth that we needed to organise a group for dam-building and digging diversion channels at the Pegleg site, while Gordon and I tried to divert more of the stream down the Oxford and County Pot sinks until more men arrived to help us.

By the time we reached Oxford Pot, Gordon and I were tired. The heavy volume of water rushed past us like a mill race as we wrestled with large blocks of limestone while waist-deep in the current. Some of the round boulders were torn from our grasp by the force of the floodwater and twice I was washed downstream towards Cow Dub, fortunately managing to regain my feet in time to prevent myself from being washed over the twenty-foot waterfall.

After a long struggle we managed to build a rudimentary barrier that directed a lot of the stream into Oxford, so we strengthened this and deepened the channel until we heard the satisfying roar of a powerful waterfall below. A grey dawn revealed two grey men, utterly exhausted as we surveyed our handiwork. We had halved the amount of water flowing down the valley and would have achieved much more with some assistance.

We were so tired that we collapsed as we tried to climb the steep bank, and I think it was only my anger that kept me going. Arriving at the farm, I threw the door open and played hell with the group sitting round the fire – and everyone else – as I demanded to know where our support group was. 'And while you lot have been sat in here round the bloody fire, Gordon and I have been up to our waists all night in the bloody gill.'

Eventually, Reg calmed me down and explained that no one knew what was going on because the runner I sent back had got lost – and when found, he had forgotten his message. After mugs of hot tea I calmed down and a group was sent to Oxford Pot to finish the diversion channel and deepen it with explosives.

Down at Pegleg a circular dam was erected around the cave entrance using corrugated iron sheets. Men hung onto these in the strong current, while others anchored them with rocks. Eventually, much to everyone's amazement, twenty-four hours after they descended the hole the two trapped cavers were saved, suffering from exposure but otherwise quite fit. They had managed to reach the highest point in a large cavern at the end, where they sat on a ledge and watched the water rise until it was lapping at their refuge – another two feet and it would have all been over.

I CONSULTED MY HOROSCOPE and it said 'Keep away from water', so with my trusty team I began digging in the depths of Gavel Pot, where a rock slope blocked the way on. It came about like this . . .

Several of us were convinced that the Leck Fell caves and potholes would somehow connect with Ease Gill Caverns. Gavel is situated high on Leck Fell, beginning as a large, open-air shaft almost 450 feet in circumference that was formed when the cave roof collapsed millions of years ago, producing a large rock slope that blocked any continuation.

Walking the moors, quite by accident I was looking at the slope when I saw a pair of eyes staring back at me. At first I thought it was Old Nick, but on scrambling down I came face to face with a billy goat. Being a gentleman and lover of all things hairy, I organised an impromptu rescue. I removed my best ginger Harris tweed jacket and placed it under the goat's belly, before tying a special sling knot around it with our rope. The lads up above soon had the goat pulled out, and I retrieved my jacket.

What a stink! No one would walk with me, no one would talk to me, and when we called at the pub on the way home, it emptied. I was left standing at the bar, alone except for a fat Labrador bitch which seemed to be on heat and kept rubbing itself against my legs while giving me an adorable smile.

The goat belonged to Arthur Sweatenham, the gamekeeper for Lord Shuttleworth, who owned the land. Its release was fortuitous, as while I was rescuing the goat I noticed a draught coming out from the rocks in the rock slope near the cave wall. The following weekend we commenced our dig.

So here we were, having been told to keep away from water, removing rocks from the lowest point in the slope then passing them up and seemingly making good progress. As we went further, the cave wall became undercut and formed a right angle on a joint. There was an old tree trunk in the chamber so I manoeuvred it into position across the exposed angle of the walls, providing a safe position to work. Then we found another, much longer tree trunk and plonked that further up the slope, and as I passed rocks to the lads above, they passed them back to Bill Leyland who built a wall behind the trunk.

This is one reason why I was a decorator. I would have made a lousy engineer, for digging at the bottom of a loose rock slope is not a very sensible thing to do. I was about six feet down, wrestling with a rock, when the whole slope avalanched. I popped my head out of my hole just in time to see Bill, sitting on his tree trunk, hurtling towards me on a moving carpet of rocks. I leapt out of the hole like Bugs Bunny and, with footwork which would not have disgraced Fred Astaire, I tap-danced on the shifting rocks until they ground to a standstill – the pungent smells of broken limestone and frightened Jim hung in the air. It was obvious that a different approach was needed, as the slope was now higher than it had been before we started!

We set to again and started heaving rocks out. The ladies arrived; they had brought a paraffin stove and suggested we had a brew of tea. I volunteered to bring the water from the stream which entered from Short Drop Cave; an easy climb and a short, easy traverse gained the waterfall, where I filled the pan and began working my way back, pan in one hand and the other in my pocket, as nonchalant a figure as could be imagined.

A split second later I was in fast-forward mode as my numbed brain tried to cope with the moss-covered walls flashing past. The sunlight abruptly gave way to darkness as a floor of broken rock jumped up to meet me.

My mind was a kaleidoscope of mixed emotions. Foremost was a need for survival, for I knew that the steep slope of loose rock overhung a sixty-foot drop to the streamway so, instinctively, I relaxed my body when I hit the rock. Something struck me in the ribs, knocking all the breath out of my lungs as I slid towards oblivion.

I tried to postpone the rapidly approaching end of Jim Eyre by digging in with my feet, elbows, hands, fingers, knees, nails and teeth, as I slid rapidly in an avalanche of rock towards Jesus. Fortunately, Jesus didn't want me and I stopped, in complete darkness, on the edge of the sixty-foot sheer drop. I experienced great difficulty in breathing, I couldn't move and I inwardly cursed myself for being so bloody stupid.

I heard a faint shout: 'Jim's fallen!' Then nothing seemed to happen until I vaguely heard someone climbing down the rift; then a shower of rocks came trundling down, some of which hit me, as a hazy figure climbed cautiously down the slope and stood on my outstretched hands when he tried to peer over the edge.

'He's gone over,' said a voice.

'Bloody 'ell,' answered his mate, 'what are we going to tell Rose?' All this time I was trying to breathe and say something to denote my presence, like, 'Get off my hands.'

After a heroic effort I managed a groan. 'Hell, he's here,' said Tommy Leigh. 'Are you alright, Jim?'

No answer.

'He's dead!'

'He's not, I just heard him groan.'

The two clubmates eventually assisted me into the main daylight chamber, where Rose had hysterics. Later, when she found out that I was likely to survive, she called me a silly sod and asked, 'Where's my pan?'

I expect this, my first fall, could be called part of the learning curve. I had learned to take heed of my horoscope: 'Keep away from water', which also means water in pans. I had learned to keep both hands free when traversing. I had learned that all the fallen climbers and cavers in heaven can be distinguished from the other angels by the surprised looks on their faces. And I learned from a man in a white coat that I had fractured two ribs.

Chapter 15

Travel Broadens the Mind

MOST CAVERS in the 1950s and '60s were avid readers of Casteret, Chevalier and the other great French speleologists whose epic accounts of exploration in huge French cave systems stirred the blood, and made our own caves seem like rabbit holes. The heroic exploits described in *Subterranean Climbers*, *The Darkness Under the Earth* and other superb autobiographies gave me an itch I longed to scratch.

My chance came in 1961 when I found out that a group of cavers were heading for the French Pyrenees, intending to descend Casteret's ice cave, the Grotte Casteret. In no time, together with Rose, I found myself on a coach hired in Yorkshire with a Yorkshire driver and a load of Yorkshire potholers – which gave me the chance to brush up on a foreign language.

Trundling across France with this load of unwashed northerners, the coach tinkling musically to empty beer bottles rolling from side to side, was my idea of heaven. It was great fun; Ernie, our driver, was never quite sure where he was. Exclaiming, 'Foreign bastards, driving on the wrong side,' he would pull up on a different road from the one he should have been on to consult a map, while the coach disgorged a bunch of wild men. We would descend on the village shop with wild cries of 'Mus-yor, mus-yor, beer silver plate,' then shovel loads of strange coins on the counter and wave fistfuls of paper money at the bemused proprietor.

Grubby fingers would snatch at beer bottles as fast as they were passed over, then a confused reckoning would take place as the proprietor had to write down the amount for each customer, because the silly sods couldn't understand him, and then remove the necessary amount from each customer because the silly sods couldn't add up. By the time the wild men had said 'Mercy bunkup, mus-yor,' and gone out of the door, the proprietor was left in a daze, standing looking at a battered old coach which rolled down the road in a cloud of dust while he muttered 'Anglais, Anglais.'

Being cavers, we had to visit the amazing karst country of the Massif Central and undertake the tourist trip in Padirac with its waterways and blue, subterranean lakes. Slowly moving across the scenic beauty of La Belle France, even the most philistine among us couldn't fail to be impressed. In particular, the caves of Lascaux left a deep and lasting impression which remains with me to this day.

We didn't realise how lucky we were to wander in this remarkable cave. There was no queue and hardly any restrictions, unlike today when people have to be content with a replica; indeed, in the second millennium everything in life seems to be a replica. Gazing at the Lascaux paintings I was awestruck at the skill of these primitive people who, using basic tools and pigments mixed from the earth, had created works of art that far excel anything produced by the pretentious modern 'artists' who exhibit in Tate Modern.

I emerged from the cave feeling as though I undergone a religious experience. Then, as we passed through Lourdes I had a religious experience of another kind when I saw the trade in human suffering – the sick and the dying clutched desperately at commercialised religion, and I felt sick at the religious hypocrisy of the place.

Gavarnie was a picture postcard of a village, situated under the imposing limestone cliffs of the Cirque de Gavarnie, a natural amphitheatre 2,000 feet high in the Marboré Massif. Waterfalls fell from the snow-covered peaks at the head of the cirque, descending through thin wisps of cloud, swaying and twisting like the transparent veils of a harem dancer before bursting onto the rocks below.

We loaded our rucksacks and began the walk up towards the Brèche de Roland, where the mythical French sword-wielding giant had cut a gap in the Pyrenees between France and Spain. The higher we climbed the more impressive became the scenery, with dazzling white snow contrasting against the grey and gold of jagged cliffs and the azure blue of the sky. To me, the feel of the warm sun on my back and the magnificent surroundings were overpowering, and I felt exhilarated as I climbed upwards, drawn by the cliffs above, rent asunder by a giant.

I followed young Geoff, who was bounding on in front clad only in a pair of boxer shorts and soft boots with his trusty sheath knife in a belt around his waist. This, plus the T-shirt he was carrying, was how he left Yorkshire – the ultimate lightweight traveller. The only other possession I ever saw him with was a French supermarket carrier bag containing a large loaf, a chunk of cheese and a bottle of beer.

We spent the night in a French refuge, seven in a bed plus an industrious French flea, before climbing up to the Brèche in glorious sunshine. We passed below the Casque du Marboré which stands sentinel above the high cliffs that separate France from Spain, a well-known smugglers' route.

Beyond the Brèche the steep, snow-covered cliffs changed dramatically into a more arid wilderness of karst that, with less snow, sloped away gently to merge in a hazy distance. Keeping close to the foot of the cliffs we maintained a lookout for Spanish border guards who, we had been told, shot first and asked questions after. A dark shadow at the foot of a cliff face soon revealed the Grotte Casteret, a cave found in 1926 by Norbert Casteret and his wife Elizabeth.

Norbert and his wife were tough cookies who thought nothing of sleeping outside the cave at an altitude of around 10,000 feet, without sleeping bags or decent clothing (Elizabeth wore a knee-length skirt). Having discovered the highest ice cave known at that time, they explored it without crampons, almost coming to grief in the process.

It was a strange feeling, walking under the twenty-foot-high arched roof of the cave, because the sheet of ice that stretched before us was unblemished, just as Casteret described it all those years ago.

The beauty of ice caves is that they are continually replenishing; the partial thaws and refreezing keeps the mirror-like surfaces free from blemishes and permanently virgin. We were looking at frozen history; the sights ahead were exactly as Norbert and Elizabeth had seen them.

With crampons on our feet we approached two large ice columns, heralding a world of frozen cascades and fluted curtains which flashed and sparkled in our lamplight as we moved into the Salle Maud, a larger chamber named after one of Casteret's daughters. Obviously she was a chip off the old block, for it is not everyone who will insert their body into a low, downward-sloping letterbox in ice, not knowing what lies ahead.

To quote Casteret, 'I watched Maud lying prostrate on the ice, forcing her way through a very narrow opening close to the floor. . . . her knees and boots slithered on the smooth surface of ice. She continued to make headway, and only her feet remained visible, when she suddenly spread her legs and made frantic efforts to brake with her heels against the rock. Instinctively I leaped forward, caught hold of her feet, and pulled her back.' Just as well, because Maud was about to dive over a vertical 50 foot ice fall.

After fastening a ladder to three ice pitons, I followed in Maud's footsteps and slid on my stomach through the low opening. I immediately gathered speed and shot away from the ladder, completely out of control, and over the brink of the ice wall, where my flight was arrested by my lifeline. I pendulumed onto the ladder and climbed awkwardly down using my instep crampons, which allowed me to get a toehold on the round alloy rungs and reach the base of a magnificent frozen miniature Niagara – an apt name, given by Casteret.

It was exactly as he had described it: fifty to sixty feet high with horizontal stratifications, alternating between clear and opaque and over 150 feet long. It was an amazing sight, especially when two of the team found that they could walk behind the solid waterfall. Their lights from behind created a wonderful effect; the whole ice fall became semi-transparent and as they moved it glowed and shimmered with a beautiful green luminosity.

The sloping ice sheet of the floor led us on, down to more chambers with ice columns that were so clear they were almost invisible. Following the underground glacier I encountered several large, octagonal ice crystals, described by Casteret as fossilised ice, eight inches in diameter and structured like spiders' webs. The glacier was slowly but surely filling the far reaches of the cave, as was demonstrated near the end where ice snouts forced their way into the innermost recesses. Several years previously some French speleologists had left orange markers here, and these were now entombed in the ice, several feet below.

Leaving the Grotte Casteret, a group of us went prospecting and discovered several previously unknown ice caves at a slightly higher altitude, set back on a broad ledge that ran along the cliff face, east of the Casque. I noticed ice and meltwater behind a loose rockfall and heaved out a slab of rock to reveal a small hole and an icy draught. It was man-sized, so I pushed my body in and found I was pointing head-first down an ice slope.

Not wishing to commit hara-kiri I rapidly retreated, then re-entered feet first. Once through, before I had time to clamber to my feet, I was off on the bobsleigh of my life as I shot down the ice on my backside, vainly trying to stick my axe in the hard ice. I zoomed down for fifty feet and, just as it seemed that I was about to come to a sticky end where the roof lowered to meet the ice, I suddenly careered round a bend and arrested my headlong descent where the ice levelled out at a pile of frozen snow and ice that had fallen from above.

I was joined by the rest of the group, who descended in a more orthodox fashion, and we progressed through several chambers, up giant cascades and past crystal-clear icicles that were several feet thick. In one place they almost blocked the cave. We came to a large, frozen pool which seemed to have a wet surface. I was leading when suddenly I broke through the ice into a foot of water and, below it, another ice layer.

I wasn't too keen on taking an ice bath at this altitude, so I moved slowly forward, prodding the ice with my trusty axe. The reason for the melting ice became apparent when we felt a draught of warm air and, rounding a corner, we saw daylight.

Unfortunately, the narrow passage contained a canal of ice slush and water. After several tentative attempts to climb round it on the smooth walls, with one cautious attempt to walk through it – which came to an abrupt halt when the icy water lapped up to within an inch of my testicles – I desisted.

Reluctantly, we returned from this world of ice caves and dazzling snow, to the mundane world below. The journey was enlivened by young Geoff, who passed me at great speed, going backwards while lying on his stomach, hanging grimly onto his trusty sheath knife which, although very useful for slicing bread, wasn't much use as an ice axe. We watched the figure in red shorts grow smaller and smaller, until his headlong flight came to a stop. He picked himself up and we heard a crazy laugh as he began laboriously cutting steps in the steep, hard snow while he struggled back up to rejoin us on the traverse.

FRANCE, WITH ITS SUBTLE FRAGRANCE OF STALE PERFUME, Gauloises cigarettes and open drains, captured my soul and I vowed to return – for who could resist the sheer excitement of a visit to a French bog.

Why can't we have some of these in England? A visit to the 'bog' in England is a very boring part of life, but in France – Oo, la la – who knows what you will meet? It can be like a scene from the writings of Sade, with a seemingly innocuous hole in the floor waiting to trap the unwary with a huge tidal wave, which washes you and everything else out of the bog door when you pull the string.

I rapidly found that all French bogs were booby traps and, no matter what you did with that string you were always enveloped in a tidal wave. On one occasion I even tied another length of string to the existing one and pulled it from outside, but achieved the same result.

We rapidly formed a 'bog advance guard' from our hardier characters; on behalf of the rest, they would try the bog first. I was performing this vital task in a remote village when I was almost killed in action. I took the appropriate deep breath of fresh air, opened the door and stepped inside. There was no floor, just a gaping black pit over which I dangled, grimly hanging onto the door knob while my feet pedalled furiously over the evil-looking cesspit, which winked and bubbled at me from ten feet below.

But there were also good days, and my red letter day – my finest hour – came in a little village outside Montignac.

We had found a little cafe. It was a beautiful day and, after a beer, I investigated the long shed with the sacking curtains in the garden. It was a collector's item – a French three-seater, circa 1928. The sun-warmed wooden seat was smooth to the touch and short sackcloth curtains between the nicely polished holes turned it into a sort of confessional box, where you could chat to your neighbour and discuss events of the day (or each others' bowel movements).

I sat there daydreaming when a hand came through the curtain and grasped mine. I looked at the hand in amazement: it was soft, well manicured, wore a pretty ring and obviously belonged to the young lady in the next compartment. She whispered through the sacking into my left ear in a soft, sexy voice, 'Ah, chéri, mon amour,' and my hand was given an affectionate squeeze.

The fair sex have never found me irresistible, so I presumed the young lady next door thought I was her boyfriend. Not wishing to discourage her, I gave her hand a little squeeze in return, and said, 'Pass the paper, luv.'

This, and other adventures where strange young ladies join you in the shower then ask you to wash their backs, released a sudden yearning to revisit the Mediterranean of my war years. The following year saw my return as the leader of the grand-sounding Anglo-French Speleological Expedition to the Maritime Alps, which consisted of six cavers and my wife. It was a stroke of genius for, as far as I was aware, no other expedition had ever been organised to the French Riviera, especially a caving one!

A battered Ford van eventually ground to a halt in a cloud of steam and smoke in Draguignan, a small historic town in Provence. Now came the funny bit, for never had an expedition been arranged on such a casual basis: one letter to a small French caving group which rejoiced in the name of the Amicale Speleo Group. I had arranged to meet them at a filling station in the town square the day before we arrived, a meeting which, of course, failed. Nevertheless, we had found the filling station, which was next to a bar so we soon settled down and watched life go by.

After a while our attention was drawn to a crew-cutted gent who kept emerging from the depths of the filling station to peer at us, before going back inside again. He seemed to be shaking his head in disbelief. Some time later we noticed him looking inside the van and eventually he approached us. 'Bonjour,' he said. 'Monsieur Jeeme Eerie?'

'Oui', I answered in my best French. It was Maurice Fraisse, our host.

After shaking hands all round we found that he couldn't speak English and I couldn't speak much French. After several embarrassed silences, I unearthed the secret of instant multi-lingualism by getting more beer down our necks, then we found we could converse with an easy volubility that could bankrupt all language teachers. Maurice made a phone call and we were soon joined by more French cavers and the Mayor, the President of the club, who brought along his beautiful daughter. She oozed sex, spoke delightful English and gave rise to delightful visions which made me go all wobbly at the knees.

We were taken past fields of lavender to the small village of Ampus, about nine miles away in the foothills of the Maritime Alps. Here we found, much to our aston-ishment, that a new campsite had been constructed purely for us. Showers, cooking facilities, toilets and even electricity had been laid on. We were being treated like VIPs and I wondered if, perhaps, I had overdone the bullshit when I wrote my original letter – especially when the Mayor of Ampus brought us fresh bread every morning.

Late in the afternoon of the following day, it was all systems go. Maurice arrived with a cavalcade of cars containing reporters and, only half understanding what was going on, we grabbed a load of caving gear and ladders, for it seemed we were going caving. Following five other cars, we headed into the mountains. It was dusk when we left the village and it soon became dark as we followed the rear lights of the car in front, almost choking in its cloud of dust as we zigzagged steadily up the mountain around hairpin bends with awesome drops.

The cars stopped on a flat plateau overlooking the Grand Canyon du Verdon, the longest and deepest gorge in Europe. Quite near the edge of the 2,000 foot drop, Maurice pulled back a large slab of rock to reveal a hole about eighteen inches in diameter. I dropped a stone down the shaft – it fell for a hundred feet before it hit a ledge and ricocheted further into the depths.

The reporters grew very excited as Maurice shook me by the hand and pronounced, 'Très profond – vous descendez,' and flashbulbs began popping off all over the place. This was weird. The French are used to potholes for, having the world's deepest at that time, speleology was almost a national sport – so what was so special about this hole? A hundred feet of ladders were lowered – then, as Jim Newton was handing me a wire belay, he managed to drop all the belays down the shaft! It was like fluffing an opening night.

'Oh shit,' said Jim in his best French. Fortunately, our resourceful Maurice came up with some stiff fencing wire. I didn't like it, Jim didn't like it, but what could we do surrounded as we were by such an avid audience? Maurice fastened the ladders on the wire, twisted it round the rock which had formerly covered the hole, sat on it and said 'Okay, Meester Jeem.'

I squeezed through the hole and began descending the ladder. The top section of the shaft was covered in pink calcite, coral-like formations, and as I descended I began to forget that the ladder was suspended on a bit of fencing wire.

The shaft started to bell out and jagged ledges jutted into the shaft below. The air seemed stale and, as I climbed lower, I could smell something unpleasant. As I passed the small ledges I noticed that they were several inches deep in old but live .303 bullets, and I became uneasy. The stench of rotting flesh was almost overpowering as I stepped off the ladder onto a broad, sloping ledge at a hundred feet, carefully avoiding the live ammunition and a cluster of very dead sheep that smiled at me. A rock just missed me and was followed by a shout from above; it seemed the reporters were curious. I shouted up, 'Moutons morts; bullets live.'

Much to everyone's amusement, Dave Hall soon reached me with more ladders. I clipped on another hundred feet and descended further into that foul shaft. Approaching two hundred feet I discerned a vague shape crouched in a corner at the foot of the shaft, but fortunately for my jangled nerves it turned out to be an old German great-coat with no one inside it.

The base of the shaft was an evil mess of rotted sheep carcasses and ammunition of all calibres. I wondered what else lay under the lethal assortment and was reluctant to step off the ladder.

The shaft narrowed and sloped off to the right. I carefully made my way across, pulled out a few rocks and animal skulls and slid head first into a continuation of the shaft. Pulling out more debris, I enlarged the opening and managed to find some clean air blowing out. Encouraged by this and the near-vicinity of the deep Verdon Gorge, I slid lower and cleared the shaft further, until a howling draught was blowing through.

The hole would definitely repay a bit more digging, but I retreated as I hadn't come to France to dig my way through a sheep's graveyard. On the surface I was inundated with questions, and it turned out that the shaft was of great local interest because during the war the retreating Germans had thrown a variety of objects down the hole, then blocked it with a large boulder. This had given rise to all sorts of stories, from bodies to buried treasure. There were plenty of bodies, but what else lay down there was not going to be retrieved by me.

One reporter, keener than the rest, wanted to know if he could take photographs of the shaft. I looked at his fancy footwear and made a mock play about feeling his arm muscles, then dolefully shook my head.

The French have a great sense of humour and everyone enjoyed my little joke, before I said okay and stuck a borrowed helmet on his head, gave him a light and tied him on. It was hilarious watching him struggle into the entrance of the hole and take his first tentative steps down the ladder. I knew he was going to have problems and expected to pull him out before he went very far.

However, Jim and the others kept carefully lowering him; as Jim remarked, he was certainly not climbing the ladder and, looking down the shaft, I could make out the reporter clinging desperately to the ladder with his hands while his legs waved about all over the place. He began shouting and I asked Maurice to look down and translate.

'Is he okay?' I asked, somewhat concerned.

'Ah, oui,' said Maurice and put his thumb up. He then turned to the locals and said something else, whereupon they all burst out laughing. After a while Jim and the lads on the lifeline reckoned that the intrepid reporter must have reached the ledge and held the line taught while we waited for him to take his photographs. And we waited, and waited, and waited. I looked down the hole and made out a light on the ledge, then shouted down several times but received no answer. Again I asked Maurice to find out what was happening, and after a lot of confused shouting he explained, aided by one of the reporters who spoke some English, that the man below 'was not well,' and that he needed assistance.

Vous êtes departez

'Right, Jim, start pulling him up, steadily,' I said. As the team began pulling on the rope, a loud shout from came from below. 'Non, non-assist!'

We obviously had a 'leetle problem,' as somebody said. I tied on another rope and went down. I was confronted with our intrepid reporter, standing on the ledge and holding onto the cave wall with his head facing away from the pitch, looking steadfastly at a stalactite. He was terrified. I put a hand on his shoulder, 'Ça va?' I asked in my slang French.

'Non, non,' he replied. 'Je suis perdu.'

He was shaking like a leaf. I tried to convince him that he was not lost, by tugging on his lifeline, whereupon he gave a yell and clung even more fiercely to the rock. 'Photo?' I asked. He dolefully shook his head.

I took hold of his camera, which was hanging round his neck, and suggested that I take a picture of him.

'Non, merci, non.' I suggested he take a photograph of me. 'Non non non!' I asked if he would like to go to the bottom of the shaft and he almost had a heart attack.

'Ah, mon dieu, non, non, non.' I asked him if he would like to go up the shaft. He nodded his head vigorously: 'Oui. Oui, oui.'

Okay. We had been playing silly buggers long enough, so I shouted to Jim to pull the lifeline up slowly. I gave my fellow 'caver' a pat on the shoulder, pointed up and said something like, 'Vous êtes departez,' just as the line tightened. He clung to the wall with even more desperation as, slowly but surely, he was yanked off the ledge, shouting in panic. I placed his hands and feet on the ladder rungs and everything seemed alright until he suddenly wrapped his legs around the ladder like a long-lost lover and wouldn't let go. The ladder was being dragged up with him, so I hastily stood on the bottom and unwrapped his legs. Shouting 'Up, up,' to the men above, I held the ladder grimly as the unwilling reporter's hands were dislodged from their vice-like grip on a rung. He floated upwards like a pantomime fairy, though with less grace, and his patent leather shoes never even touched the ladder.

The following day our hosts arrived at our campsite clutching bundles of French newspapers. Brigitte Bardot and the Riviera jet set had been pushed to the back pages by the reports on Les Spéléo Anglais in front-page headlines in some, and double page spreads in others. There were fanciful stories and photographs of our moonlit caving trip, our campsite, the young reporter being extracted from the hole and what great achievements were still to come. There was even an article on what we ate and drank: 'Ze Eenglish bread and jam and tea.'

We later met our guide to the region. He was nineteen years of age and a fairly serious student – Jean-Claude Giroux didn't drink, but we soon corrupted him. We explored several potholes on the Grand Plan de Canjuers and sinks along the Artuby river, which drops into the Verdon Gorge, and traversed the gorge itself. This was an unforgettable experience, as were our days off when we zoomed away to the Riviera. Well, the lads needed a rest.

Photographico silver plate?

At St Tropez we made another major discovery: Tahiti beach, with its palm trees, golden sand and over a mile of totally naked, gorgeous women, laid out end to end. It was almost too much for us to bear – you never saw sights like this where we came from, especially Morecambe in 1962. Apart from it being too bloody cold, one never seemed to bump into naked ladies in England, especially any that were laid out for inspection like some sort of supermarket for the erotically deprived.

The erotically deprived must be even more so in Bradford, because we watched with awe and admiration as Pete, our ambassador for Bradford, approached a gorgeous specimen of naked female pulchritude and set up his tripod and camera.

The young lady looked up at this apparition before her, wearing a crew-cut and off-white, oil-stained knee-length shorts, black socks and black hobnailed boots while clutching a long, French loaf and a pot of jam. Hardly the epitome of Riviera chic, Pete was obviously years ahead of his time and had anticipated British grunge before anyone else. Pete smiled his greasy lop-sided smile and pointed at his camera, saying in his best French, 'Photographico silver plate?' The young lady smiled and said, 'Oui.'

AFTER A FEW MORE DAYS, accompanied by Jean-Claude, we headed for Gap and set up camp in the orchard of our next host, Jean Tourres, a flour-mill owner. We met more members of the Amicale Speleo Group, ready for more caving trips.

The town of Gap is overlooked by the Grand Ferrand, a 9,000 foot peak which dominates a high plateau where several cave systems drain the mountain slopes. They resurge some 6,000 feet lower at the Sources des Gillardes, a large rising where all the year round a strong volume of water emerges under pressure. It is impossible to enter the rising as the water wells up from a wilderness of huge boulders, but across the valley the Puits des Bans, another large rising, is accessible for a few weeks in the summer. Max Ailkard, one of the group, was once deep in this giant artesian well when the water began to rise, so he beat a quick retreat.

I had a dog named Max; he was quite mad. I have met several cavers called Max, and they were all quite mad. It didn't take me long to realise that the French variety was also quite mad, as Max led the way into the chaos of rock that covers the entrance to the Puits des Bans.

Once through the entrance pools, the cave floor fell away at a 45 degree angle over smooth deposits of flowstone and deep gour pools, before widening into a huge rift. The angle steepened and the floor and sides became non-existent, leaving two cave walls that fell away at an angle of 55 degrees.

Max was moving at an incredible speed, jumping from ledge to ledge as he worked his way down this giant rift and I was struggling to keep up. He eventually halted where a large rock had jammed across the rift and we hung on for the others who were now spread out, way above our heads. Looking up, I realised how vulnerable we were if anything fell.

Once everyone had arrived, Max picked up a rock, saying 'Attention!' before hurling it into the blackness below. We listened, awestruck, as we heard the rock rumbling and falling for several hundred feet before stopping with a far-off booming noise.

Our faces must have been a picture, as Max grinned and leapt after the rock. Not quite having Max's faith in flying, I peered over the edge of the small ledge we were standing on and saw the rift dropping away at an even steeper angle. There were several good holds, but a slip would have been fatal. Jean Tourres became most concerned about the complete lack of safeguards. Max's light glimmered far below and I carried on after him; Jean still muttered, 'Très dangerous.'

Several places were completely vertical and I had to resort to back-and-footing. We continued in this fashion, climbing, chimneying and sliding down and down, and I thought of the struggle we would have climbing back out. I met Max on a ledge by a bank of flowstone; he explained that this was where the rising water began to chase him on his last exploration. 'Ahead is unexplored.' I looked down the black hole and listened intently – I was sure I could hear rushing and gurgling water, swirling up the shaft towards us.

'The water rises fast,' said Max. I nodded glumly, trying to visualise the statistics of a 3,000 foot head of water and wondered what the weather was like outside.

We had trouble trying to pass the flowstone, for it was overhanging and offered no handholds. Further along the ledge a small crack enabled us to swing underneath and continue down the shaft, which seemed never-ending.

At last a change took place: the walls appeared wet and the steepness of our descent grew less acute. The elongated rift changed into a large borehole passage, still descending but gradually levelling off, and pools began to appear. The tunnel-like passage felt more sinister and, as the ceiling and walls were covered in mud, I became aware that I was walking through a gigantic sump which was normally filled with rushing water. I considered what would happen if there was a thunderstorm on the mountain far above.

The passage levelled off and banks of large, rounded stones littered the passage, then the cave came to life where cascades of water trickled down the walls, splashing into deep pools. It was very cold. Max and I waded waist-deep through pools that became deeper and longer, until the way on was barred by a continuous sheet of water. I eventually managed to traverse along the edge, around a bend in the passage. Ahead, the tunnel stretched as far as our lamps would reach, with dapples of light shimmering on the round, mud-covered roof – reflections from the deep, blue canal that blocked the way on. The ceiling was ominously sloping down. Max was frustrated: 'Un bateau,' he said.

'Oui,' I answered. 'Un submarine.'

The almost vertical 700 foot climb up the entrance rift proved very tiring and, at one point, quite dangerous when Max dislodged a large slab of rock directly above my head. I saw the slab roll from under his feet as he shouted a warning. Three men below me were directly in its path and, as it slithered off the ledge, I reached out before it gained any momentum and managed to deflect it as it hurtled into space. The rock hit a ledge and split into fragments, narrowly missing the group.

Spread out in this deep rift, we were extremely vulnerable to anything or anybody that fell from above, so we closed up and climbed together. I found myself in the lead and, after climbing on calcite nodules that kept breaking under my weight, I worked my way across the rift to a safer route. We had all been climbing steadily for some time when I realised that the angle of the shaft walls seemed much steeper than I remembered on the descent and I wondered how we had climbed down them. At one stage I struggled to climb further because the walls had become suddenly vertical, devoid of holds and quite close together. A muttering, in French and English, rose on the air as an exasperated Jim Newton shouted, 'How the bloody hell did you get up here?'

Max said, 'Oh Meester Jeem, I think you find new cave.' I had, for suddenly the tight rift ended and I popped into a large, muddy chamber filled with stalactites and stalagmites, and a spacious cavern beyond which seemed to go on and on.

Our lights were beginning to fade so Max insisted that we must rejoin the others – wisely, as it turned out, for it took considerable time to retrace our route down the precipitous cleft, then traverse a hundred feet before we reached the correct route. Emerging into warm sunshine, we joined the rest of the group swimming in a turbulent mountain stream.

More caves were explored on the shoulder of the Grand Ferrand by opening some of the snow-blocked shafts. But, unfortunately, time was running out and we had to return to England, though we promised to return to La Belle France the following year. With our new French caving friends we could then explore the cave potential on a high plateau above the Cirque d'Archiane in the Vercors.

A GREAT MANY PLANS WERE MADE and laid and a strong expedition was organised in 1963 for the expected deep potholes of the Plateau de Tussac, and the river caves below. However, when Rabbie Burns said: 'The best made schemes o' mice an' men gang aft a-gley,' he must have been referring to me.

On our arrival at Gap, Jean Tourres had some bad news. Heavy winter snows still blocked the shafts we had intended to explore, so we sat around our campfire late into the night discussing Jean's alternative, which meant moving the expedition to the Dévoluy Massif in the Hautes-Alpes.

More cavers were following us from Britain and were already en route to Châtillon. Jean produced a map of the new area and a circle of the approximate venue, with instructions and an arrow which said 'we are here', was added in lipstick (not mine). Jean hastily departed for Châtillon, where he would ask the mayor to inform all arriving members of the Archiane Expedition of the new destination. What a wonderful political system the French have. I could never imagine an English mayor doing anything like this – opening stress centres for dysfunctional lesbians, yes, but helping foreign cavers? The poor sods would more likely be arrested.

When Jean returned, our convoy of vans and motorbikes left Gap on the road to Veynes. Turning off onto a mountain road we were soon among majestic peaks dominated by the Pic de Bure, rearing up from a pyramid of scree and snow that overhung the narrow road which clung to the side of the gorge as we climbed higher. The road narrowed and we skirted around rockfalls, our vehicle wheels spinning on the loose edge of a precipitous drop as we drove over the Col du Festre at 4,700 feet and down into the valley beyond. It was a sort of Alpine Shangri-La, where a rough track zigzagged up the mountain to end at a huddle of farmhouses which rejoiced in the pleasant name of La Villard-Joli. What a glorious place – I was half pleased that the other expedition had been cancelled.

With typical French hospitality, the farmer dashed out and scythed the grass in a small field so that we could camp in comfort. It was a magnificent area – it had everything but a pub. Ah, but what was that faded sign over the door of one of the buildings? Cafe? It was, and soon we had drunk the landlord's entire stock of beer while he entertained us with music in the form of an old wind-up gramophone and one battered copy of the *Blue Danube* waltz which he played over and over again. We had all died and gone to heaven.

Jean Tourres did not believe in wasting time, so at seven the next morning we loaded up his battered jeep with equipment and followed it on foot to the snow-line, several thousand feet higher. We collected our heavy packs and climbed a steep moraine until we reached the col between the peaks of Grand Ferrand and Tête de l'Aupet. Before us was a huge basin, an amphitheatre that stretched for several miles and swept up the peak ahead. Numerous large depressions and open shafts were visible and at 7,000 feet the situation seemed ideal.

Full of enthusiasm, we set about exploring the terrain which, although full of promise, proved at the end of a long and tiring day to be disappointing as all the shafts

At La Villard-Joli in 1963: George Cornes, wearing a woolly hat, is sitting with Jim on his left

were blocked with deep snow and ice. In the evening we staggered back to camp to find things had happened in our absence.

Our friendly landlord had been more constructive than us, for he had stocked 'le pub' with the latest pop records, umpteen crates of freshly imported beer, lots of shiny new glasses and lots of shiny buxom lasses, all dressed up in their Sunday best. From then on, every evening our idyllic campsite became the focal point for the scattered community, as the young and not so young congregated in the cafe to dance with, and be entertained by, 'Ze crazy speleos Anglais.'

The rest of our expedition arrived during the night, after touring halfway round France following a thick line of lipstick that wiped out towns and villages on a map where one centimetre equals two kilometres. Their first words of greetings were:

'Who drew that bloody map?' and 'Who's the stupid sod that used lipstick one kilometre thick?'

I placated mad Max (yes, another one) with a beer and, 'Well, you see, we hadn't got a pencil.'

During the days that followed, as our search spread across the mountain, we discovered several potholes and two impressive ice caves. One contained large chambers of ice and spectacular ice columns and crystals, as well as a series of large broken caverns which, unfortunately, were blocked by a rock fall about a thousand feet down. With some digging and rock-moving the cave could have been extended, but we had not gone there to dig – especially when the local hop awaited.

Some old hotels and inns have ghosts; our cafe at Villard-Joli had a haunted wheelbarrow. The toilet facilities consisted of the greenest, most environmentally friendly, large, evil-smelling, manure heap imaginable, which was cleverly situated outside the cafe. The wheelbarrow was always parked alongside it. Everyone knew it was there and always avoided it when they stepped out to have a pee, but the haunted wheelbarrow seemed to move on its own and every night someone tripped over the handles and dived into the manure. One night I made a mental note of its position and detoured around the cafe to approach the manure heap from behind, then tripped over a wheelbarrow's handles and fell into the dung.

I asked old Jacques if we could have a priest to exorcise the haunted wheelbarrow, and he asked, 'Which one? We have two.'

Every morning we woke with the sunrise and started our trek up the mountain before the sun rose too high. Jean drove his jeep over terrain that was so steep that he needed two of us to lie on the bonnet, to prevent the vehicle from tipping over backwards. We grimly hung onto this mechanical bucking bronco as it charged like a demented automaton straight at seemingly perpendicular karst, until the engine stalled and we thankfully slid off.

Jean-Claude found another *chourun*, or hole, in a deep depression on the steep slopes of the Tête de l'Aupet and, loaded down like mules, we struggled up towards him. Disturbed jackdaws created quite a fuss, wheeling, diving and shrieking as we interrupted their privacy while looking down on an irregular hole more than sixty feet in diameter and sixty feet deep with a snow floor that had melted into weird pinnacles. In several places, well-like holes and crevasses revealed bluish depths. Dropping a ladder, I tied on a lifeline and climbed down onto the glistening snow plug. The small pinnacles I had viewed from above now towered over me, so I cautiously approached the crevasses and holes and I found one near the foot of the ladder that looked quite deep.

One hundred feet of ladder had been dropped into the shaft and, of this, forty feet lay on the snow. Not expecting anything to come of it, I lowered the end into this icy well and climbed down. Much to my surprise, the hole continued beyond the end of the ladder and I returned to the surface. Several more ladders were fastened on and another of the team descended. As I lined him down, I found the sound-deadening effects of the frozen snow to be quite remarkable – leaning over the hole I could barely hear the whistle signal denoting the return of a very mystified Peter Faulkner who, shaking with cold, described the ice hole still continuing below.

We fastened on even more ladders, until we had 200 feet hanging down this icy pit. Jim Newton, who had changed into caving gear, took down the field telephone. After a while he telephoned to say that he was at the bottom, and that it was 'bloody fantastic.'

I rapidly changed and took my turn to set off, finding the effect of climbing down the three-foot diameter, circular hole in the compressed snow quite disturbing and very claustrophobic. Apart from the deadly silence, the fact that I was descending through such a massive snow plug made me wonder what would happen if it suddenly collapsed. I was relieved when, after 180 feet, the snow tube broke into a large ice chamber. It was bisected by a bridge of ice and huge ice curtains hung over large shattered ice blocks that littered the floor.

A cascade of water suddenly hit me, then at 220 feet I landed in a large, rock-strewn chamber. Looking for the others, I found a steep snow slope leading down to an even steeper scree slope, where the lights of my companions were far below. Steadily making my way towards them, I saw that we were in an enormous cavern and felt that we had hit the jackpot. Unfortunately, the cavern sloped down to a cross-rift which was blocked by rock debris. Cursing our luck, we retreated back to the snow plug.

Pete tied on the lifeline and rang the surface. He was climbing past the ice bridge when he excitedly shouted that there was a black expanse beyond; he informed the lifeline party that he was going to try to swing across to the bridge, then thread the ladders over the other side.

Jim and I watched with interest as Pete began his Tarzan imitation, but unfortunately he flew off course and swung into an ice wall. He hurt his shoulder, so I contacted the surface and asked them to assist Pete up the snow tube, as he was obviously in considerable pain and couldn't use his right arm. While the casualty was being assisted out, I started prodding around in the chamber below the ice bridge and found a narrow gap between the rock wall and the ice. I managed to squeeze in and climb the wall, until I could pass over the ice barrier. Ahead lay blackness.

Although I had a good light, I could see no roof or walls, only a snow slope that fell away steeply at my feet for as far as I could see. It continued upwards past me, to join the ice plug near the bridge; it was a subterranean snow mountain, leading to caverns measureless to man.

Having no ice axe, I clung to the exposed rock of the wall and kicked large, cowardly steps in the frozen, crystalline snow. I slowly descended, stopping frequently for a rest and further amazing probings with my light. The steep slope seemed never-ending and I looked back to see Jim's light, twinkling like a star far above as he followed me down.

After descending for over 300 feet I reached a section of black ice and rubble at the end of another huge cavern, where a fault plane crossed the terminal wall – at this point it was 150 feet high and over 60 feet wide. The rift in the floor contained two more pitches of 90 feet and 45 feet, but the rift below was partially blocked by debris – a disappointing end to a promising and unusual cave system. We later estimated that the main cavern, two-thirds of which lay under the snow, must have been over 1,000 feet long with a maximum height of over 500 feet.

After a night spent at our alpine Palais de Danse we returned to the *chourun*, where we were surprised to find a tremendous change had taken place. Several new holes had opened in the surface snow and a long, deep crevasse and treacherous snow bridge had appeared, where the day before there had been solid ice. A surveying party descended the now much-widened ice tube, to find water running freely. Large masses of ice had fallen from below the ice plug and the ice bridge had gone.

It was obvious that the snow and ice must have been balanced at a critical temperature, just on or slightly below freezing. The passage of our bodies through the snow had upset the equilibrium and started a temporary chain reaction thaw. We made a hurried survey before the thousands of tons of snow and ice could move and block the shaft.

A group of chamois, silhouetted against the rich gold of the setting sun, gazed down on us from the shoulder of the Grand Ferrand, hypnotised into statuesque poses by the curious objects far below. A jackdaw screeched and the spell was broken; one by one the chamois fled the skyline, the telephone crackled into life and we tightened the safety rope for the last time.

Chapter 16

Variety is the Spice of Life

RETURNING FROM FRANCE, it was back to work to earn more money – and back to surveying Ease Gill Caverns and Lancaster Hole. Just as Topsy kept on growing, the combined system was spreading and made the original British Speleological Association and Northern Pennine Club surveys totally inadequate. I decided that a complete survey and description of this extensive series of passages and caverns were required, and that we in the Red Rose Cave & Pothole Club were the ones to do it.

For a small club this was a mammoth task and, but for the enthusiasm of Peter Ashmead, it would never have been completed. Peter was a young, not very experienced caver who always struggled with low-paid jobs that never realised his true potential. I was unimpressed when he said that he could produce the survey as I thought it would be beyond him – but, fortunately, I was proved wrong.

For six years the front room of the Ashmead's small family house was taken over by a huge, home-made table. On this sat the master survey of the Ease Gill System, as it was slowly and meticulously plotted, week after week.

It would be good to say that my self-imposed task of writing the detailed topography could be called meticulous, but it wasn't. With my small team of dedicated followers, every weekend saw me down Ease Gill, furiously scribbling in little red notebooks while directing my minions into all sorts of nooks and crannies.

'How wide do you reckon this passage is?'

'About fifteen feet.'

'What's up there? Is it a shadow, or is it a passage?'

'Could you have a look under that block?'

'Can you hear the stream?'

'Hey there's a passage here – never seen that before!' The topography study would then be abandoned and everyone would go off exploring, upsetting the surveyors with descriptions of their discoveries as 'tight, wet and 'orrible', or 'a squeeze through loose boulders leading to a hairy drop down to the stream'. Each Sunday night I returned from Ease Gill via, of course, a few après-caving pints of beer in the local hostelry. On chucking out my bag full of wet gear I would look in total amazement at the soggy, mud-covered scrawl in my notebook. 'Did I write this? What does it all mean?'

I would sit looking at the demented scribbling and strange little diagrams, like those seen on Egyptian tombs, and scratch my head in complete bafflement at something that a few hours previously had been obvious. If, as happened quite often, I arrived home tired and went straight to bed, leaving writing up my notes until a few days later, I was faced with pages that could outwit the Enigma code-breaking machine.

It was inevitable that, giving a cave of this nature such a close scrutiny, many unexplored passages would be revealed. As the survey grew, obvious – and some not so obvious – leads were found, such as one discovered during an official Cave Research Group visit when a group of cavers literally walked into a new passage.

When my team made its exit after a long session surveying we did not know that the Cave Research Group party had used our ladders to enter the system, so when we de-laddered the entrance pitch we were blissfully unaware of the other cavers' existence. We were informed of our error by a police constable in the Whoop Hall, where we were singing along to the refrain of 'The Threshing Machine' and risqué verses from 'Mister Doddlem'.

'Ah, I thought you lot would be in here. We've had a report of some cavers overdue up at Bull Pot Farm.' We thanked the constable and offered him a drink. 'Sorry lads, I'm on duty.' It looked like we were as well, but we could still get another round in. It was a good night and, as someone said: 'They'll keep – but this beer won't.'

When we eventually went to 'rescue' the missing cavers, we discovered that one of them was a leading light in the caving world – the well-respected Arthur Gemmell – and he was quite indignant about the whole affair. I can still see Arthur, in his steamed-up glasses, glaring at me like a ruptured owl when I told him that it was one of his rescuers who had removed the ladders. 'You're . . . You're . . . Incompetent,' he said, 'and drunk!'

Diamond Hall stood out like a sore thumb on the survey, so much so that I began digging there and soon excavated a low, tight crawl. It was blocked after several yards by a small calcite boss with a small hole in the centre – ideal for stuffing with gelignite. I pressed a good amount of this pink, marzipan-smelling stuff into the hole and fixed the detonator before crawling back to the safety of Diamond Hall, from where I set off the charge.

I never wore gloves for caving and was unaware of the unpleasant side effects that can be caused by handling gelignite. While waiting for the dense fumes to clear, I whiled away the time by eating a packet of crisps, licking the salt (and traces of gelignite) off my fingers. Soon, I pushed my way past the wreckage of the calcite boss and struggled along the low, fume-filled passage that lay ahead until I came to another obstruction. Returning to the chamber, I felt rather peculiar and within minutes I had a blinding headache and thought I was going to be sick. My legs suddenly seemed very weak and, much to my embarrassment, I fell over.

Not known for my sympathetic reaction towards weak cavers, I received none from Wilf Taylor – whose life I sometimes made a misery – or from the others in the group. 'Come on Ers – get off your bum,' was the nicest thing said to me that day, but they half-carried and half-dragged me, between bouts of being violently sick, the considerable distance from Oxbow Corner to the foot of the Lancaster Hole pitch. A Northern Pennine group which happened to be on the fell hauled me up the shaft like a sack of potatoes and dumped me on the moor, an abject heap of spew-gurgling misery.

During the early sixties it seemed that everyone wanted to go caving. Casterton Fell and the caves it contains began to suffer from an increase in novice caving groups, which produced numerous callouts, and damage to both Bull Pot Farm (in those days rented to a gentleman farmer) and the unique formations found in Lancaster Hole.

Events came to a head when we rescued a group of young cavers missing in Lancaster Hole. They were soon found, sitting around a tent inexplicably pitched underground, above Fall Pot – reading caving books! As we shepherded the adventurous youths back up the entrance shaft, which at that time was still rigged with rigid metal ladders, I heard a shout. I looked up, just in time to see a sword clattering off the ladders in a shower of sparks; it was on a direct flight path towards my right ear. Not wishing to do a Van Gogh, I hastily moved. In the stunned silence that followed, a thin, piping voice shouted down: 'Could you bring my sword back, mister?'

Even in this enlightened age, my answer is unprintable.

The following week the gentleman farmer's lady wife turned up at their little place in the country to find three potholers in her bath. She was not amused, especially when one callow youth asked, 'Could you wash my back, love?'

IN 1962 AN ERA ENDED when Eli Simpson died, leaving behind a legacy of unique cave exploration, politics and intrigue. It was ironic that the Casterton and Leck fells were closed to all cavers within a few months of old Cymmie's death, which no doubt would have caused him a wry chuckle. It was obvious that the caving organisations needed to control a rapidly deteriorating situation so, after consulting my Access to the Countryside Act 1947, I convened a meeting of all the major northern clubs and we formed the Council of Northern Caving Clubs, which as a responsible body arranged an access agreement with the fells' landowners. It has worked reasonably well ever since.

Working under a system of controlled access run by cavers for cavers allowed for a slight bending of the rules now and then, which enabled us to continue with the survey and topography without blocking access for others. Once again I found myself in strange, uncharted places, only this time I was perched on a stemple with George Cornes like two bedraggled, exotic-looking birds, peering at the black, uncharted waters of the Graveyard Sump forty feet below.

'Ah, Jim lad,' said George in his best Long John Silver voice. 'Oi reckon, if you fell off 'ere, you'd get the underground diving championship.'

I didn't answer, as I was trying to work out how the hell I had placed myself into this position with an Oxford lunatic.

'Now, Jim lad, oi wants you to lean out as far as you can and screw this other stemple into position,' said George. 'If you falls off, young Gordon will 'ave you dangling like the man on the flying trapeze.'

I looked at Gordon Batty, straddled precariously on another stemple behind us, clutching my lifeline. He didn't look too happy. 'What do you reckon?' I asked.

'Cornes is bloody mad – he always has been,' said Gordon. 'If you fall off, what am I supposed to do?'

'Ah,' says George, 'oi 'ave thought of that. You jump off. Mind you, you've got to jump the other side of your stemple – don't jump the same side as Ers, or else you'll both end up in the sump.'

The looks of total incomprehension on our faces stopped him.

'Ar, now, if you thinks about it, one will balance the other and you'll both dangle over the sump,' said George.

'Then what?' I asked.

'Well, oil go off and get the cave rescue,' said George.

'You've already got three of the cave rescuers here,' I reminded him.

'Ah well, oil get the other lot,' said George.

That was our first attempt at climbing over the Graveyard Sump. I should have known better than to become mixed up with the Pennine club – the NPC were all crazy and George was the worst of the lot. I realised that I would never reach middle age if I hung about with Cornes, but who could resist George's magnetic appeal when

'Now, Jim lad, oi wants you to lean out as far as you can and screw this other stemple into position,' said George

he confessed that, 'Last night, oi dreamt oi was a choirmaster and you, Ers, was my favourite choirboy.'

His Svengali-like appeal drew me back and the following weekend saw me again making that death-defying traverse, clinging onto smooth, black slimy walls with my feet on one wall and back on the other. Clutching at yet another stemple, I advanced towards the rubble bridge that clung tenaciously to the rock some forty feet above the sump.

Perched on the last stemple, I weighed up the gap to the last jammed rock in the bottom of the steep, frozen avalanche – and leapt across. The rock held and I cautiously made my way up the steep slope of hanging death to the black expanse that beckoned high overhead, mentally praying to all the gods to prevent the unstable rock pile from moving. Climbing like a cat, carefully testing every foot and handhold, I crept up to behold a large funnel-shaped space surrounded by huge, angular blocks, seemingly suspended in space. A light flashed below me – it was George, who for once was speechless. My probing light revealed a way on through a gap in the rockfall, but it was suicidal and this time I retreated.

AS ONE GOES THROUGH LIFE, advancing years are supposed to endow one with more wisdom. Lying prone under a beer barrel, with beer dripping from a leaking spigot onto my head, I wondered why this sensible sort of reasoning did not seem to apply to me – and who would have thought that a wet mop could be wielded with enough force to unseat a rider and flatten her mount, and send them both skidding along the beer-soaked floor to end up in the bar under three barrels mounted on a bench.

We had been invited to a 'do' by a caving and mining club in an ancient Masonic hall in the ancient market town of Ulverston, birthplace of Stan Laurel and Hartley's beer. Both were guaranteed to have you falling about laughing.

The day was spent grovelling in glutinous, red ochre clay in old mine workings; it aged me ten years as I crept under tons of hanging 'deads' left by long-gone miners, who had the dangerous habit of propping up mountains of unstable rock on twigs and bits of wood. This probably contributed to their early demise, a state I didn't wish to emulate.

Eventually, our hosts desisted in showing us their peculiar form of masochism and deemed it reasonable, after washing in cold water (which still left us looking like Red Indians) that we should be entertained. After a tour of olde worlde pubs that specialised in very strong ale, we were treated to a display of black magic which ended in their club hut (a derelict building and our place of residence) with a duel between two inebriated cavers using red-hot pokers.

We eventually arrived at the Masonic hall. There, triggered by looking at the stern faces peering down on us from ornate picture frames – or perhaps because of the Hartley's XB bitter – we thought we would hold a jousting contest. Four men were the horses and four young ladies were jockeys armed with wet mops.

It made her realise how desirable she must be

With native cunning I picked a well-endowed lass, who looked as though she had been brought up on the end of a mop – but it turned out that she had never even seen one before, which is how I ended up under a beer barrel.

Meanwhile, a middle-aged lady stepped out of her bath and was amazed, and no doubt a little gratified, to find that she had a couple of peeping Toms. The fact that her bathroom was three storeys above the ground and that the two lusters after female flesh were clinging to the church steeple opposite, made her realise how desirable she must be for young men to take such risks for a glimpse of her naked charms.

Ah well, 'twas ever thus and, thinking of Helen of Troy, whose face launched a thousand ships, the lady approached her window to discover that she had launched a thousand slips. One youth gave a cry of anguish and fell off and the other slid onto an adjoining roof. Fortunately for the youth who was airborne, he flew through the air, did a graceful backflip and landed on the top of a dinky little sports car that was parked below. It was transformed into a sort of tin jelly mould, with an inside-out view of a human bum, two hands and two feet. The shaken climber staggered away, groaning in pain but alive.

By then the strange goings on at the old church had been brought to the attention of the local constabulary by our friendly middle-aged lady. Back at the party we had reached the stage, as people do, where four well-endowed young ladies were dressed in four tiny bikinis and four inebriated youths were down to their Y-fronts, and we were all trying to pass the large church front-door key, which was tied to a piece of string, through places it had never been before. This was accomplished by threading the string down through the bikini tops and bottoms, up some Y-front legs and gently pulling.

This was a good game, inducing lots of girlish giggles as the key passed by on its voyage of discovery before diving down some Y-front and encountering a different ball game. It was particularly enjoyable for the person pulling the string – me.

'Allo allo allo – what 'ave we 'ere?'

Then, preceded by a loud knocking on the door, an authoritative voice shouted, 'Open up, it's the police.' The door opened and there stood PC Blodge. 'Allo allo allo – what 'ave we 'ere?' he said, then went silent as Sandra tried to stuff one of her wayward breasts back into her bikini top.

'Well, I, er, well,' he muttered. I could imagine his mind racing as he tried to grasp the situation – peeping Toms, defiling property, beer on unlicensed premises, under-age drinking? Underage sex? An orgy!

Then he peered strangely at Jim Newton (who prefers to be known as Mr X) and said, 'Why, it's Jim Newton – it's me, Bill Blodge.'

It turned out that he and Jim went to school together and were both on the rugby team. They greeted each other like old Mafia pals (though without the kissing as Jim, although being a man's man, knows where to draw the line).

'Take off your helmet and have a beer!'

After a wild night we retired to our Hotel Derelicto for a night of agony, as our air conditioning worked overtime. The temperature outside fell to minus six and the wind brought flurries of snow through the pane-less windows, blowing them out through a hole in the roof.

Morning came with the cry of 'Brew up.' Lots of confused stumbling around followed: 'Where's the Primus?' 'Where's the pan?' 'Where's the tap?' A long period of silence, then, 'Bloody tap's frozen solid.'

'There's some water in the boot of my car.' I threw the keys. Sound of footsteps coming back.

'It's frozen solid,' and I was handed a plastic bottle, frozen hard. I stuck it in my sleeping bag and hugged it, desperate for tea. Sometime later, shaking with cold, I handed the bottle of melted water to Pete, who filled the pan on the stove and we watched as the life-giving liquid began to boil. Pete fumbled for some tea in a rucksack, then turned and knocked the pan off the stove. He vanished in a cloud of steam, curses and hurled boots. We were saved by Rose's hot-water bottle.

Two days later the headlines in the local paper read: 'Perverts frighten local woman. Peeping Tom falls off church steeple. Hooligans invade Ulverston.'

THE SWINGING SIXTIES were highlighted by an increase in the caving population, better equipment, new lightweight clothing and the beginning of 'packaged cavers'. As commercialised sport took hold, silly sods crawled around in cardboard caverns on television. Educational establishments, university caving clubs and outdoor pursuits centres blossomed; schoolteachers were sent on courses to be taught how to become leaders in caving and climbing activities by self-appointed 'experts' who hadn't a clue and even less experience. 'Sport for all' (and death for some) became compulsory and the mountain rescue teams were kept busy.

Cave rescues, in our area alone, increased from three a year to thirteen and the Cave Rescue Organisation was in business with a vengeance as cavers fell down pitches or became trapped by floods with monotonous regularity. Our hard-working secretary, Brian Boardman, established invaluable records through his incident reports; nothing escaped his attention and the mind boggles with one that stated: 'Divers recover trousers containing valuables.'

There must be a story in this, I thought. Might it bear a relationship to the report: 'Divers attempt to recover handbag'? Could it have been a lovers' tiff? Perhaps the caver was divested of his trousers on the strength of a promise and, when she refused, he chucked her handbag in the river; she retaliated by chucking in his trousers, complete with wallet and car keys, and their faithful dog was so upset by all this that . . .

The next incident report read: 'Large dog collapsed with heart attack.' Another mentioned the rescue of a 'well-equipped female hiker' – could she have been the owner of the handbag?

The public service role of the CRO was very much in evidence as, apart from the numerous serious cave rescues, the rescue team became a general troubleshooter for the area. We developed into a free, general emergency service which undertook everything from looking for escaped lunatics (excluding MPs – they come under Special Branch) to rescuing ducks.

Incident 652 read: 'Nine ducks trapped down narrow hole, six rescued' – by a very small caver, I presume.

Strange things happen in the caving world. I was once climbing a ladder out of Alum Pot when I looked up to see a lady descending. From the state of her black stockings proceeding upwards past voluminous skirts to end at a thin band of flesh before being swallowed in blue baggy knickers, she could have been none other than Old Mother Riley. All was revealed in Brian's incident report: 'Twelve-year-old novice and mother unable to climb 80 foot pitch.'

Apart from the six ducks, we saved 52 lambs, 40 sheep, 21 dogs, 5 calves, 4 cows and 1 bullock, as well as playing Sherlock Holmes in 'The Strange Case of the Headless Helmet'. 'Blood in pool and fleshy stale air smell at bottom of pitch', we were told, and we were asked to investigate. It wasn't the only odd request. We helped the police search the caves and mines of the Attermire area, looking for someone who was under arrest in Morocco. He couldn't be found, but instead we discovered 'a female pseudo-hiker who collapsed with a form of hysteria'.

The 'pseudo-hiker' had probably been reading Brian's incident reports – though I never did find out what a female pseudo-hiker was. Perhaps she was a transvestite on a bike.

Even allowing for Brian's laconic prose in the incident reports, we did receive some odd callouts. I was helping on a fell search for a man reported missing by his wife and mother-in-law. 'We were walking on the fell when he suddenly vanished,' said the young lady's mother, an extremely dominant person. I was not really surprised when, searching the moor several miles away, I came across a furtive figure crouched in a shakehole. 'Keep going,' he said. 'Don't tell anyone you've found me. I'm escaping from the mother-in-law!'

Generally, all the minor incidents and false alarms were attended to by those members of the CRO who lived locally. Now and again I was involved, though, and on one occasion – looking at the bloated carcass of a long-dead cow that was conducting a macabre dance thirty feet above my head – I found my enthusiasm waning.

'The rope's stuck,' came a shout from above.

'Well, lower it down a bit and try again,' I shouted.

The daylight was almost eclipsed as the cow's body jerked downwards, then stopped as the lads heaved on the ropes again. Suddenly, I heard a yell as the rope broke and the dead beast hurtled towards me and, together with my mate, I dived for cover. The bloated carcass hit the floor only inches away with a mighty 'Splat!' and we were literally covered in the exploded contents of the cow's guts.

'Shit,' said my mate.

'Yes it is,' I replied, 'and we're bloody well covered in it!'

ASK ANY MEMBER OF A CAVE RESCUE TEAM, 'How many accidents are avoidable?' The answer will probably be that most caving accidents are not accidents in the true sense of the word, but lapses in judgement and therefore avoidable.

Simpson's Pot in Kingsdale is a popular sporting cave. It has everything: five hundred feet of low, hands-and-knees-sized passage leading to a flat-out crawl in water, then on to nine pitches of varying degrees of difficulty, a duck, traverses and a series of winding passages that connect with Swinsto Hole and Kingsdale Master Cave.

A young caver was following the well-traversed route established by hundreds of cavers before him when, pulling himself up on a well-polished handhold on a large slab of rock that overhung the seventh pitch, the slab – which had been there for thousands of years – suddenly fell, severely injuring the unlucky man.

What was a nice 'sporting' cave now turned into a cave rescuer's nightmare. We struggled to ease the pain-wracked victim through the low beddings and pendulum him along the narrow traverses. We had men balanced above and men jammed in the crevices below, as we manhandled the bulky stretcher through the restricted streamways with only inches to spare.

In one area the passage is bisected by a sixty-foot-deep, well-like shaft. Bob's Pit, as it is known, had two baulks of timber jammed across the top to allow an easy traverse, but unfortunately they caused the stretcher to jam. The beams had to be removed and were substituted by two volunteers, who lay full-length across the gaping hole while the injured caver, encased in bamboo and metal, was dragged painfully across their backs. Looking down a sixty-foot drop while lying prone, bearing a weighty stretcher that is suddenly plonked on your back, was an extremely uncomfortable experience, as judged by the groans and grunts of 'Hurry up!'

After a long struggle we began to move through the last section along the five hundred foot entrance crawl, which suddenly seemed lower and wetter than usual. Our steady progress was brought to a halt in front of a pool. I demanded to know what the hold-up was, and was informed that the passage was blocked by someone in front.

I pushed forward and found a bloke in blue overalls fiddling with a camera and obstructing the passage. Without hesitation, I shoved the press reporter to one side and instructed the stretcher-bearers to move forward, carefully ensuring that the heavy stretcher pushed the prat off balance. Both he and his camera went into the five-foot-deep pool, where a couple of the lads used him as a stepping stone.

This Simpson's Pot rescue was the result of a genuine unforeseen occurrence. It could have happened to me, as I too had several times heaved my body onto that unstable-looking slab and each time thought, 'One of these days, this is going to move.' But then, for me, it never did.

Another hazard was caused by grant-aided hill farmers, who cut drainage channels on the fells as part of yet another government directive that had no end product – apart from almost instantaneously directing huge volumes of water down potholes when it rained, flushing cavers out like panic-stricken frogs.

This practice of 'gripping' caused flood callouts to increase dramatically, and some of the easier, more accessible caves were turned into death traps for the unwary. This was illustrated when the CRO was called upon to rescue a total of thirty-seven cavers from Alum Pot in two incidents within three days. One group was completely trapped and the other consisted of distraught schoolchildren, who had been left by their school-teachers in a rapidly flooding cave while they went for assistance. By the time the rescuers entered, the children were suffering from varying degrees of hypothermia and shock; they were brought out through a nearby oxbow that bypassed the stream passage. This was a good example of a little knowledge being a dangerous thing – leaders of novice groups should always familiarise themselves with a cave before they take their charges underground.

This is but one example of incompetent parties requiring rescue and at the time I wrote several strong articles condemning these practices, but to no avail. Alum Pot added to its grim total when, only two months after the multiple rescues, a young caver fell eighty feet to his death.

THERE'S ONE THING ABOUT CAVING – you soon find out who your friends are.

Young Mabel was enjoying her caving experience in Upper Long Churn Cave with a group of friends and a nice leader, when she was introduced to the joy of Dr Bannister's Handbasin. This water chute plunges into a five-foot-deep pool and little Mabel enjoyed the exhilarating slide, but due to recent rain the pool was deeper than normal. As Mabel hit the water her light went out; she splashed about in the gloaming and found land, which was – unfortunately – a ledge behind the waterfall.

At this point one wonders if little Mabel suffered from BO or something, because no one noticed her sudden departure, and only when the nice leader shepherded his flock back to his van did he realise that he had an empty seat.

'Who sat here?' he asked.

'Mabel,' came the reply.

'Where is she?'

'Dunno – you should know, you're in charge.' Panic, swiftly followed by a stricken telephone call to the police.

'I think I've lost Mabel – her Mother will be awfully upset.'

We quickly established that Mabel had been swallowed up by a cave, so one of our lads found himself in Dr Bannister's Handbasin, feeling around and shouting, 'Coo-ee.' He was soon answered by Mabel who, though only young, had an enquiring mind and wanted to know: 'Why has everyone buggered off and left me?'

IN 1963, APART FROM OTHER INCIDENTS, there were eight callouts for cavers trapped by flooding, including four on one Sunday evening in November.

A day of torrential rain continued well into the night, as members of the CRO battled away on the mist-shrouded slopes of Penyghent to extricate cavers from the flood-lashed depths of Little Hull Pot and Hunt Pot. With more sense the trapped cavers wouldn't have been there, but there they were and it was our job to bring them out, so we split into two groups.

The Little Hull party had been caught on its way out, whereupon four of its six members had managed to fight their way to the exit. This left two of their colleagues trapped in a cave which the guidebook described as: 'A strenuous pot, only to be done in fine and settled weather.'

When we arrived at the entrance it was submerged under several feet of water, so we set to building dams upstream and digging diversion channels to send the water down sundry shakeholes on the moor. We filled sandbags and stacked them to form a pool deep enough to submerge our pumps and, together with some firemen, we ran hoses across the moor into other sinks. Eventually, a few inches of airspace appeared, allowing two of us to enter the 150 foot long entrance passage. The report we received from the cavers who had made it out was that one man was trapped on a ledge on the big pitch, which required 135 foot of ladder, and the other was below him. Given the weather conditions, time was precious.

Crouching and crawling along the wet passage, with water streaming from the roof, we hoped the dams would hold. Reaching the big pitch, I looked over to see a caver in an alcove. I shouted down just as a wall of water came tearing out of a side passage, hit me on my back and almost knocked me down the drop.

'Bloody hell. Give them a ring and tell them to find another hole to pump into,' I shouted to my mate, who had the field telephone.

After various other outdoor plumbing experiments, which brought water in from all sorts of unexpected places, the team eventually stopped the deluge and, joined by more rescuers, we brought the two lads out.

Meanwhile, the Hunt Pot team was struggling. As we joined them, we took in the sight of a stream swollen almost to the size of a river that thundered down the narrow ravine of the pothole's entrance. Two groups of rescuers were standing on the brink, tugging at lifelines which hung down the drop in the hope that someone might tie on and be pulled up.

This frantic underground, blind fishing hadn't received a bite – it was a bit futile without communications. Three of the team had gone down and they, too, had been swallowed by the gaping plughole of Hunt Pot and not been heard of again.

At last we succeeded in sending the field telephone down and were relieved to hear that the trapped cavers had been located in a side passage between the thundering waterfalls of the entrance rift. They had been huddled in this wet, draughty, narrow crevice for eleven hours; we hauled them out like stranded fish.

In the meantime, another callout had been received for Marble Steps Pot, so a rescue group set off while we recovered the last of the trapped cavers. The victims of Marble Steps had been forced to abandon all their gear and 'fight like hell' to escape from the floodwater that overwhelmed them in the restricted depths of the Intestines, a name that speaks for itself.

Unfortunately for one of these lads, he hadn't avoided his date with destiny – it was only postponed. A week later six cavers from the same group descended Marble Steps to retrieve their tackle. The weather was still unfit, but they reckoned that they could dash in and out fairly quickly. However, the Intestines route consists of awkward climbs and a twisting crawl; it is not a place where a caver can move quickly.

Mike McShea's girlfriend stayed above Stink Pot, just before the restricted section, to keep an eye on the water level and give a warning if it rose. The three men were well into the Intestines when one of them thought he heard a scream from above. Mike Myers went back to check; he was gone for some time and Graham Lyon felt worried enough to say to Mike McShea that they should return. Mike could not be persuaded so Graham set off alone, a decision that saved his life. The floodwater hit him just as he emerged from a low crawl into the base of the last inclined pitch. He had to brace his body against the wall of water as it hit him and, with water backing up to his head, he half-scrabbled and half-floated up the pitch, against the torrent of water.

Mike McShea stood no chance. He clambered desperately into the highest part of the restricted passage, waiting for the flood pulse to subside. Unfortunately for him, the flooding continued . . .

The first member of the rescue team found that the floodwater in the higher levels of the cave passage above Stink Pot was within three inches of the roof. Water pumps from the Settle and Bentham Fire Brigades were used to enable members of the rescue team to penetrate the flooded passages. The body of the trapped potholer was found near the top of Pillar Box pitch, lying on his back with his head partly submerged. Lifting him out of the entrance pitch, I felt something touching my leg. I looked down at Mike's hand and the gold ring on his finger as it moved in a futile gesture, still trying to grasp at a life that had been so carelessly thrown away.

Again, we asked ourselves why cavers take such risks with flooding. Some risks in caving are an acceptable – some might say an essential – part of the attraction of cave exploration, but to descend any active water sink in bad weather is to court disaster. It is not sport, it is not even thrilling. For the unfortunate victim, it must be sheer terror and he does not even have the satisfaction of telling his mates about it afterwards.

SOMEONE AT CASTERTON SCHOOL must have read my ensuing article, warning of the dangers of inexperienced groups being taken underground by leaders who lack expertise and experience. The Honorary Secretary of the Northern Pennine Club, who at that time was Colin Green (I believe because he was the only one who could write), approached me in the Flying Horse-shoes and said,' Ah, it's Mr Jim Eyre.' His craggy face lit up when he told me that the Pennine had been asked to take a party of pupils from Casterton School down Alum Pot.

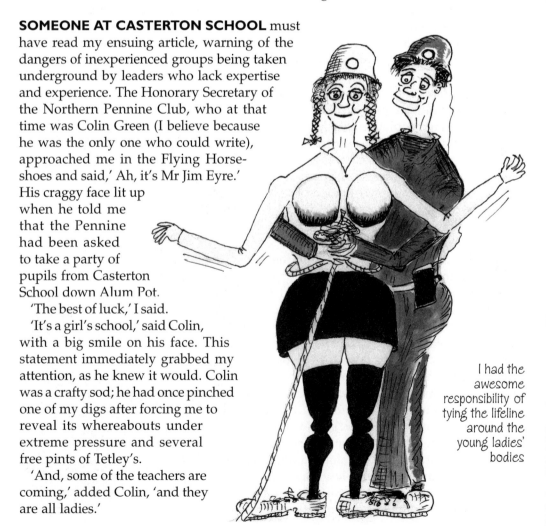

I had the awesome responsibility of tying the lifeline around the young ladies' bodies

'The best of luck,' I said.

'It's a girl's school,' said Colin, with a big smile on his face. This statement immediately grabbed my attention, as he knew it would. Colin was a crafty sod; he had once pinched one of my digs after forcing me to reveal its whereabouts under extreme pressure and several free pints of Tetley's.

'And, some of the teachers are coming,' added Colin, 'and they are all ladies.'

'Ah,' I said. 'Fancy a pint, Col?'

For the NPC it was a surprisingly large turnout. When the coach disgorged all these rather well-developed young ladies in hockey gear, there was a stunned silence. Then, when it disgorged their teachers, there was an even greater stunned silence. This must have been the safest caving trip on record: the young ladies were assisted over every little obstacle and one caver outdid Sir Walter Raleigh by throwing himself into a pool to prevent a young lady from becoming wet. 'Just walk across my back,' he said. It was disgusting.

At the Double Shuffle Pool the young dears were surrounded by willing cavers, who placed their dainty feet on the right holds and held their hands, giving a little push to a shapely bum now and again. But when we reached the pitches, it was time for the really experienced cavers to take over and, having rigged the ladders and stationed fellow 'guardians' at various danger points, I had the awesome responsibility of tying the lifeline around the young ladies' bodies. This required a deft touch and is something that could never be done today, as it would certainly end up in court with a charge of molesting or attempted rape.

A few girlish giggles always accompanied this operation, as in several instances with the senior girls it was problematical where to tie the knot – above or below the breasts – and the girls' advice was sought. That induced more giggling.

The Dollytubs, an easy forty-foot pitch, lived up to its name in a manner that the old timers who named it could never have imagined. One bloke had perched himself precariously on a small ledge halfway down, just so that he could prevent the ladder twisting on the rock flake. He carefully chaperoned each young lady past, with a look on his face like an overfed spaniel as he stared at our charges with large, soulful eyes and asked each one if she was alright. The two chaps clinging steadfastly to the bottom of the ladder were there 'To stop it swinging about,' while steadfastly trying not to look up at the long, black, stocking-clad legs and exposed thighs that headed their way.

It was embarrassing and it became even more so helping the lasses down the Greasy Slab, as this was definitely a case of 'hands on'

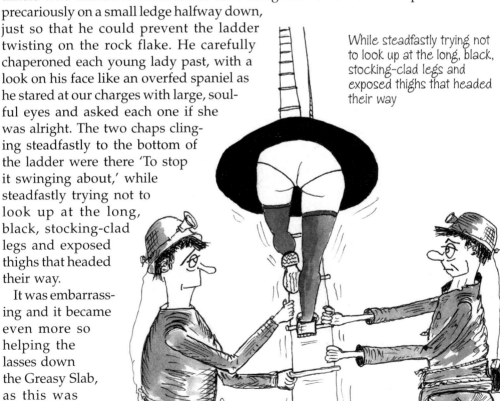

While steadfastly trying not to look up at the long, black, stocking-clad legs and exposed thighs that headed their way for a slip here would have resulted in an eighty-foot fall. I lost count of how many young ladies ended the short climb with their legs wrapped around my neck. It's a good job I was made of stern stuff.

We brought them all over the rock bridge and down to the bottom of the daylight shaft. The return was harder but, thanks to the stout lifelining team, the young ladies, now looking more like refugees from St Trinian's with torn skirts, holey stockings and mud-streaked faces grinning at us in a manner that belied their tender years, were hoisted up and shepherded out.

Everyone enjoyed themselves, especially the lecherous sods (who shall remain anonymous). It was a delightful day out, a case of jolly hockey sticks and let's make it an annual event.

I DECIDED THAT I LIKED YOUNG LADIES better than small boys. I am not a lover of small boys (strictly in the 1960s meaning) – they are generally spotty, truculent and don't smell as nice as young ladies. When I was offered one to use on a practice cave rescue, I wasn't too keen.

I mean – you don't know where they've been.

This particular small boy had been knocking around with Ron Bliss, who used him as a photographer's model in his caving photographs. Not that Ron liked small boys all that much, but it was all he could get because none of *us* would pose for him.

Before I proceed much further in this narrative, I should point out that the reason I needed a small boy was that, as an underground rescue controller, I was concerned about the number of cavers entering Ease Gill Caverns, given the restricted nature of some of its passages and the loose areas.

An accident resulting in a stretcher-bound casualty would cause problems for the rescue team, so I needed to know how we would overcome them. It would be better to use a small, live boy than a nearly dead, twelve-stone caver – if the stretcher became stuck with a small, live boy in it, we could always kick him out and tell him to walk, whereas a nearly dead, twelve-stone caver would take very unkindly to this sort of suggestion.

It is not very pleasant being fastened into a stretcher, then manhandled up pitches and through twisting restricted cave passages, but against my better judgement I accepted Ron's offer of his protégé. He was, as I suspected, spotty, truculent and called Leslie.

Mention that name now and I shudder. Everyone has a favourite name and a few general dislikes, like Septococco or Bolonicuss, which are never very popular at christenings. However, hearing the name Leslie brings me out in a cold sweat. We started the exercise with a bright and chirpy Leslie, quite comfortable and strapped inside the stretcher about half a mile from the cave entrance.

We were soon being tested by small climbs and pitches, low crawls and traverses. Leslie proved to have the ideal body – light – and was uncomplaining. After a while I stopped the exercise to remove him from the stretcher, offer him a hot drink and some exercise, after which he happily climbed back into the stretcher and away we went again.

During a period of very severe testing of our stretcher-removal skills, where we had to negotiate several problems, I was quite proud of young Leslie. He quietly put up with the strange positions in which we were forced to place the stretcher. Then, in one extremely tortuous section of passage, the stretcher handlers got into difficulties and the head of the stretcher ended up lower than its foot. 'Keep the head up,' I ordered. As the stretcher levelled off, I suddenly realised that Leslie, who had been most vociferous, was now extremely quiet.

I traversed over the handlers and looked at Leslie's homely face – it was pale and wan and the coloured bits that should have been in the middle of his eyes were missing. He looked like a small Greek statue. Instant panic.

We lowered Leslie to the ground, rapidly released him from the stretcher and I began shaking him – no response. I slapped his face and his

He was spotty, truculent and called Leslie

eyes went from tilt to normal, then the coloured bits reappeared. Leslie came round and jumped to his feet, shouting, 'You've tried to kill me,' then fell over in a dead faint!

'Oh Christ!' I remember saying. 'He really is a stretcher case now.'

We carefully picked Leslie up and placed him in the stretcher. Just as we were tightening the straps, he came round. 'Let me out, let me out!' he yelled hysterically, obviously in some distress. We took the lad out of the stretcher, but he collapsed in a heap again and sat on the cave floor shaking violently, as though he was having a fit. I don't know about Leslie, but I felt that I was about to have one! Here we were with a body that refused to lie down and refused to stand up.

I talked to Leslie and calmed him down, then suggested that we should all head out of the cave, but I couldn't get much sense out of him. He refused to move and just sat there, shaking.

'Put him in the stretcher,' I said, which triggered Leslie into more hysterical shouting as he tried to prevent us from touching him.

I realised that we had a fairly novel and potentially serious situation developing. I sent Mike Bateson out of the cave to obtain some hot drinks from Bull Pot Farm and alert the CRO ambulance. Then, despite Leslie's protestations, we half-carried, half-dragged him through the rest of the cave to the foot of the first of the two small entrance pitches. He refused to let us haul him up the pitch and refused to try to climb it.

Increasingly exasperated, I stationed three of the team above the pitch and put a rope on Jack Proctor, a well-built, strong member of the group. We hoisted Leslie, also tied to a rope in case the silly sod decided to leap off, onto Jack's back. Then, assisted from above, Big Jack climbed the eighteen-foot pitch with his shouting burden, who almost throttled him in the process.

At the top we took over and literally pushed, pulled and dragged the lad to the surface. Mike, who had run two miles to the farm and back again clutching the hot drinks, came gasping into view.

'Here you are Leslie, drink this,' said Mike.

'Don't want it,' said Leslie. I'm sure Mike was tempted to kick him back down the hole.

After being half-carried across the fell, our intrepid schoolboy hero made a sudden and quite miraculous recovery, and we thought that was that. Unfortunately, it wasn't . . .

The following day dear Leslie appeared as a star in several national newspapers, with headlines proclaiming: 'Patient, fifteen, blacks out in mock pothole rescue', and 'Mock rescue became the real thing', followed by a lurid account by Leslie telling how the rescuers, led by Jim Eyre, nearly strangled him as the stretcher caught him in the throat and that 'he was often carried upside down in the cold and damp'. I almost choked on my egg and bacon when I read that the intrepid Leslie stated: 'I'll have another go at being rescued, and I'll be potholing again next week.'

Not with me you won't, matey.

I HAD BEEN AWARE FOR SOME TIME that I should have picked another sport, for Mother Nature hadn't designed me to be a caver. Well, not a caver in English caves. I was the wrong shape: long, awkward and fairly skinny, with sticky out bits and hip bones that wouldn't look out of place on a camel.

I was continually frustrated by the ability of some of my plumper colleagues to progress, amoeba-like through tight crevices and crawls as their body fat squelched around them, while my progress was always marred by

Big Jack climbed the eighteen-foot pitch with his shouting burden, who almost throttled him in the process knocking shoulder and hip bones. It was in this sort of position that I now found myself, after spending several weekends clearing a low, silted-up crawl in Car Pot on the slopes of Ingleborough.

At Car Pot a short entrance pitch ends in a tight letterbox with, immediately underneath, a tight, low crawl that leads off at right angles. After sixty feet this opens onto a series of pitches that end at a 130 foot pitch that drops into a large passage, which could – we hoped – be joined to the Gaping Gill system. The crawl had been blocked for several years but now, after a lot of hard work, we had cleared it and two of my Red Rose clubmates were slithering on ahead. Alas, they were slithering without me, for I was stuck – not permanently, but nevertheless stuck.

I lay in several inches of water with my face pressed into the gravel, blowing bubbles out of the side of my mouth as, with one arm stretched in front holding my helmet, I rolled and thrashed from side to side swearing every swearword I could think of.

This was the fourth time I had been stuck in this bloody crawl and it was at exactly the same place, beside a little knobbly stalagmite boss which was now inserted into my hip bone.

'Push!' I shouted to my personal assistants, who were on the end of my secret weapon – a set of drain rods joined to a specially made T-piece which was attached to my boots. They rammed the metal against my hobnailed boots and I shot forward – one and a half inches.

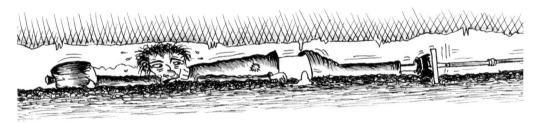

Push!

'Again,' I shouted.

They pushed again and I distinctly heard the clunk of bone on rock as I felt a sharp pain in my right hip bone.

'Bugger it!' I shouted. 'Try again,' and with another heave from the lads I wriggled and thrutched and swore, but to no avail.

'Sod it, I'm coming out,' I shouted.

My buddies withdrew my home-made ramrod and I began to follow it out. But, after a bit of casual wriggling, I hadn't moved. The wriggling became more extreme and I found, to my consternation, that I was still in the same position. Someone shouted from the end of the crawl and I gave a non-committal grunt as I laboured to free myself, but only succeeded in jamming one arm.

A light approached from the end of the crawl as the two men in front returned in a cloud of steam, accompanied by lots of grunting and two 'bloody 'ells' when they saw that their line of retreat was blocked by an outstretched hand holding a helmet and the bulk of something vaguely human with its face buried in the gravel.

'Bloody 'ell, is that you Jim?' asked Mike. 'What are you doing?'

'Praying. I'm bloody stuck,' I muttered.

'Shit – are you sure?'

'Of course I'm bloody sure – do you think I like lying here?'

'Oh! What about me and Tom – we can't get out.'

'Give me a push.'

'What are you doing?'
'Praying. I'm bloody stuck.'

There followed a frantic struggle for several minutes as Mike pushed and I squirmed and wriggled until we both stopped, exhausted. Needless to say, I hadn't moved. By this time the lads outside the crawl realised that something was amiss, so Tommy Leigh crawled in behind me and looped a rope around one foot.

After a rest I tried again to free my body from the cold embrace of the fossil crinoids and, after an almighty battle assisted by my gallant comrades, pushing and pulling and swearing, I gradually came free and floundered backwards to perform another acrobatic manoeuvre to rise up the letterbox and out.

Later that evening, after quenching the thirst of my chortling rescuers with several pints of ale, I decided to organise an expedition to Yugoslavia, a land of mystery, intrigue and lots of giant caves – the sort that you can't become stuck in. Accordingly, I contacted the world's only professional cavers, the Karst Research Institute in Postojna.

I had almost forgotten about it when, several weeks later, I received an invitation to join some Yugoslavian speleologists on a caving expedition. My life was about to change again!

Chapter 17

Yugoslavia

I **LOOKED UP** at this formidable, khaki-clad giant of a woman who peered down at me through the open van window. She had first attracted my attention by leaping out of a small sentry box in the middle of a dark forest, still dripping with rain-drops falling from the wet branches. She had since held my undivided attention with the muzzle of a rifle, which gently nudged my chin.

'Passaport. Visa,' she thundered, glaring at me as though I had just run over her pet cat. Her huge, khaki-enclosed breasts rocked the van as she peered inside. 'Out!' she commanded and gestured me round to the back doors, which I opened to expose a huge pile of caving ladders and ropes.

She swiftly took a step back and aimed the gun at me again. 'Vos is dis?'

'Speleo,' I said. She obviously didn't understand, so I said 'Karst Institute Postojna,' and showed her the letter of invitation with the official stamp.

'Also?' she said, pointing at Jim Newton and Young Les, who were standing beside Jim's BMW motor-cycle, still glowing hot after the struggle up the rough one-in-three gradient of the Wurzen Pass.

'Ja, also,' I answered.

She minutely examined all the documents and passports before returning them. This Slovenian Brunhilde then pointed into darkest Yugoslavia and said, 'Go!'

'Passaport. Visa,' she thundered

A short distance down the road we encountered the official customs post, where we changed our money and, thanks to a bonus from Marshal Tito, we became instant dinar millionaires.

Leaving the post behind us, with the mist gradually clearing, we found ourselves in a beautiful country. The snow-capped Julian Alps glistened in the sunlight, rising above a multi-shaded patchwork of green fields and dark green forests of conifers. The road ahead snaked down into Austrian-type scenery, passing quaint churches with their distinctive onion-shaped domes and picture postcard chalets decked with flowers.

Northern Slovenia was a legacy from the old Austro-Hungarian Empire and, as such, its culture had hardly changed. It was far removed from the austere, grim communist state that we expected in 1964 and we felt a bit like Alice going through the keyhole as we passed sweet-smelling meadows and quaint hamlets.

Having had a long journey, with Jim and Les on the motorcycle being particularly tired, we pulled off the road at an official campsite as it was forbidden to camp anywhere else. The rutted track led to a field containing a wooden hut, embellished by a string of coloured lights, four long tables, eight forms and a ladies and gents toilet that was discreetly camouflaged by thick bushes.

The hut was the office and the bar. I handed our passports to a surly individual who suddenly materialised, as they do in communist countries. He proceeded to fill in mountains of paperwork and bash it repeatedly with a stamp, which is also what they do in communist countries, with a vigour not seen anywhere else. We pitched our tents, had a meal, then headed for the bar.

My life is littered with mistakes and this decision was one of them. Several things led to my downfall. I was pleasantly tired, the evening was pleasantly warm, the people were pleasantly friendly and the local booze was pleasantly cheap. Soon, our table was stocked with Črni-var – a local black or dark-red wine which we found very palatable. Then my grammar-school-educated brain slipped into gear; wasn't Yugoslavia the land of slibbovitch or slivovitz or something, the world-famous plum brandy?

After some discussion with the friendly barman, I came away with several slivovkas – colourless, harmless-looking fluid in very small glasses. I made the appropriate toast and knocked mine back in the approved fashion, trying not to convey to my companions my complete loss of an ability to breathe, speak or move as liquid fire hit my guts and lungs at the same time.

A frozen grin appeared on my face as I tried to whisper how good it was, but Jim, Les and Rose had no unfulfilled taste desires, or imagination. After a little sip (or sniff) they declined my invitation to drink what the natives drank and carried on sipping at their wine, pulling faces and plonking lemonade in it.

'When in Rome, do as the Romans do,' I quoted, as in a show of bravado I downed another tot of nitro-glycerine.

'This isn't Rome,' said Rose sniffily, 'and you are going to end up pissed.' Which is precisely what happened.

I drank all the slivovitz, most of the wine and some more slivovitz offered by friendly Slovenians as we drank lots of toasts, which one must join in. I then executed a kind of slow-motion samba towards the gents, after which there was a blank period in my life until I was reborn, clutching a luminous insect – glow-worm or firefly, I will never know. Suffice it to say, like Moses, I had found a bush on fire with burning luminosity and, like him, I didn't get burned. I wonder if old Moses had been on the slivovitz?

I staggered around our fellow campers with my own electric light, then passed peacefully away for forty-eight hours.

THE KARST RESEARCH INSTITUTE had been set up by the state to study the geology and problems affecting the environment; it was now a world-famous organisation and a foremost caving authority. Its offices were housed in a large museum in the centre of Postojna, which was in the process of being either dismantled or rebuilt. Picking our way through the builders' rubble, we eventually tracked down my contact, Professor France Habe, a dapper little man with a neat moustache and a lively personality. He introduced us to his colleagues: Rado Gospodarič and Peter Habič, both of whom spoke excellent English and looked as we imagined Yugoslavians should look – big, burly and crew-cutted.

We were taken across the square to a delightful restaurant where we met other members of the staff and had a great meal. This was also where, in spite of my protestations, we were introduced to pear brandy – another form of slivovitz that, according to our new friends, was much smoother than the stuff that had laid me out for two days.

'Ah, Mr Jim, this will repair your brain,' said Rado.

Twenty-five miles from Postojna is a heavily forested area of karst centred on a little village called Hrušica, which was the scene of severe fighting between the Germans and Yugoslavian patriots during the Second World War. Following the Yugoslav's battered old Renault van we pulled up at the partially ruined village, where we were shown bullet and mortar holes in the brickwork of the old inn. The grizzly owner of the place told us the sort of tales that patriots love to tell, while the van was loaded with cardboard boxes full of food and several large bottles of the local black wine.

We continued on our way along the dirt road, deep into the forest until, eventually, we pulled up in a clearing beside a log cabin which belonged to local woodcutters. It was to be our headquarters for the next eleven days while we explored the area's caves.

Later that evening, when all our chores were done, we sat around the pine table and were served by Professor Habe in his chef's apron and tall, white hat. His cooking was excellent and, helped down with copious glasses of Črni-var, it made for a memorable evening. Warmed with wine and the soft glow from oil lamps, we exchanged stories of our lives, got to know each other better, bullshitted about our caving exploits and, as always, swapped swear words.

One man, in particular, stood out from the rest. Lois was six and a half feet tall and well built, with black, oily hair brushed back from a brown, oval, good-looking face and dark eyes that were always twinkling with fun. Of Italian descent, Lois had worked in a circus for many years, later becoming a stuntman for a film company before joining the Karst Research Institute as a general handyman and troubleshooter. He was extremely strong and his party trick was to lift his body up on two fingers; it was an unwritten rule that Lois was always the first to descend any unexplored shaft. Although he spoke no English, Lois had a nimble brain and a great gift of mime. We sat entranced, listening to his stories which, with the odd German or Italian word, were mimed with extravagant gestures. With his brilliant sense of humour, Lois soon had us laughing uncontrollably.

During the days that followed, the friendly giant Lois and our diminutive comedian Les became firm friends. Les used to make a fool of his non-comprehending buddy by saying things like, 'Lois, I think you're a big slob,' and other insulting remarks while smiling up at him. Of course, Lois would smile back, not understanding that he was being made the butt of a joke and slightly bemused by everyone laughing.

One day, as we returned from caving, I asked Peter to translate what Les said. While we were sitting around the table that evening, Les was poking fun at his big, smiling friend when Lois stood up, picked Les up with one hand and hung him on a coat hook by the back of his anorak. He left him there, ranting and raving while we had our supper, occasionally and with great pantomime giving him a sip of wine and tweaking his nose.

THE SURROUNDING FOREST covered a mass of karst which was honeycombed with large, open shafts in a corroded landscape of fluted limestone and jagged crevices hidden by thick undergrowth, making walking hazardous. Every day we trekked into the woods to explore and survey caves as we found them.

The institute only possessed ladders constructed from very thick fencing wire and heavy, wooden rungs. There was one thick wire belay, which was fastened to the nearest tree. I often wondered what they would do if there were no trees.

Our lightweight ladders were a boon to the expedition and were a source of wonder to Lois, who kept shaking his head as he tried to snap them with his hands, inferring that they were weak. The Slovenians, with the exception of Professor Habe, were very strong and every morning they threaded their heavy ladders onto a newly felled, trimmed tree trunk, then two of them would hoist the load onto their shoulders and march off into the forest. We could carry twice as much electron ladder in our hands.

Carrying primitive ladders made from fencing wire and round hardwood rungs, during the 1964 Yugoslavia expedition. Young Les is on the left with Lois third from left and Peter Habič on the far right. Photo: Jim Eyre

Every time we found an unexplored shaft, Lois took command and looped his only belay round a tree, fastened on the ladders and descended, always insisting that he had to be the first 'to test them'. I soon became fed up with this and set up a rival 'pit-bagger's club' by exploring our own shafts. Most of these large holes were blocked by debris, tree trunks and rocks, and they rarely went below 200 feet, which prevented us from reaching the extensive river caves that lay below.

On one occasion Peter discovered what he thought was a deep shaft and led us to it. About thirty feet across, it had smooth, sheer walls and looked promising. As usual, Lois took out his one belay and wrapped it around the nearest tree, began fastening ladders on, then descended it. After some time he shouted up and the ladders were pulled to the surface, where another ladder was fastened on and the lot was lowered down again. A little while later he shouted up once more and this complicated manoeuvre would again take place.

I was intrigued when this happened for the third time and wondered where Lois went when his ladders vanished – I presumed that there must be ledges in the shaft. However, Lois's faint signal soon indicated that he had reached the bottom, so I tied on and followed. The walls of the shaft were smooth and completely devoid of ledges, so I was puzzled about what Lois had clung to when we pulled the ladders up. Perhaps he could levitate.

Looking down at the motley conglomeration of fencing wire, firewood and electron ladder that hung below my feet, I felt rather uneasy that all the good ladders (ours) were last on the line. In a perverse sort of way I considered that I was much more secure on our electron ladders, ignoring the fact that in this instance they were fastened to a load of rubbish.

Reaching the bottom I stepped into a jungle of dead trees and undergrowth, where I was immediately grabbed by a jubilant Lois. He explained to me that we had passed the hundred metres depth, a personal record for him and a local record. He shook me vigorously by the hand and, from a string around his neck, produced a flask containing slivovitz to drink a toast.

In my case, I knew that if I drunk much of that stuff I would never return to the surface, but it was an insult to refuse – especially a chap like Lois, who was bursting with excitement. I took a delicate swig.

'No, no, Jim – more,' and he shoved more jet fuel down my throat, before he tied on and sailed up the ladders like an orang-utan with a rocket up its bum.

I undertook a light-headed wander around the base of the shaft, where I found a rift descending to further depths which Lois had missed. There was no telltale draught, so it was probably blocked.

The rope and several rocks came down, with an indecipherable shout. I tied on and realised that I could have drunk all the offered slivovitz, because these lads didn't believe in ladder climbing: I was literally plucked off the ladders and sailed up the pitch like a pantomime fairy, to be greeted at the top by Lois – who came rushing towards me with outstretched hand and more slivovitz – and the four burly Slovenians who had looped the rope over a tree branch and were grinning furiously at my bemused expression. It became even more bemused when I noticed that the rope had almost sawn through the branch.

The mystery of how Lois had clung to the smooth walls of the shaft when the ladders were being extended was explained to me by Rado: Lois would find a little crack in the limestone, hammer in a peg and tie himself on with a bit of fencing wire he carried around his waist. I couldn't imagine myself swinging about gaily on the end of a piece of fencing wire on a 350 foot shaft, especially hanging on one of Lois' home-made pegs!

DURING THE SECOND WORLD WAR many German parachutists were dropped in this area. Some were blown onto the karst and one unfortunate parachuted straight down one of these deep shafts. I wonder what his feelings were, as he watched the circle of sky diminishing above him and the smooth, rocky walls of his tomb closing in on him. I could imagine his frantic search for a way out and his final collapse into total despair as his life ebbed slowly away while he crouched in the one small patch of sunlight, vainly trying to warm his weakening body.

This was how Lois found him. Several years after the war ended Lois descended a deep, open shaft and noticed an old German greatcoat bundled up against the cave wall where it was illuminated by a patch of sunlight. As Lois approached he noticed some shrivelled boots and the stark white of bleached bones. A helmet and rifle lay alongside the tattered remnants of a field-grey uniform that clung to the bones underneath, and a skull that gave him a lopsided grin as it leaned against the rock, sightless eye sockets still staring upwards for the rescue that never came.

Lois also noticed the para's watch, which had slid down the wrist bones. He picked it up, wound it and it has kept perfect time ever since on Lois' wrist.

RETURNING TO OUR LOG CABIN one evening, we found that all the tables had been placed on the road, lined up with jars of wild flowers on them and with a large bonfire burning nearby. It was obvious that there was to be some sort of celebration when a motorcyclist came roaring into the camp carrying fresh meat, and dozens of bottles of wine appeared from somewhere.

As the evening shadows lengthened, with the bonfire blazing and the wine flowing freely, we were handed sharpened sticks and chunks of meat. We barbecued these before basting the tender morsels with a special sauce made by our brilliant chef, Professor Habe.

It was a magical evening as we sat around the table in the middle of the road, lit by the orange glow of the bonfire and small oil lamps. The reason for our impromptu party was revealed: someone must have remarked that it was Rose's and my wedding anniversary, for we were sat at the head of the table and each Slovenian member of the expedition brought us a little gift, in some cases a few wild flowers, and gave a small speech.

I shall always remember this strange scene in the depths of the forest – it could have come straight out of Grimm's fairy tales, especially when a car appeared and the driver found the road blocked. No problem. Being Yugoslavian, he shook us all by the hand and joined in.

TWO DAYS LATER WE LEFT HRUŠICA, having explored and surveyed many deep shafts. We gave the woodmen back their hut and descended off the plateau, then explored several large river caves situated in low-lying poljes (temporary lakes with underground outlets, which transform into fertile valley basins).

The Slovenian karst is honeycombed with spectacular river caves and, wearing wetsuits, we pushed into unexplored passages and joined two cave systems by forcing our way through a low, dripping crawl in slimy mud. The roof suddenly lifted and the passage enlarged as we entered a large river passage with black, polished walls and a rounded roof, carved into thousands of scallop-shaped indentations by aeons of floodwaters.

The expanse of darkness beckoned and with shouts of elation we followed the swiftly flowing river as it swirled over large, black, rounded stones, past huge stalactites and calcite curtains, down a fast-flowing cascade into a deep pool. However, our feelings of elation were soon squashed when the roof lowered and froth appeared, circling slowly in the black malignant waters of the sump that barred our way.

The following day Peter took us to another large polje, where a surface river sank in a series of evil-looking holes, each slimy with rotting vegetation. Les discovered an old rectangular boat near one of these; it was very heavy and seemed very old, but we reckoned it would float. We dragged it to an open hole where a narrow canal flowed underground; we launched it and, surprise surprise, it floated. Rado remarked that it looked like a floating coffin as, with shouts of exhilaration, three of us jumped into our fine craft and set sail along the uncharted waters of our River Styx.

But, we rounded a corner and our fine seaworthy vessel went down with all hands. One minute it was there, the next it sank like a stone, leaving three very confused cavers floundering in the deep, cold water, swimming for our lives. This amused our audience outside, which watched us emerge from the dark confines, puffing and blowing.

'Ah, Jim, where is your yacht?' asked Rado.

WE MADE MANY FIRM FRIENDS on this our first visit to Yugoslavia and I have returned several times when driving to other expedition destinations in Greece, Turkey and Iran. I have always been made welcome, both on the outward and the return journey, and I have caved with members of the institute many times.

Two thousand, nine hundred and ninety-nine caves had been discovered in Slovenia when, above Tolmin near the Italian border in the Julian Alps, an expedition located the three thousandth: Poloska jama. The expedition was exploring this cave in 1966 when, returning from an expedition to Greece, I arrived on the scene.

The weather was atrocious and the car ground its way up the steep track, lurching from side to side with wheels spinning and the wipers hardly able to cope with the torrential rain, as we made our way over the summit towards a quagmire of an army camp. Anyone reading army recruiting posters should have made sure they didn't join the Yugoslavian one – the poor sods were lying prone in small bivi tents and were so desperate to keep out the driving rain that they had covered their tents with newspapers. Lying full length in three inches of water, pissing wet through, is not helped when a crazy Englishman comes around enquiring after speleologists. I received a mouthful of Serbo-Croat swear words and a hand pointing up the next mountain, which could just be seen through the mist.

The track eventually petered out at a large farmhouse where, almost straightaway, I bumped into Peter and Rado. They had just returned from the cave and, after lots of handshaking, backslapping and telling Rose how beautiful she was, I introduced them to the other two cavers with me: Alan Thomas and Ron Bridger.

We entered the farmhouse to be introduced to the farmer. The inevitable bottles of

Črni-var were produced and we sat by the huge fireplace in the large, high-ceilinged room, bathed in the firelight's glow, as we caught up with each other's lives again.

A huge shiny copper container, almost filled with milk, was suspended over the fire on a black, cast-iron pivot. The bearded farmer stood stirring the liquid with a large ladle almost obscured in steam and smoke, with sweat dripping into the milk off his large, hooked nose. I presumed he was making cheese. This large bulky man in his black, shiny leather apron, his ruddy face lit by the flickering flames and reflected in the highly polished copper bowl, would have made a perfect picture and I cursed the fact that my camera was packed away in the middle of my rucksack.

We were taken to a nearby barn which bore a crude sign over the door depicting a cross-eyed cow, and a sign which read Hotel Moo. Wide gaps in the old floorboards let up the warmth, stink and slurping noises from the cows below. Sorting out our gear we rejoined Peter, Rado and more Slovenians, some of whom I remembered from the year before: more backslapping, then in walked Lois who welcomed me like a long-lost brother before looking round for Young Les. He was most disappointed when I told him Les wasn't on this expedition.

We had a fine evening and Ron and Alan were soon swilling down slivovitz and wine with gay abandon, in spite of my dire warnings that it was loony broth. It was the small hours of the morning when we eventually staggered into the Hotel Moo.

Strange noises in the night woke me up. I had become used to the cows grunting, snorting, farting and the occasional splatter of crap, but this was the noise of two souls in anguish as my two companions took turns in honking onto the unfortunate animals below, between moans of 'Never again.'

Daylight came with the agony that only an unreformed drunk can experience. I rolled over and looked at Ron and Alan's faces. Cast in the mould of pre-dawn innocence, saliva drooling from slack, open mouths, faces devoid of any sign of intelligence, they would not be exploring caverns measureless to man this morning. I hurriedly gathered my caving gear together, finding my Nife cell flat, then hurriedly chased around the other cavers and managed to borrow one.

It was a fine day and I chased up the track, trying to catch the group of cavers who were far ahead. With heaving lungs and throbbing head, I narrowed the gap but failed to join them before they entered a heavily wooded area below the screes of the white cliffs. By then I knew I couldn't catch them, so I took a bearing on the two black openings in the cliff face, one of which must be Poloska jama, before I plunged into the semi-darkness of the forest and struggled steeply uphill over loose earth, leaves and roots that snatched at my ankles.

Finally, I arrived at the entrance to the cave, bathed in sweat, and met with a group of Slovenians who were filling their carbide lamps and packing bags. Rado was in charge of this group and his face lit with a beaming smile when he saw the state I was in.

'Ah, Jim, too much wine? Where are your friends?'

'Kaput,' I answered. This raised a laugh and I followed them into the cave, unaware that at that very moment Alan and Ron with their outsize hangovers were struggling manfully up the hill in their effort to join us. The stage was set . . .

The main passage of Poloska jama consisted of a large, spherical, tunnel-like bore-hole that sloped steadily upwards into the heart of the mountain. Devoid of formations, it seemed to me to be ominously like a flood tunnel, clean and water-washed by periodic flooding. The fifteen-foot-wide passage climbed steadily and became larger where cross-joints had formed chambers, and several passages led off into the darkness. I followed Rado and his group to a large cavern, where another group was surveying with Peter.

Yet another team was deep in the cave, pushing on with the exploration and leaving markers for the slower surveying team. Working our way further into the cave, we split up. Peter's group disappeared down a hole in the floor, while Rado plus four others and I carried on for several hundred yards up the main passage to where more passages were encountered as the cave became more complex. Rado and three of his team then decided to explore a left-hand fork, leaving Georgio, one of the younger Slavs, and me to push on in the hope of contacting the exploration party in front.

Confused? Not as confused as young Georgio and I were as we passed several junctions and alternative routes appeared every few yards, until we stopped where two equally obvious routes split the main passage. We expected the routes to converge again later, as had happened previously, so I waved Georgio on through the lower route while I climbed into the passage overhead. As soon as the scraping of Georgio's boots had died away, I experienced a sense of foreboding. The passage I was exploring came to an abrupt end at a large rockfall. My light shone into another passage overhead and a roomy hole leading under the rock pile.

'Which way?' I stuck my head underneath. It looked a bit dodgy, so I climbed into the more stable passage above, which soon inclined to forty-five degrees and twisted and turned like a snake as I scrambled upwards. My light flickered and I banged it with my hand to improve the contact. I reckoned that Georgio and I were only about half a mile from the entrance when we split up, so I wasn't unduly concerned and pushed on upwards to the base of a vertical climb up a chimney.

Thrusting my way up for twenty feet or so, I noticed that my light was becoming dimmer, but put it down to a bad contact for I had been assured that it was fully charged. By now I was in the grip of exploration fever, as for some time I had realised that I was the only person to have entered this part of the cave, and the adrenalin was flowing. At the top of the climb a roomy, horizontal gallery led off in both directions; I opted for the left-hand route for it appeared to be growing larger and continued in the general direction of the passages below.

After one hundred yards or so the passage split. The left-hand side seemed more promising, so I scratched a mark on a rock before pushing on with my solo exploration. This took me still deeper into the mountain and also became more complicated when I entered a chamber from which three different routes led on.

'Ah, this is where Jim gets lost,' I thought. 'Eeny, meeny, miny, mo – which way should I go?'

I decided on the right-hand passage because I could detect a faint draught, so I built a small cairn at its entrance and carried on. After a while the passage increased in height and led to the foot of another rift, which I chimneyed up into another tunnel leading off in both directions. I was beginning to have a niggling doubt in my mind that perhaps I should turn back and look for some support. 'Ah, well, a little further; I'll definitely turn back at the next junction,' I told myself as I headed right.

All the passages that I had followed were featureless, like some of the high-level passages in Lancaster Hole. I took careful note of anything unusual, like an oddly shaped rock or a joint in the roof or the large chamber in which I suddenly found myself. It led into another two large chambers. Well, they might have been small chambers, because for some time my light had been becoming dimmer and, in spite of me continually slapping it into spasms of stronger output, it had now stopped responding to my coaxing.

Ahead, a large passage beckoned. I decided to take a quick look and then head back at top speed before my light faded but, as I advanced, my light – which had become very dull and yellow – suddenly deteriorated and sank like the setting sun. I hastily began retracing my steps, but to my dismay I found myself in a chamber with no way on. I had taken a wrong turning.

My lightbulb now glowed like a cigarette end so I switched it off to allow the cell to partially recharge, and sat there in pitch darkness trying to whistle a jolly little tune. Nothing came out, as my mouth was bone dry. What relief when I switched on and could see the route. Moving as fast as I dared, I entered another chamber with a passage leading off – but alas, it was not the way I had entered. Damn!

The light was yellowing again and, like a rat running around in circles, once again I retreated, confused and not too happy at my fumbling along like a blind man in the dim yellow glow, only able to see a couple of feet. Once again I had to switch the light off to enable it to regenerate a fraction of its power.

I sat on the dry mud of the floor in complete blackness and cursed myself for borrowing a light of unknown quality, then going on a solo exploration in an unknown cave – even a novice wouldn't do something so bloody daft! I thought of my mates, laughing when they found me. If they found me. I shuddered: perhaps I wouldn't be found. If someone began searching for me at this very instant, it would be a long time before I was located; even with luck on the side of the searchers, no one would know where to start looking. The young, inexperienced Georgio was the last caver I had been in contact with and he hadn't seen the route I took after leaving him. He might not even be aware that I was missing, as he didn't know me.

Sitting in the dark, I concluded that my situation could become serious, and come what may I must find my way back into the vicinity of the main passages which lay somewhere below. I switched my light on again and it responded with a feeble glow, enabling me to reach another chamber but still unable to find the way on in the fading glow. I sank down on my hands and knees and found an imprint of my vibram soles in the dry mud; my footprints came out of a passage concealed by a dip in the roof and a large block. I scurried onwards like a frightened rabbit, in case it disappeared. My light went out; taking care to switch it off, I sat once more in the dark.

Each wait was now becoming longer, for rapidly diminishing returns from the recovering battery; within a very short space of time the cell would be totally defunct and I wouldn't be far off the same state, as I was growing cold with the enforced inactivity. The darkness of a cave is absolute, the blackest of black, and in my condition it was overpowering and pressed on me with a presence that I could feel, like being buried alive.

Luckily, I was wearing a luminous watch, which was some comfort as it gave my eyes something on which to focus in the oppressive dark. Being able to time my actions prevented me from becoming too disorientated, though I was still desperate enough to try to see with the luminosity of the watch – but even using my imagination this didn't work. I decided to try out a new technique. This involved switching my light on briefly and memorising the passage ahead, then switching it off and feeling my way forward on my hands and knees for as far as I could. This system worked quite well, as it enabled me to move more frequently and kept my body heat up.

I concentrated hard on trying to recreate the route in my mind. Having negotiated a chamber by one brief flash and crawling round the perimeter while feeling the walls, I found the way on and, after checking in the dull glow with my face inches from the next footprint, I switched off and sat back, elated. The waits were, however, becoming even longer, and the glow of the bulb more feeble. Then, after another hands and knees crawl along a floor in the darkness, I stopped and switched the light on. Nothing.

I curled up into a corner of the rock and wished that I hadn't given up smoking, for in a situation like this the glow of a cigarette end could be enough to see a foot of cave passage. Health-wise, a smoker's cough is better than being dead. I hopefully switched the light back on again: nothing.

Thinking of cigarettes reminded me of the time when, for a bet, I chain-smoked my way from one cave entrance to another with no light and no helmet. In fact, I was dressed in casual wear, Hush Puppies and all, and won the bet in spite of falling into a pool. Ho-hum.

I looked at my watch and realised that even its luminosity was fading; I had been sitting still for fifteen minutes. I switched the light on and was rewarded with a feeble glow; I could just make out a hole in the floor ahead. I remembered climbing up a rift and traversing across two others. Was it here or in the passage below?

In the dark by the edge of the hole, I realised that if I attempted to climb down the wrong one I could be in serious trouble. Feeling around, I found a small piece of rock. I dropped it – it seemed to land about twenty feet lower. I had been talking to myself for some time now and, strange as this may seem, this was helping me to rationalise things more, because there's always two sides to every problem. 'Yes, Jim.'

Talking out aloud had helped with route-finding and now, my alter ego and I discussed whether this was the right hole and asked each other if there was a boot mark on the other side. The next time my light came on, I saw the faint sign of a vibram sole and in the brief yellow glow I quickly traversed over to another hole a few feet further on. Switched off, I sat there for a long time and realised that a faint draught blew from below – this must be the way.

Sitting, shivering, I listened intently for any sound from other cavers. There was nothing: no murmuring of a faraway stream, no dripping water, nothing, just the silence and oppressive blackness of the tomb. I again groped around for a rock to throw down: nothing. I searched at the lip of the shaft and found a loose piece of wall, then spent several minutes levering it away with my fingers before dropping it down the shaft. It fell for about twenty feet and then bounced further. My mind was in a whirl as I tried to reason what the other drop was. Perhaps I was wrong – but the air currents must be coming up from the main cave. It seemed like an hour since I last looked at my watch; it was twenty minutes. It was now or never.

I switched on and in the feeble glow began climbing down the shaft, feeling for holds with my feet. The light faded to nothing and plunged me into darkness while I was straddled across the rift. I swore. There I was, perched above bugger all in the bloody dark, in a foreign country in a bloody cave that hadn't even been explored. How bloody silly could you get?

Clinging like a limpet, all my weight was on my left leg, which was lower and seemed to be on a good foothold. My other foot kept slipping and with my hands I felt around desperately for a better hold. Success. I grasped the jug-handle with relief and clung there, waving my right leg about in desperation until it found some sort of a hold. Jammed in this position, I turned off my headlamp switch, which I had forgotten about. As the Americans say, I hung in there for what seemed like hours, but wasn't.

After an interminable wait, my hands started to cramp and I realised that I was going to either fall off or shout 'Geronimo' and jump. I tentatively tried the light switch and a dull glow revealed a broad ledge eight inches below my left foot, before the light went out again. I carefully reached down and thankfully placed my foot on it, then tapped around with my boot. It was quite a big ledge – in fact, it extended right across the shaft. It was the bloody floor!

I sat down, rubbing my aching hands and not knowing whether to laugh or cry; I had been hanging on for grim death eight inches above the floor!

I lay down and tried to sleep, but only succeeded in dozing off for brief periods. There should be another climb down somewhere, which should take me to the large, steeply inclined passage from the rock collapse. Which way, left or right? With these thoughts running through my mind – or what was left of it – I decided to follow the faint air current.

After a long wait, I switched on and was rewarded with a dull, orange glow. I scampered for several feet on my hands and knees, before the other shaft was revealed and the sun set again. I was plunged into darkness once more. The draught was stronger here and, finding a small piece of rock, I dropped it. The distance seemed right and the rock rolled and bounced after it fell. This was the way – it had to be.

Sod it! I was going to climb down in the dark while I still had enough strength left. I carefully levered my body over the edge and felt on the opposite wall with my feet for good footholds and, with my back braced against the other wall, I worked my way lower, inch by inch in the pitch darkness. I found it surprisingly easy relying on touch alone, until my questing feet found space! Panic. I carefully lowered my body further and searched lower with one extended leg – it encountered the floor and I dropped down.

Quite pleased with my climb in the dark, I allowed myself the luxury of a brief switch on and off. It appeared to be the right passage, so I sat on my backside and fumbled my way down the steep slope for what seemed a long way. I became uneasy and had to use all my powers of reason and common sense to stop going into a blind panic. Eventually, it levelled off and my 'light' revealed a rockfall.

My panic subsided as I now knew where I was. I was talking to myself quite freely now: 'I'll just feel my way round this rock, keep heading down, I don't think there's any more side passages, this boulder's loose.' I felt my way slowly down until the slope of rubble stopped and I stood on clean rock.

I tried the light and, in the brief glow of the filament, I could just make out the junction where Georgio and I had separated. I was back in the known cave! Keeping hold of the wall I groped slowly forward: feel with hands and feel with feet, in a sort of sliding, shambling movement. When I got confused, which was often, I switched on and saw ahead for about eighteen inches; the rest was guesswork.

During my slow, tedious progress I realised that my body had adapted to my surroundings and for some time now I had become aware that I could see in the dark. Sure enough, instead of pitch black, there was now a heavy grey and, very vaguely, I could make out the passage wall. 'I'm going mad,' I thought. Gradually, my numbed mind realised that the shape of the passage could be defined, and rounding a bend reflected light lit up the cave.

Shouting madly, I burst around another bend into a large chamber lit by a solitary carbide lamp. Beside the lamp lay a half-eaten loaf, a chunk of cheese and a half-empty bottle of wine. Surveying equipment was scattered around and two cameras stood on tripods, ready for a photograph.

What had happened? It was like an underground *Marie Celeste*. Where had everyone gone? Perhaps there had been an accident. Perhaps they were looking for me. Perhaps the cave was flooding.

This last thought chilled me to the marrow and I listened intently for the faint rumbling that would herald the approach of floodwaters – but all was silent. The bread and cheese, followed by the wine while basking in the glow of a friendly light, were the ultimate happiness for a trapped subterranean Robinson Crusoe who had just emerged from Hades. I sat there, quietly belching and dwelling on my sudden good fortune.

Thus fortified, I took the light and began to make my way out of the cave, until I came to a deep pool which I recognised. A section of the passage was flooded for about twelve feet to a depth of eight feet. On the way in we had swung across it using a hand-traverse on an overhang, which left our feet swinging in space. I hung the large carbide lamp on the back of my belt, then carefully traversed out to the first handhold and launched myself over the pool, swinging like Tarzan from one hold to the other.

Unfortunately, the lamp on my belt also began to swing and bumped against my backside several times. This burned it rather painfully, before the lamp snuffed itself out

I launched myself
over the pool,
swinging like Tarzan
from one hold to
the other

on my flesh, exposed by my burning trousers. Anyone who has hung by his hands over a deep pool in total darkness, suffering with a smouldering bum, will sympathise with my predicament. I desperately fumbled for more holds, until by chance my swinging feet encountered a ledge and I worked my way across to land at the other side of the pool.

'Bloody hellfire,' I shouted. 'What more can go wrong?' I unhooked the hissing lamp, which was spewing out stinking carbide gas, and flung it into the darkness of the cave behind me.

I sat down once again in pitch darkness and I swore for ten minutes, loud and long without using the same swear word twice.

During my enforced isolation in the cave, the Yugoslavs had returned to the farm for a meal. Ron and Alan had also returned, independent of the Yugoslavs; they thought I was with another party in the cave, and Rado and the group I had entered the cave with thought I was with the two English cavers. I probably wouldn't have been missed until later that evening . . .

Meanwhile, luckily for me, a small group of Yugoslavs had decided to undertake a late trip to finish some exploration. Late in the day they returned to the cave and I gradually became aware of the faint sound of approaching cavers. Gradually, the first flicker of light appeared, which burst upon me as they came round a bend in the passage. They stopped dead. I don't know what Serbo-Croat is for 'What the bloody hell is that?', but that's what they said when they saw the lightless apparition that greeted them with eyes like red frogspawn and arms open wide, advancing towards them.

After a stunned silence, one touched me on the arm and asked, 'Ah, Meester Jeem, what for you cave all alone with no light?'

There was no answer to that.

Anyone who has hung by his hands over a deep pool in total darkness, suffering with a smouldering bum, will sympathise with my predicament

By the Same Author

'Lancaster Hole and the Ease Gill Caverns, Casterton Fell, Westmorland'. *Transactions of the Cave Research Group of Great Britain*, Vol 9 (2), March 1967, pp61-123 (with Peter Ashmead)

The Cave Explorers. Stalactite Press, Calgary. 1981, viii+264pp

Race Against Time. A history of the Cave Rescue Organisation. Lyon, Dent. 1988, 208pp (with John Frankland)

'The Ease Gill Cave System'. *British Cave Research Association*, Speleo-History Series (1). 1989, 48pp

Right In It. Mendip Publishing, Castle Cary. 1992, 80pp

References and Further Reading

The following sources are recommended for further reading. Extracts based on the author's previous writings, and from other sources, appear in this book with grateful thanks to the authors and publishers for permission

ASPIN, Jack & JOWETT, Alan. 1952. *The Caverns of Upper Ease Gill*. Northern Pennine Club, Leeds, 23pp

BOON, J.M. 1977. *Down to a Sunless Sea*. Stalactite Press, Edmonton, 105pp

CASTERET, Norbert. 1954. *The Darkness Under the Earth*. Dent, London, xiv+168pp

CHEVALIER, Pierre. 1951. *Subterranean Climbers*. Faber and Faber, London, 223pp

GEMMELL, A. & MYERS, J.O. 1952. *Underground Adventure*. Blandford, London, 141pp

TAYLOR, Wilf in ST LAWRENCE, Hugh (ed). '50 Years. Anniversary journal 1946-1996'. 1996, *Red Rose CPC Journal*, (10), pp8-9

Publisher's Notes

Jim's descent of Flood Entrance Pot as part of a BSA meet 'on 15 September', as detailed on a postcard (see p113), has been the subject of previously published reports. These attribute the year as being 1946, presumably because the group always caved on a Sunday and 15 September 1946 was a Sunday.

However, while writing this book Jim noticed that his honourable discharge from the navy – according to his demob papers – took place on 23 September 1946 and thus the descent could not have occurred on 15 September that year. In general it took servicemen a long time to readjust to civilian life and it is clear that the trip took place in 1947. The postcard can no longer be found to check the date, leaving several possibilities for the day or month being incorrectly quoted: the date on the postcard and of the trip might therefore be 14 September 1947 (a Sunday), or Sunday 15 June (the only Sunday falling on a 15th that year).

Credit for the discovery of Lancaster Hole (see p123) has been scrutinised in recent years. Wilf Taylor, writing in the Red Rose CPC 50th anniversary journal, reproduces an entry from Bill Taylor's diary for 29 September 1946. Most literature credits George Cornes as having first noticed the drafting hole, but Bill clearly states that it was he who first saw the grass quivering in the wind. Appendix 2f in Jim Eyre's *The Ease Gill Cave System*, pp46-7, is written by George Cornes and covers the same intriguing question. George does not claim the discovery but acknowledges that edited reports in 1947 made it appear that it was he who first noticed the hole; George himself only refers to 'our find'. The somewhat academic question of which man 'discovered' Lancaster Hole by reason of noticing moving grass is avoided in this book, instead crediting the discovery to both men.

There are discrepancies in published accounts of the time given for the death of Neil Moss in Peak Cavern (see p198). In *Race Against Time* when Jim returns to the chamber all was silent and Neil had, therefore, already died. A major article in *Descent* (62) states that the time of death is uncertain but was some time in the morning of Tuesday 24 March 1959 and could have been as early as midnight; the inquest stated 3 a.m. However, in *The Cave Explorers* Jim wrote that he was present when Neil died. The poignant fact that Jim's group was present and heard Neil's breathing falter and stop is specifically confirmed by Jim.

And for our American readers, please note that 'fag' is British slang for a cigarette.

Index